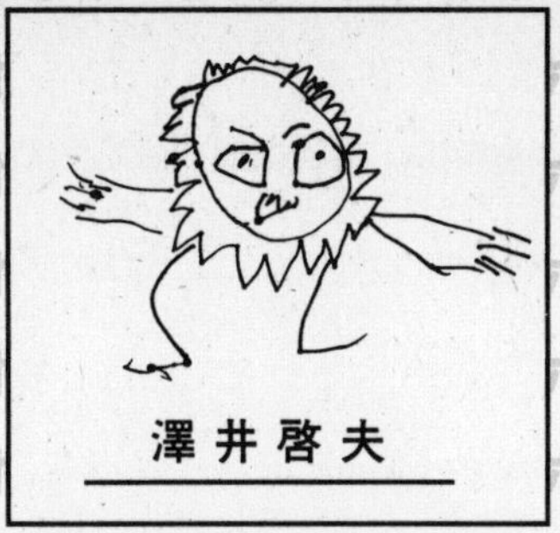
澤井啓夫

The other day, I went back to Fukui, my hometown, where I hadn't been for over three and a half years. While I was there, my nephew, who just turned 4 years old, drew a picture of Poppa Rocks for me. I was very happy. It really cheered me on.
(His drawing is above.)
-Yoshio Sawai

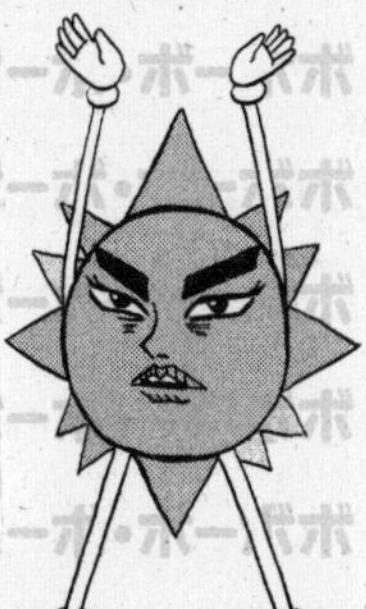

Yoshio Sawai was born in 1977 in Aichi Prefecture. He made his debut with a story called ***Yamanaka Shuukatsugeki*** (Smelly Action Story in the Mountains). ***Bobobo-bo Bo-bobo*** began serialization in ***Weekly Shonen Jump*** in 2001. Sawai's irreverent and wacky humor inspired several video games and an anime series which debuted in Japan in November 2003.

BOBOBO-BO BO-BOBO VOL. #4
SHONEN JUMP Manga Edition

STORY AND ART BY
YOSHIO SAWAI

Translation/Tetsuichiro Miyaki
Adaptation/Ian Robertson
Touch-up Art & Lettering/William Schuch
Design/Sean Lee
Editor/Daniel Gillespie

VP, Production/Alvin Lu
VP, Sales & Product Marketing/Gonzalo Ferreyra
VP, Creative/Linda Espinosa
Publisher/Hyoe Narita

Published by VIZ Media, LLC
P.O. Box 77010
San Francisco, CA 94107

10 9 8 7 6 5 4 3 2 1
First printing, June 2010

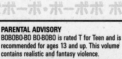

PARENTAL ADVISORY
BOBOBO-BO BO-BOBO is rated T for Teen and is
recommended for ages 13 and up. This volume
contains realistic and fantasy violence.

ratings.viz.com

www.viz.com

THE WORLD'S
MOST POPULAR MANGA

www.shonenjump.com

BOBOBO-BO BO-BOBO

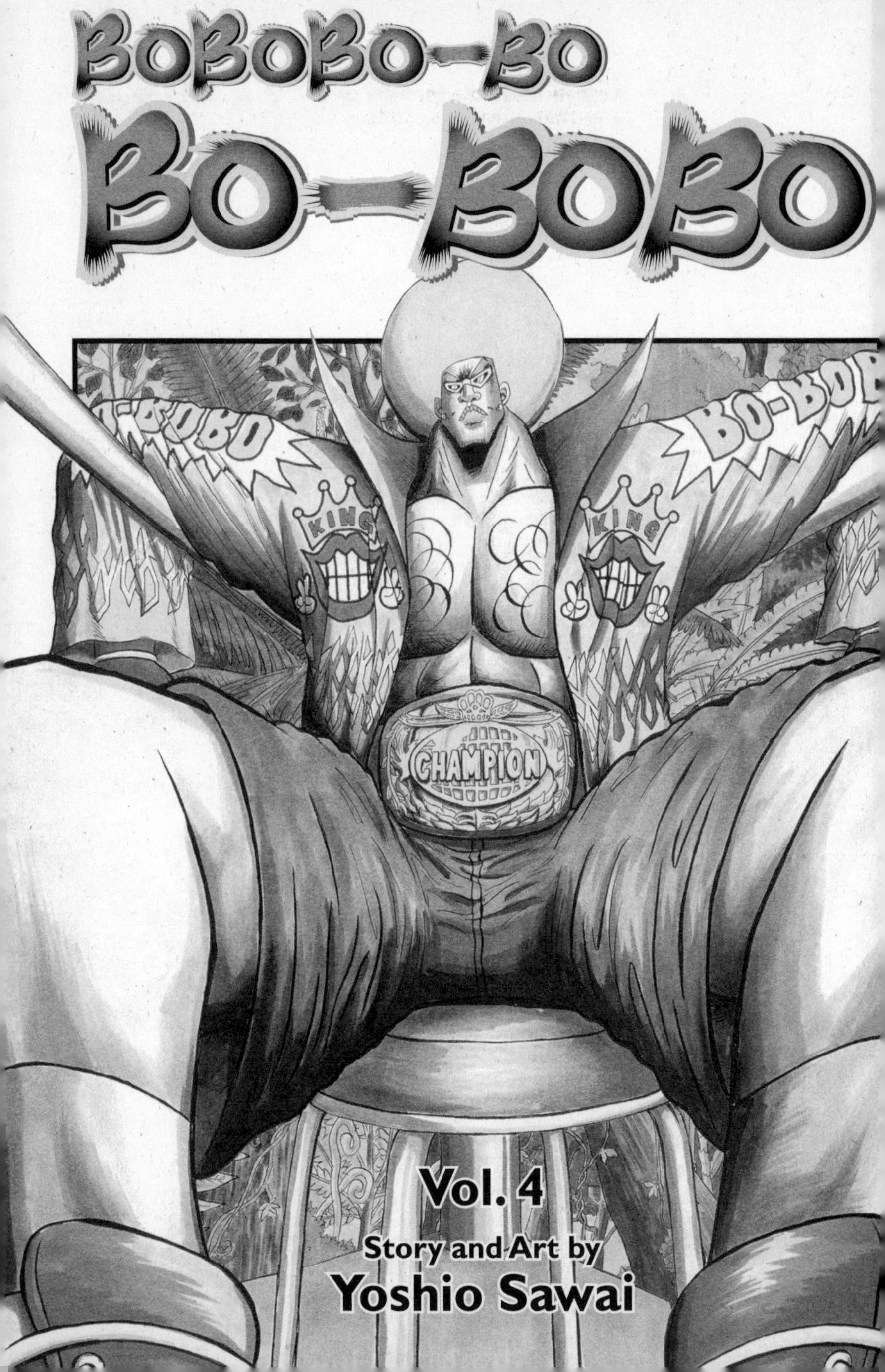
KING
KING
CHAMPION

Vol. 4

Story and Art by
Yoshio Sawai

•CHARACTERS•

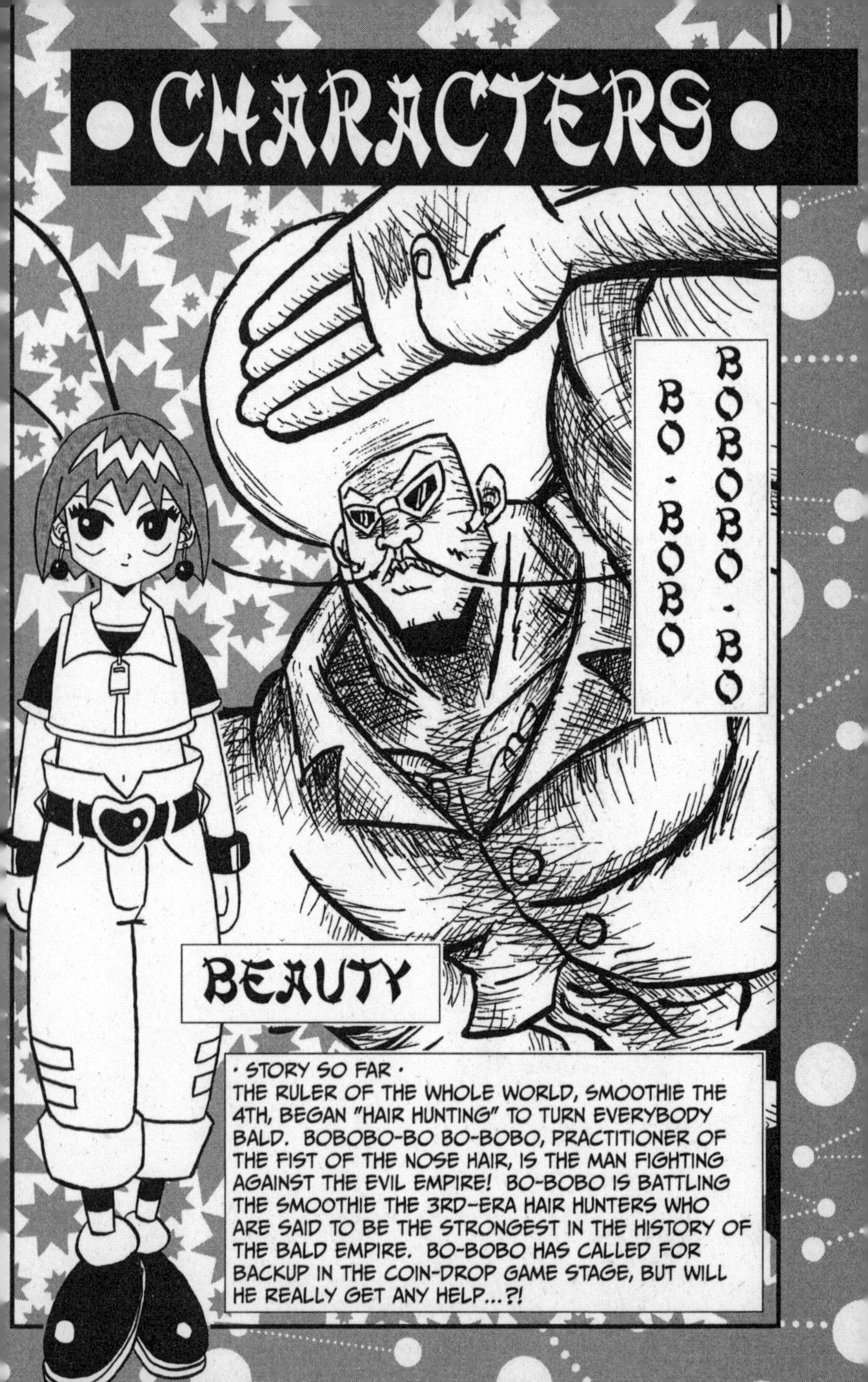
BOBOBO-BO BO-BOBO
BEAUTY

· STORY SO FAR ·

THE RULER OF THE WHOLE WORLD, SMOOTHIE THE 4TH, BEGAN "HAIR HUNTING" TO TURN EVERYBODY BALD. BOBOBO-BO BO-BOBO, PRACTITIONER OF THE FIST OF THE NOSE HAIR, IS THE MAN FIGHTING AGAINST THE EVIL EMPIRE! BO-BOBO IS BATTLING THE SMOOTHIE THE 3RD-ERA HAIR HUNTERS WHO ARE SAID TO BE THE STRONGEST IN THE HISTORY OF THE BALD EMPIRE. BO-BOBO HAS CALLED FOR BACKUP IN THE COIN-DROP GAME STAGE, BUT WILL HE REALLY GET ANY HELP...?!

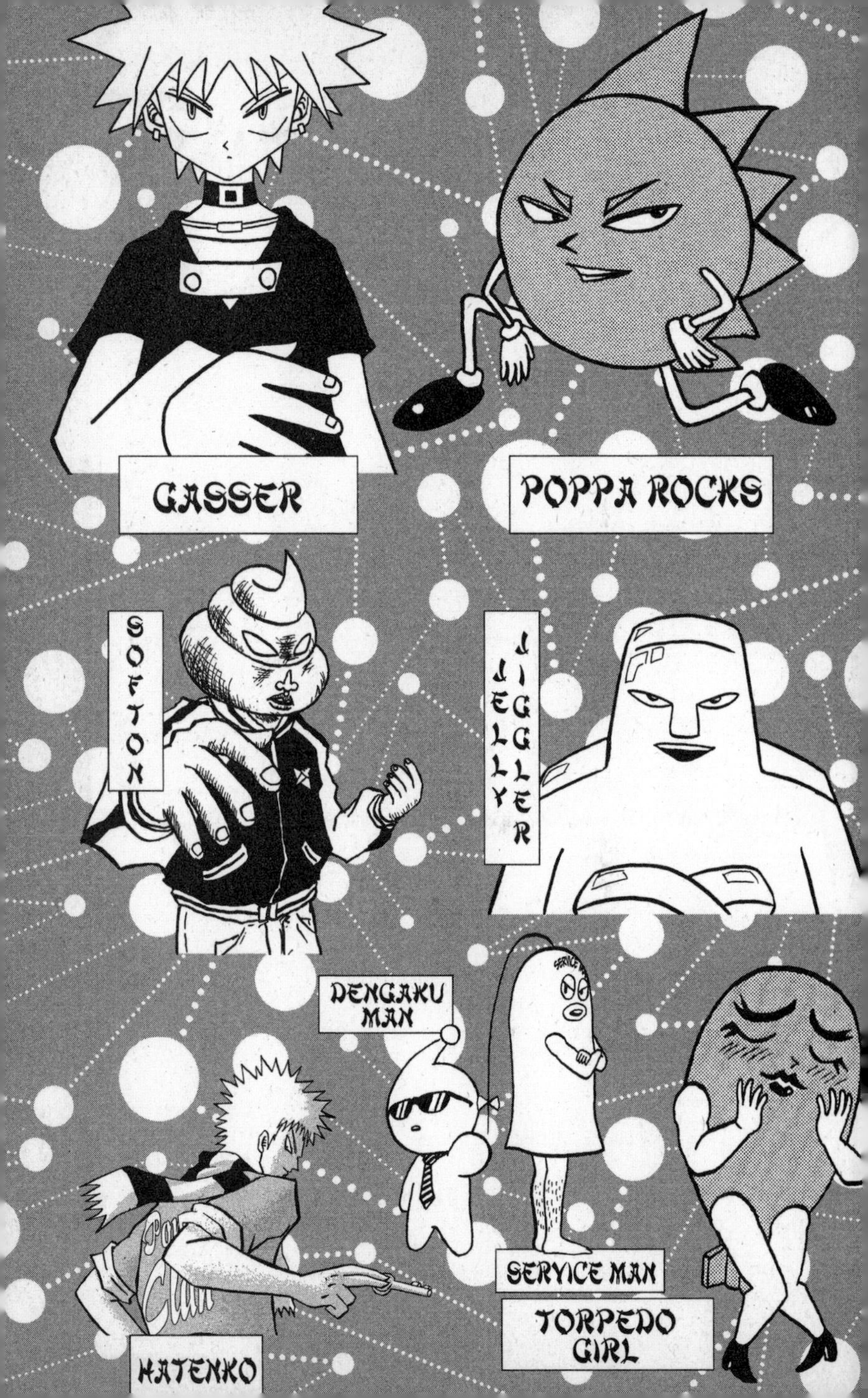
POPPA ROCKS
GASSER
JELLY JIGGLER
SOFTON
TORPEDO GIRL
SERVICE MAN
DENGAKU MAN
HATENKO

BOBOBO-BO BO-BOBO

CONTENTS

Chapter 34: Maximum Service! The Great Escape!! 7

Chapter 35: Who the Devil Are They?! Goemon Is in Shock!.................. 23

Chapter 36: Rem Rem Rem Rem.. 39

Chapter 37: The Great Sleep Battle!!! 55

Chapter 38: Bo-bobo World Nightmare 75

Chapter 39: Lambada, Member of the Big Three, Appears!...................... 91

Chapter 40: Polygon of the Valley of the Nose Hair 107

Chapter 41: Retro Games Are Go!.. 123

Chapter 42: Bo-bobo vs. Hanpen 139

Chapter 43: The Two on the Top.. 155

Chapter 44: Confusion Battle!! The Chaotic 9 Oden in Sangaria 170

Bobobo-bo Bo-bobo Extra Story

Bo-bobo Nose Hair Theater 7 186

Chapter 34: Maximum Service! The Great Escape!!

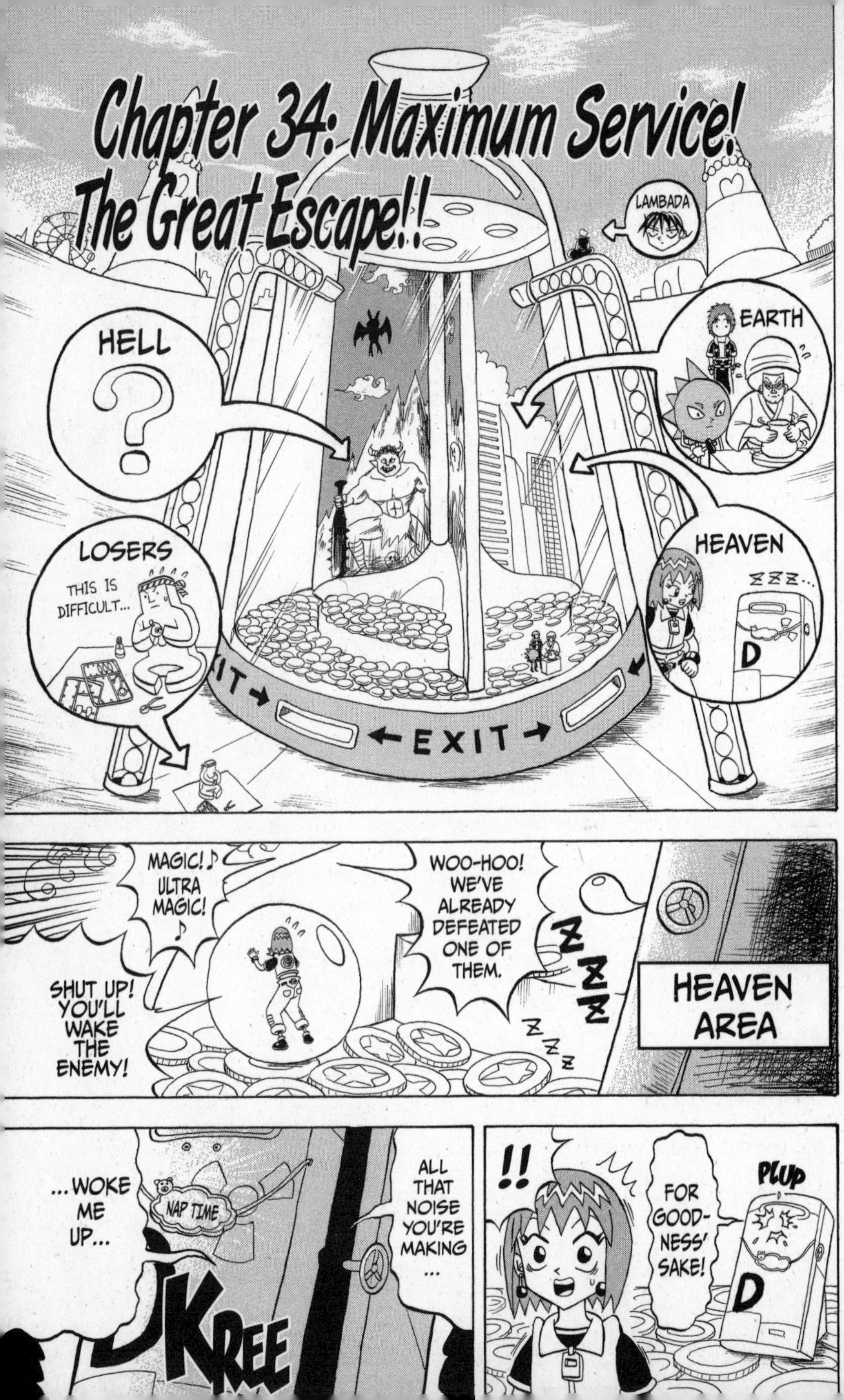
LAMBADA
EARTH
HELL
?
HEAVEN
ZZZ...
D
LOSERS
THIS IS DIFFICULT...
EXIT→
←EXIT→
HEAVEN AREA
ZZZ
ZZZ
WOO-HOO! WE'VE ALREADY DEFEATED ONE OF THEM.
MAGIC!♪ ULTRA MAGIC! ♪
SHUT UP! YOU'LL WAKE THE ENEMY!
PLUP
FOR GOOD-NESS' SAKE!
D
!!
ALL THAT NOISE YOU'RE MAKING ...
...WOKE ME UP...
NAP TIME
KREE

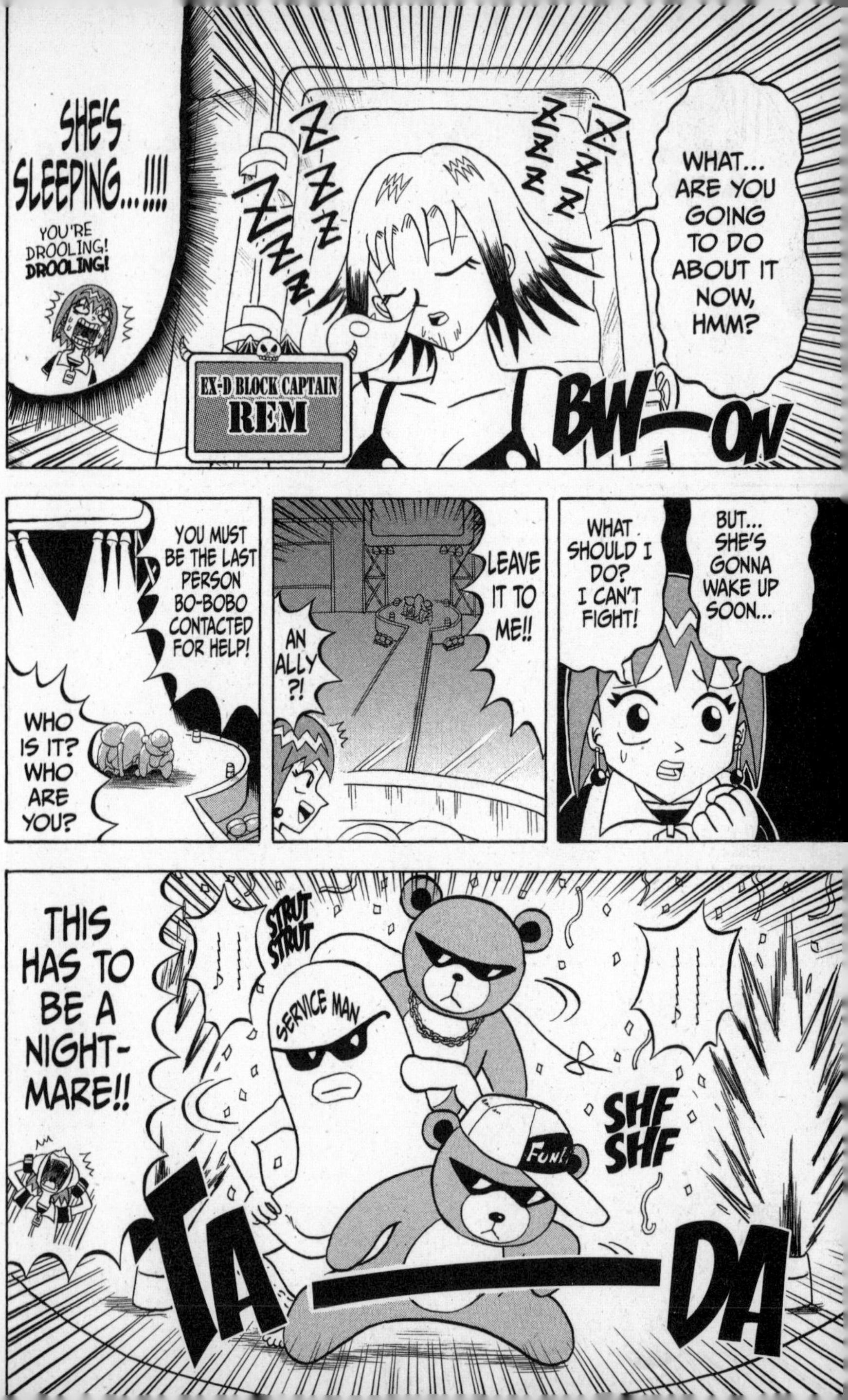
WHAT... ARE YOU GOING TO DO ABOUT IT NOW, HMM?
ZZZZ
BW—ON
EX-D BLOCK CAPTAIN REM
SHE'S SLEEPING...!!!!
YOU'RE DROOLING! DROOLING!
BUT... SHE'S GONNA WAKE UP SOON...
WHAT SHOULD I DO? I CAN'T FIGHT!
LEAVE IT TO ME!!
AN ALLY?!
YOU MUST BE THE LAST PERSON BO-BOBO CONTACTED FOR HELP!
WHO IS IT? WHO ARE YOU?
SHF SHF
STRUT STRUT
SERVICE MAN
FUNK
TA—DA
THIS HAS TO BE A NIGHTMARE!!

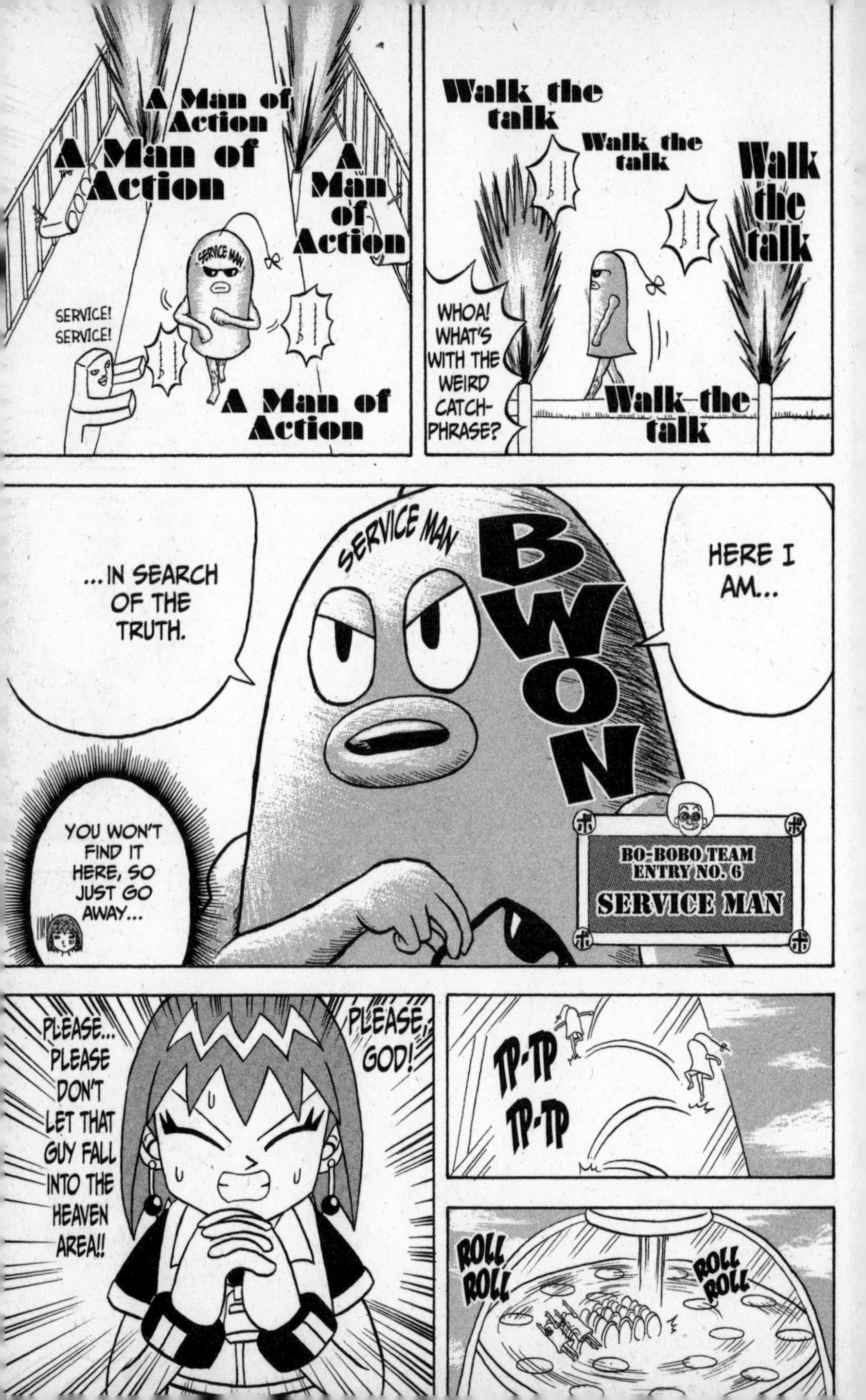

Walk the talk
Walk the talk
Walk the talk
WHOA! WHAT'S WITH THE WEIRD CATCH-PHRASE?
Walk the talk
A Man of Action
A Man of Action
A Man of Action
SERVICE MAN
SERVICE! SERVICE!
A Man of Action
HERE I AM...
BWON
SERVICE MAN
...IN SEARCH OF THE TRUTH.
BO-BOBO TEAM ENTRY NO. 6
SERVICE MAN
YOU WON'T FIND IT HERE, SO JUST GO AWAY...
TP-TP TP-TP
ROLL ROLL
ROLL ROLL
PLEASE, GOD!
PLEASE... PLEASE DON'T LET THAT GUY FALL INTO THE HEAVEN AREA!!

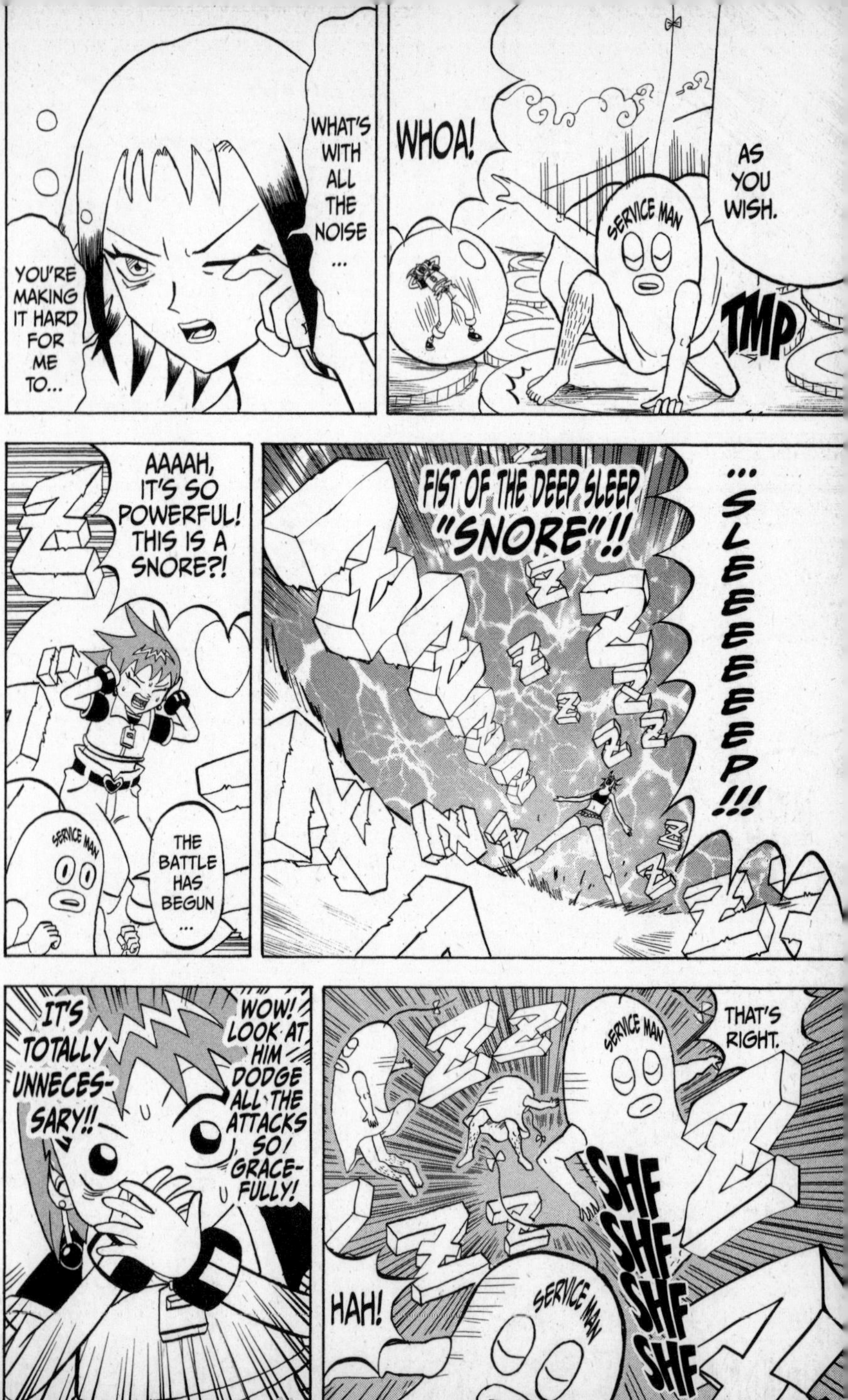
AS YOU WISH.
WHOA!
SERVICE MAN
TMP
WHAT'S WITH ALL THE NOISE ...
YOU'RE MAKING IT HARD FOR ME TO...
...SLEEEEEEEP!!!
FIST OF THE DEEP SLEEP "SNORE"!!
AAAAH, IT'S SO POWERFUL! THIS IS A SNORE?!
SERVICE MAN
THE BATTLE HAS BEGUN ...
THAT'S RIGHT.
SERVICE MAN
SHF SHF SHF SHF
HAH!
SERVICE MAN
WOW! LOOK AT HIM DODGE ALL THE ATTACKS SO GRACEFULLY!
IT'S TOTALLY UNNECESSARY!!

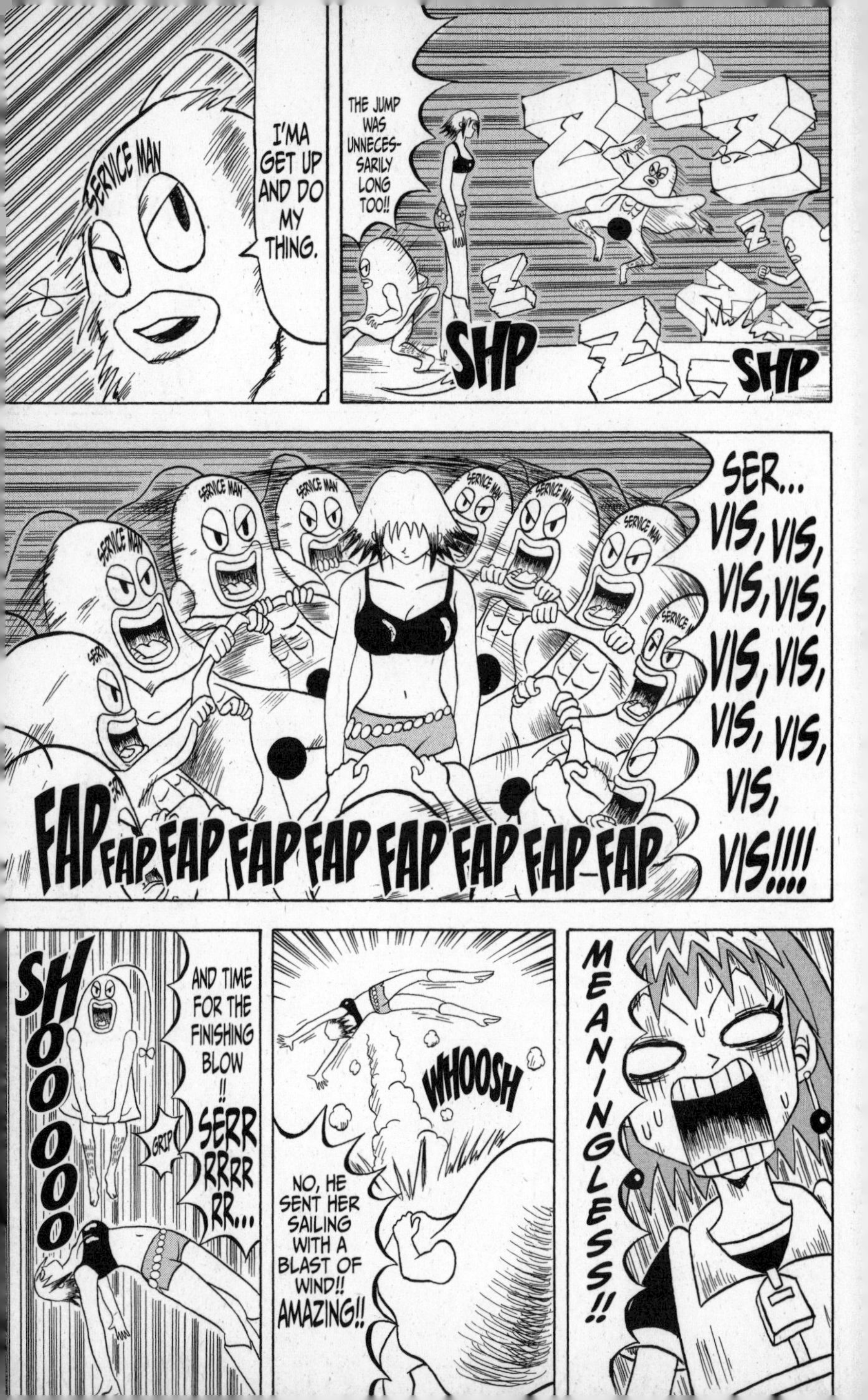
THE JUMP WAS UNNECES-SARILY LONG TOO!!
SHP
SHP
SERVICE MAN
I'MA GET UP AND DO MY THING.
SER... VIS, VIS, VIS, VIS, VIS, VIS, VIS, VIS, VIS, VIS!!!!
SERVICE MAN
SERVICE MAN
FAP FAP FAP FAP FAP FAP FAP FAP FAP
MEANINGLESS!!
WHOOSH
NO, HE SENT HER SAILING WITH A BLAST OF WIND!! AMAZING!!
AND TIME FOR THE FINISHING BLOW!!
SERRRRRRRR...
GRIP
SHOOOOOO

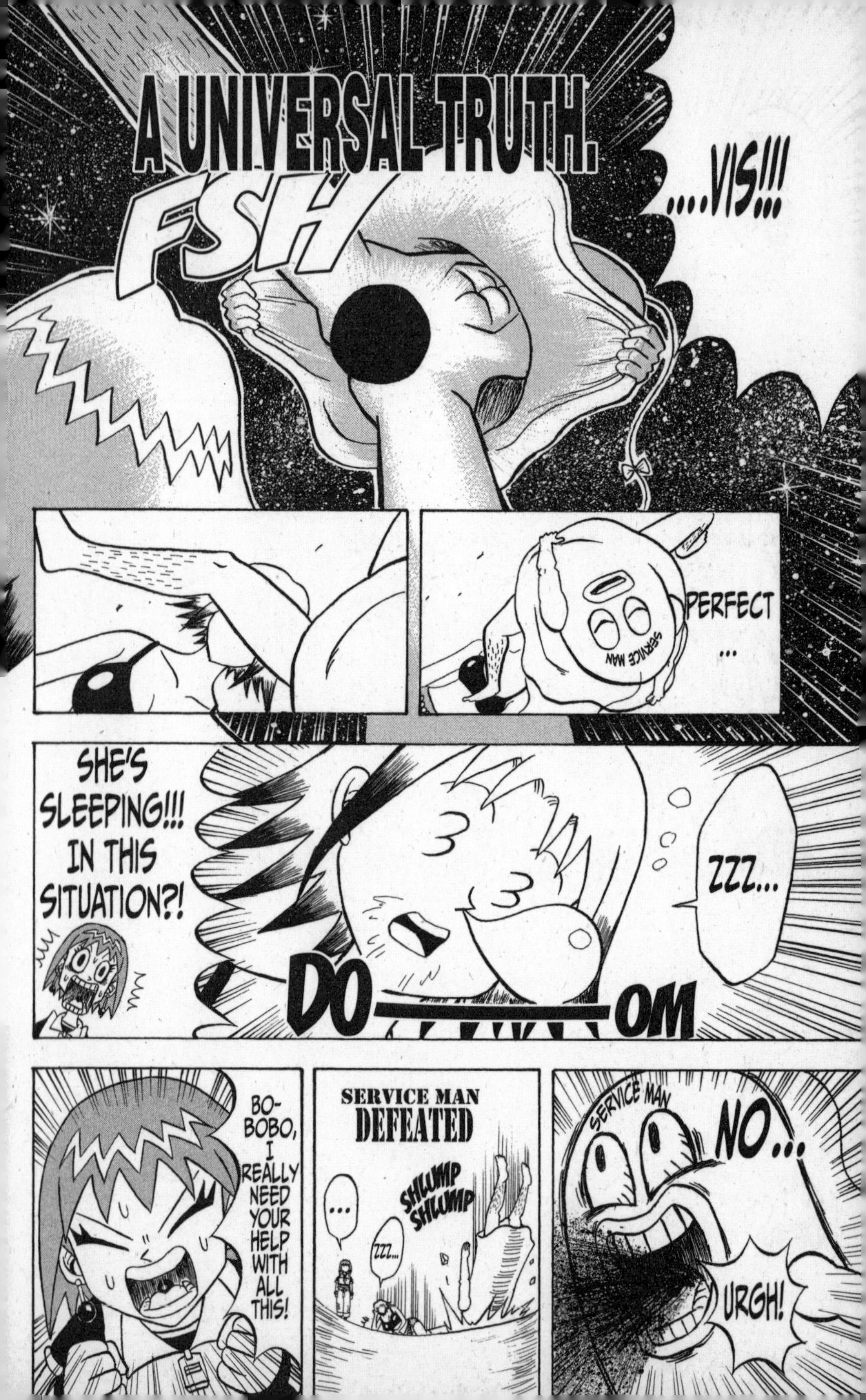
A UNIVERSAL TRUTH.
....VIS!!!
FSH
PERFECT ...
SERVICE MAN
ZZZ...
DO——OM
SHE'S SLEEPING!!! IN THIS SITUATION?!
SERVICE MAN
NO...
URGH!
SERVICE MAN DEFEATED
SHLUMP SHLUMP
...
ZZZ...
BO-BOBO, I REALLY NEED YOUR HELP WITH ALL THIS!

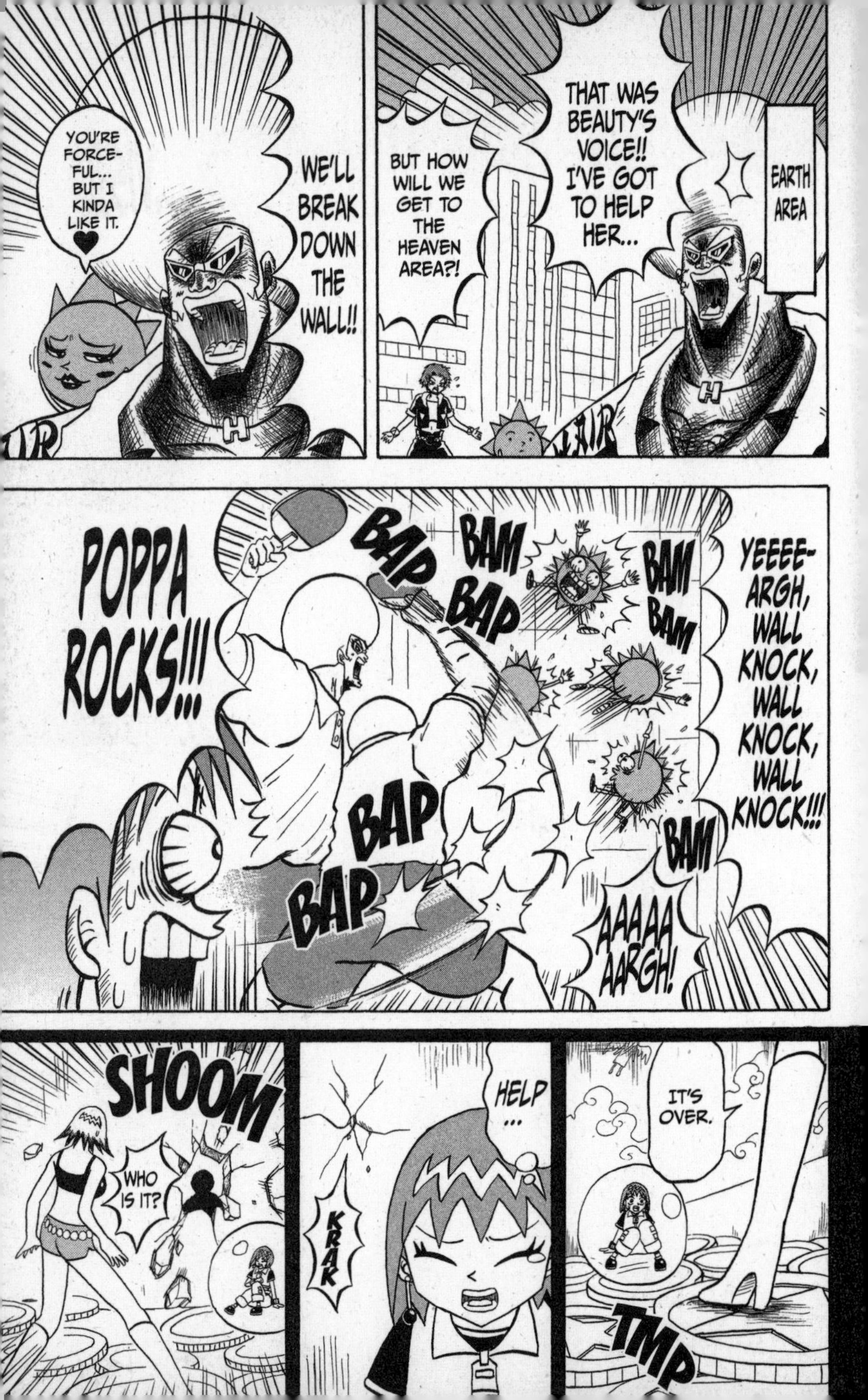
EARTH AREA
THAT WAS BEAUTY'S VOICE!! I'VE GOT TO HELP HER...
BUT HOW WILL WE GET TO THE HEAVEN AREA?!
WE'LL BREAK DOWN THE WALL!!
YOU'RE FORCE-FUL... BUT I KINDA LIKE IT.
YEEEE-ARGH, WALL KNOCK, WALL KNOCK, WALL KNOCK!!!
BAM
BAM
BAM
BAM
BAM
BAP
BAP
BAP
BAP
AAAAA AARGH!
POPPA ROCKS!!!...
IT'S OVER.
TMP
HELP...
KRAK
SHOOM
WHO IS IT?

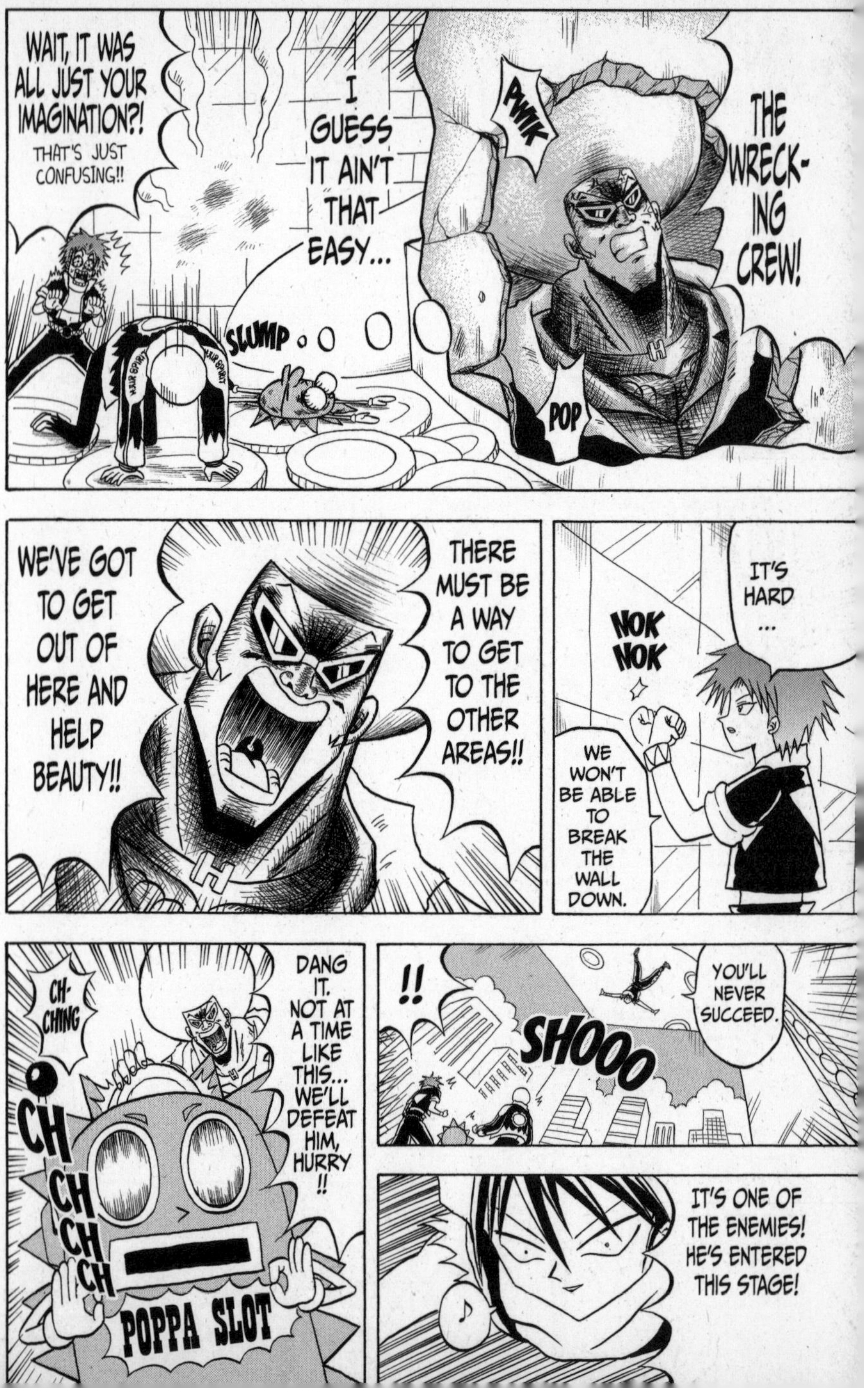
THE WRECKING CREW!
PWIK
POP
I GUESS IT AIN'T THAT EASY...
SLUMP
WAIT, IT WAS ALL JUST YOUR IMAGINATION?!
THAT'S JUST CONFUSING!!
IT'S HARD ...
NOK NOK
WE WON'T BE ABLE TO BREAK THE WALL DOWN.
THERE MUST BE A WAY TO GET TO THE OTHER AREAS!!
WE'VE GOT TO GET OUT OF HERE AND HELP BEAUTY!!
YOU'LL NEVER SUCCEED.
!!
SHOOO
IT'S ONE OF THE ENEMIES! HE'S ENTERED THIS STAGE!
DANG IT. NOT AT A TIME LIKE THIS... WE'LL DEFEAT HIM, HURRY!!
CH-CHING
CH CH CH CH CH
POPPA SLOT

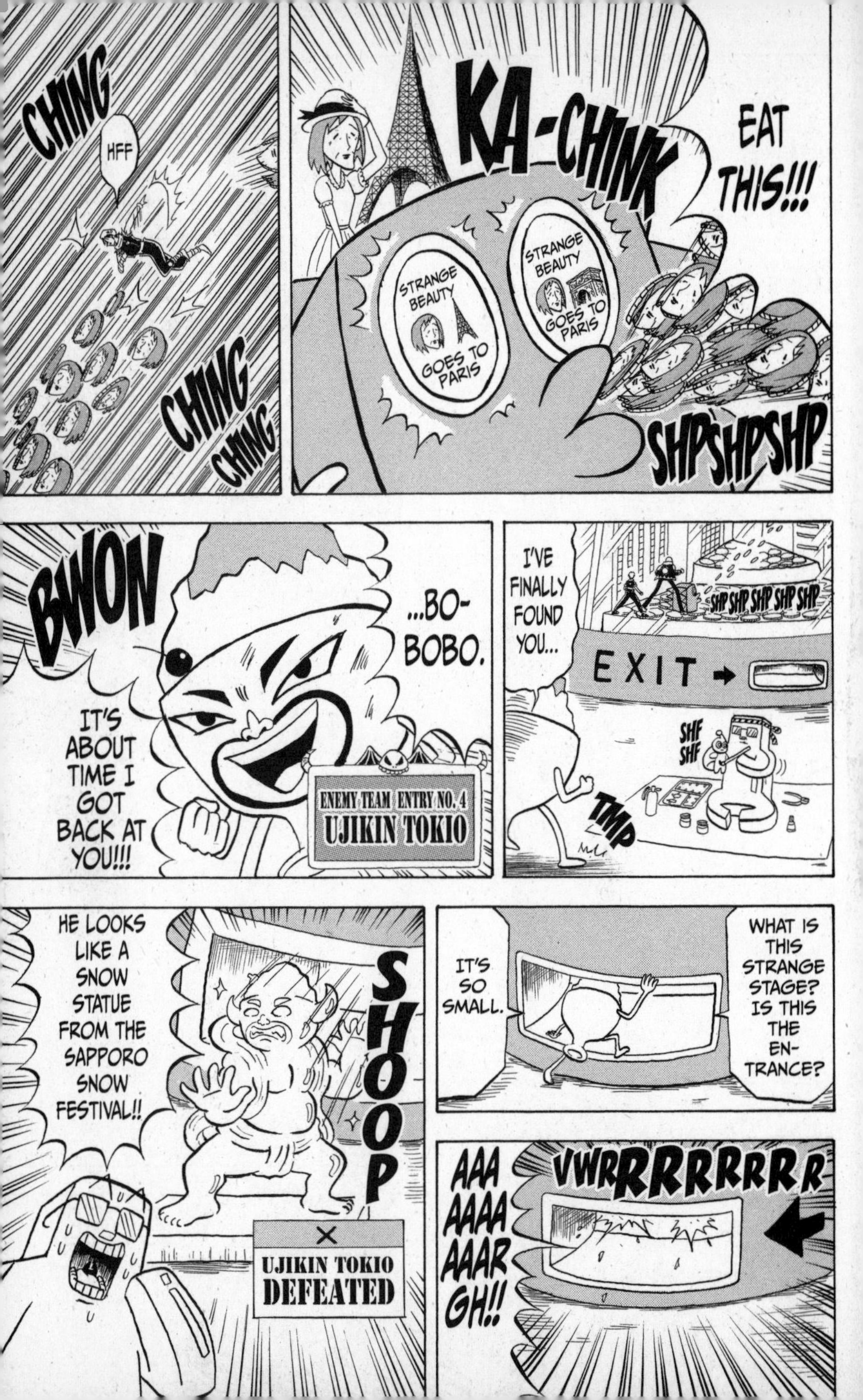
KA-CHINK
EAT THIS!!!
STRANGE BEAUTY GOES TO PARIS
STRANGE BEAUTY GOES TO PARIS
SHPSHPSHP
CHING
HFF
CHING
CHING
I'VE FINALLY FOUND YOU...
SHP SHP SHP SHP SHP
EXIT
SHF SHF
TMP
BWON
...BO-BOBO.
IT'S ABOUT TIME I GOT BACK AT YOU!!!
ENEMY TEAM ENTRY NO. 4
UJIKIN TOKIO
WHAT IS THIS STRANGE STAGE? IS THIS THE EN-TRANCE?
IT'S SO SMALL.
VWRRRRRRRRR
AAAAAAAAARGH!!
HE LOOKS LIKE A SNOW STATUE FROM THE SAPPORO SNOW FESTIVAL!!
SHOOP
UJIKIN TOKIO DEFEATED

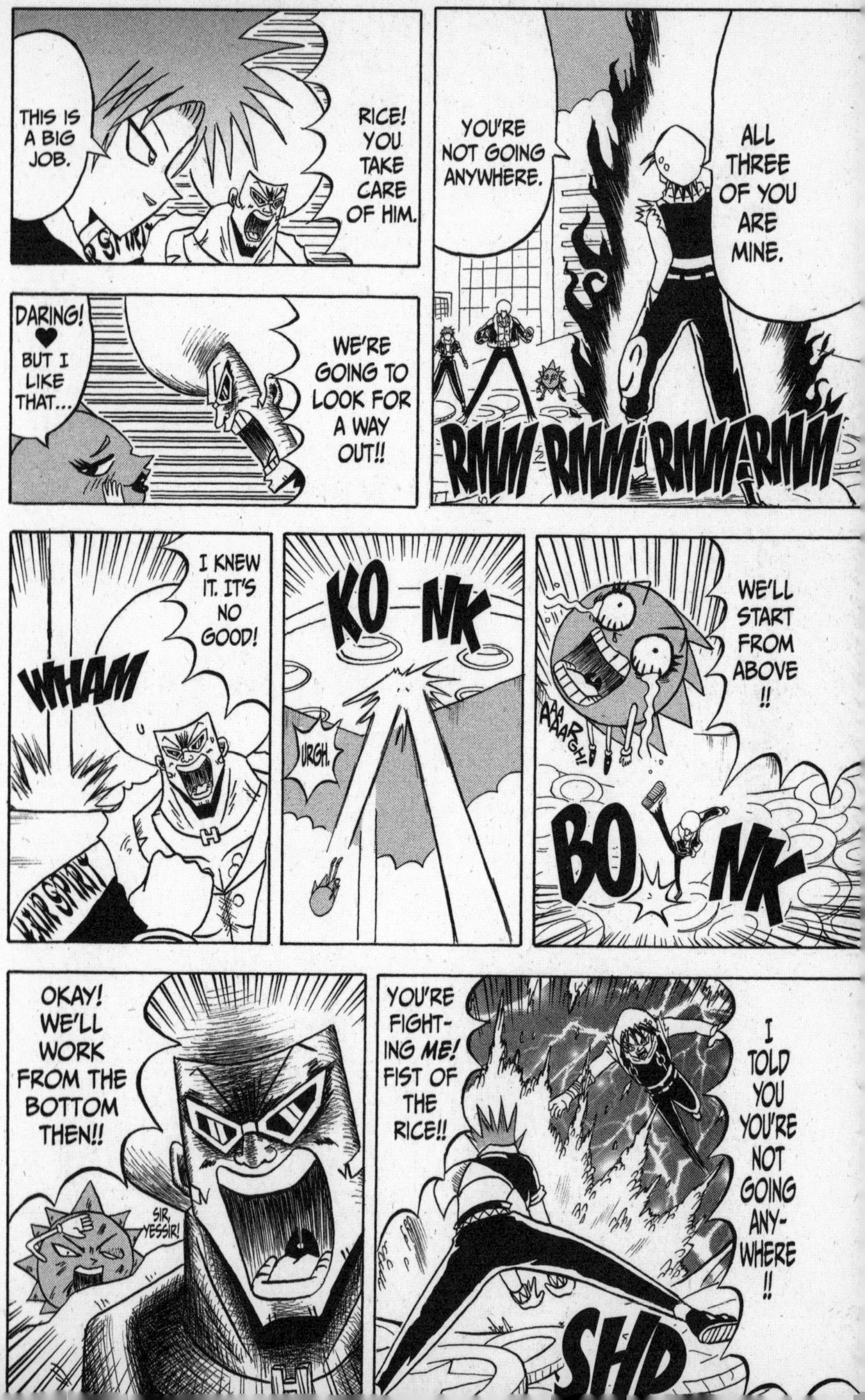
ALL THREE OF YOU ARE MINE.
YOU'RE NOT GOING ANYWHERE.
RMM RMM RMM RMM
RICE! YOU TAKE CARE OF HIM.
THIS IS A BIG JOB.
WE'RE GOING TO LOOK FOR A WAY OUT!!
DARING! ♥ BUT I LIKE THAT...
WE'LL START FROM ABOVE!!
AAAARGH!
BONK
KONK
URGH.
I KNEW IT. IT'S NO GOOD!
WHAM
I TOLD YOU YOU'RE NOT GOING ANYWHERE!!
YOU'RE FIGHTING *ME!* FIST OF THE RICE!!
SHP
OKAY! WE'LL WORK FROM THE BOTTOM THEN!!
SIR, YESSIR!

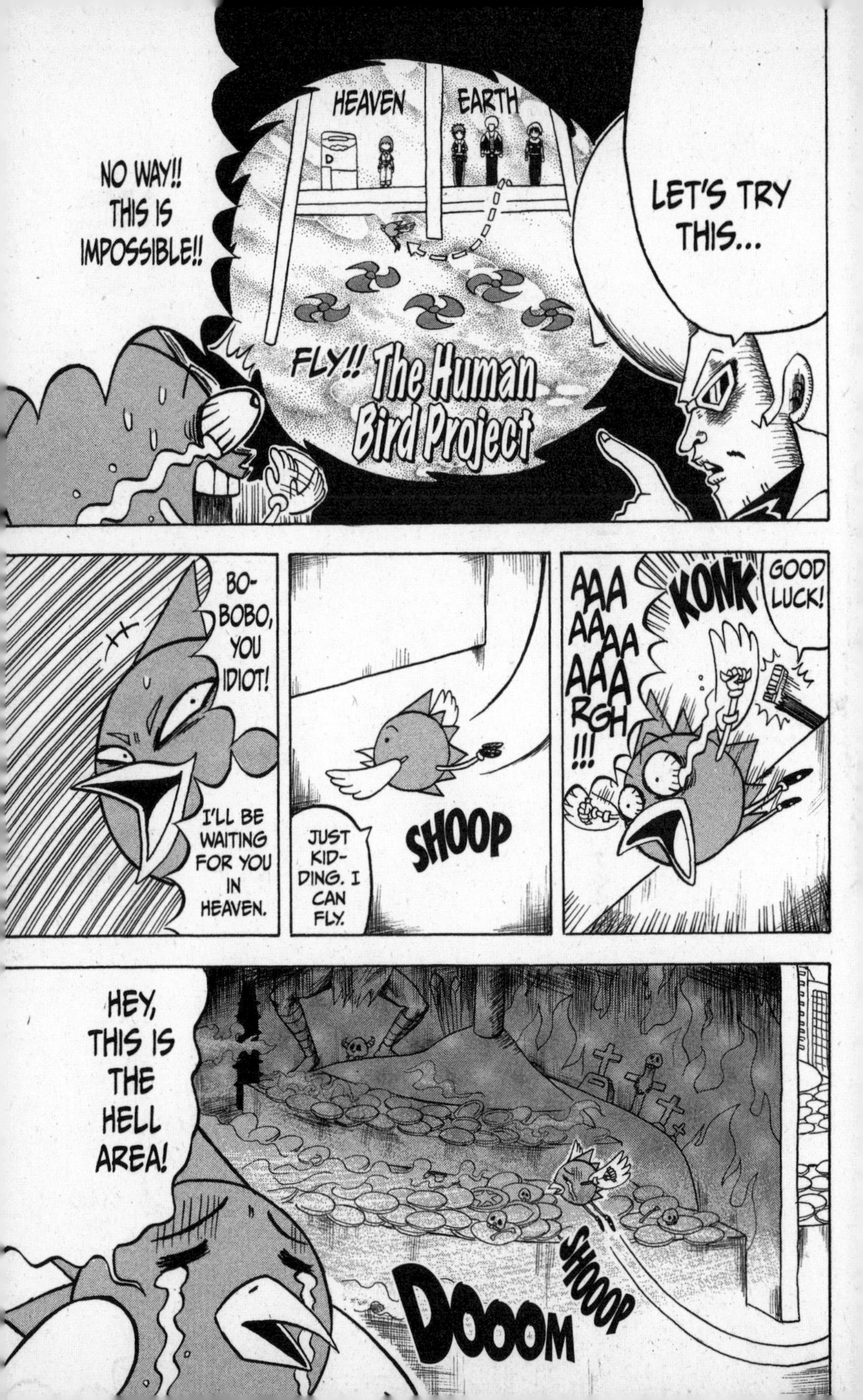
LET'S TRY THIS...
HEAVEN
EARTH
FLY!! The Human Bird Project
NO WAY!! THIS IS IMPOSSIBLE!!
GOOD LUCK!
KONK
AAAAAAAAAARGH!!!
SHOOP
JUST KID-DING. I CAN FLY.
BO-BOBOBO, YOU IDIOT!
I'LL BE WAITING FOR YOU IN HEAVEN.
HEY, THIS IS THE HELL AREA!
SHOOOP
DOOOM

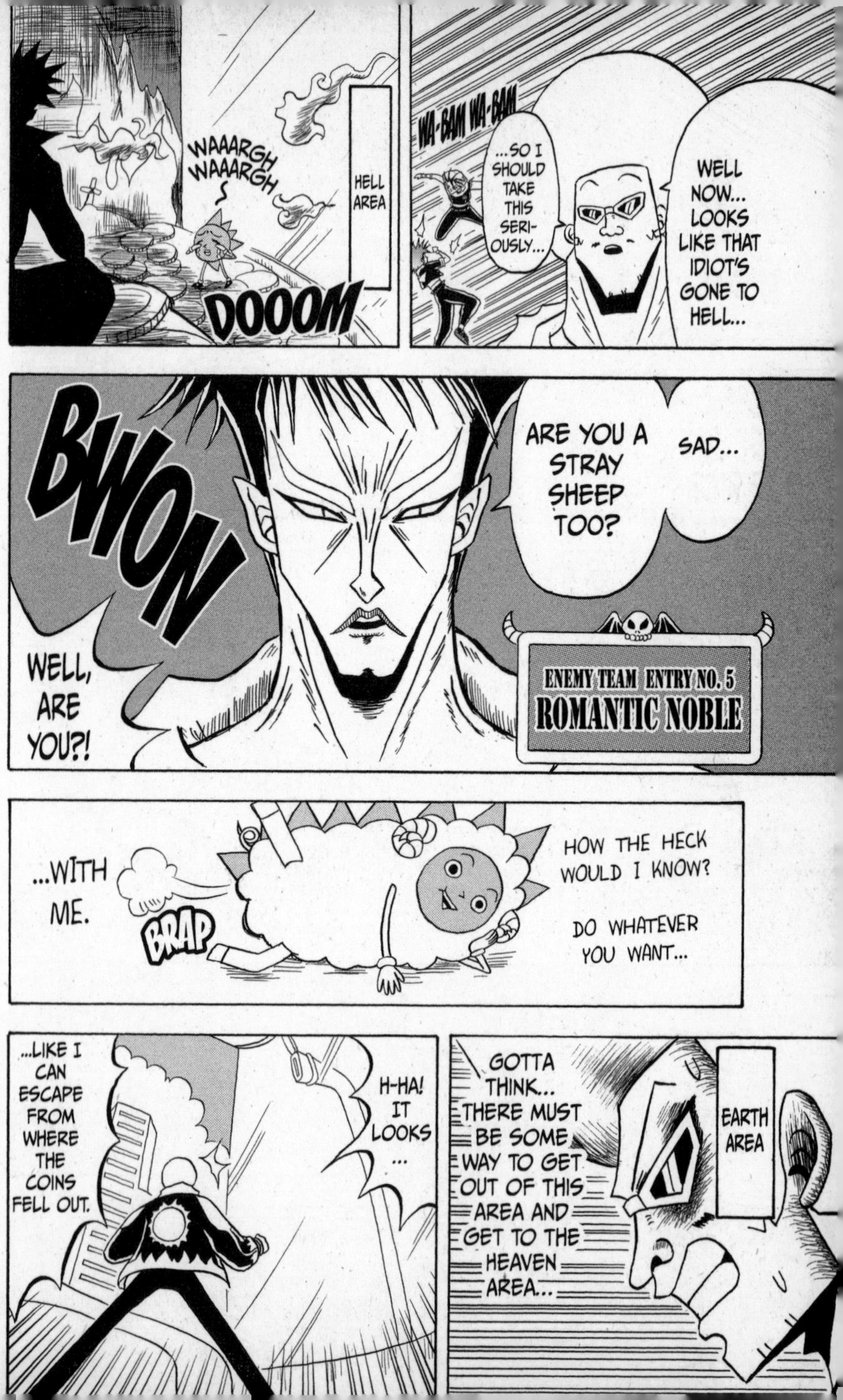
WELL NOW... LOOKS LIKE THAT IDIOT'S GONE TO HELL...
...SO I SHOULD TAKE THIS SERIOUSLY...
WA-BAM WA-BAM
HELL AREA
WAAARGH WAAARGH
DOOOM
SAD...
ARE YOU A STRAY SHEEP TOO?
ENEMY TEAM ENTRY NO. 5
ROMANTIC NOBLE
BWON
WELL, ARE YOU?!
HOW THE HECK WOULD I KNOW?
DO WHATEVER YOU WANT...
BRAP
...WITH ME.
EARTH AREA
GOTTA THINK... THERE MUST BE SOME WAY TO GET OUT OF THIS AREA AND GET TO THE HEAVEN AREA...
H-HA! IT LOOKS ...
...LIKE I CAN ESCAPE FROM WHERE THE COINS FELL OUT.

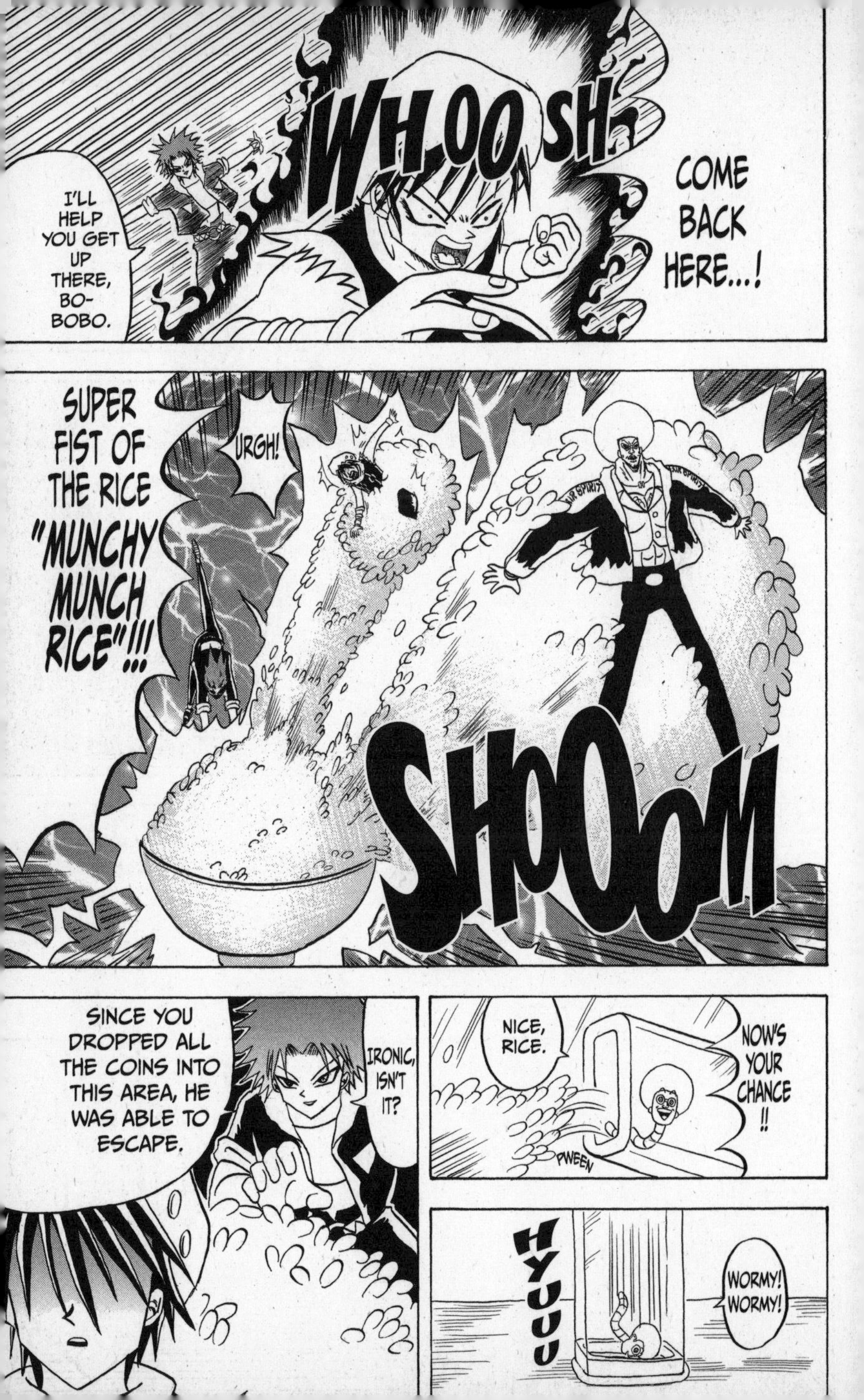
COME BACK HERE...!
WHOOSH
I'LL HELP YOU GET UP THERE, BO-BOBO.
URGH!
SUPER FIST OF THE RICE "MUNCHY MUNCH RICE"!!!
SHOOOM
NOW'S YOUR CHANCE !!
NICE, RICE.
PWEEN
WORMY! WORMY!
HYUUU
IRONIC, ISN'T IT?
SINCE YOU DROPPED ALL THE COINS INTO THIS AREA, HE WAS ABLE TO ESCAPE.

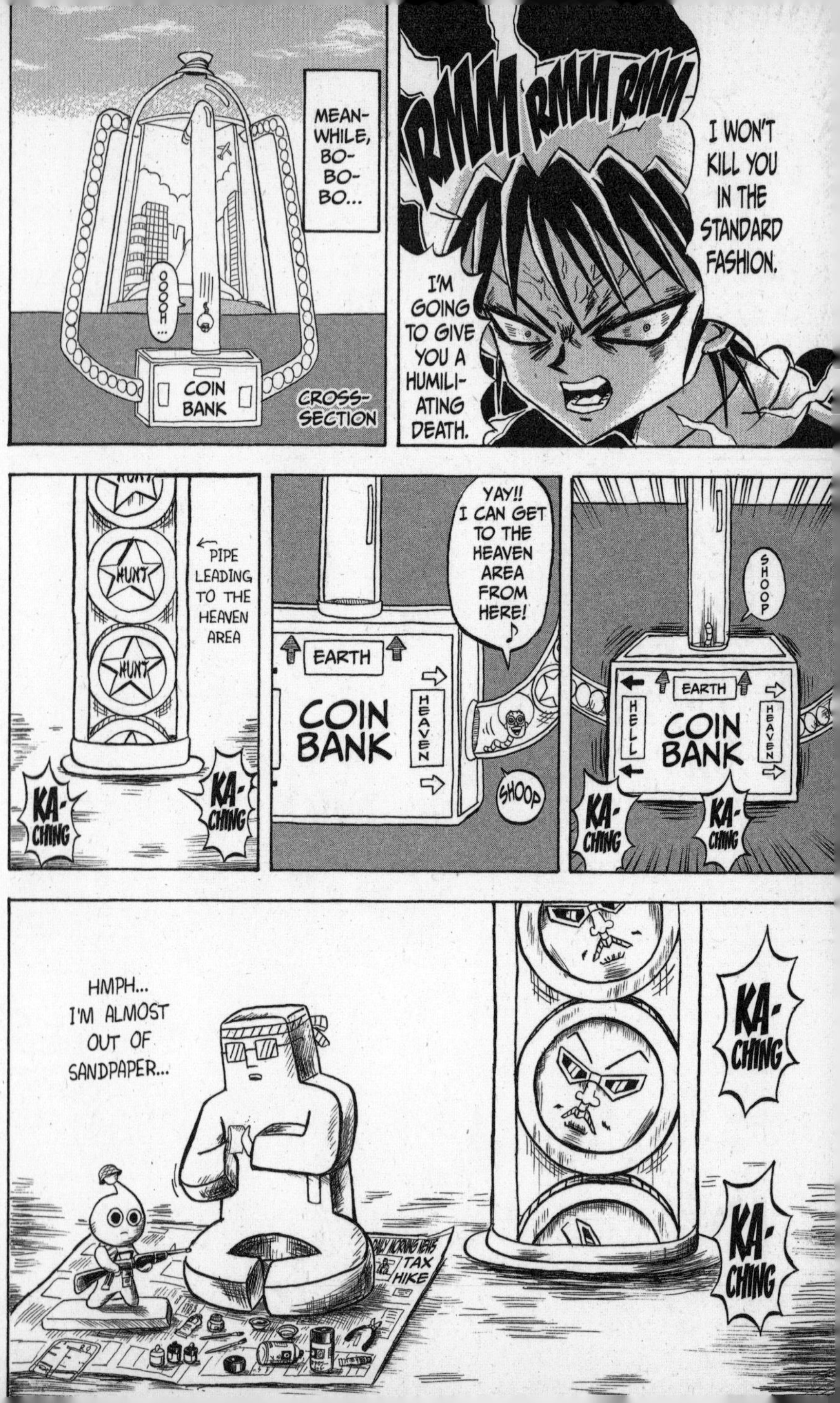
RMM RMM RMM
I WON'T KILL YOU IN THE STANDARD FASHION.
I'M GOING TO GIVE YOU A HUMILIATING DEATH.
MEANWHILE, BOBOBO...
OOOOH...
COIN BANK
CROSS-SECTION
SHOOP
EARTH
HELL
COIN BANK
HEAVEN
KA-CHING
KA-CHING
YAY!! I CAN GET TO THE HEAVEN AREA FROM HERE! ♪
EARTH
COIN BANK
HEAVEN
SHOOP
PIPE LEADING TO THE HEAVEN AREA
HUNT
HUNT
KA-CHING
KA-CHING
KA-CHING
KA-CHING
HMPH... I'M ALMOST OUT OF SANDPAPER...
DAILY MORNING NEWS
TAX HIKE

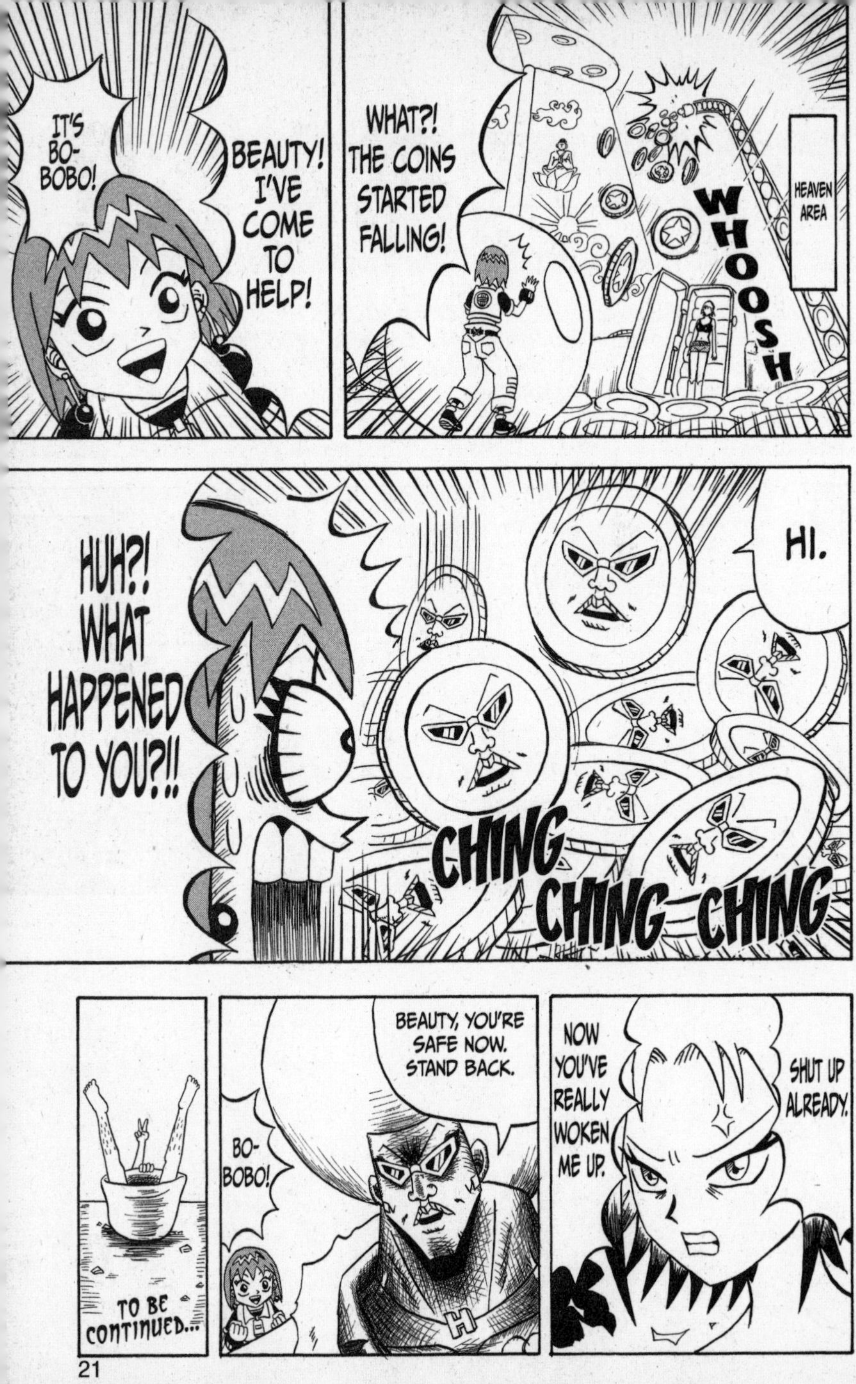
HEAVEN AREA
WHOOSH
WHAT?! THE COINS STARTED FALLING!
BEAUTY! I'VE COME TO HELP!
IT'S BO-BOBO!
HI.
CHING CHING CHING
HUH?! WHAT HAPPENED TO YOU?!!
SHUT UP ALREADY.
NOW YOU'VE REALLY WOKEN ME UP.
BEAUTY, YOU'RE SAFE NOW. STAND BACK.
BO-BOBO!
TO BE CONTINUED...

Bo-bobo Q & A?!!

HEY, EVERYBODY!! LONG TIME NO SEE!! AND NICE TO MEET YOU!! THE Q & A CORNER IS FINALLY BACK. ANYTHING RANGING FROM QUESTIONS ABOUT THE CHARACTERS IN *BO-BOBO* DOWN TO PERSONAL QUESTIONS FOR SAWAI-SAN HIMSELF! HE'S GOING TO ANSWER YOUR QUESTIONS.♥

Q. MR. SAWAI, I REALLY LIKE THE COVER ILLUSTRATION FOR VOLUME 6, BUT WHICH IS YOUR FAVORITE COVER SO FAR? PLEASE TELL ME.

(Tokyo, Dengaku Sukiyaki)

A. I LIKE ALL OF THE *BO-BOBO* COVER ILLUS-TRATIONS. I'VE GOT A SPECIAL ATTACHMENT TO EACH OF THEM. SO, I'D LIKE TO TELL YOU MY FEELINGS FOR EACH OF THOSE ILLUSTRATIONS WHETHER YOU LIKE IT OR NOT.

IT ALL STARTS ON PAGE 38!!

YOU, THERE.

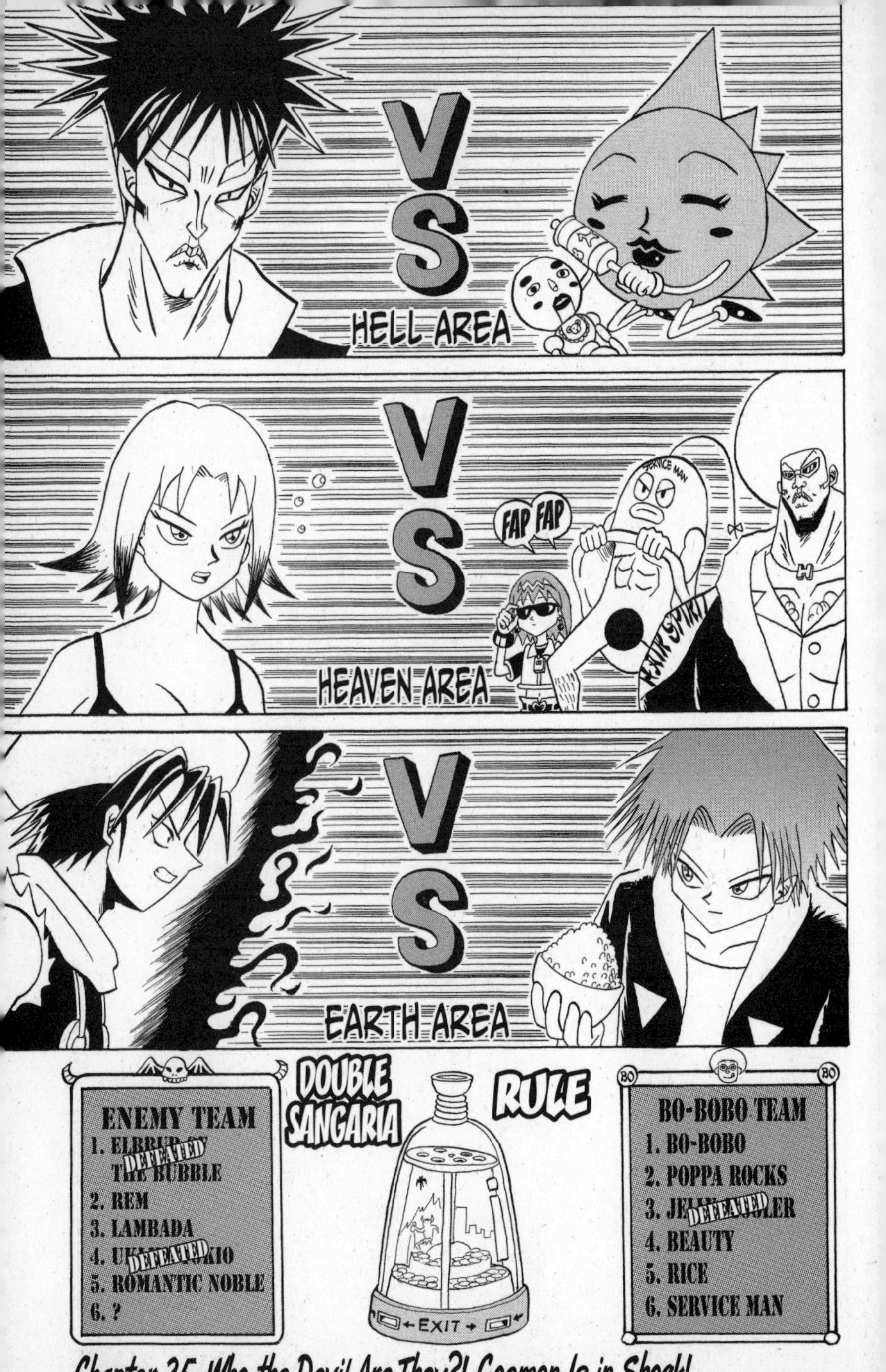
VS
HELL AREA
SERVICE MAN
FAP FAP
HAIR SPIRIT
VS
HEAVEN AREA
VS
EARTH AREA
BO BO
BO-BOBO TEAM
1. BO-BOBO
2. POPPA ROCKS
3. JE DEFEATED LER
4. BEAUTY
5. RICE
6. SERVICE MAN
RULE
DOUBLE SANGARIA
EXIT
ENEMY TEAM
1. ELBRU DEFEATED
THE BUBBLE
2. REM
3. LAMBADA
4. U DEFEATED KIO
5. ROMANTIC NOBLE
6. ?

Chapter 35: Who the Devil Are They?! Goemon Is in Shock!

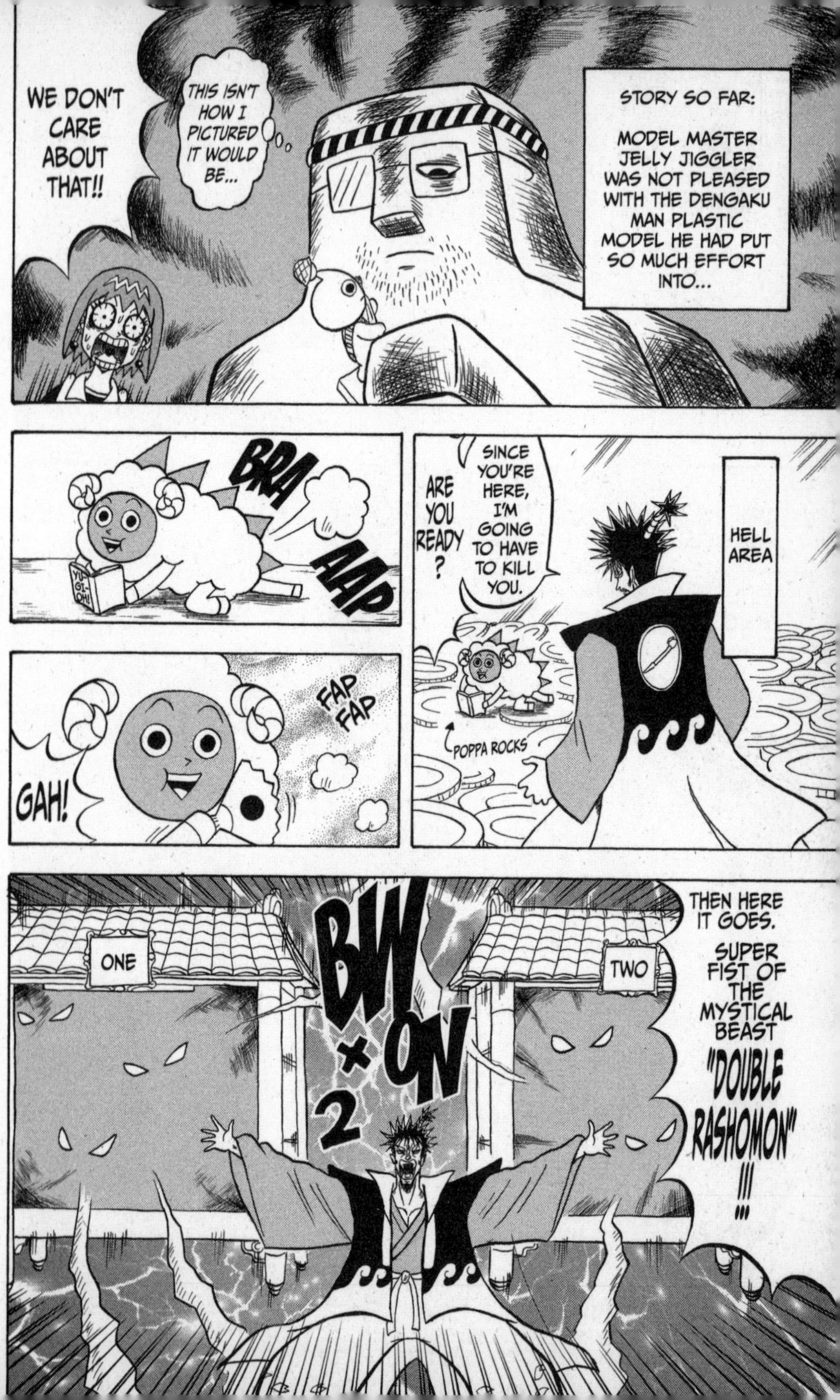
STORY SO FAR:
MODEL MASTER JELLY JIGGLER WAS NOT PLEASED WITH THE DENGAKU MAN PLASTIC MODEL HE HAD PUT SO MUCH EFFORT INTO...
THIS ISN'T HOW I PICTURED IT WOULD BE...
WE DON'T CARE ABOUT THAT!!
HELL AREA
SINCE YOU'RE HERE, I'M GOING TO HAVE TO KILL YOU.
ARE YOU READY?
POPPA ROCKS
YU-GI-OH!
BRAAAP
FAP FAP
GAH!
THEN HERE IT GOES.
SUPER FIST OF THE MYSTICAL BEAST "DOUBLE RASHOMON"!!!
TWO
ONE
BWON ×2

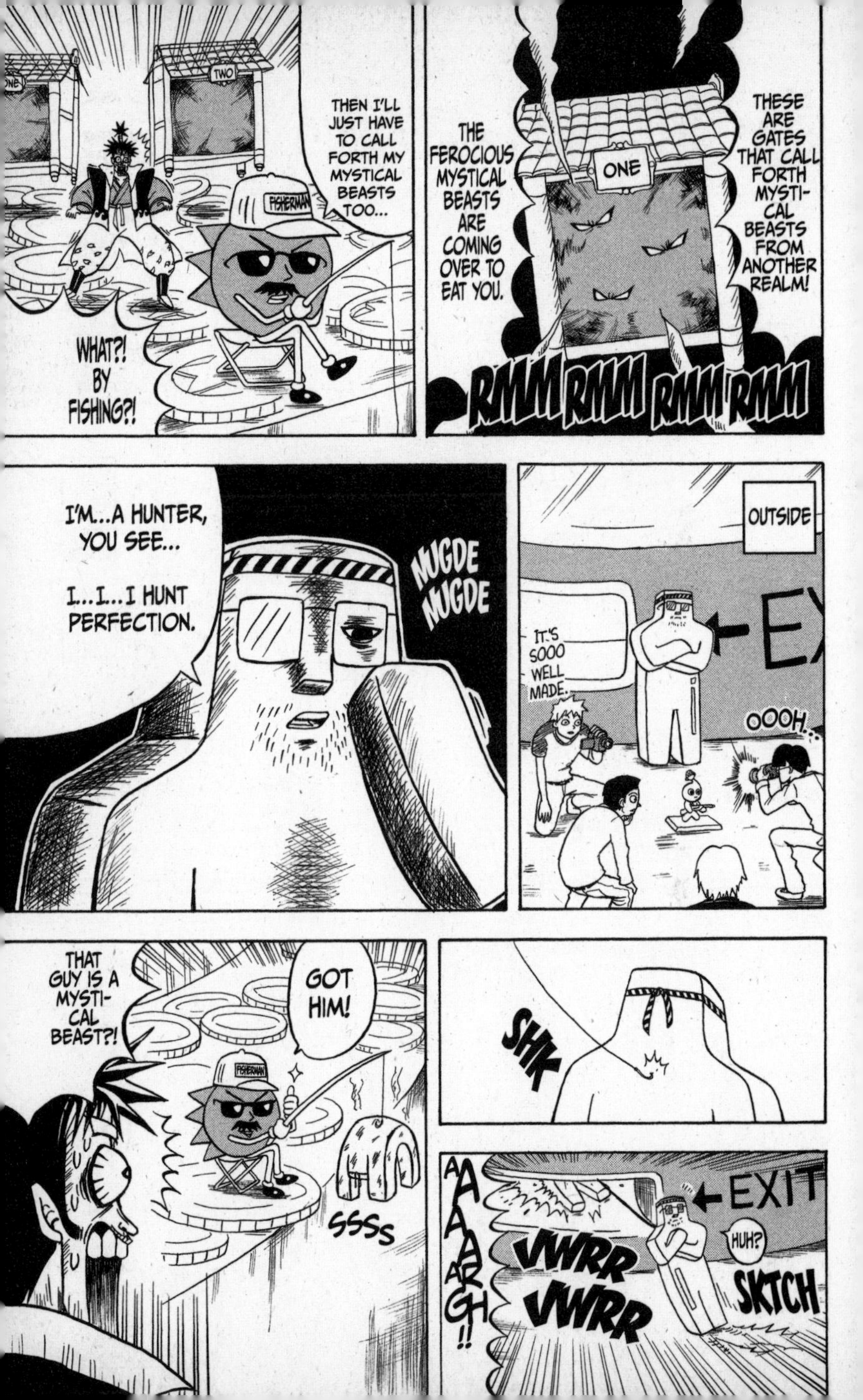
ONE
THESE ARE GATES THAT CALL FORTH MYSTICAL BEASTS FROM ANOTHER REALM!
THE FEROCIOUS MYSTICAL BEASTS ARE COMING OVER TO EAT YOU.
RMM RMM RMM RMM
TWO
ONE
THEN I'LL JUST HAVE TO CALL FORTH MY MYSTICAL BEASTS TOO...
FISHERMAN
WHAT?! BY FISHING?!
OUTSIDE
←EX
OOOH...
IT'S SOOO WELL MADE.
MUGDE MUGDE
I'M...A HUNTER, YOU SEE...
I...I...I HUNT PERFECTION.
SHK
←EXIT
HUH?
SKTCH
VWRR VWRR
AAAAARGH!!
GOT HIM!
THAT GUY IS A MYSTICAL BEAST?!
FISHERMAN
SSSS

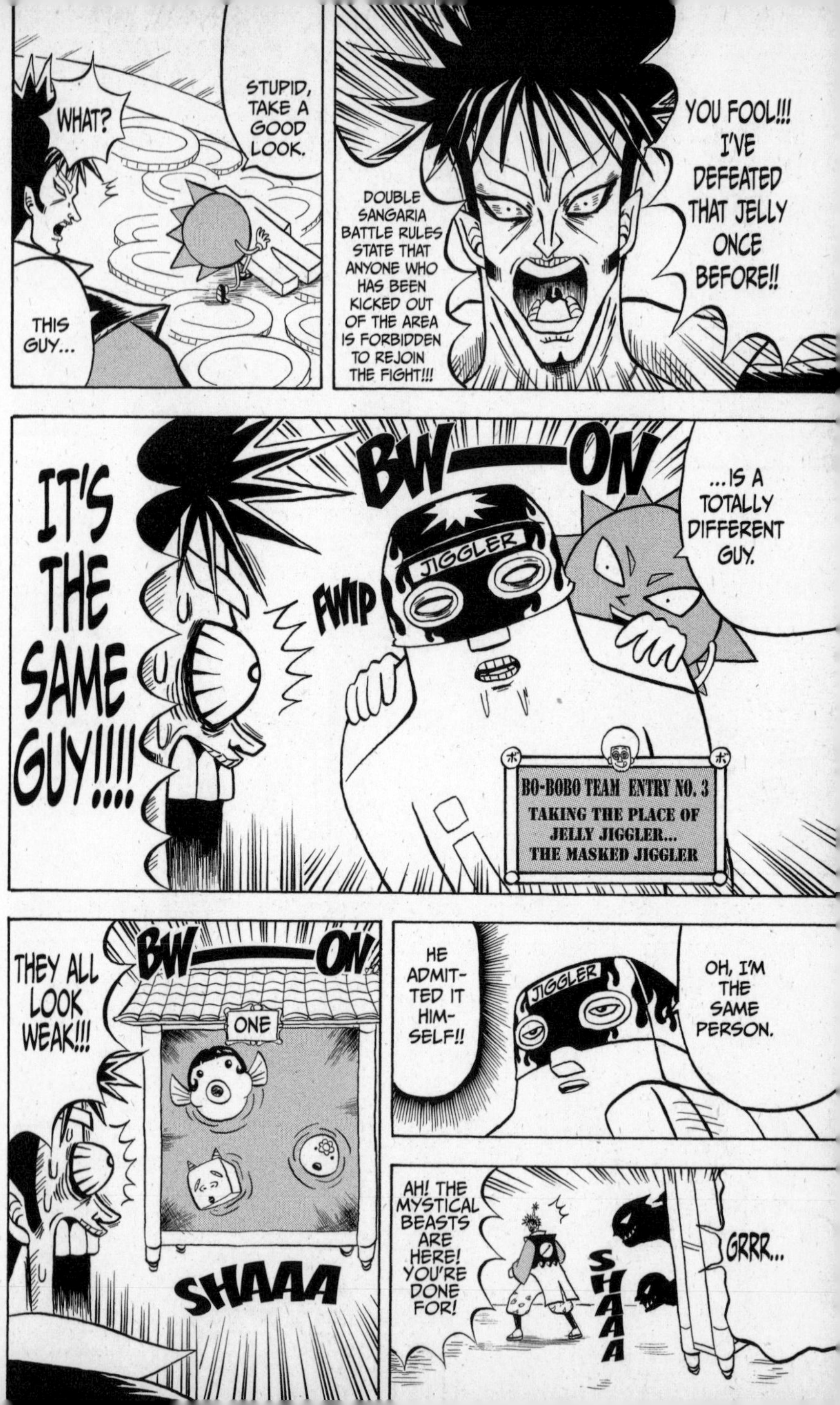
YOU FOOL!!! I'VE DEFEATED THAT JELLY ONCE BEFORE!!
DOUBLE SANGARIA BATTLE RULES STATE THAT ANYONE WHO HAS BEEN KICKED OUT OF THE AREA IS FORBIDDEN TO REJOIN THE FIGHT!!!
STUPID, TAKE A GOOD LOOK.
WHAT?
THIS GUY...
...IS A TOTALLY DIFFERENT GUY.
BW—ON
JIGGLER
FWIP
BO-BOBO TEAM ENTRY NO. 3
TAKING THE PLACE OF JELLY JIGGLER... THE MASKED JIGGLER
IT'S THE SAME GUY!!!!!
OH, I'M THE SAME PERSON.
JIGGLER
HE ADMIT-TED IT HIM-SELF!!
GRRR...
SHAAA
AH! THE MYSTICAL BEASTS ARE HERE! YOU'RE DONE FOR!
BW—ON
ONE
THEY ALL LOOK WEAK!!!
SHAAA

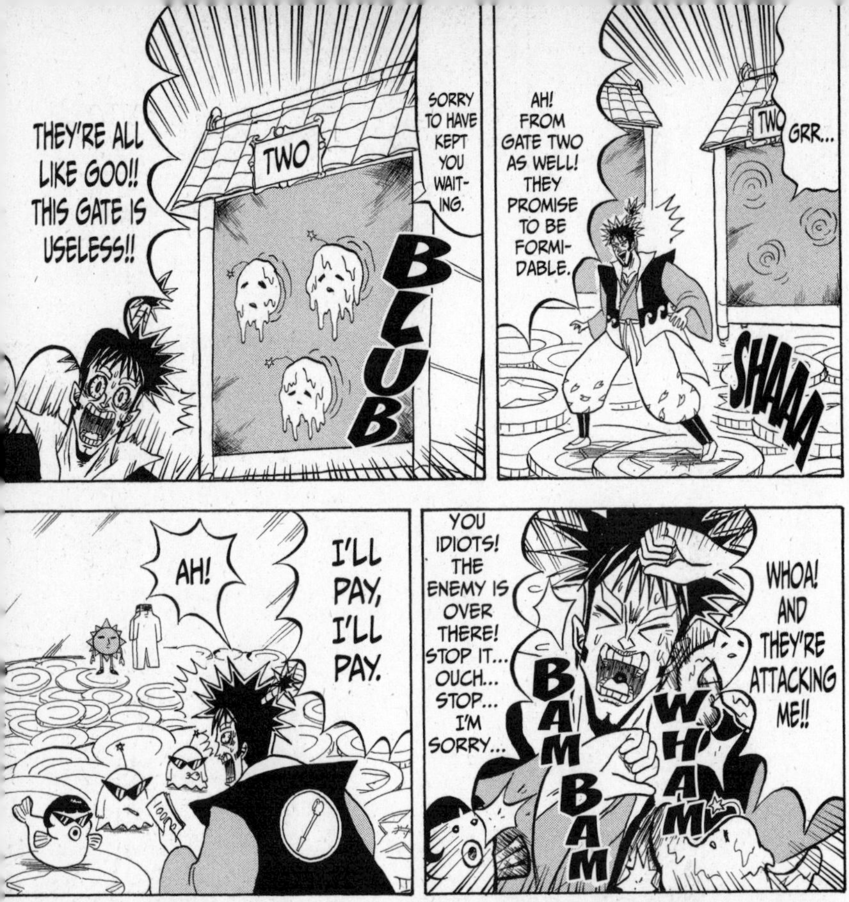
GRR...
AH! FROM GATE TWO AS WELL! THEY PROMISE TO BE FORMIDABLE.
SHAAAA
SORRY TO HAVE KEPT YOU WAIT-ING.
BLUB
THEY'RE ALL LIKE GOO!! THIS GATE IS USELESS!!
TWO
WHOA! AND THEY'RE ATTACKING ME!!
WHAM
YOU IDIOTS! THE ENEMY IS OVER THERE! STOP IT... OUCH... STOP... I'M SORRY...
BAM BAM
I'LL PAY, I'LL PAY.
AH!

Goemon is a heroic bandit from Japanese folklore.

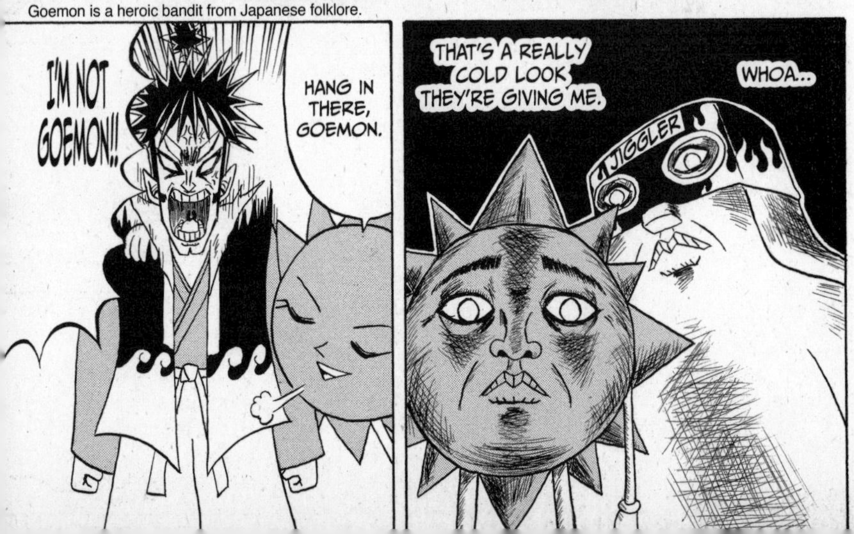
WHOA...
THAT'S A REALLY COLD LOOK THEY'RE GIVING ME.
JIGGLER
HANG IN THERE, GOEMON.
I'M NOT GOEMON!!

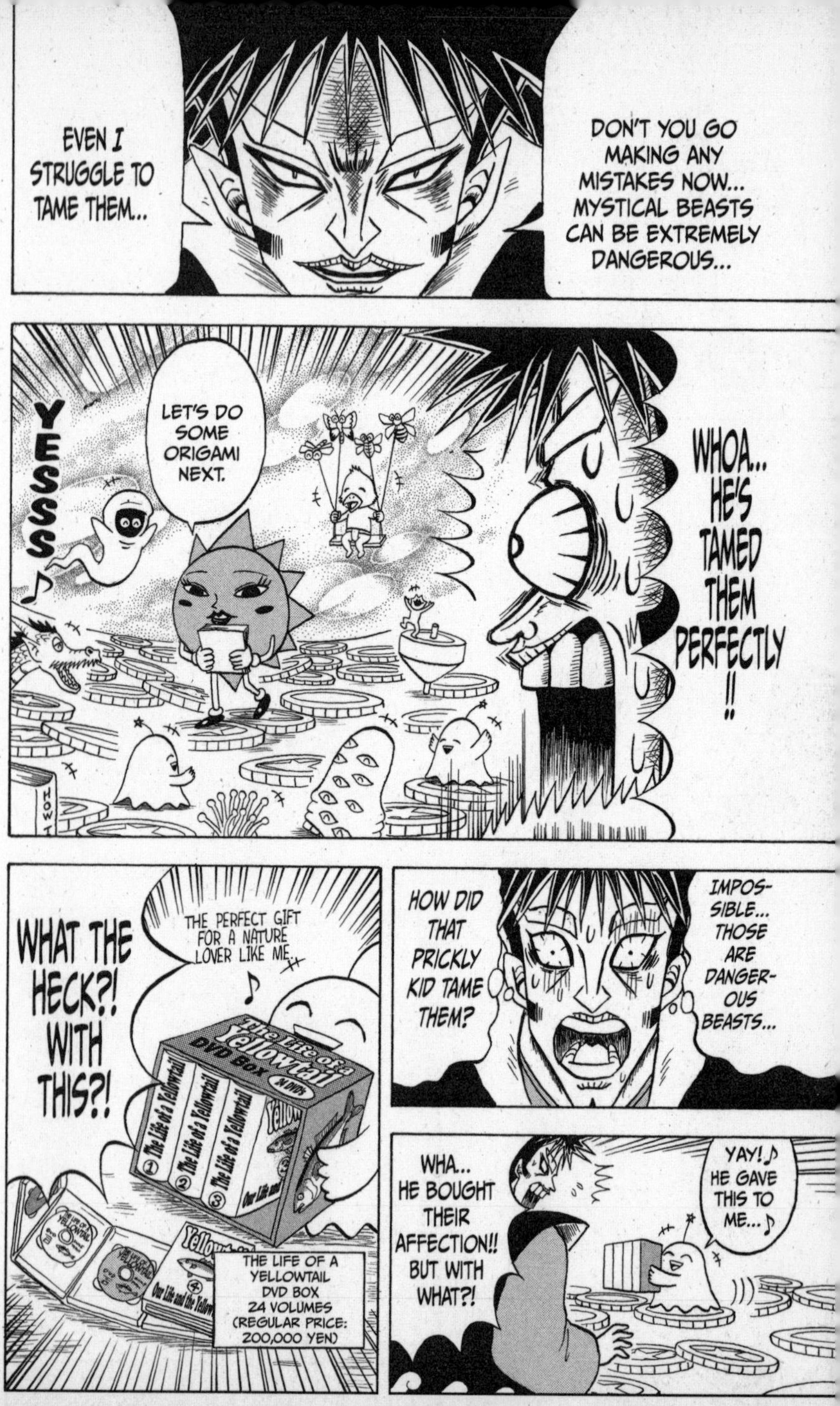

DON'T YOU GO MAKING ANY MISTAKES NOW... MYSTICAL BEASTS CAN BE EXTREMELY DANGEROUS...
EVEN I STRUGGLE TO TAME THEM...
WHOA... HE'S TAMED THEM PERFECTLY!!
LET'S DO SOME ORIGAMI NEXT.
YESSS ♪
HOW T
IMPOSSIBLE... THOSE ARE DANGEROUS BEASTS...
HOW DID THAT PRICKLY KID TAME THEM?
YAY! ♪ HE GAVE THIS TO ME... ♪
WHA... HE BOUGHT THEIR AFFECTION!! BUT WITH WHAT?!
THE PERFECT GIFT FOR A NATURE LOVER LIKE ME. ♪
WHAT THE HECK?! WITH THIS?!
The Life of a Yellowtail DVD Box 24 DVDs
The Life of a Yellowtail ①
The Life of a Yellowtail ②
The Life of a Yellowtail ③
Our Life and the Yellowtail ④
THE LIFE OF A YELLOWTAIL DVD BOX 24 VOLUMES (REGULAR PRICE: 200,000 YEN)

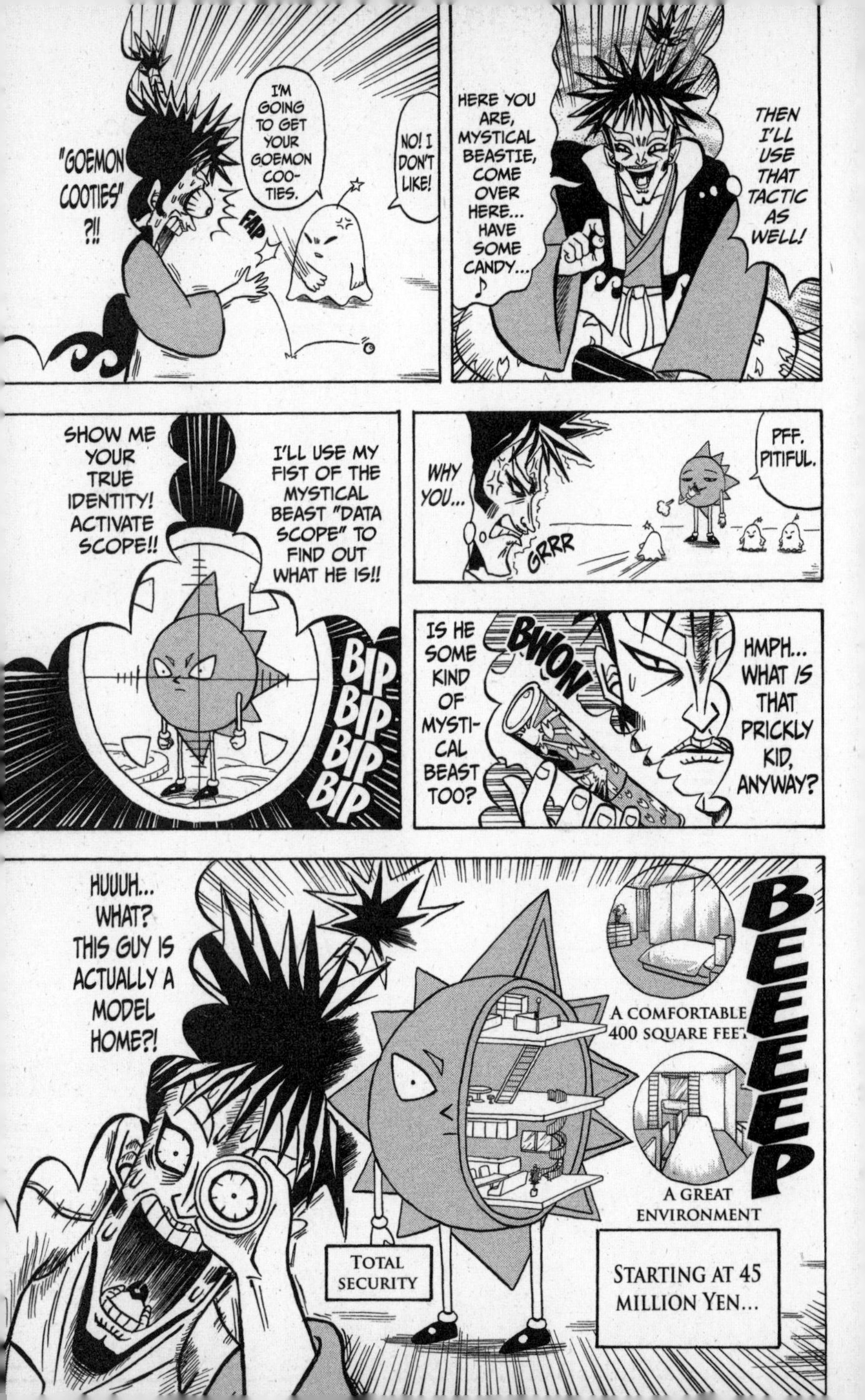
THEN I'LL USE THAT TACTIC AS WELL!
HERE YOU ARE, MYSTICAL BEASTIE, COME OVER HERE... HAVE SOME CANDY... ♪
NO! I DON'T LIKE!
I'M GOING TO GET YOUR GOEMON COO-TIES.
FAP
"GOEMON COOTIES" ?!!
PFF. PITIFUL.
WHY YOU...
GRRR
HMPH... WHAT IS THAT PRICKLY KID, ANYWAY?
BWON
IS HE SOME KIND OF MYSTI-CAL BEAST TOO?
I'LL USE MY FIST OF THE MYSTICAL BEAST "DATA SCOPE" TO FIND OUT WHAT HE IS!!
SHOW ME YOUR TRUE IDENTITY! ACTIVATE SCOPE!!
BIP BIP BIP BIP
BEEEEP
A COMFORTABLE 400 SQUARE FEET
A GREAT ENVIRONMENT
STARTING AT 45 MILLION YEN...
TOTAL SECURITY
HUUUH... WHAT? THIS GUY IS ACTUALLY A MODEL HOME?!

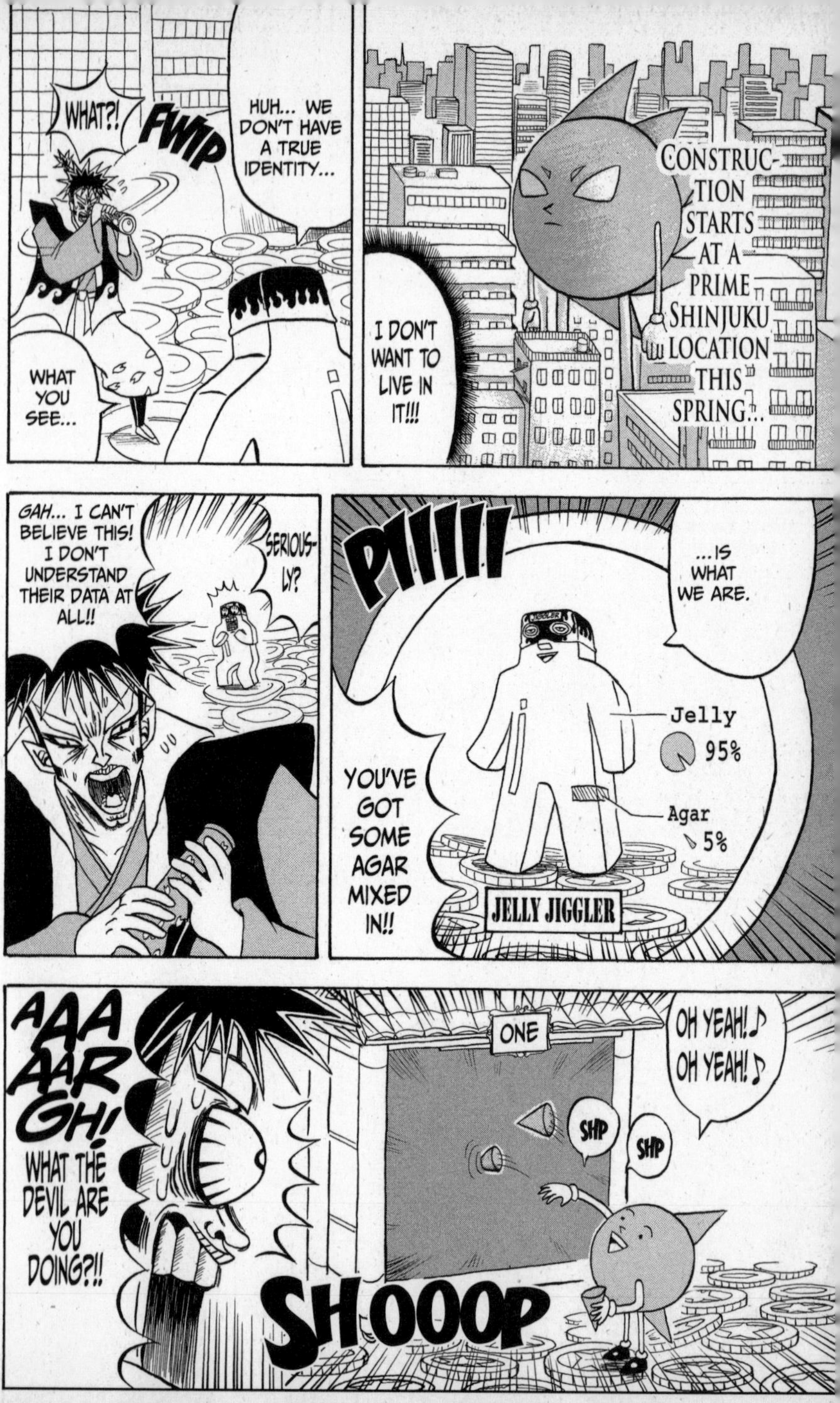
CONSTRUCTION STARTS AT A PRIME SHINJUKU LOCATION THIS SPRING...
I DON'T WANT TO LIVE IN IT!!!
HUH... WE DON'T HAVE A TRUE IDENTITY...
FWIP
WHAT?!
WHAT YOU SEE...
...IS WHAT WE ARE.
PIIII
Jelly 95%
Agar 5%
JELLY JIGGLER
YOU'VE GOT SOME AGAR MIXED IN!!
SERIOUSLY?
GAH... I CAN'T BELIEVE THIS! I DON'T UNDERSTAND THEIR DATA AT ALL!!
OH YEAH!♪ OH YEAH!♪
ONE
SHP
SHP
SHOOOP
AAAAARGH! WHAT THE DEVIL ARE YOU DOING?!!

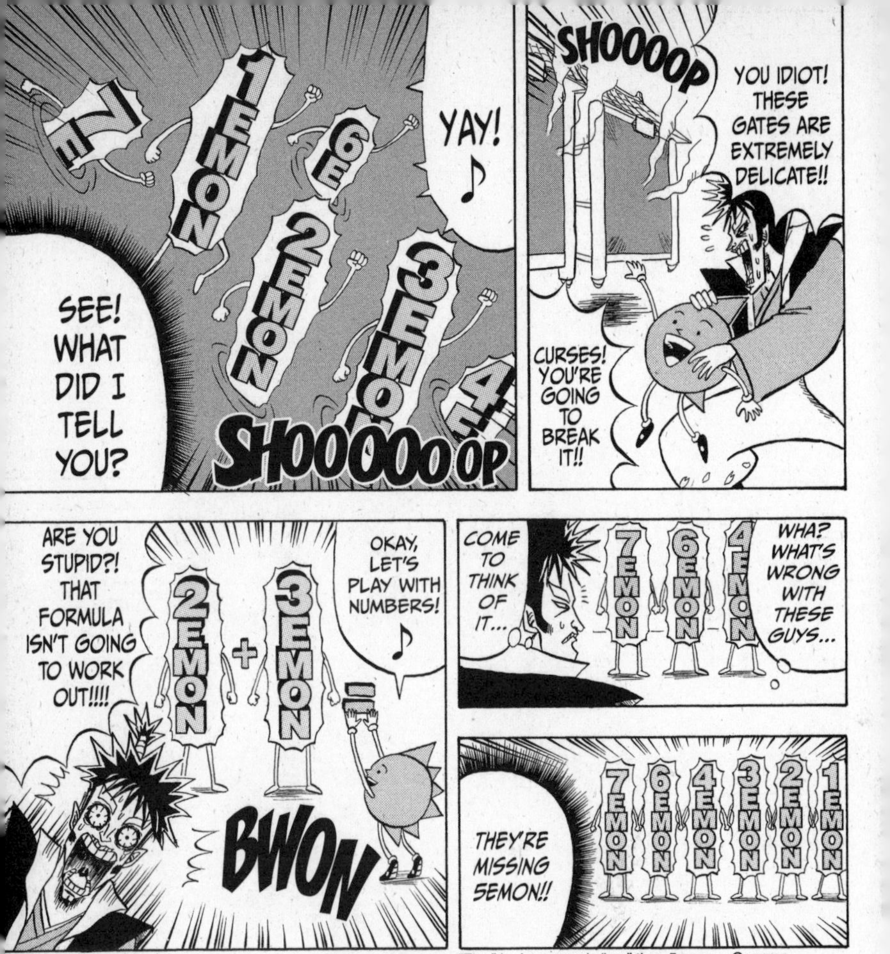
SHOOOOP
YOU IDIOT! THESE GATES ARE EXTREMELY DELICATE!!
CURSES! YOU'RE GOING TO BREAK IT!!
YAY! ♪
7E
1EMON
6E
2EMON
3EMO
4E
SEE! WHAT DID I TELL YOU?
SHOOOOOOOP
WHA? WHAT'S WRONG WITH THESE GUYS...
COME TO THINK OF IT...
7EMON
6EMON
4EMON
THEY'RE MISSING 5EMON!!
7EMON
6EMON
4EMON
3EMON
2EMON
1EMON
OKAY, LET'S PLAY WITH NUMBERS! ♪
ARE YOU STUPID?! THAT FORMULA ISN'T GOING TO WORK OUT!!!!
2EMON
+
3EMON
=
BWON

"Five" in Japanese is "go," thus 5emon = Goemon.

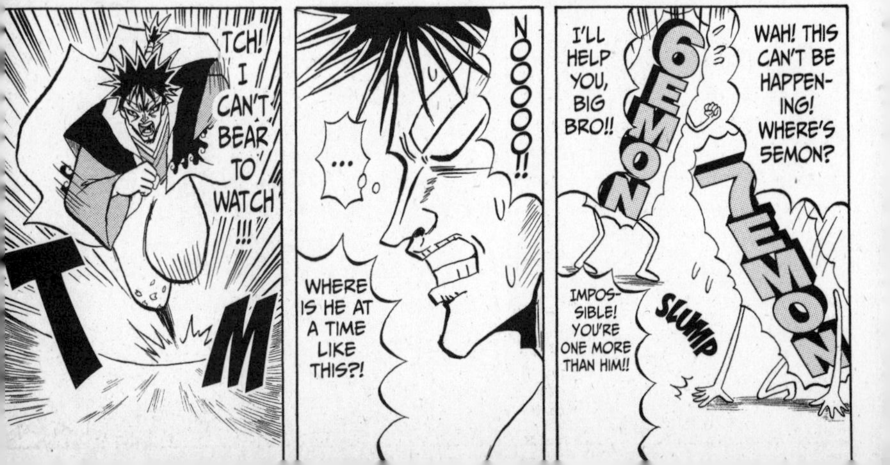
WAH! THIS CAN'T BE HAPPEN-ING! WHERE'S 5EMON?
I'LL HELP YOU, BIG BRO!!
6EMON
7EMON
IMPOS-SIBLE! YOU'RE ONE MORE THAN HIM!!
SLUMP
NOOOOO!!
...
WHERE IS HE AT A TIME LIKE THIS?!
TCH! I CAN'T BEAR TO WATCH!!!
TM

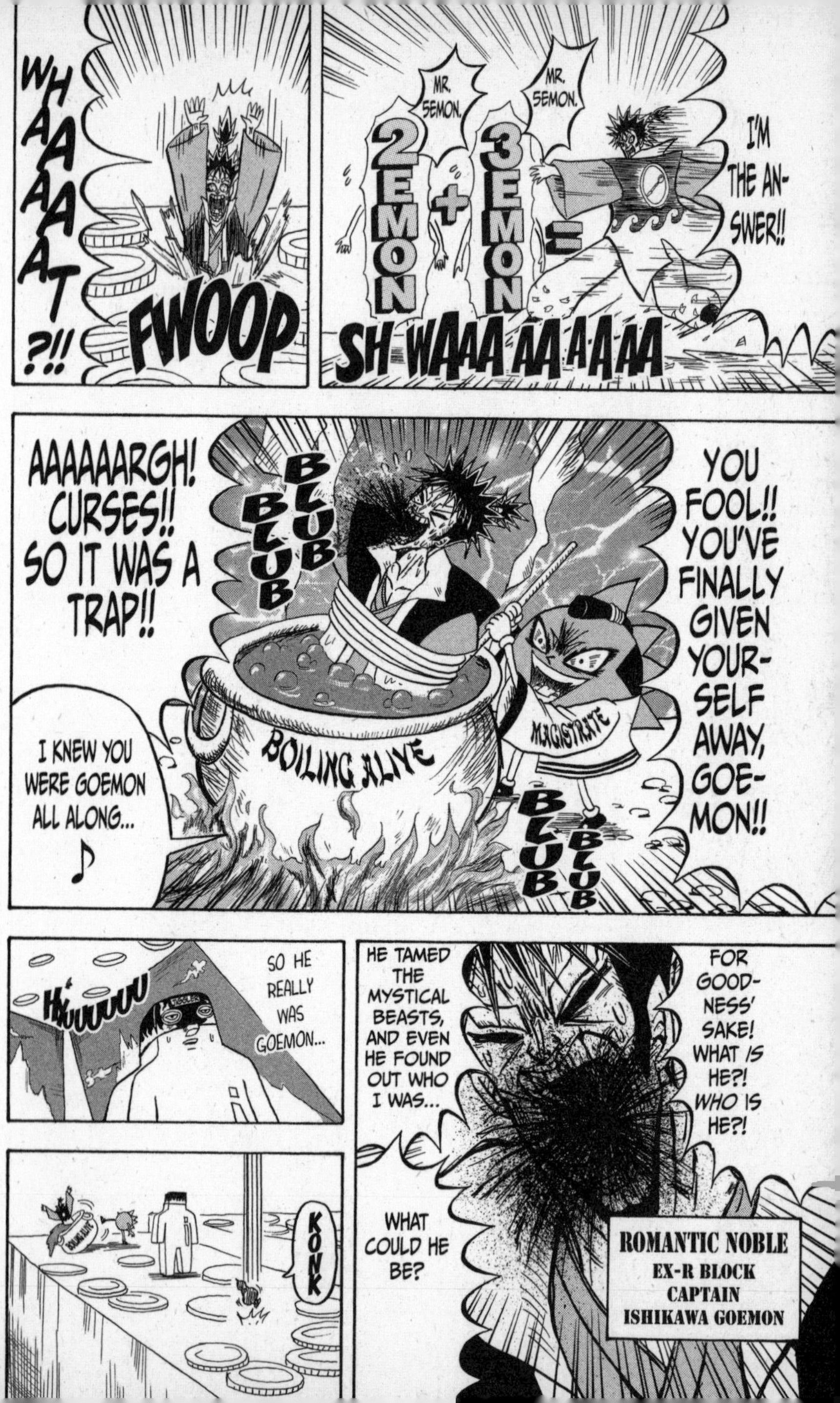
I'M THE ANSWER!!
MR. SEMON.
MR. SEMON.
2EMON + 3EMON =
SHWAAAAAAAAAA
WHAAAAAAT?!!
FWOOP
YOU FOOL!! YOU'VE FINALLY GIVEN YOURSELF AWAY, GOEMON!!
AAAAAARGH! CURSES!! SO IT WAS A TRAP!!
BLUB BLUB
BLUB BLUB
MAGISTRATE
BOILING ALIVE
I KNEW YOU WERE GOEMON ALL ALONG... ♪
BLUB BLUB
FOR GOODNESS' SAKE! WHAT *IS* HE?! *WHO* IS HE?!
HE TAMED THE MYSTICAL BEASTS, AND EVEN HE FOUND OUT WHO I WAS...
WHAT COULD HE BE?
ROMANTIC NOBLE
EX-R BLOCK CAPTAIN
ISHIKAWA GOEMON
SO HE REALLY WAS GOEMON...
HIUUUUU
KONK

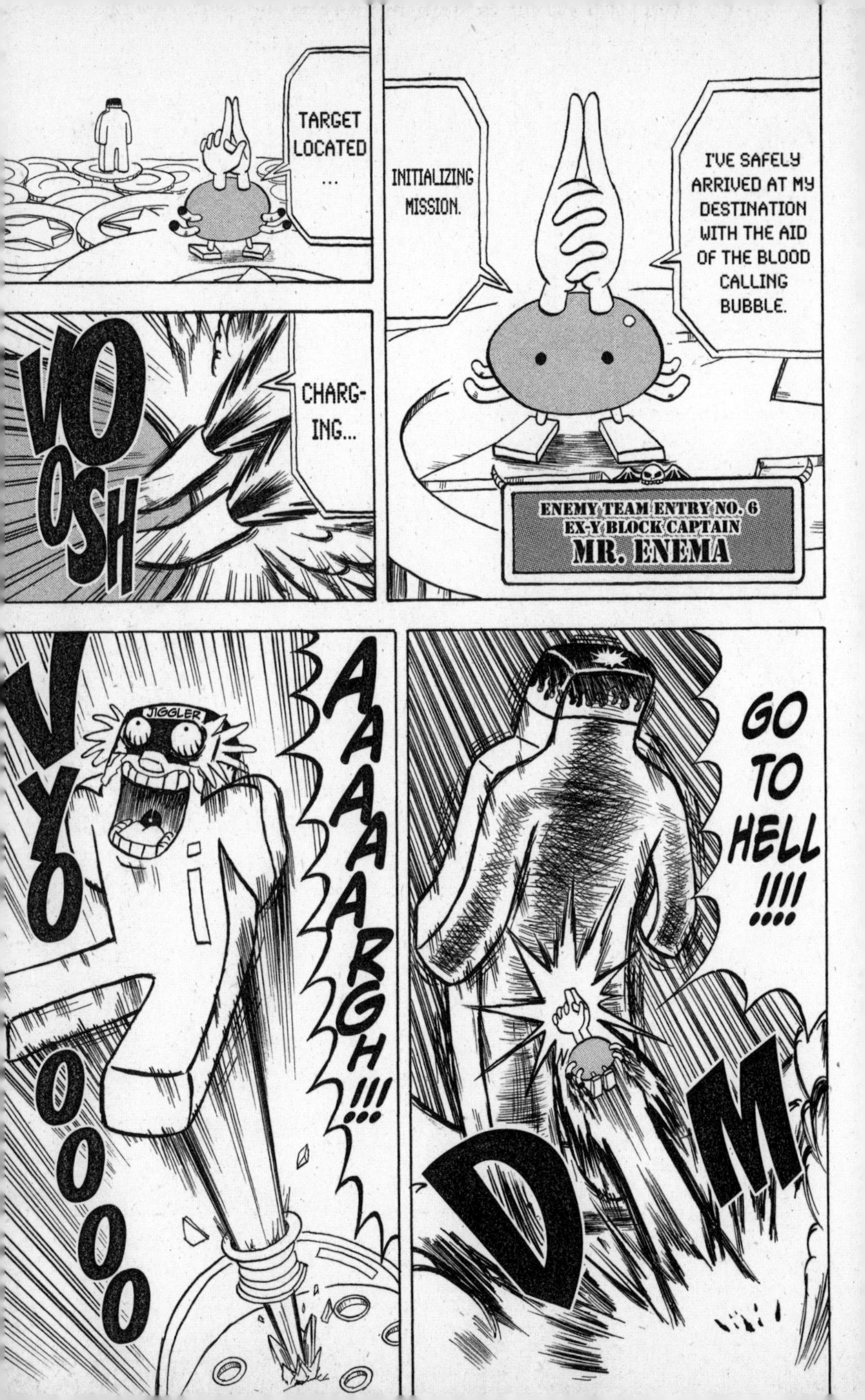
I'VE SAFELY ARRIVED AT MY DESTINATION WITH THE AID OF THE BLOOD CALLING BUBBLE.
INITIALIZING MISSION.
ENEMY TEAM ENTRY NO. 6
EX-Y BLOCK CAPTAIN
MR. ENEMA
TARGET LOCATED ...
CHARG-ING...
VOOSH
GO TO HELL!!!!
DIM
AAAAARGH!!!
JIGGLER
VYOOOOOO

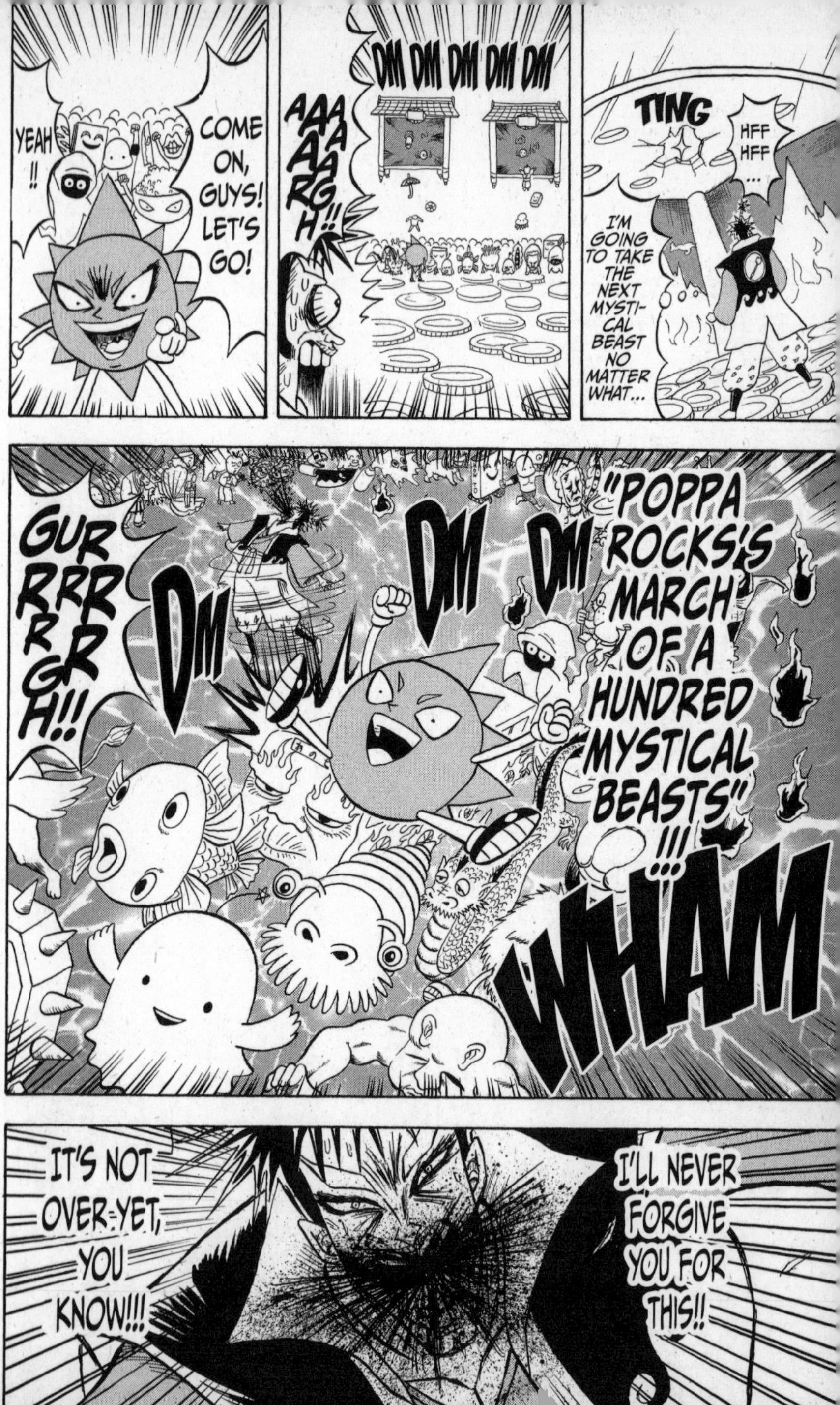
TING
HFF HFF...
I'M GOING TO TAKE THE NEXT MYSTICAL BEAST NO MATTER WHAT...
DM DM DM DM DM
AAAAAAARGH!!
COME ON, GUYS! LET'S GO!
YEAH!!
"POPPA ROCKS'S MARCH OF A HUNDRED MYSTICAL BEASTS"!!!
DM DM DM
GURRRRRRGH!!
WHAM
I'LL NEVER FORGIVE YOU FOR THIS!!
IT'S NOT OVER YET, YOU KNOW!!!

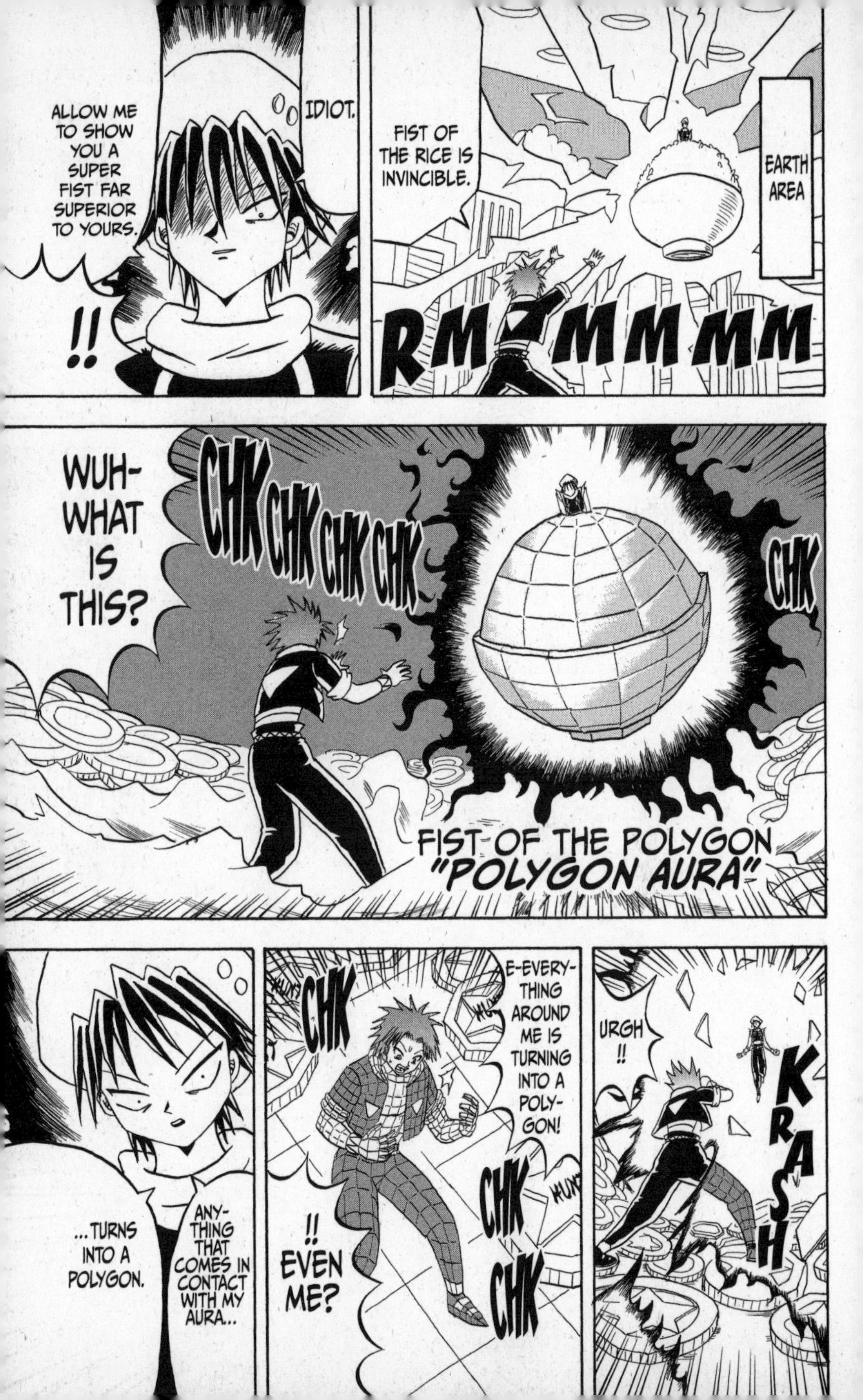
EARTH AREA
FIST OF THE RICE IS INVINCIBLE.
RMMMMMM
IDIOT.
ALLOW ME TO SHOW YOU A SUPER FIST FAR SUPERIOR TO YOURS.
!!
CHK
CHK CHK CHK CHK
WUH-WHAT IS THIS?
FIST OF THE POLYGON "POLYGON AURA"
KRASH
URGH !!
E-EVERYTHING AROUND ME IS TURNING INTO A POLYGON!
CHK
CHK
CHK
!! EVEN ME?
ANYTHING THAT COMES IN CONTACT WITH MY AURA...
...TURNS INTO A POLYGON.

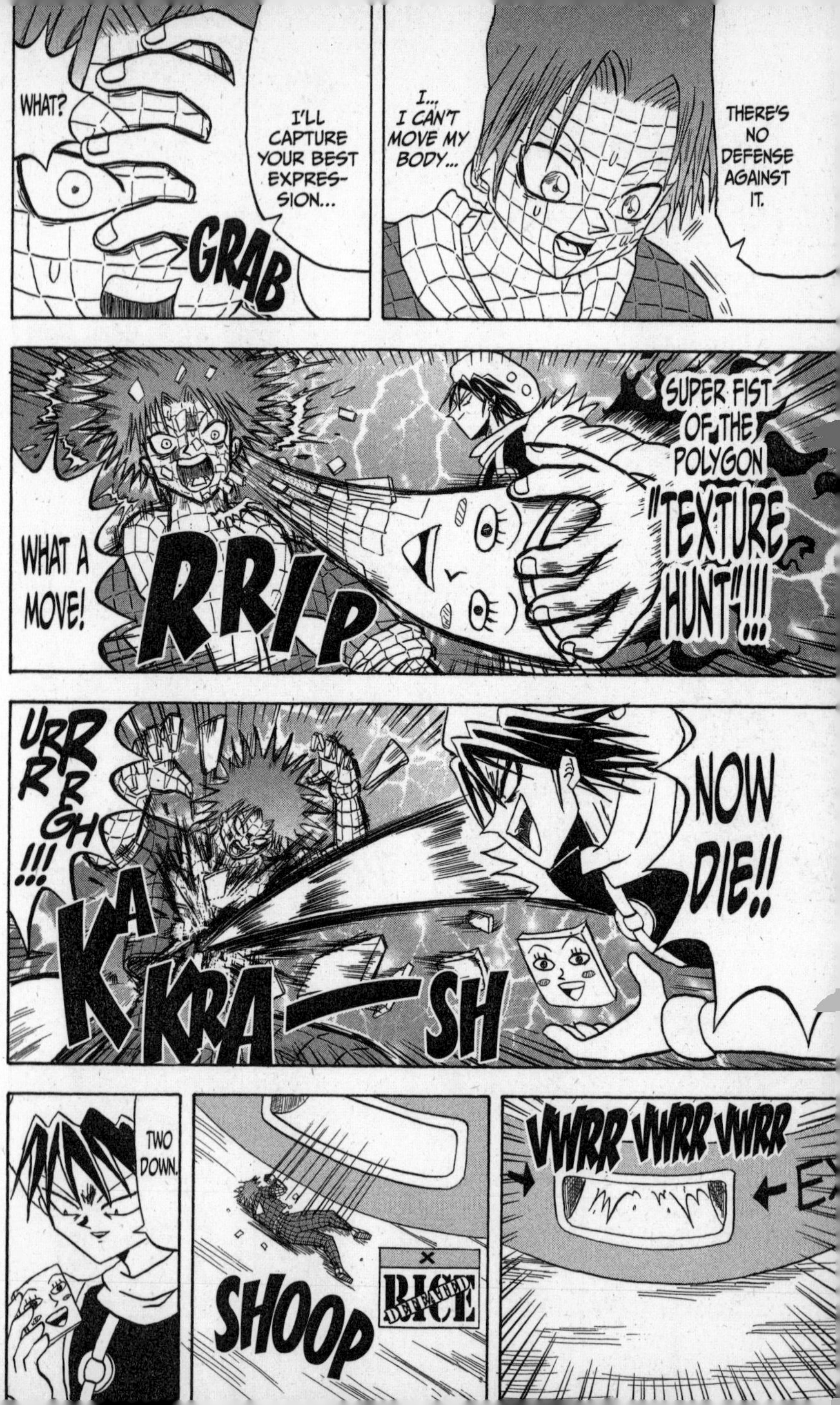
THERE'S NO DEFENSE AGAINST IT.
I... I CAN'T MOVE MY BODY...
I'LL CAPTURE YOUR BEST EXPRES-SION...
WHAT?
GRAB
SUPER FIST OF THE POLYGON "TEXTURE HUNT"!!!
RRIP
WHAT A MOVE!
NOW DIE!!
URRRRGH!!!
KA
KKRA—SH
VWRR VWRR VWRR
SHOOP
×
RICE
DEFEATED
TWO DOWN.

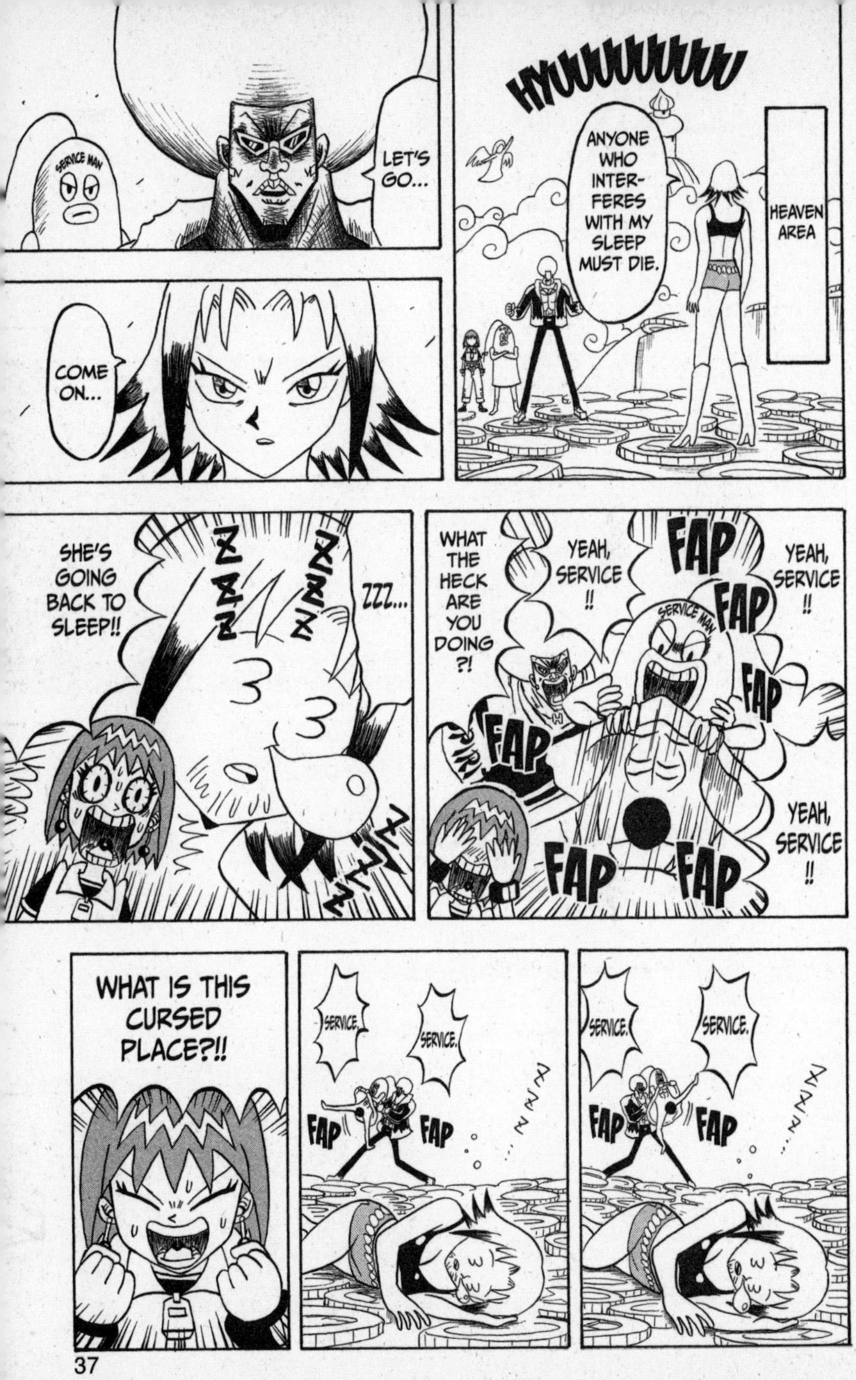
HYUUUUUUU
HEAVEN AREA
ANYONE WHO INTER-FERES WITH MY SLEEP MUST DIE.
SERVICE MAN
LET'S GO...
COME ON...
YEAH, SERVICE !!
FAP
FAP
SERVICE MAN
YEAH, SERVICE !!
WHAT THE HECK ARE YOU DOING ?!
FAP
FAP
YEAH, SERVICE !!
FAP
FAP
ZZZ...
SHE'S GOING BACK TO SLEEP!!
SERVICE.
SERVICE.
FAP
FAP
SERVICE.
SERVICE.
FAP
FAP
WHAT IS THIS CURSED PLACE?!!

Bo-bobo Q & A?!!

Volume 1 THIS ILLUSTRATION IS FROM THE FRONT COVER OF THE *WEEKLY SHONEN JUMP* MAGAZINE WHEN *BO-BOBO* STARTED. BO-BOBO'S POSE IS MEANT TO BE A SHOW OF MY DETERMINATION TO "DO MY BEST!" AND "GET CRACKING!"

Volume 2 IT'S BEAUTY AND POPPA ROCKS DOING THE SAME POSE AS BO-BOBO IN VOLUME 1. THE MEANING IN EXACTLY THE SAME AS VOLUME 1, AND I'VE ADDED A VERY SMALL BO-BOBO IN THE BACKGROUND, THINKING IT WOULD BE STRANGE IF HE WEREN'T THERE.

Volume 3 LIKE THE FIRST TWO VOLUMES, THIS IS GASSER IN THE CENTER DOING THE SAME POSE AS BEFORE, BUT HE'S EMBARRASSED TO HAVE BEAUTY NEARBY, AND POPPA ROCKS AND BO-BOBO ARE DISTRACTING HIM WITH THEIR LITTLE ROMANTIC PLAY. VERY GASSER-LIKE, DON'T YOU THINK?

Volume 4 I TRIED TO GIVE IT A VERY FESTIVE IMAGE, THINKING IT WOULD BE CHEERFUL TO HAVE LOTS OF IMAGES OF BO-BOBO AND HIS FRIENDS. I THINK I SHOULD HAVE ADDED MORE.

Volume 5 THE CONCEPT OF THIS IMAGE IS "ROBOT BO-BOBO, GO!!" THIS WAS ALSO AN ILLUSTRATION I DREW FOR THE COVER OF *WEEKLY SHONEN JUMP* MAGAZINE, BUT I DECIDED TO USE IT ON THE COVER FOR VOLUME 5 SINCE I LIKED IT SO MUCH. IT WAS A PAIN TO DRAW IT.

NOTE: THE U.S. EDITION OF *BOBOBO-BO BO-BOBO* STARTS AT THE 11TH VOLUME OF THE JAPANESE EDITION.

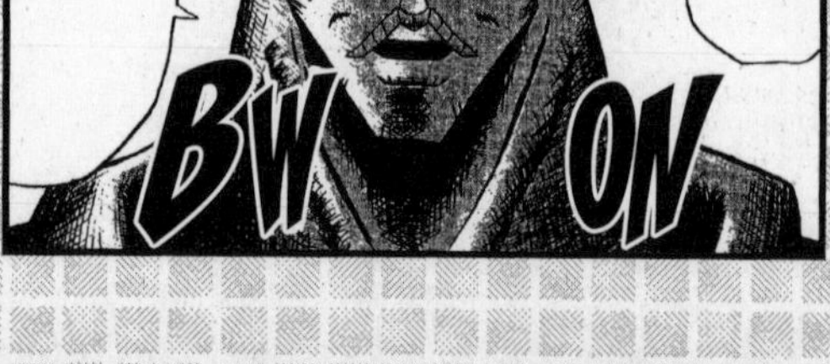
THE TRUTH...
...IS REVEALED!!
BW ON

CONTINUED...

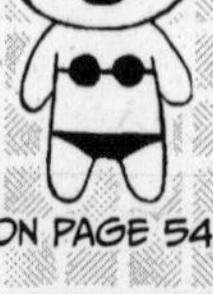

...ON PAGE 54.

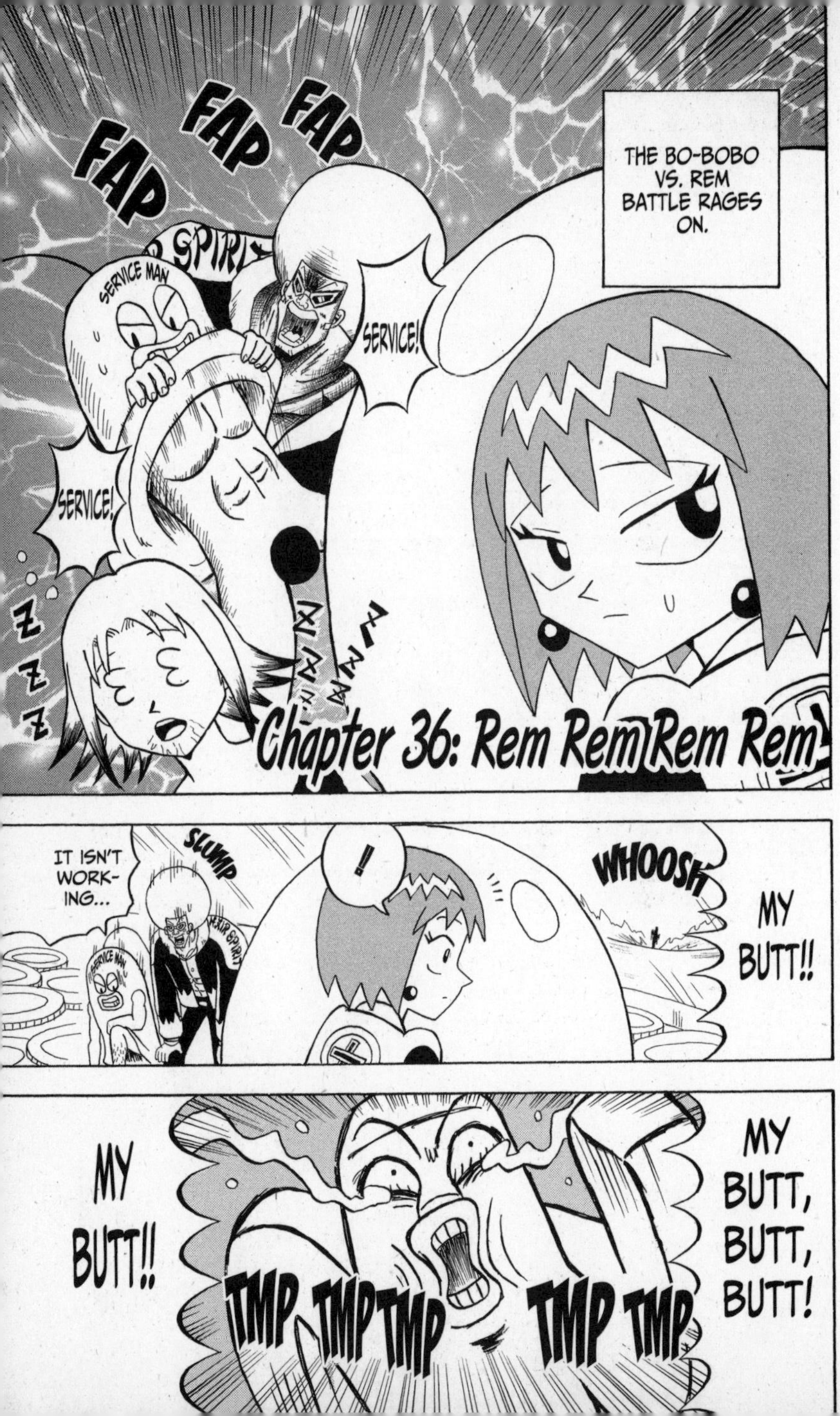
THE BO-BOBO VS. REM BATTLE RAGES ON.
FAP FAP FAP
SERVICE!
SERVICE MAN
SERVICE!
Z Z Z
Chapter 36: Rem Rem Rem Rem
MY BUTT!!
WHOOSH
!
SLUMP
IT ISN'T WORKING...
SERVICE MAN
MY BUTT, BUTT, BUTT!
TMP TMP TMP TMP TMP
MY BUTT!!

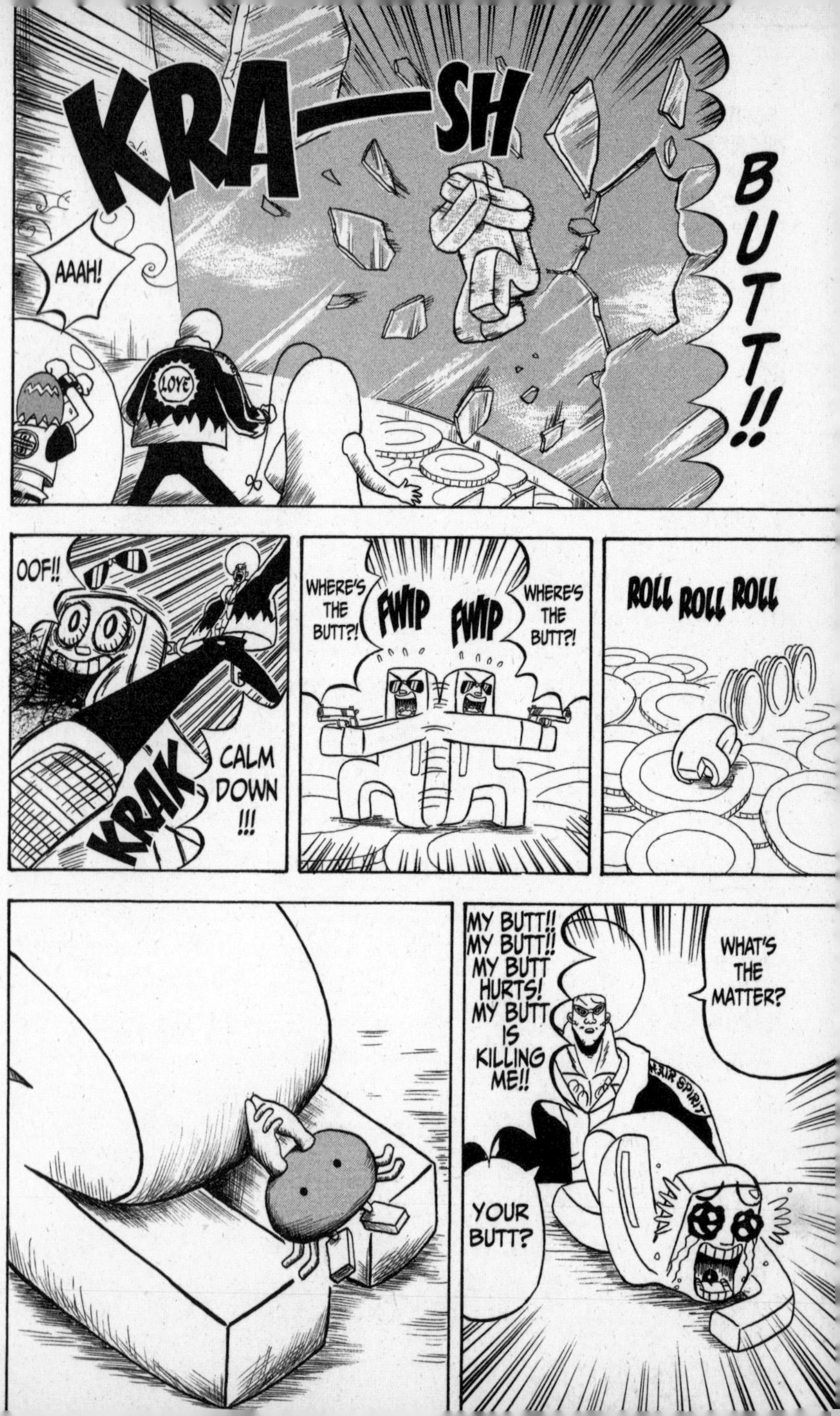
KRA—SH
BUTT!!
AAAH!
LOVE
ROLL ROLL ROLL
WHERE'S THE BUTT?!
FWIP
FWIP
WHERE'S THE BUTT?!
OOF!!
KRAK
CALM DOWN !!!
WHAT'S THE MATTER?
MY BUTT!! MY BUTT!! MY BUTT HURTS! MY BUTT IS KILLING ME!!
HAIR SPIRIT
WAAA
YOUR BUTT?

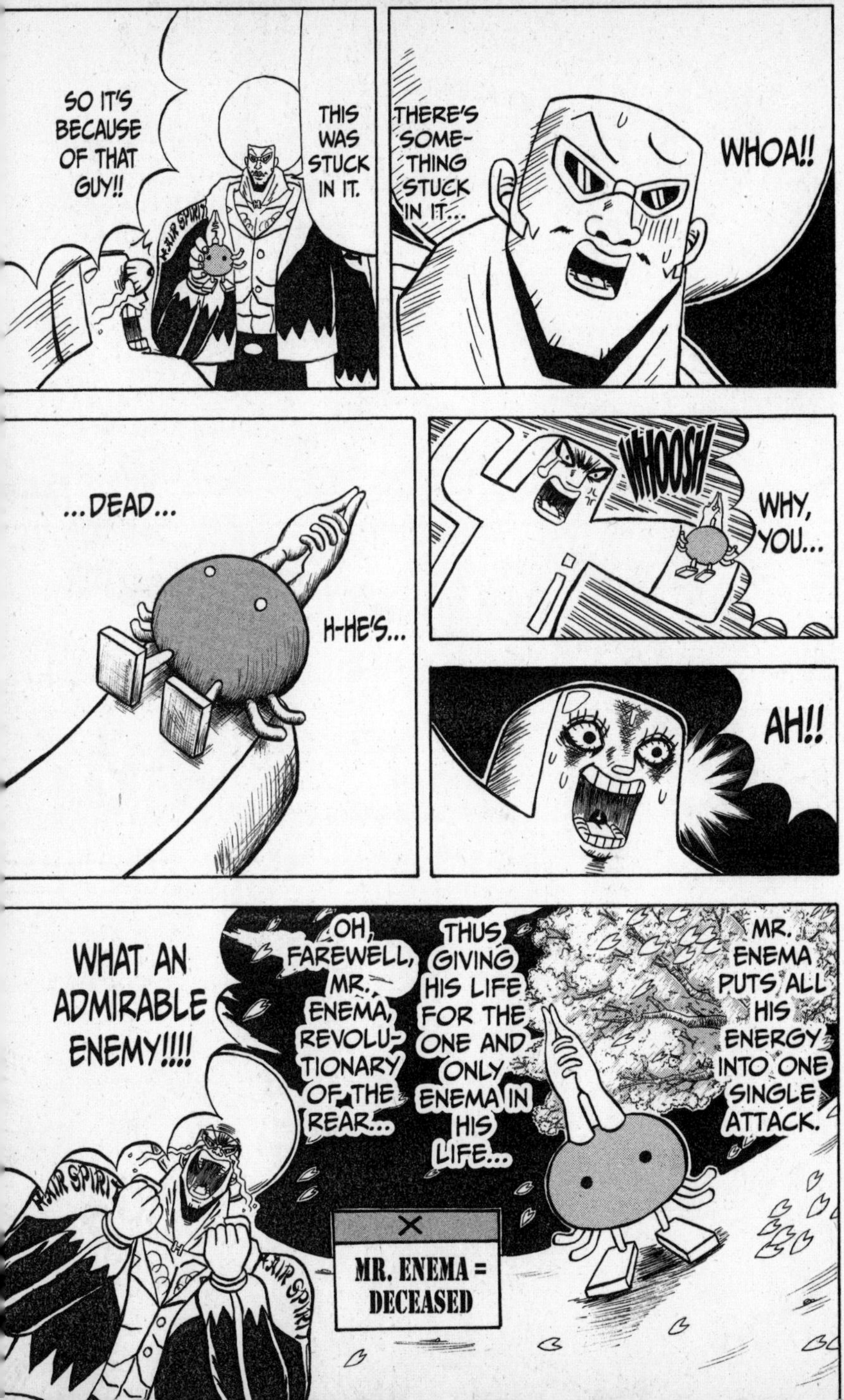
WHOA!!
THERE'S SOME-THING STUCK IN IT...
THIS WAS STUCK IN IT.
SO IT'S BECAUSE OF THAT GUY!!
HAIR SPIRIT
WHOOSH
WHY, YOU...
AH!!
H-HE'S...
...DEAD...
MR. ENEMA PUTS ALL HIS ENERGY INTO ONE SINGLE ATTACK.
THUS GIVING HIS LIFE FOR THE ONE AND ONLY ENEMA IN HIS LIFE...
OH, FAREWELL, MR. ENEMA, REVOLU-TIONARY OF THE REAR...
WHAT AN ADMIRABLE ENEMY!!!!
HAIR SPIRIT
HAIR SPIRIT
MR. ENEMA = DECEASED

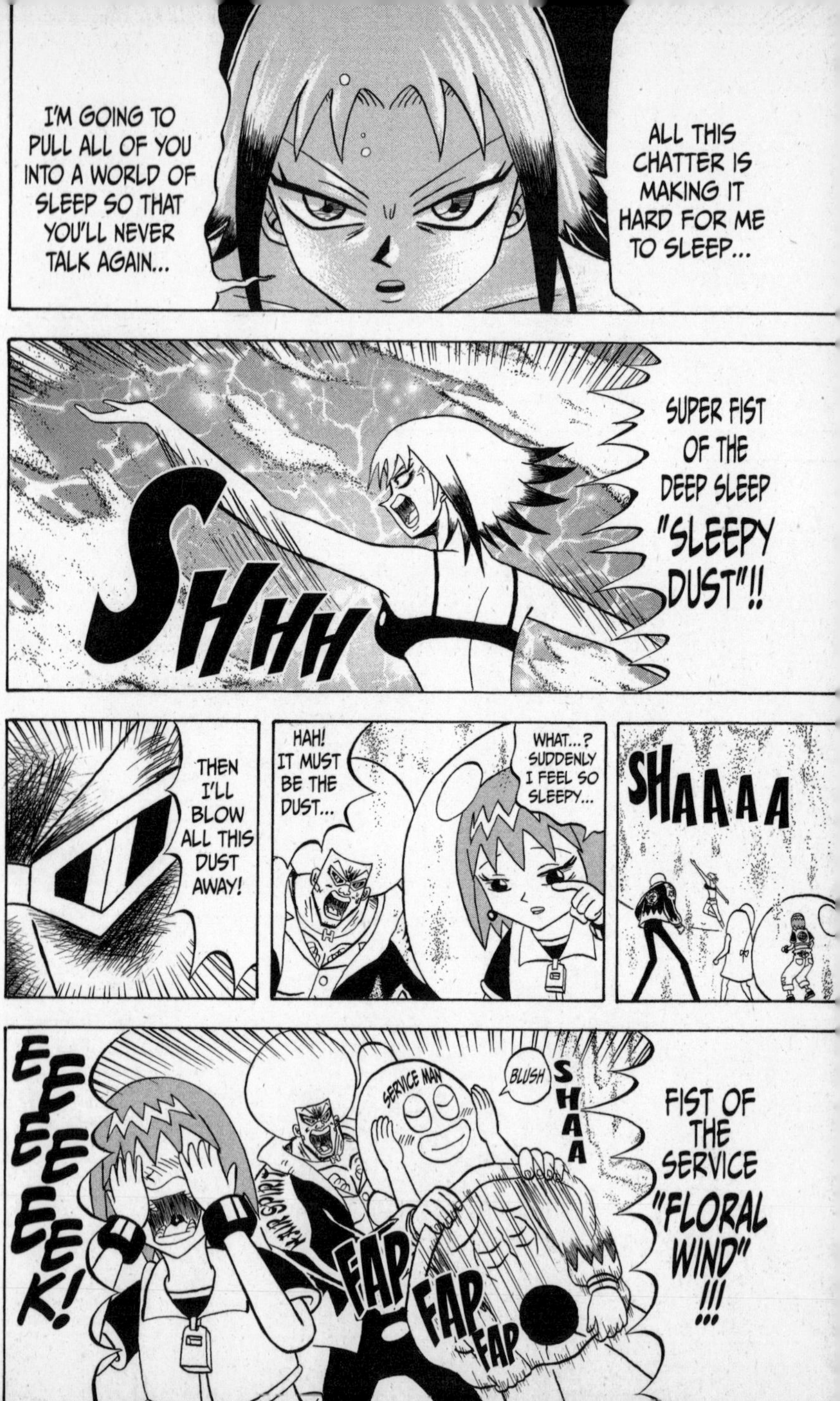
ALL THIS CHATTER IS MAKING IT HARD FOR ME TO SLEEP...
I'M GOING TO PULL ALL OF YOU INTO A WORLD OF SLEEP SO THAT YOU'LL NEVER TALK AGAIN...
SUPER FIST OF THE DEEP SLEEP "SLEEPY DUST"!!
SHHH
SHAAAA
WHAT...? SUDDENLY I FEEL SO SLEEPY...
HAH! IT MUST BE THE DUST...
THEN I'LL BLOW ALL THIS DUST AWAY!
FIST OF THE SERVICE "FLORAL WIND"!!!
SHAA
BLUSH
SERVICE MAN
FAP
FAP
FAP
EEEEEEK!

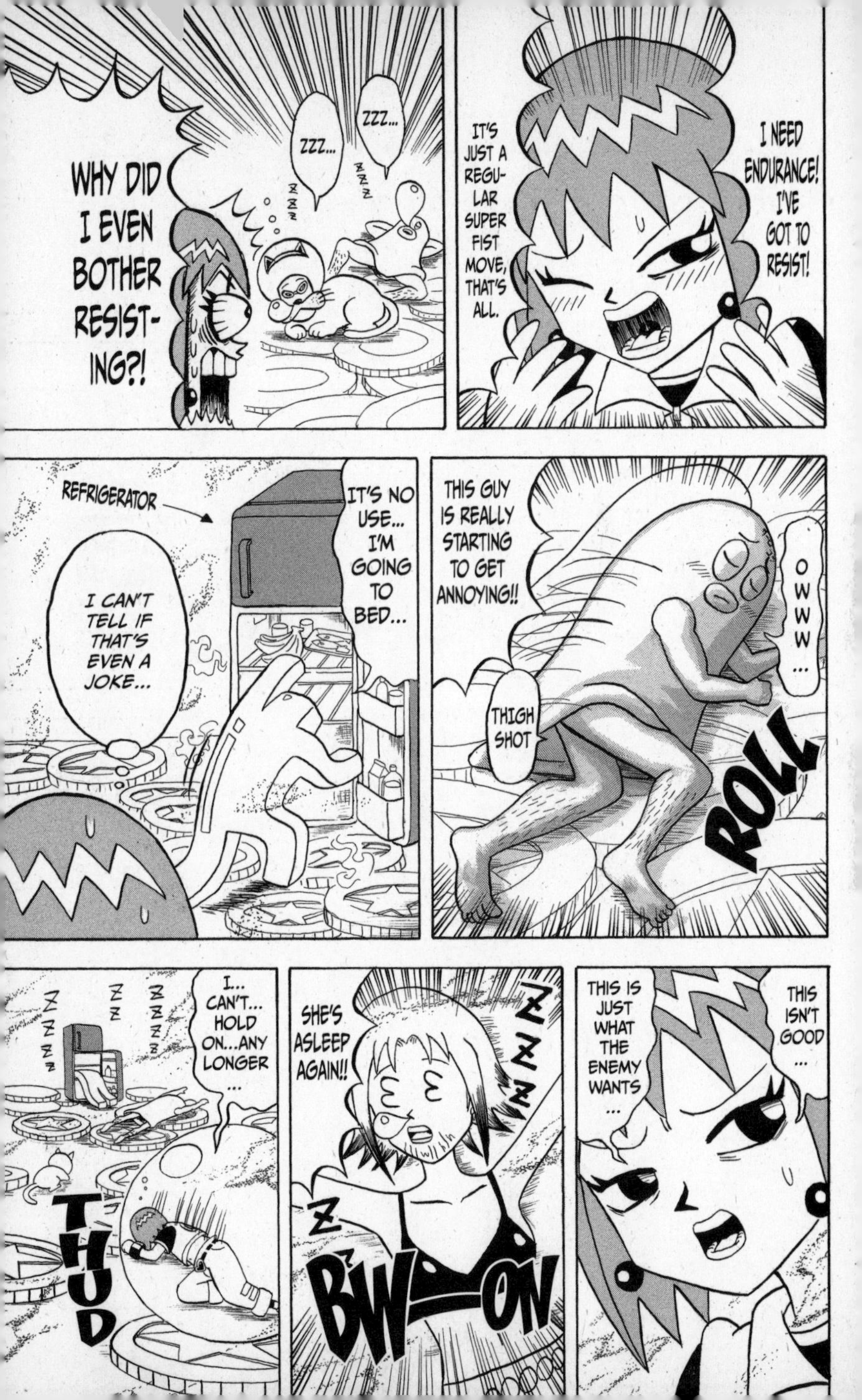
I NEED ENDURANCE! I'VE GOT TO RESIST!
IT'S JUST A REGULAR SUPER FIST MOVE, THAT'S ALL.
ZZZ...
ZZZ...
WHY DID I EVEN BOTHER RESISTING?!
OWWW...
THIS GUY IS REALLY STARTING TO GET ANNOYING!!
THIGH SHOT
ROLL
IT'S NO USE... I'M GOING TO BED...
REFRIGERATOR
I CAN'T TELL IF THAT'S EVEN A JOKE...
THIS ISN'T GOOD...
THIS IS JUST WHAT THE ENEMY WANTS...
SHE'S ASLEEP AGAIN!!
BW—ON
I... CAN'T... HOLD ON...ANY LONGER...
THUD

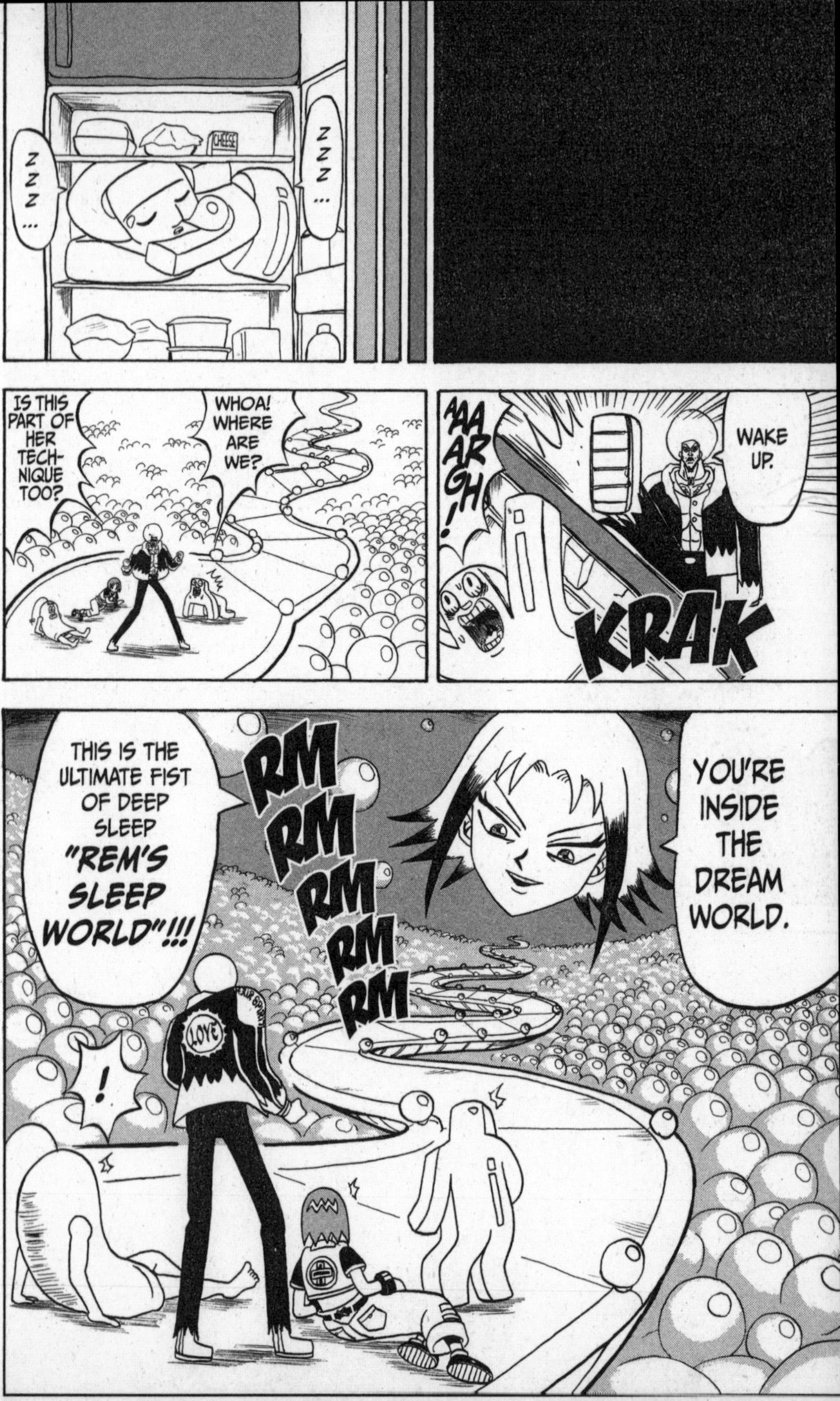
ZZZ...
CHEESE
ZZZ...
WAKE UP.
AAAARGH!
KRAK
WHOA! WHERE ARE WE?
IS THIS PART OF HER TECH-NIQUE TOO?
YOU'RE INSIDE THE DREAM WORLD.
RM RM RM RM RM
THIS IS THE ULTIMATE FIST OF DEEP SLEEP "REM'S SLEEP WORLD"!!!
LOVE
!

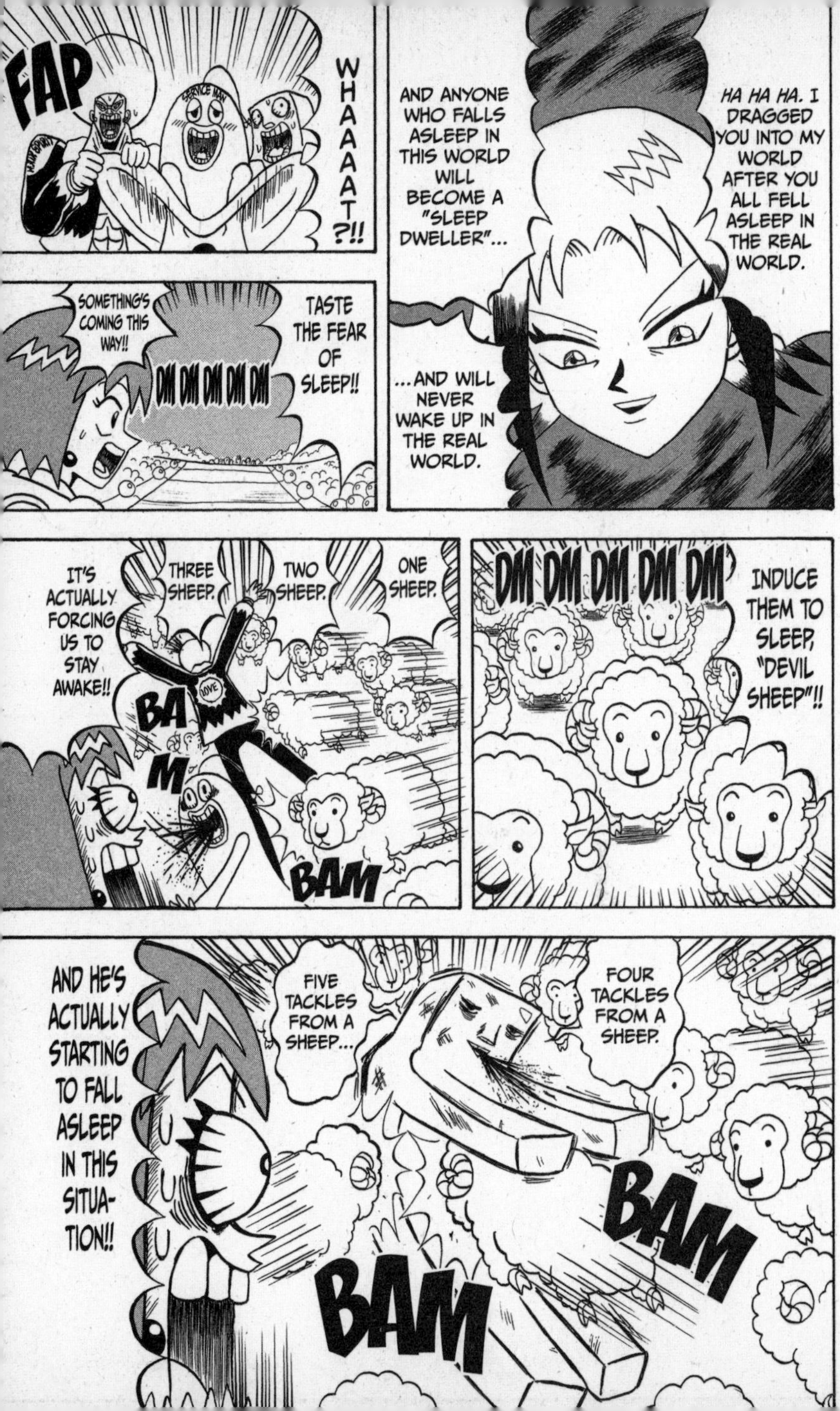
HA HA HA. I DRAGGED YOU INTO MY WORLD AFTER YOU ALL FELL ASLEEP IN THE REAL WORLD.
AND ANYONE WHO FALLS ASLEEP IN THIS WORLD WILL BECOME A "SLEEP DWELLER"...
...AND WILL NEVER WAKE UP IN THE REAL WORLD.
WHAAAAAT?!!
SERVICE MAN
FAP
TASTE THE FEAR OF SLEEP!!
SOMETHING'S COMING THIS WAY!!
DM DM DM DM DM
DM DM DM DM DM
INDUCE THEM TO SLEEP, "DEVIL SHEEP"!!
ONE SHEEP.
TWO SHEEP.
THREE SHEEP.
IT'S ACTUALLY FORCING US TO STAY AWAKE!!
LOVE
BAM
BAM
FOUR TACKLES FROM A SHEEP.
FIVE TACKLES FROM A SHEEP...
AND HE'S ACTUALLY STARTING TO FALL ASLEEP IN THIS SITUATION!!
BAM
BAM

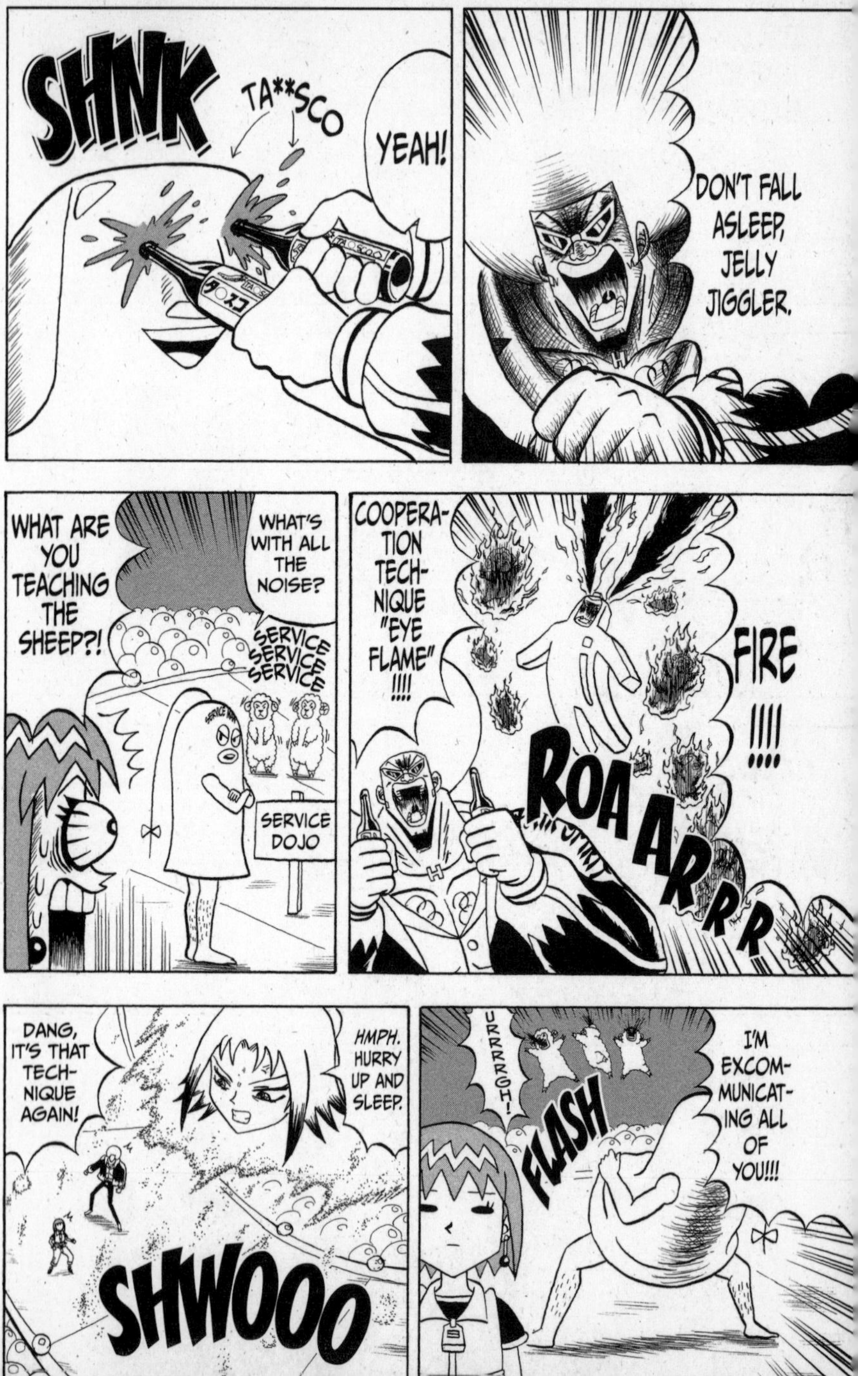
DON'T FALL ASLEEP, JELLY JIGGLER.
YEAH!
TA**SCO
SHNK
COOPERATION TECHNIQUE "EYE FLAME"!!!!
FIRE!!!!
ROAARRR
WHAT'S WITH ALL THE NOISE?
WHAT ARE YOU TEACHING THE SHEEP?!
SERVICE SERVICE SERVICE
SERVICE DOJO
I'M EXCOMMUNICATING ALL OF YOU!!!
URRRRGH!
FLASH
HMPH. HURRY UP AND SLEEP.
DANG, IT'S THAT TECHNIQUE AGAIN!
SHWOOO

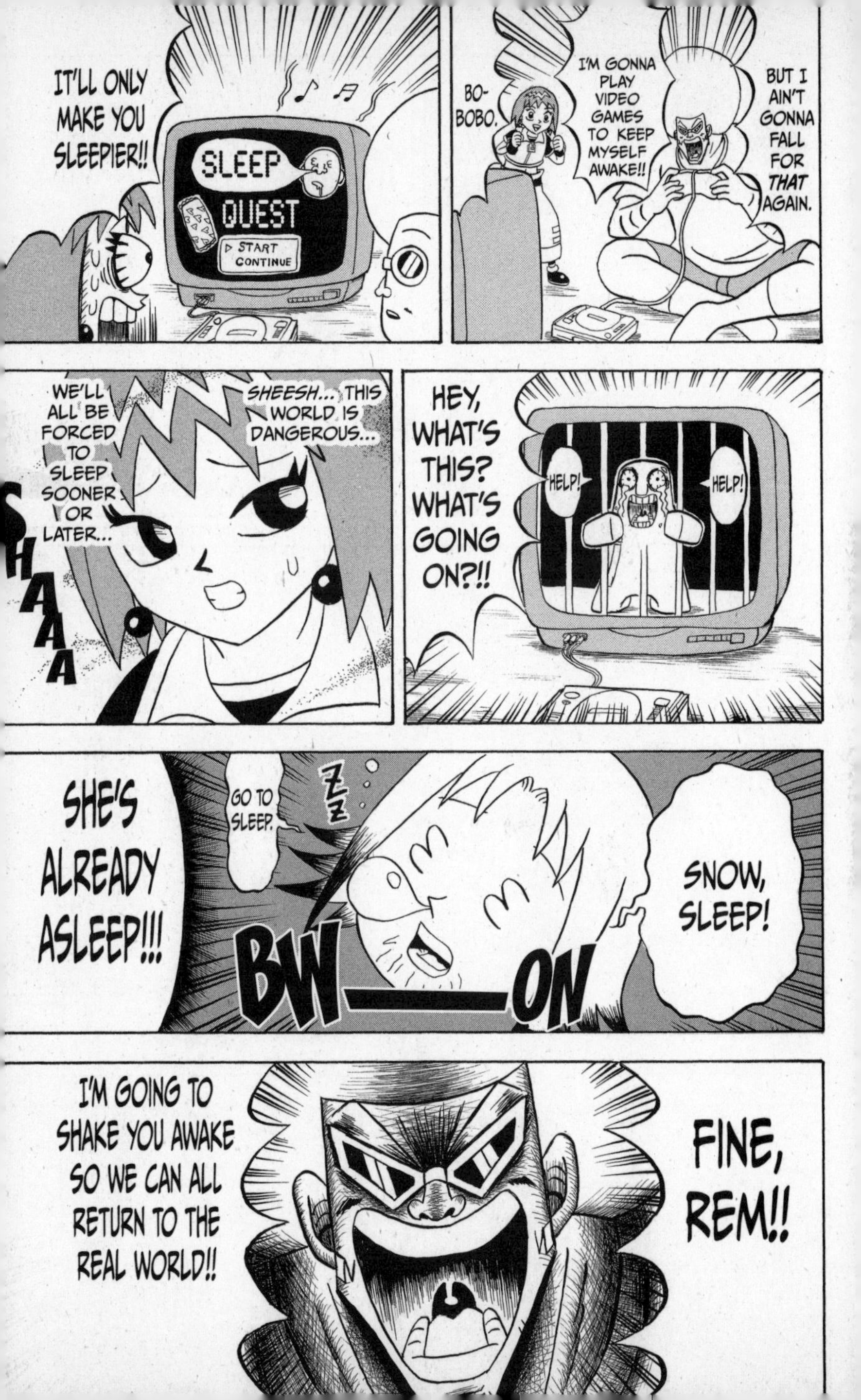
BUT I AIN'T GONNA FALL FOR THAT AGAIN.
I'M GONNA PLAY VIDEO GAMES TO KEEP MYSELF AWAKE!!
BO-BOBO.
IT'LL ONLY MAKE YOU SLEEPIER!!
SLEEP
QUEST
START
CONTINUE
HEY, WHAT'S THIS? WHAT'S GOING ON?!!
HELP!
HELP!
SHEESH... THIS WORLD IS DANGEROUS...
WE'LL ALL BE FORCED TO SLEEP SOONER OR LATER...
SHAAAA
SNOW, SLEEP!
BW——ON
ZZZ
GO TO SLEEP.
SHE'S ALREADY ASLEEP!!!
FINE, REM!!
I'M GOING TO SHAKE YOU AWAKE SO WE CAN ALL RETURN TO THE REAL WORLD!!

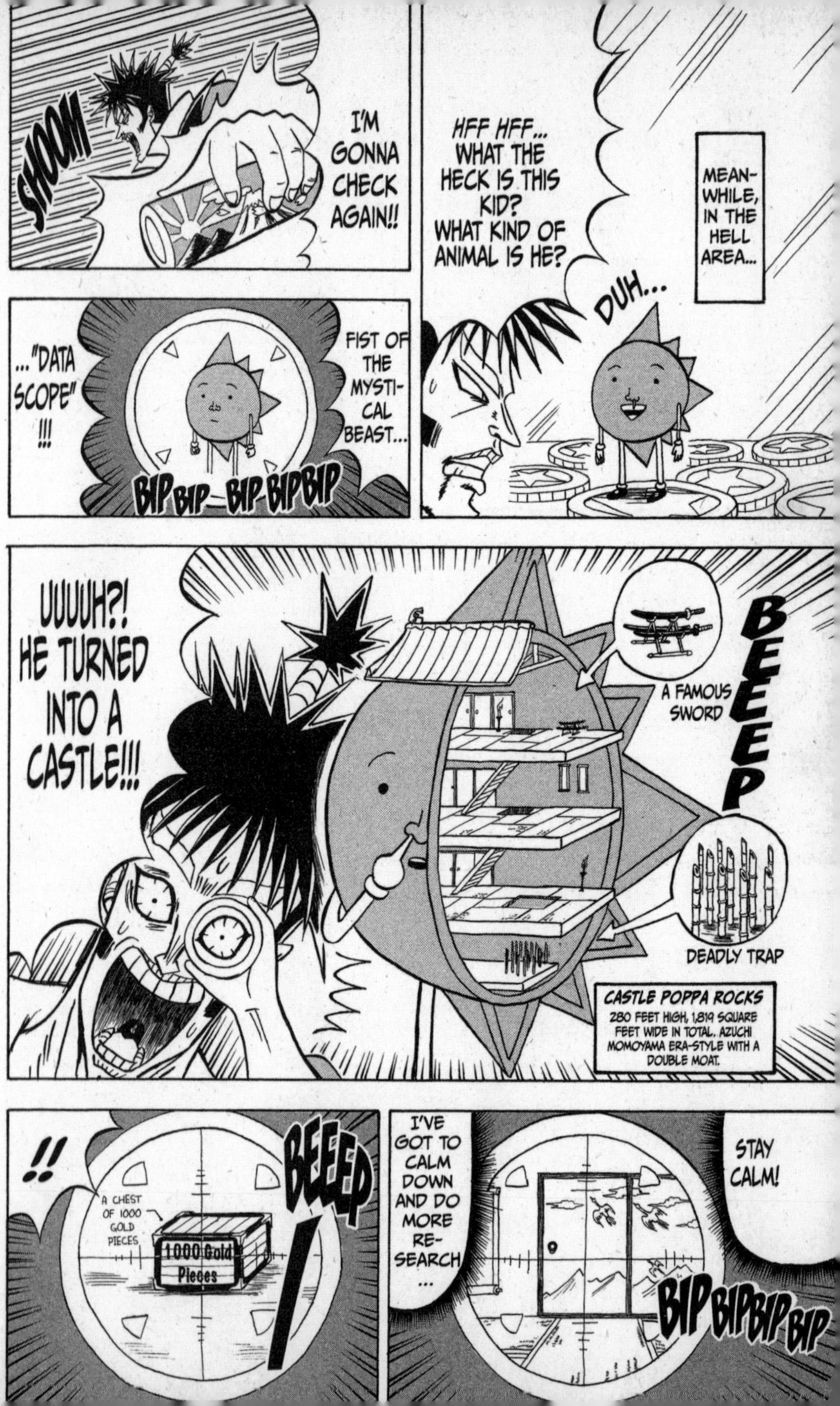

MEAN-WHILE, IN THE HELL AREA...
HFF HFF... WHAT THE HECK IS THIS KID? WHAT KIND OF ANIMAL IS HE?
DUH...
SHOOM
I'M GONNA CHECK AGAIN!!
FIST OF THE MYSTI-CAL BEAST...
..."DATA SCOPE"!!!
BIP BIP BIP BIPBIP
BEEEEP
A FAMOUS SWORD
DEADLY TRAP
CASTLE POPPA ROCKS
280 FEET HIGH, 1,819 SQUARE FEET WIDE IN TOTAL. AZUCHI MOMOYAMA ERA-STYLE WITH A DOUBLE MOAT.
UUUUH?! HE TURNED INTO A CASTLE!!!
STAY CALM!
I'VE GOT TO CALM DOWN AND DO MORE RE-SEARCH...
BIP BIPBIPBIP BIP
BEEEP
!!
A CHEST OF 1000 GOLD PIECES
1000 Gold Pieces

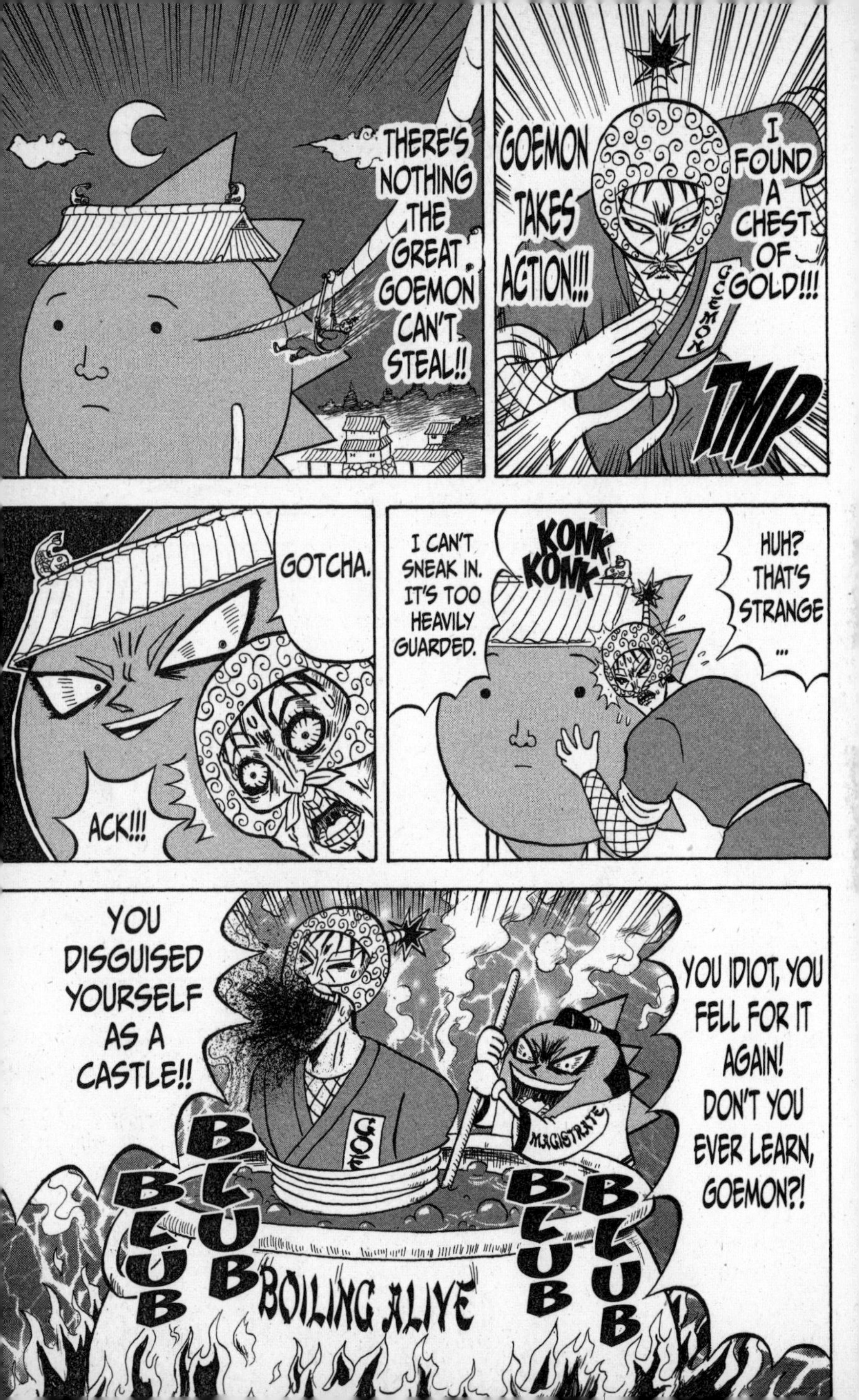
I FOUND A CHEST OF GOLD!!!
GOEMON TAKES ACTION!!!
GOEMON
TMP
THERE'S NOTHING THE GREAT GOEMON CAN'T STEAL!!
HUH? THAT'S STRANGE ...
KONK KONK
I CAN'T SNEAK IN. IT'S TOO HEAVILY GUARDED.
GOTCHA.
ACK!!!
YOU IDIOT, YOU FELL FOR IT AGAIN! DON'T YOU EVER LEARN, GOEMON?!
MAGISTRATE
BLUB BLUB
YOU DISGUISED YOURSELF AS A CASTLE!!
BLUB BLUB
BOILING ALIVE

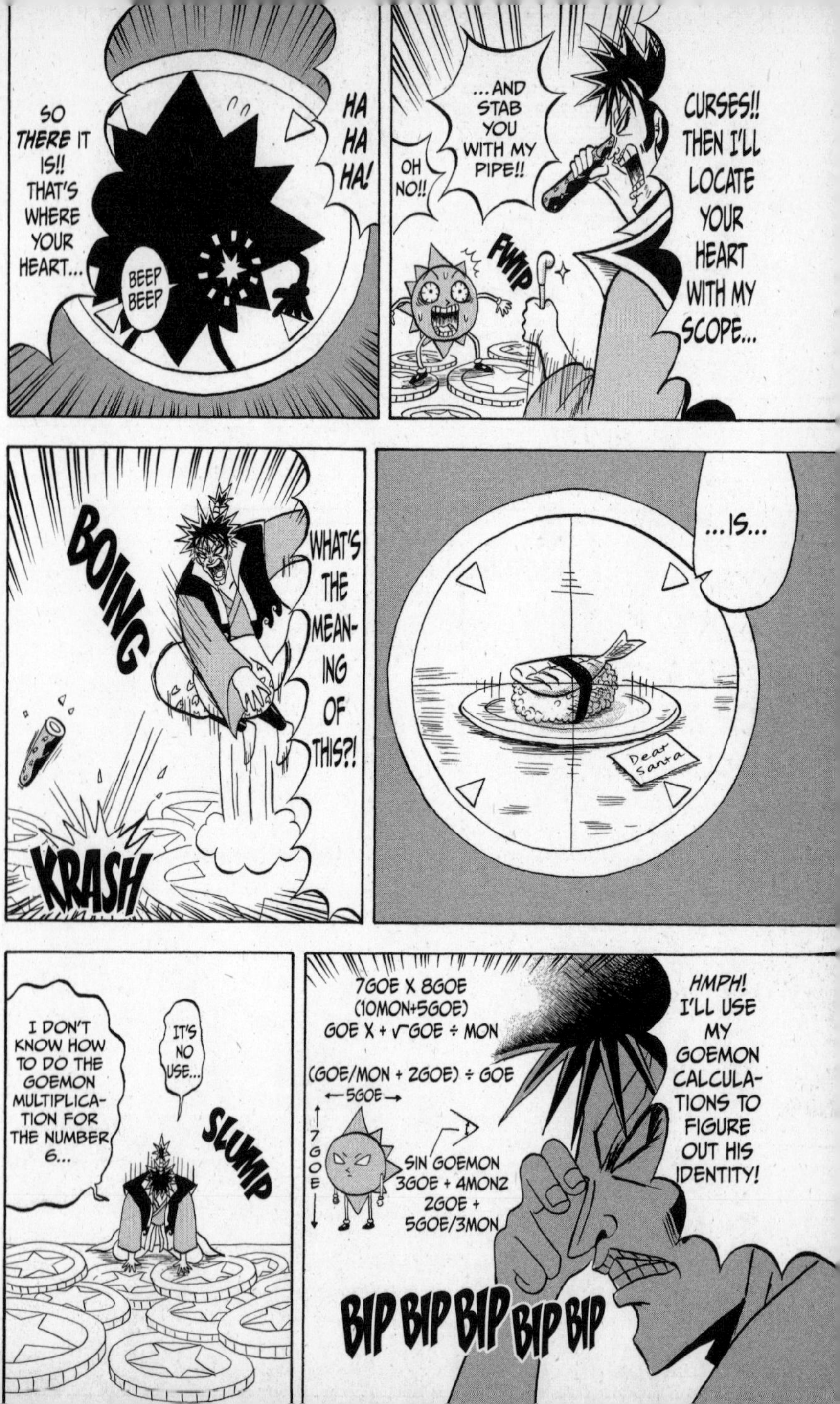
CURSES!! THEN I'LL LOCATE YOUR HEART WITH MY SCOPE...
...AND STAB YOU WITH MY PIPE!!
OH NO!!
FWIP
HA HA HA!
SO THERE IT IS!! THAT'S WHERE YOUR HEART...
BEEP BEEP
...IS...
Dear Santa
WHAT'S THE MEANING OF THIS?!
BOING
KRASH
HMPH! I'LL USE MY GOEMON CALCULATIONS TO FIGURE OUT HIS IDENTITY!
7GOE X 8GOE
(10MON+5GOE)
GOE X + √GOE ÷ MON
(GOE/MON + 2GOE) ÷ GOE
5GOE
7GOE
SIN GOEMON
3GOE + 4MON2
2GOE +
5GOE/3MON
BIP BIP BIP BIP BIP
IT'S NO USE...
I DON'T KNOW HOW TO DO THE GOEMON MULTIPLICATION FOR THE NUMBER 6...
SLUMP

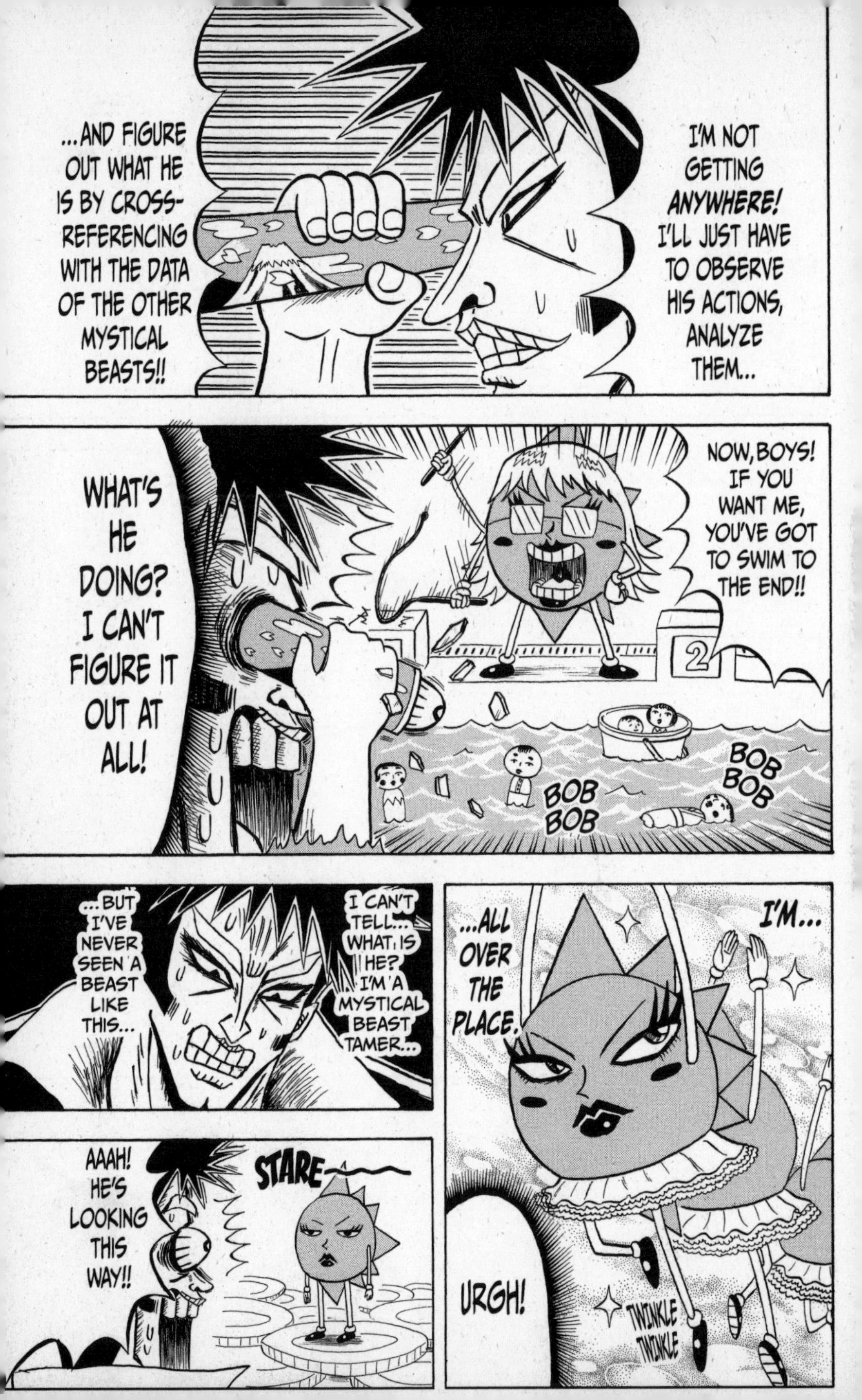
I'M NOT GETTING ANYWHERE! I'LL JUST HAVE TO OBSERVE HIS ACTIONS, ANALYZE THEM...
...AND FIGURE OUT WHAT HE IS BY CROSS-REFERENCING WITH THE DATA OF THE OTHER MYSTICAL BEASTS!!
NOW, BOYS! IF YOU WANT ME, YOU'VE GOT TO SWIM TO THE END!!
2
BOB BOB
BOB BOB
WHAT'S HE DOING? I CAN'T FIGURE IT OUT AT ALL!
I'M...
...ALL OVER THE PLACE.
TWINKLE TWINKLE
URGH!
I CAN'T TELL... WHAT IS HE? I'M A MYSTICAL BEAST TAMER...
...BUT I'VE NEVER SEEN A BEAST LIKE THIS...
STARE
AAAH! HE'S LOOKING THIS WAY!!

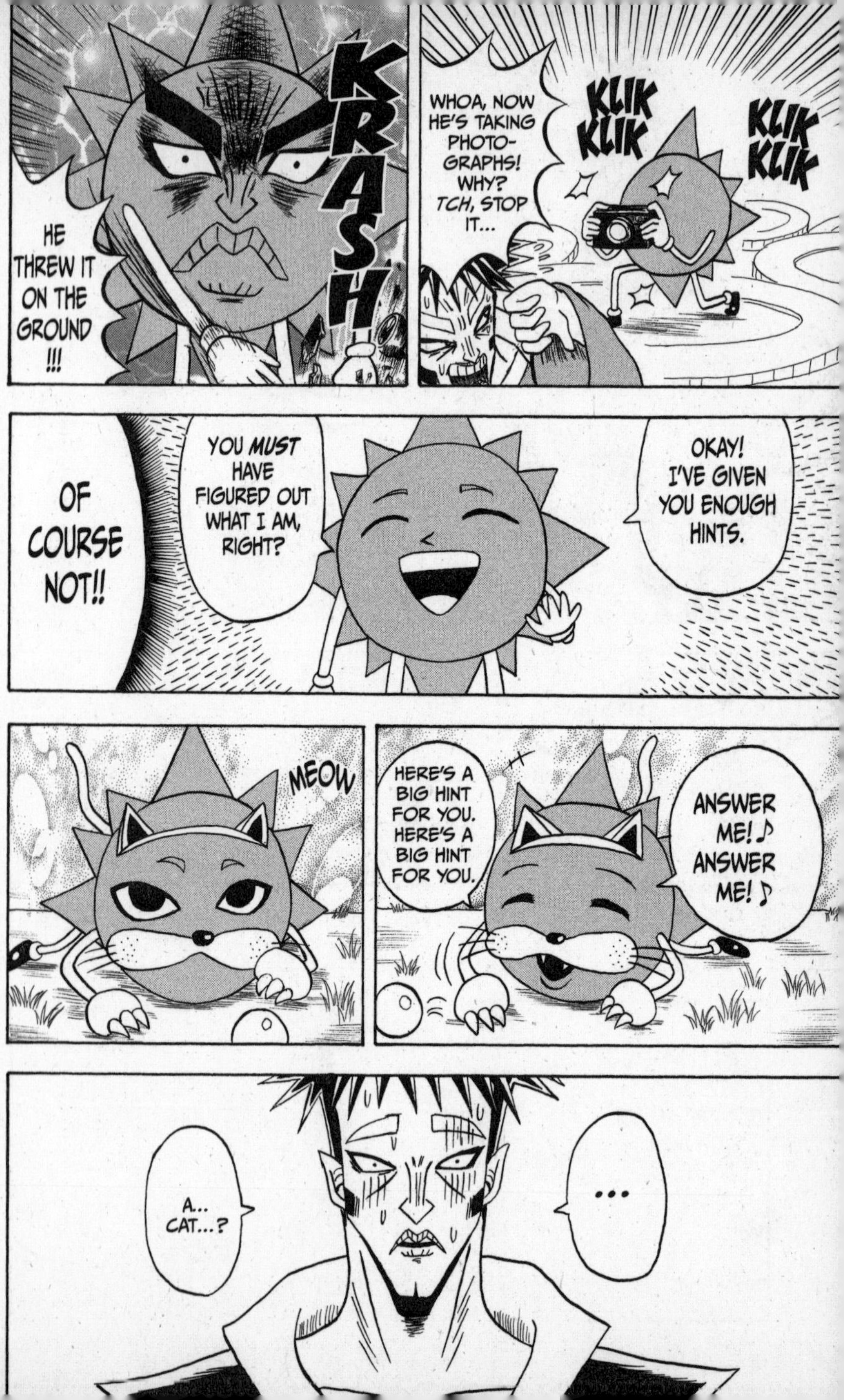
KLIK KLIK
KLIK KLIK
WHOA, NOW HE'S TAKING PHOTO-GRAPHS! WHY? TCH, STOP IT...
KRASH!
HE THREW IT ON THE GROUND !!!
OKAY! I'VE GIVEN YOU ENOUGH HINTS.
YOU MUST HAVE FIGURED OUT WHAT I AM, RIGHT?
OF COURSE NOT!!
ANSWER ME! ♪ ANSWER ME! ♪
HERE'S A BIG HINT FOR YOU. HERE'S A BIG HINT FOR YOU.
MEOW
...
A... CAT...?

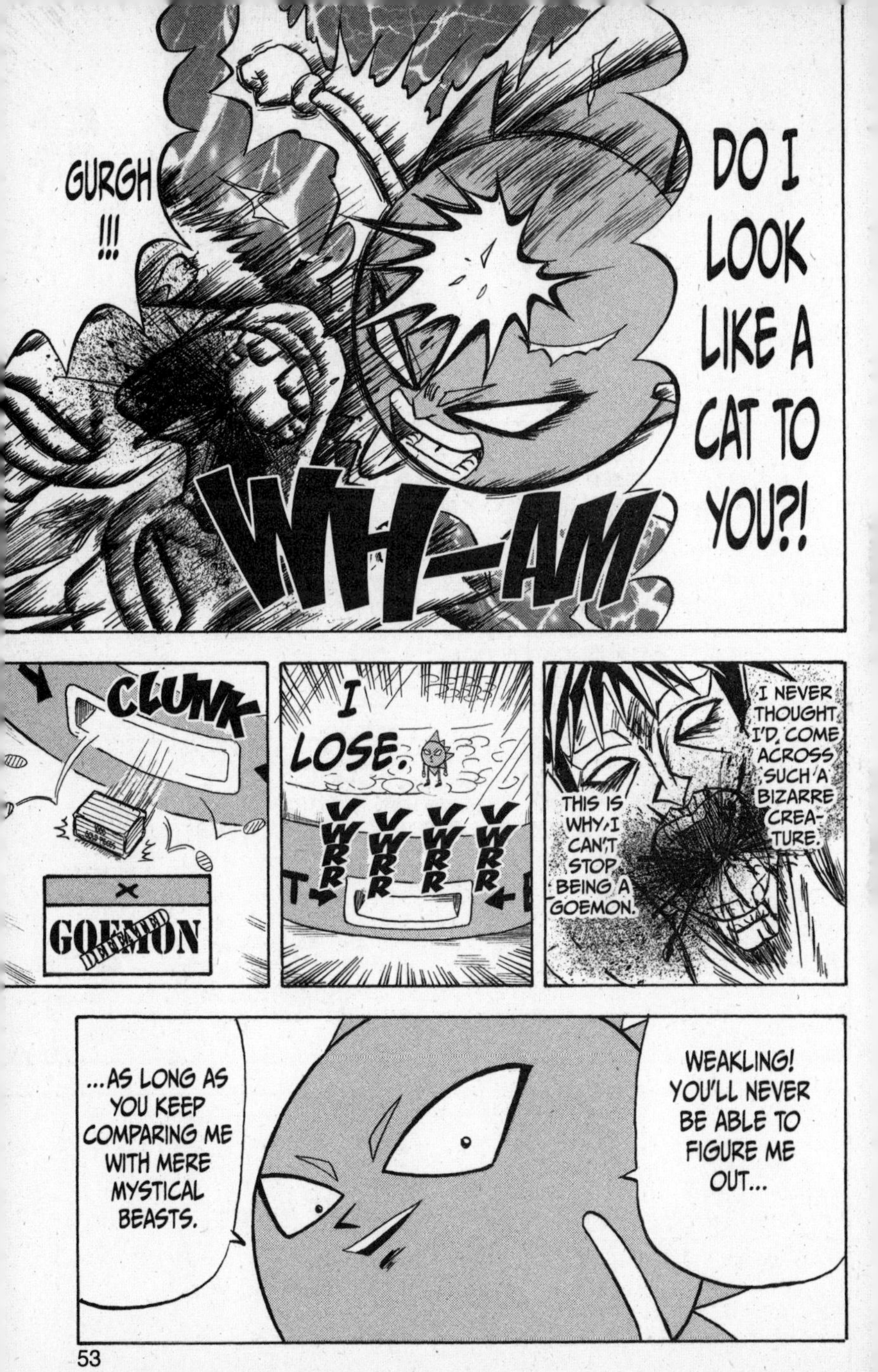
DO I LOOK LIKE A CAT TO YOU?!
GURGH !!!
WH-AM
I NEVER THOUGHT I'D COME ACROSS SUCH A BIZARRE CREATURE.
THIS IS WHY I CAN'T STOP BEING A GOEMON.
I LOSE.
VWRR
VWRR
VWRR
VWRR
CLUNK
×
GOEMON
DEFEATED
WEAKLING! YOU'LL NEVER BE ABLE TO FIGURE ME OUT...
...AS LONG AS YOU KEEP COMPARING ME WITH MERE MYSTICAL BEASTS.

Bo-bobo Q & A?!!

Volume 6
THE CONCEPT OF THIS ILLUSTRATION IS "THE ARRIVAL OF THE BEAUTIFUL TRANSFER STUDENT!" THAT'S WHY BEAUTY IS WEARING A BOY'S SCHOOL UNIFORM. THIS IS ALSO THE ONLY VOLUME WITH HATENKO IN THE ILLUSTRATION. I LIKE POPPA ROCKS'S POSE AND EVERYBODY'S REACTION.

Volume 7
THIS IS THE VOLUME WHERE BO-BOBO, POPPA ROCKS AND JELLY JIGGLER FINALLY GET TOGETHER, SO I DREW THE THREE OF THEM AS THE CENTER OF THE ILLUSTRATION TO SHOW THAT "NOW THE THREE OF THEM ARE GOING TO GET CRACKING TOGETHER." ALSO, THIS WAS THE VOLUME WITH THE FEARFUL BATTLE AGAINST RICE, SO I TRIED TO GIVE IT A BATTLE MANGA-LIKE ATMOSPHERE. I'M GLAD I SUCCEEDED IN GIVING RICE A REALLY MENACING LOOK.

Volume 8
IN THIS VOLUME, I DREW BEAUTY AND GASSER AS THE MAIN CHARACTERS IN THE COVER ILLUSTRATION AND HAD THEM WALK AROUND SOME KIND OF RUIN. IT'S SUPPOSED TO GIVE YOU THE FUN ATMOSPHERE OF BO-BOBO'S JOURNEY.

Volume 9
I TRIED TO MAKE EVERYBODY LOOK COOL IN THIS ONE. THIS IS SOFTON'S FIRST APPEARANCE IN A COVER ILLUSTRATION, ALTHOUGH HE'S KIND OF SMALL IN IT. THIS WAS ACTUALLY AN ILLUSTRATION THAT WAS USED FOR A POSTER FOR *V JUMP*, BUT I LIKED IT A LOT, SO I DECIDED TO USE IT FOR VOLUME 9 AS WELL.

Volume 10
THIS IS AN IMAGE OF POPPA ROCKS COMPLETELY IGNORING THE RISING TENSION BETWEEN BO-BOBO AND HALEKULANI AS HE PLAYS AROUND IN HALLELUJAH LAND. YOU'LL FIND DENGAKU MAN DRAWN ON THE BADGE POPPA ROCKS IS WEARING, AND JELLY JIGGLER IS ALSO HIDDEN AWAY AMONGST THE MONEY IN THE BACKGROUND.

WE NEVER KNEW THAT!!

CONTINUED ON PAGE 74!!

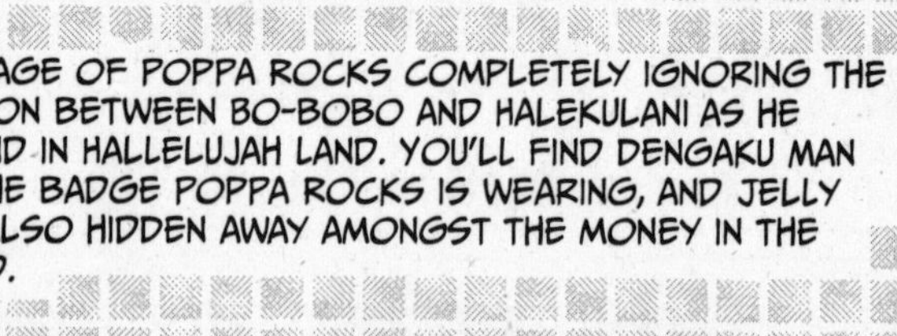

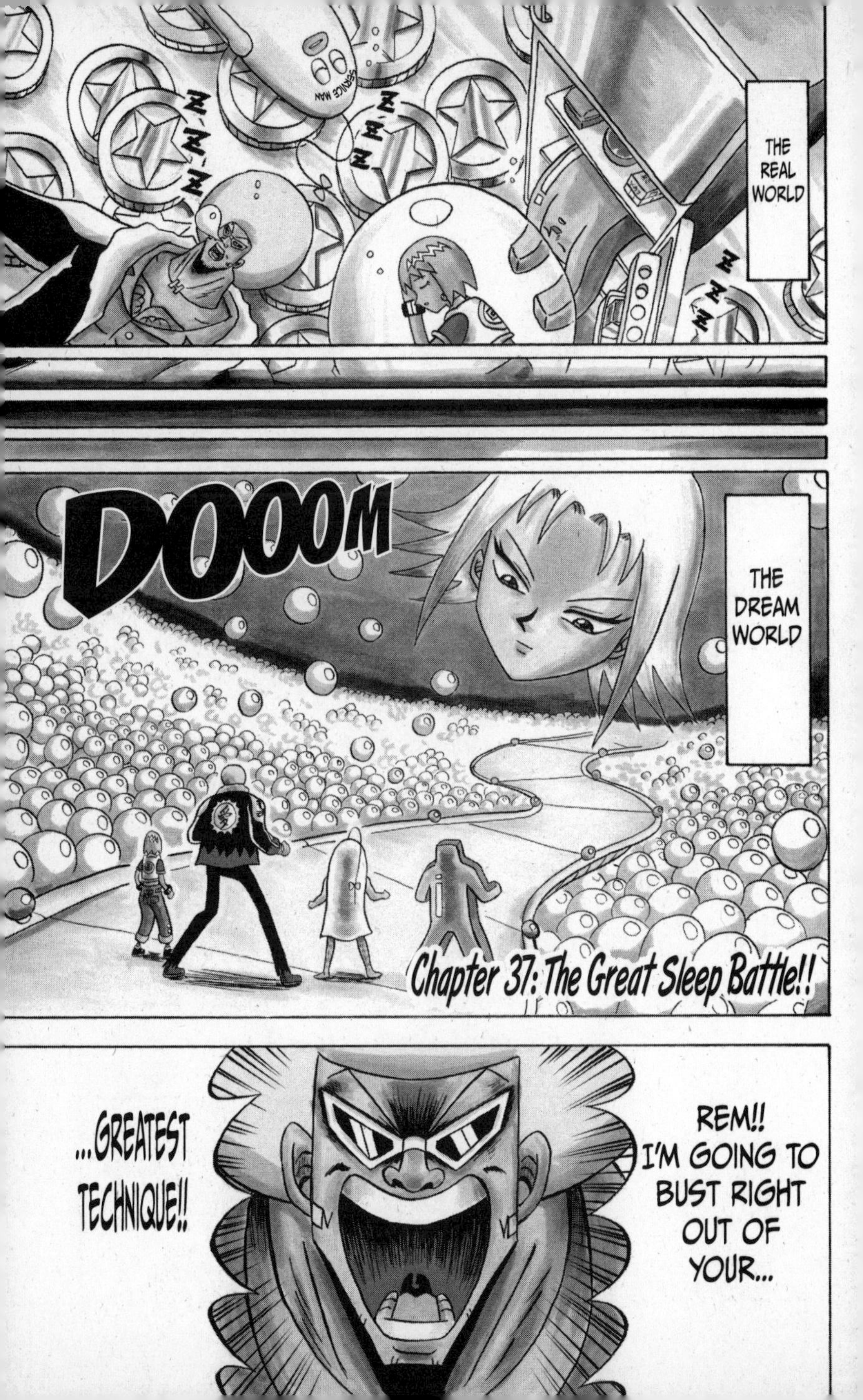
THE REAL WORLD
THE DREAM WORLD
DOOOM
Chapter 37: The Great Sleep Battle!!
REM!! I'M GOING TO BUST RIGHT OUT OF YOUR...
...GREATEST TECHNIQUE!!

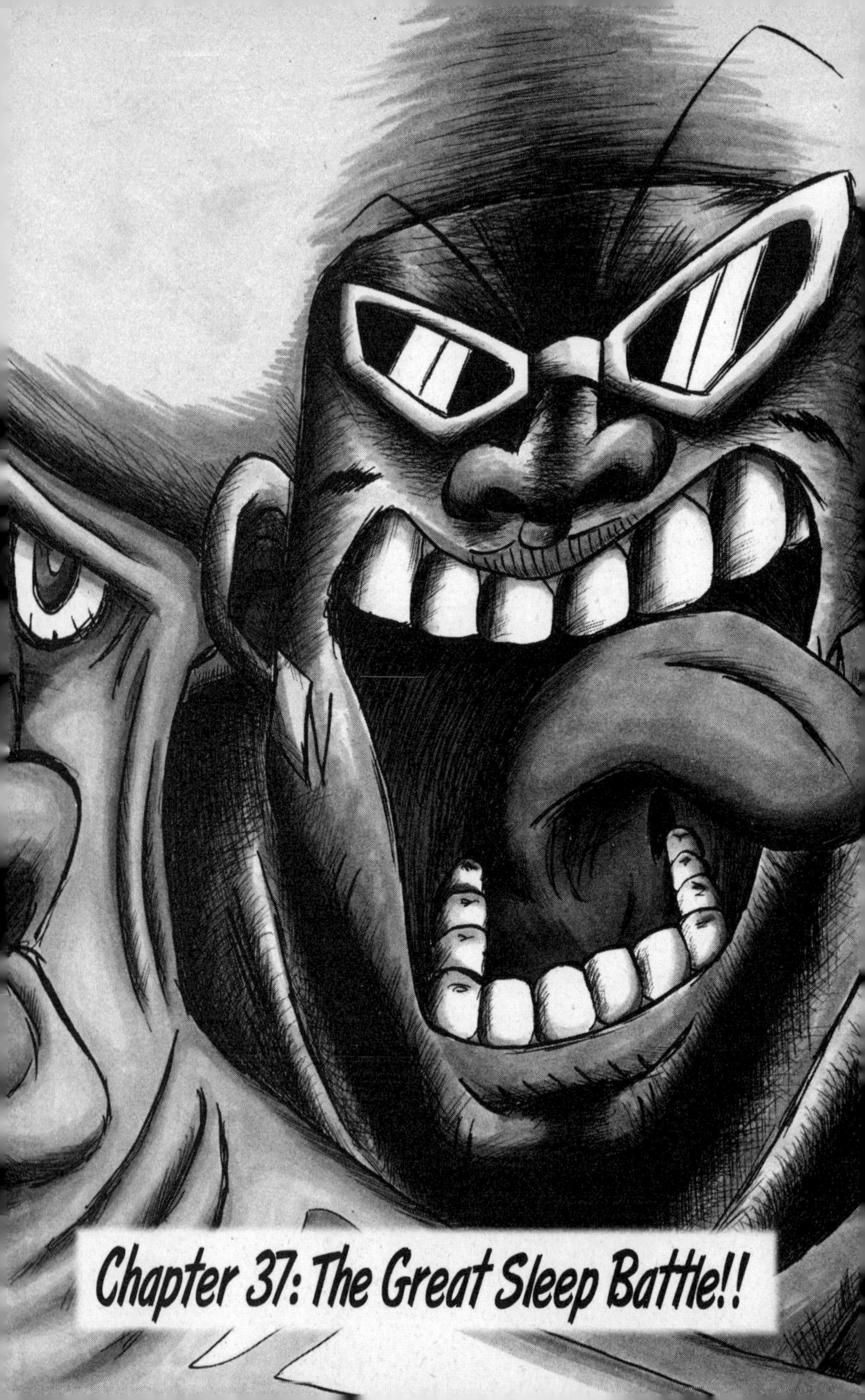

Chapter 37: The Great Sleep Battle!!

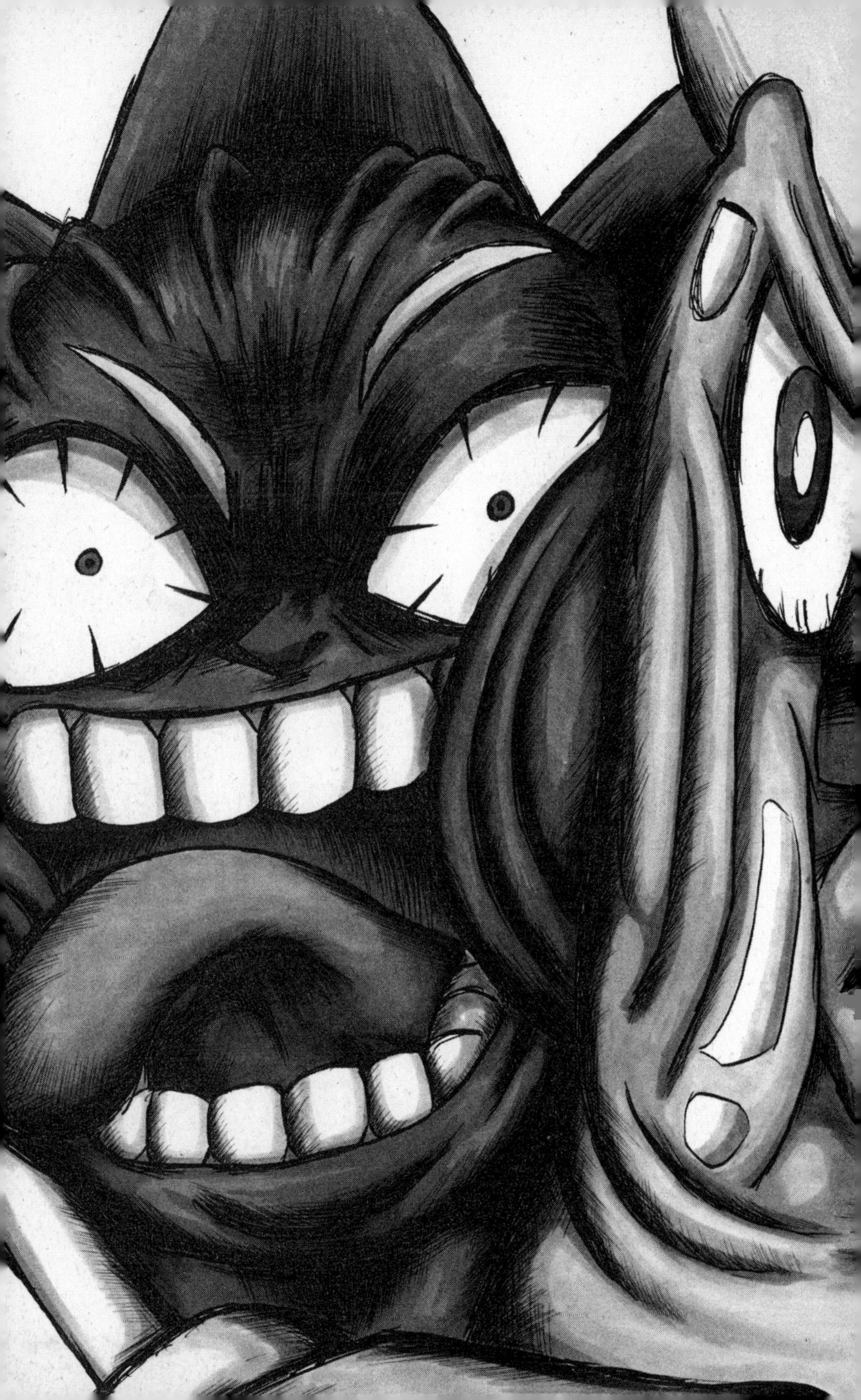

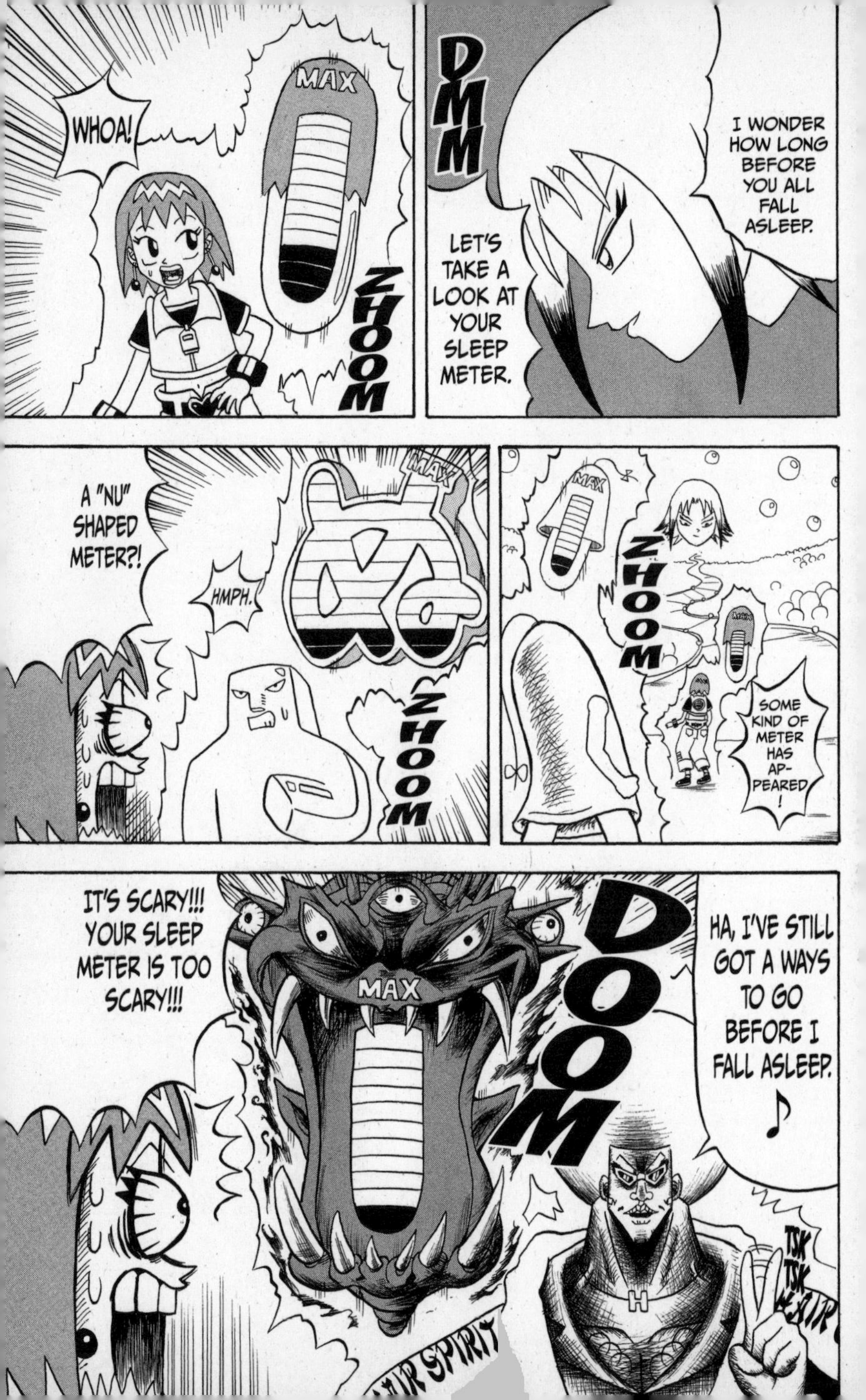
DMM
I WONDER HOW LONG BEFORE YOU ALL FALL ASLEEP.
LET'S TAKE A LOOK AT YOUR SLEEP METER.
MAX
WHOA!
ZHOOM
MAX
ZHOOM
MAX
SOME KIND OF METER HAS AP-PEARED!
MAX
A "NU" SHAPED METER?!
HMPH.
ZHOOM
HA, I'VE STILL GOT A WAYS TO GO BEFORE I FALL ASLEEP. ♪
DOOM
MAX
IT'S SCARY!!! YOUR SLEEP METER IS TOO SCARY!!!
TSK TSK

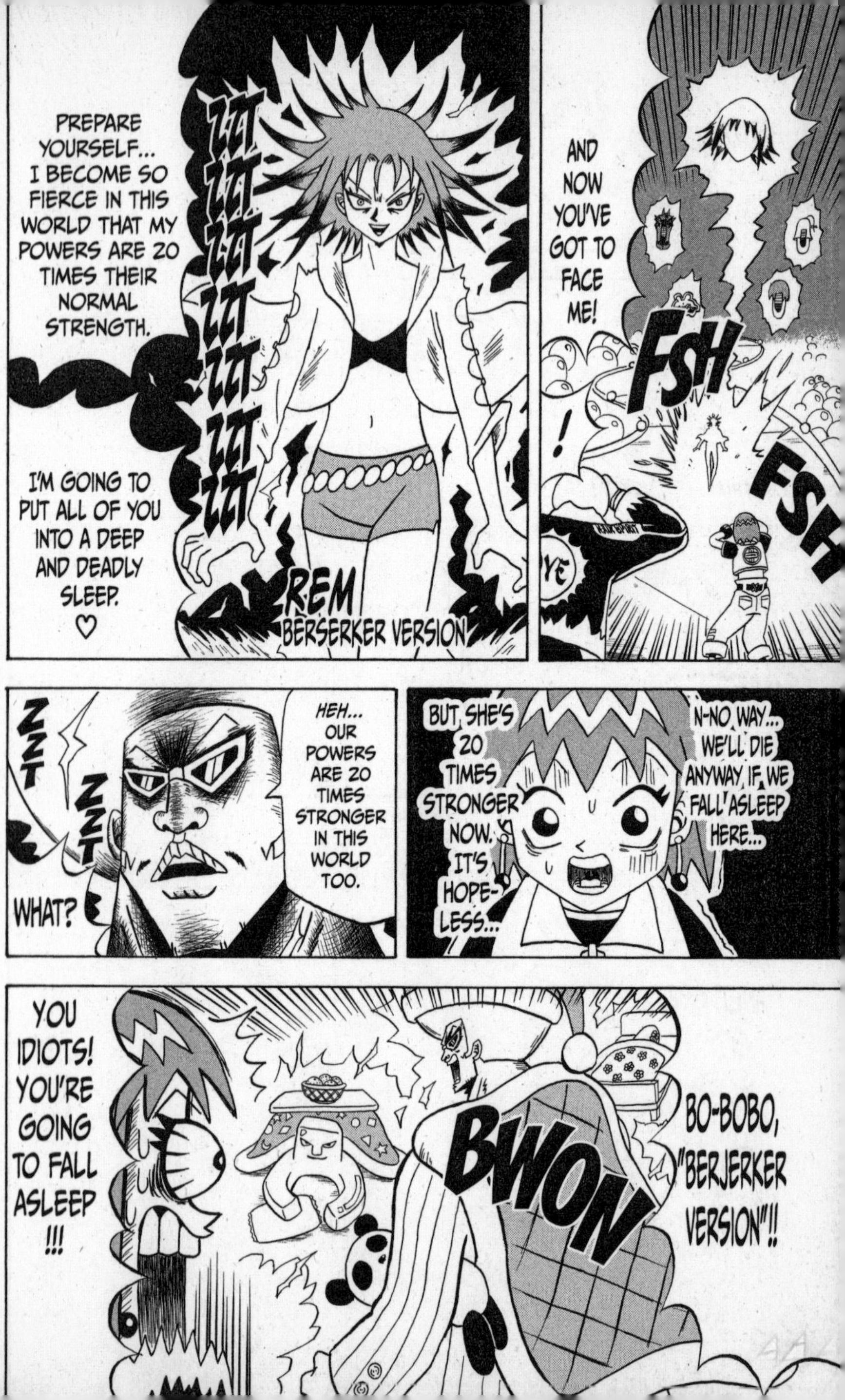
AND NOW YOU'VE GOT TO FACE ME!
FSH
!
FSH
PREPARE YOURSELF... I BECOME SO FIERCE IN THIS WORLD THAT MY POWERS ARE 20 TIMES THEIR NORMAL STRENGTH.
ZZT ZZT ZZT ZZT ZZT ZZT ZZT ZZT ZZT ZZT
I'M GOING TO PUT ALL OF YOU INTO A DEEP AND DEADLY SLEEP. ♡
REM
BERSERKER VERSION
N-NO WAY... WE'LL DIE ANYWAY IF WE FALL ASLEEP HERE...
BUT SHE'S 20 TIMES STRONGER NOW. IT'S HOPE-LESS...
HEH... OUR POWERS ARE 20 TIMES STRONGER IN THIS WORLD TOO.
ZZZT
ZZZT
WHAT?
BO-BOBO, "BERJERKER VERSION"!!
BWON
YOU IDIOTS! YOU'RE GOING TO FALL ASLEEP !!!

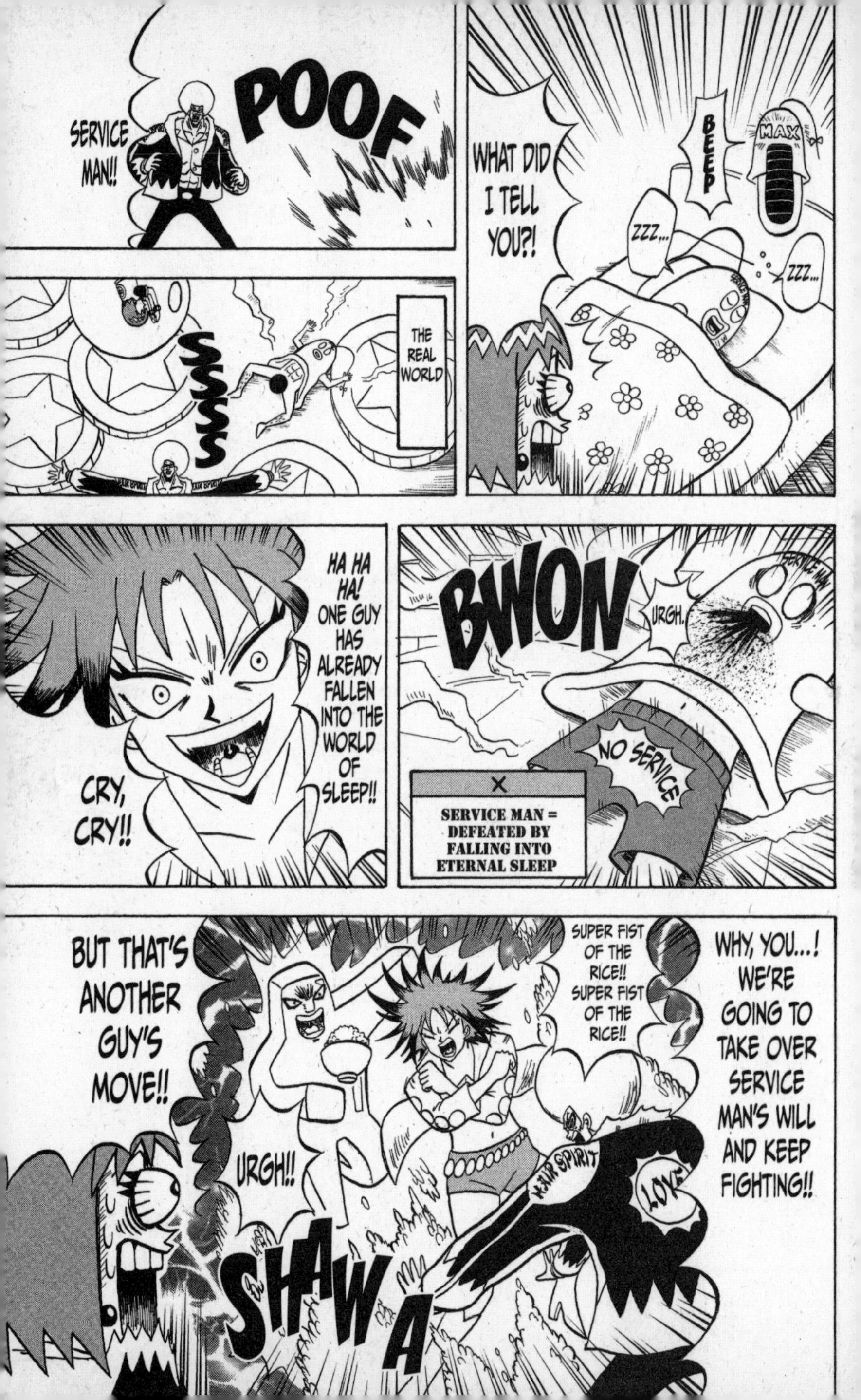
MAX
BEEP
ZZZ...
WHAT DID I TELL YOU?!
ZZZ...
SERVICE MAN!!
POOF
THE REAL WORLD
SSSSS
SERVICE MAN
URGH.
BWON
NO SERVICE
X
SERVICE MAN = DEFEATED BY FALLING INTO ETERNAL SLEEP
HA HA HA! ONE GUY HAS ALREADY FALLEN INTO THE WORLD OF SLEEP!!
CRY, CRY!!
WHY, YOU...! WE'RE GOING TO TAKE OVER SERVICE MAN'S WILL AND KEEP FIGHTING!!
SUPER FIST OF THE RICE!! SUPER FIST OF THE RICE!!
BUT THAT'S ANOTHER GUY'S MOVE!!
URGH!!
HAIR SPIRIT
LOVE
SHAWA

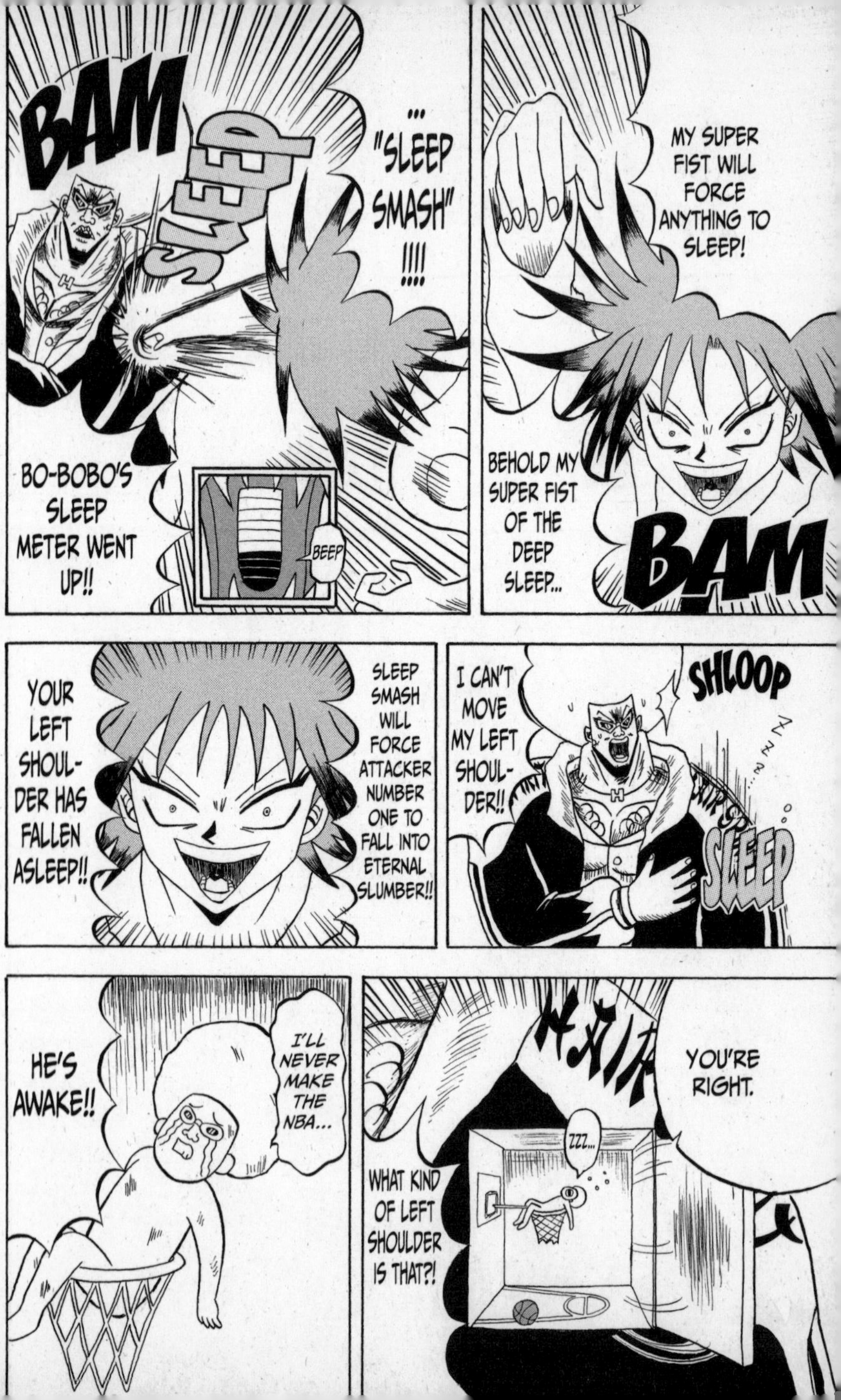
MY SUPER FIST WILL FORCE ANYTHING TO SLEEP!
BEHOLD MY SUPER FIST OF THE DEEP SLEEP...
BAM
..."SLEEP SMASH"!!!!
SLEEP
BAM
BEEP
BO-BOBO'S SLEEP METER WENT UP!!
SHLOOP
I CAN'T MOVE MY LEFT SHOUL-DER!!
SLEEP
SLEEP SMASH WILL FORCE ATTACKER NUMBER ONE TO FALL INTO ETERNAL SLUMBER!!
YOUR LEFT SHOUL-DER HAS FALLEN ASLEEP!!
YOU'RE RIGHT.
ZZZ...
WHAT KIND OF LEFT SHOULDER IS THAT?!
I'LL NEVER MAKE THE NBA...
HE'S AWAKE!!

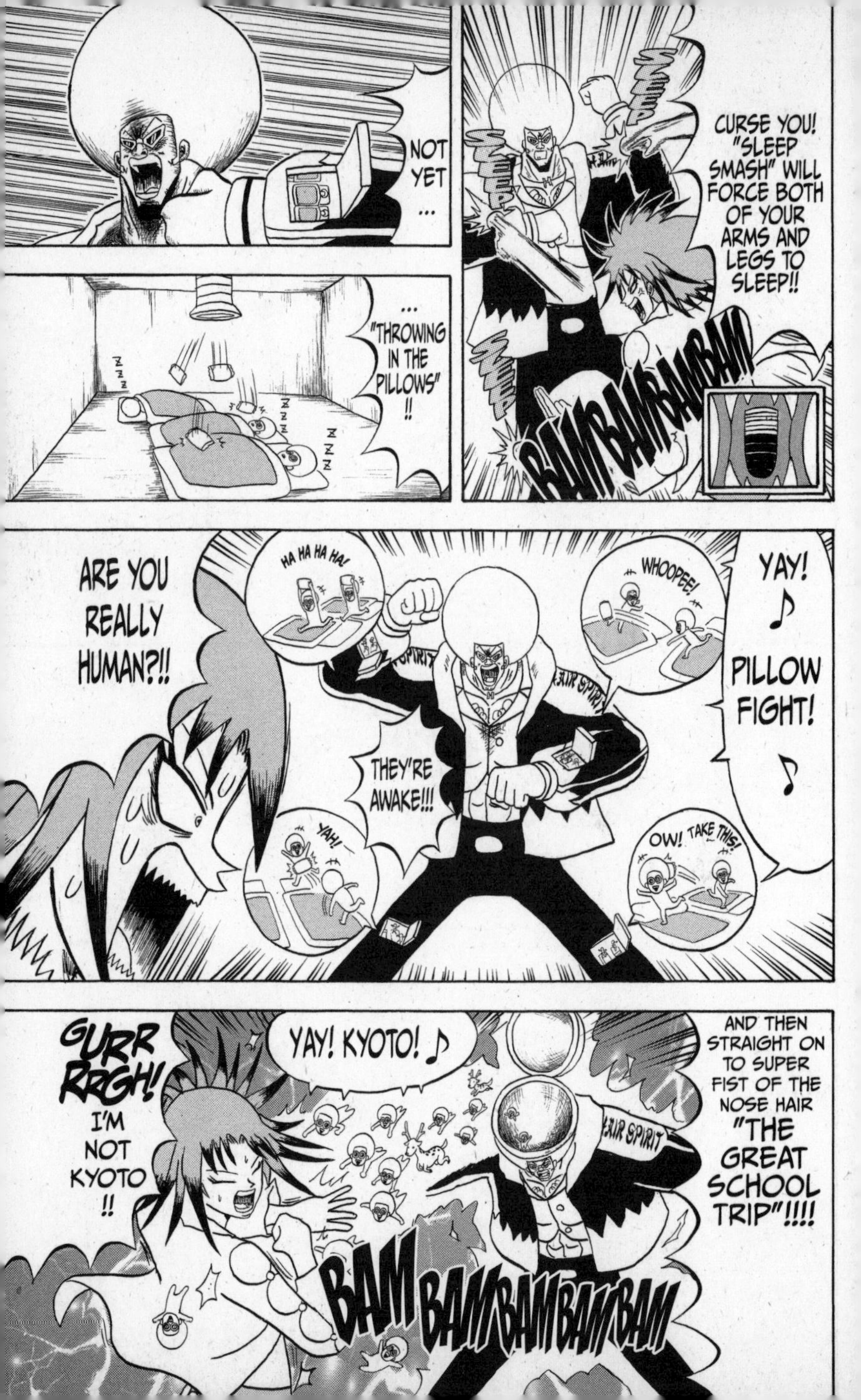
CURSE YOU! "SLEEP SMASH" WILL FORCE BOTH OF YOUR ARMS AND LEGS TO SLEEP!!
SLEEP
SLEEP
BAMBAMBAMBAMBAM
NOT YET ...
... "THROWING IN THE PILLOWS" !!
YAY! ♪ PILLOW FIGHT! ♪
WHOOPEE!
HA HA HA HA!
THEY'RE AWAKE!!!
OW! TAKE THIS!
YAH!
ARE YOU REALLY HUMAN?!!
AND THEN STRAIGHT ON TO SUPER FIST OF THE NOSE HAIR "THE GREAT SCHOOL TRIP"!!!!
YAY! KYOTO! ♪
GURRRRGH! I'M NOT KYOTO !!
BAM BAM BAM BAM BAM

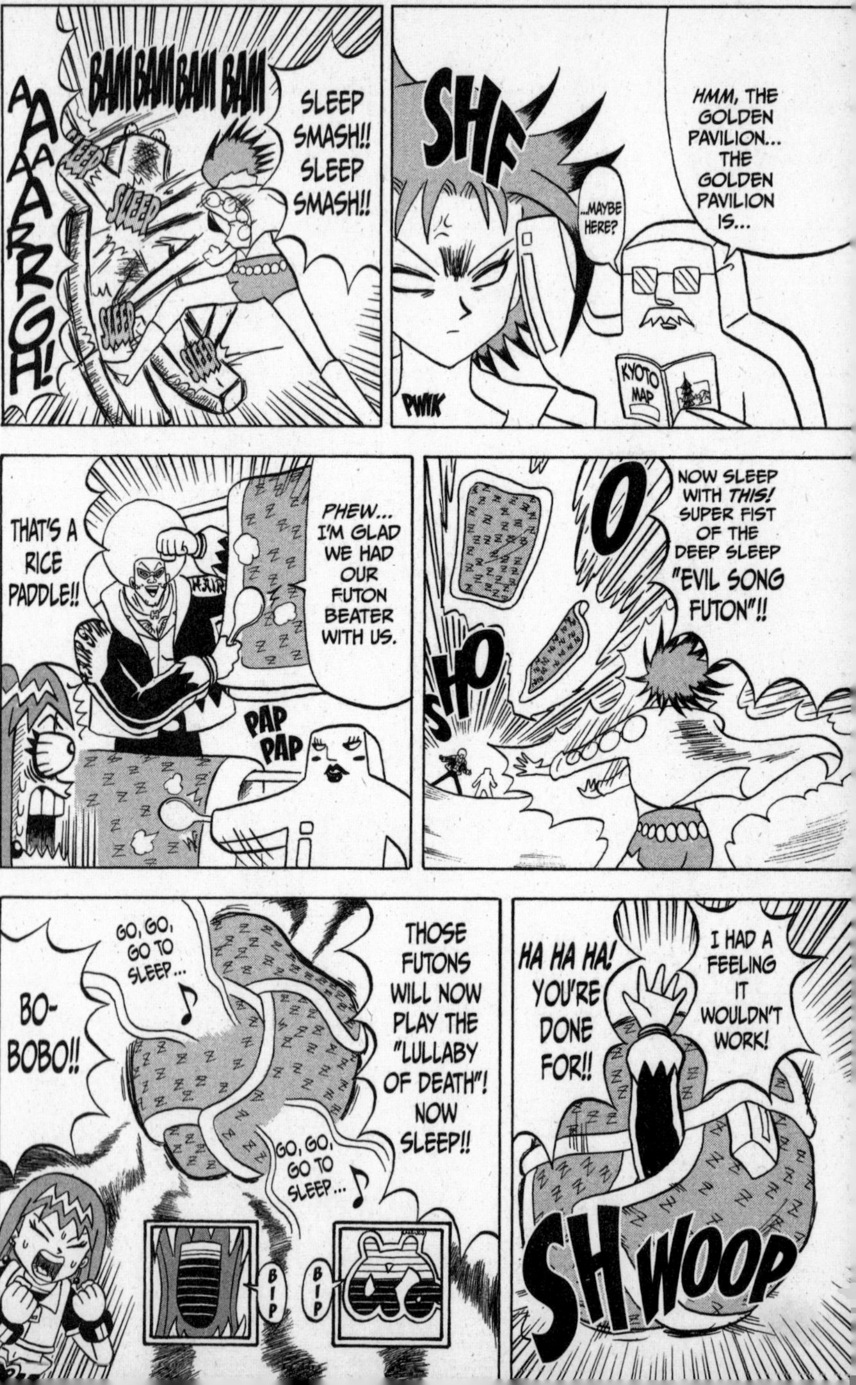
HMM, THE GOLDEN PAVILION... THE GOLDEN PAVILION IS...
...MAYBE HERE?
SHF
KYOTO MAP
PWIK
SLEEP SMASH!! SLEEP SMASH!!
BAM BAM BAM BAM
AAAAARRGH!
NOW SLEEP WITH THIS! SUPER FIST OF THE DEEP SLEEP "EVIL SONG FUTON"!!
O
SHO
PHEW... I'M GLAD WE HAD OUR FUTON BEATER WITH US.
THAT'S A RICE PADDLE!!
PAP PAP
I HAD A FEELING IT WOULDN'T WORK!
HA HA HA! YOU'RE DONE FOR!!
SHWOOP
THOSE FUTONS WILL NOW PLAY THE "LULLABY OF DEATH"! NOW SLEEP!!
GO, GO, GO TO SLEEP... ♪
BO-BOBO!!
GO, GO, GO TO SLEEP... ♪
BIP
BIP

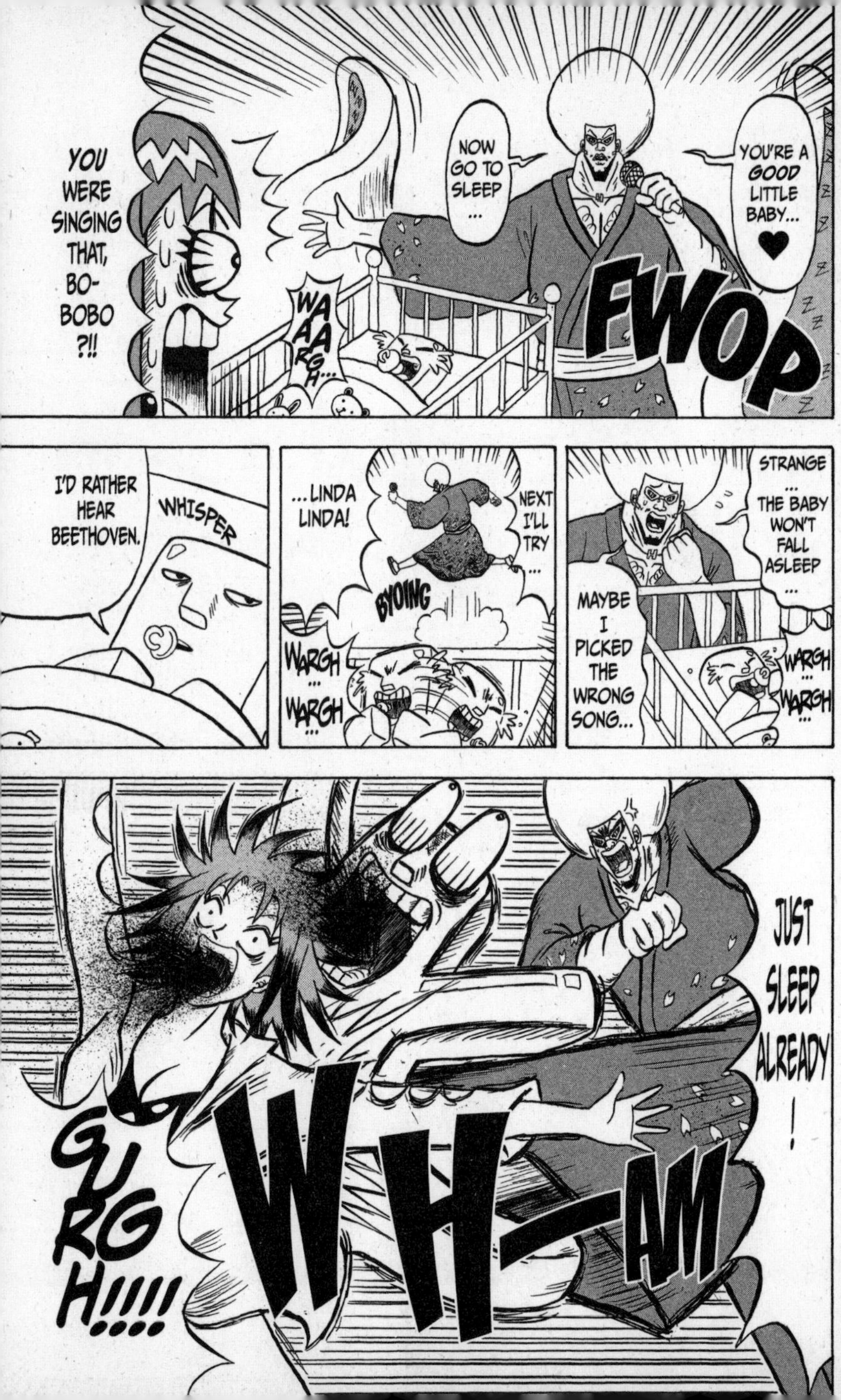
YOU'RE A GOOD LITTLE BABY... ♥
FWOP
NOW GO TO SLEEP ...
WAAAARGH...
YOU WERE SINGING THAT, BO-BOBO ?!!
STRANGE ... THE BABY WON'T FALL ASLEEP ...
WARGH ... WARGH ...
MAYBE I PICKED THE WRONG SONG...
NEXT I'LL TRY ...
...LINDA LINDA!
BYOING
WARGH ... WARGH ...
WHISPER
I'D RATHER HEAR BEETHOVEN.
JUST SLEEP ALREADY !
WH-AM
GURGH!!!!...

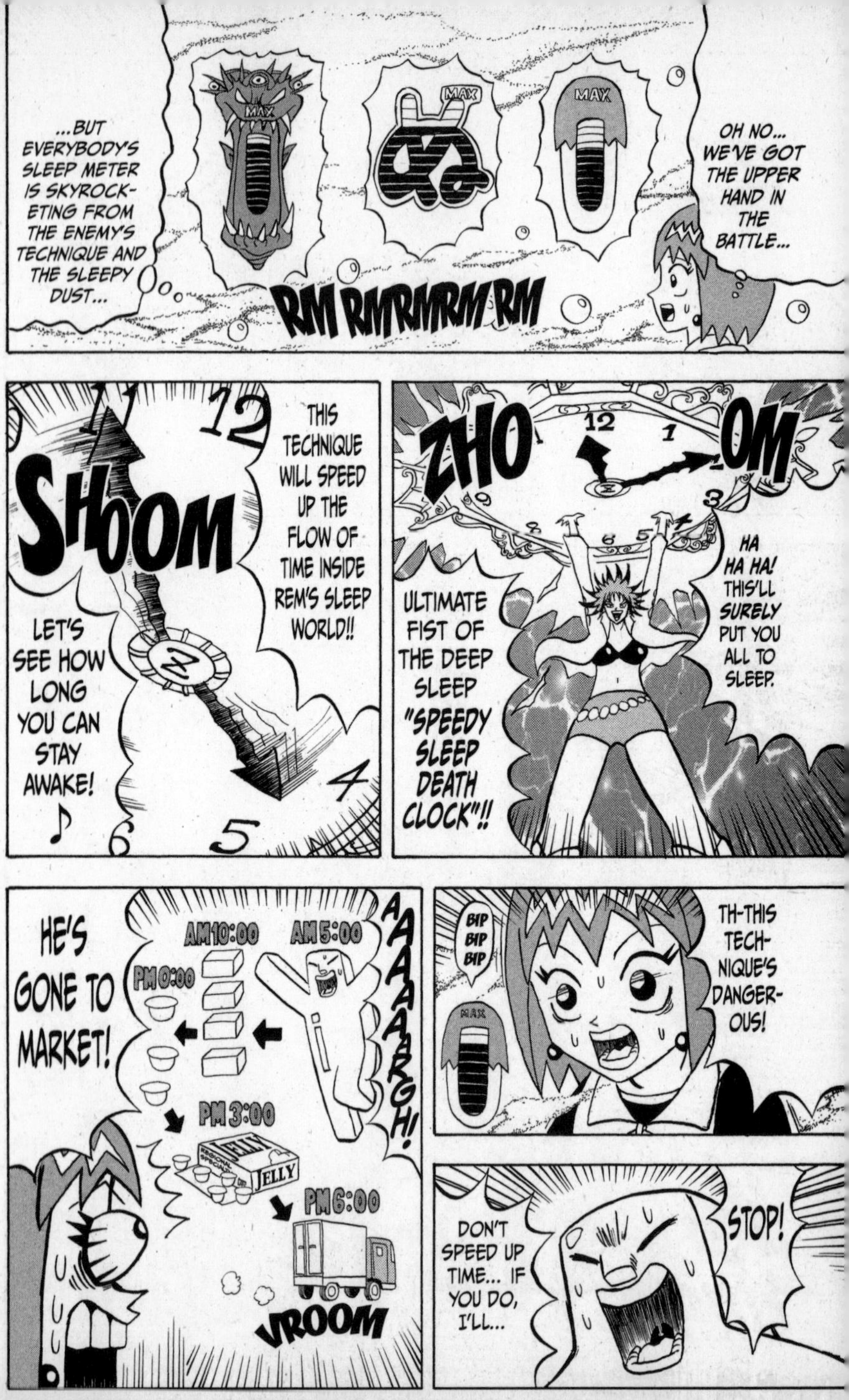
OH NO... WE'VE GOT THE UPPER HAND IN THE BATTLE...
MAX
MAX
MAX
...BUT EVERYBODY'S SLEEP METER IS SKYROCKETING FROM THE ENEMY'S TECHNIQUE AND THE SLEEPY DUST...
RM RMRMRM RM
ZHOOM
HA HA HA! THIS'LL SURELY PUT YOU ALL TO SLEEP.
ULTIMATE FIST OF THE DEEP SLEEP "SPEEDY SLEEP DEATH CLOCK"!!
THIS TECHNIQUE WILL SPEED UP THE FLOW OF TIME INSIDE REM'S SLEEP WORLD!!
SHOOM
LET'S SEE HOW LONG YOU CAN STAY AWAKE! ♪
TH-THIS TECHNIQUE'S DANGEROUS!
BIP BIP BIP
MAX
STOP!
DON'T SPEED UP TIME... IF YOU DO, I'LL...
AAAAARGH!
AM 5:00
AM10:00
PM 0:00
PM 3:00
JELLY
REGIONAL SPECIAL
JELLY
PM 6:00
VROOM
HE'S GONE TO MARKET!

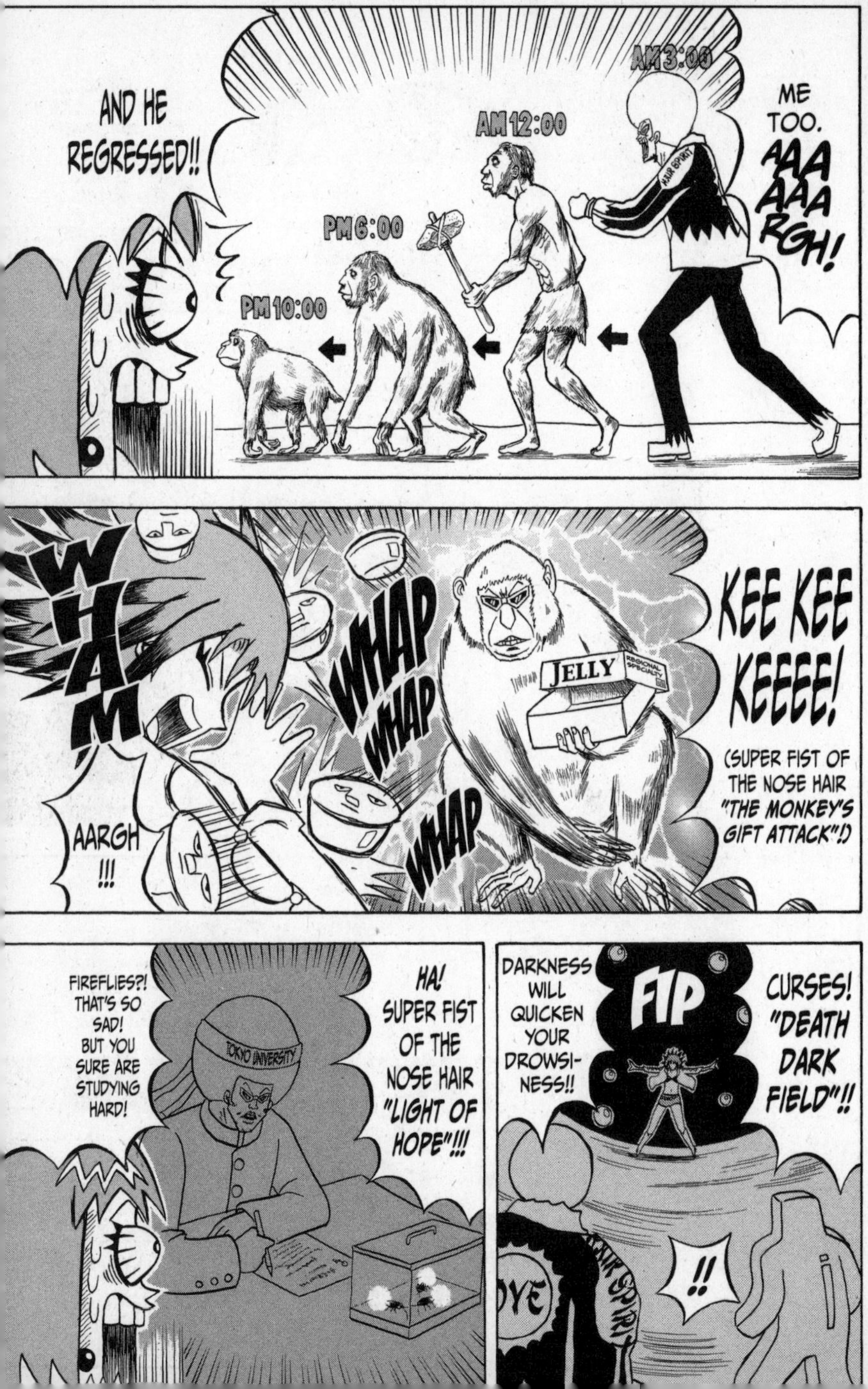

AM 3:00
ME TOO. AAAAAARGH!
AM 12:00
PM 6:00
PM 10:00
AND HE REGRESSED!!
KEE KEE KEEEE!
(SUPER FIST OF THE NOSE HAIR "THE MONKEY'S GIFT ATTACK"!)
JELLY
REGIONAL SPECIALTY
WHAP WHAP
WHAP
WHAM
AARGH !!!
CURSES! "DEATH DARK FIELD"!!
FIP
DARKNESS WILL QUICKEN YOUR DROWSI-NESS!!
!!
HA! SUPER FIST OF THE NOSE HAIR "LIGHT OF HOPE"!!!
FIREFLIES?! THAT'S SO SAD! BUT YOU SURE ARE STUDYING HARD!
TOKYO UNIVERSITY

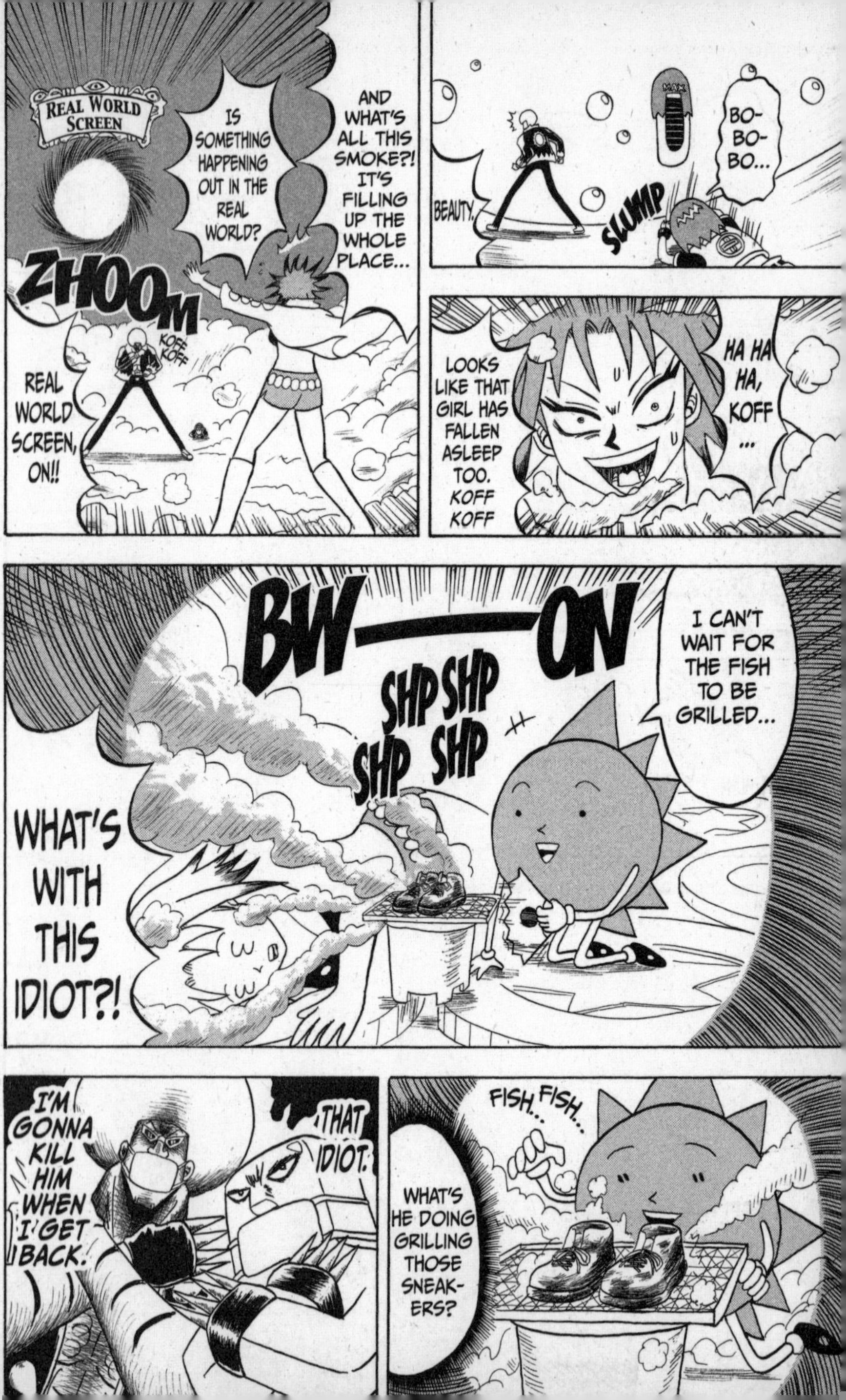
BO-BO-BO...
SLUMP
BEAUTY.
HA HA HA, KOFF...
LOOKS LIKE THAT GIRL HAS FALLEN ASLEEP TOO. KOFF KOFF
REAL WORLD SCREEN
AND WHAT'S ALL THIS SMOKE?! IT'S FILLING UP THE WHOLE PLACE...
IS SOMETHING HAPPENING OUT IN THE REAL WORLD?
ZHOOM
KOFF KOFF
REAL WORLD SCREEN, ON!!
I CAN'T WAIT FOR THE FISH TO BE GRILLED...
BW——ON
SHP SHP SHP SHP
WHAT'S WITH THIS IDIOT?!
FISH... FISH...
WHAT'S HE DOING GRILLING THOSE SNEAKERS?
THAT IDIOT.
I'M GONNA KILL HIM WHEN I GET BACK.

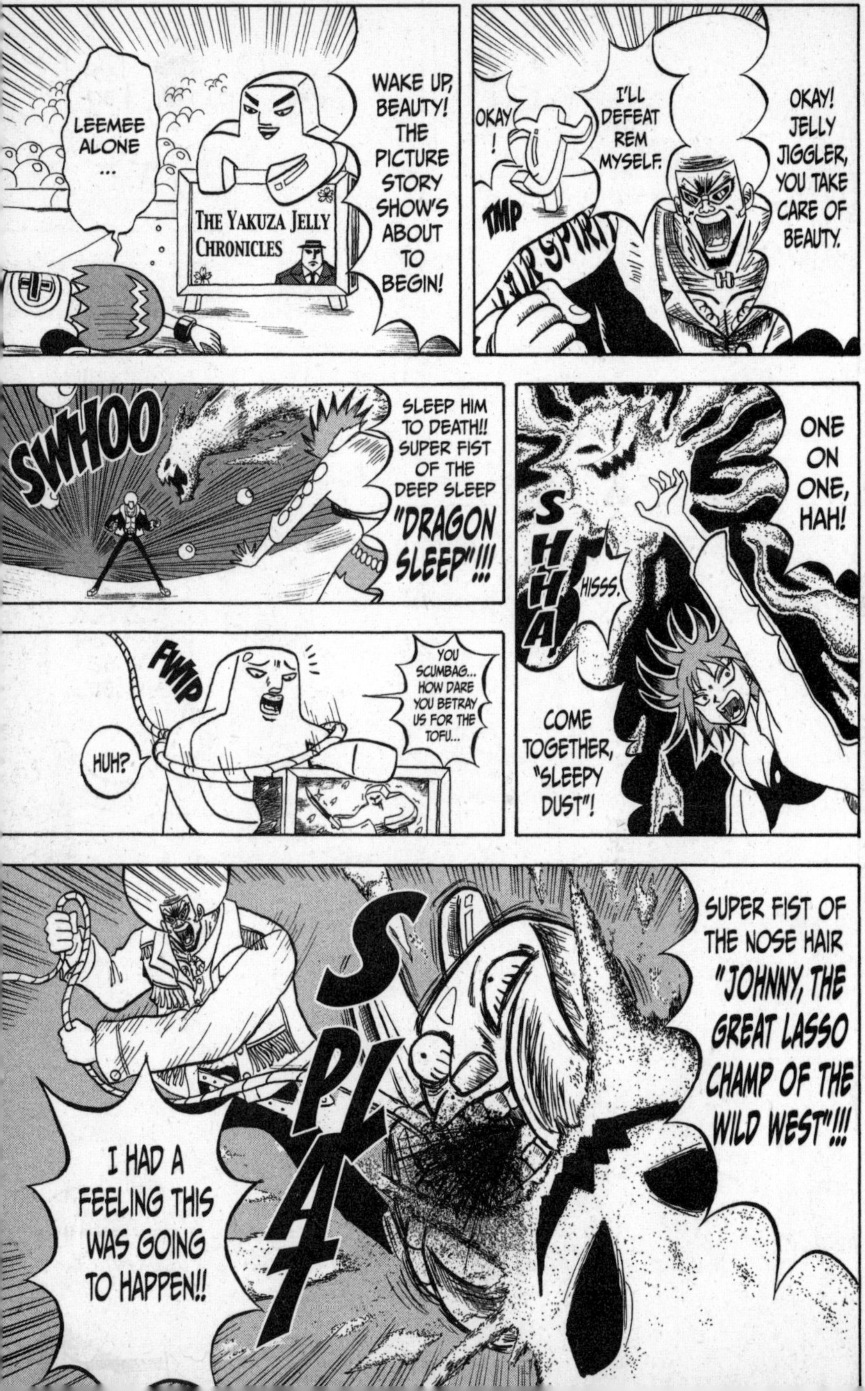
OKAY! JELLY JIGGLER, YOU TAKE CARE OF BEAUTY.
I'LL DEFEAT REM MYSELF.
OKAY!
TMP
WAKE UP, BEAUTY! THE PICTURE STORY SHOW'S ABOUT TO BEGIN!
THE YAKUZA JELLY CHRONICLES
LEEMEE ALONE ...
ONE ON ONE, HAH!
SHHHA
HISSS.
COME TOGETHER, "SLEEPY DUST"!
SLEEP HIM TO DEATH!! SUPER FIST OF THE DEEP SLEEP "DRAGON SLEEP"!!!
SWHOO
YOU SCUMBAG... HOW DARE YOU BETRAY US FOR THE TOFU...
FWIP
HUH?
SUPER FIST OF THE NOSE HAIR "JOHNNY, THE GREAT LASSO CHAMP OF THE WILD WEST"!!!
SPLAT
I HAD A FEELING THIS WAS GOING TO HAPPEN!!

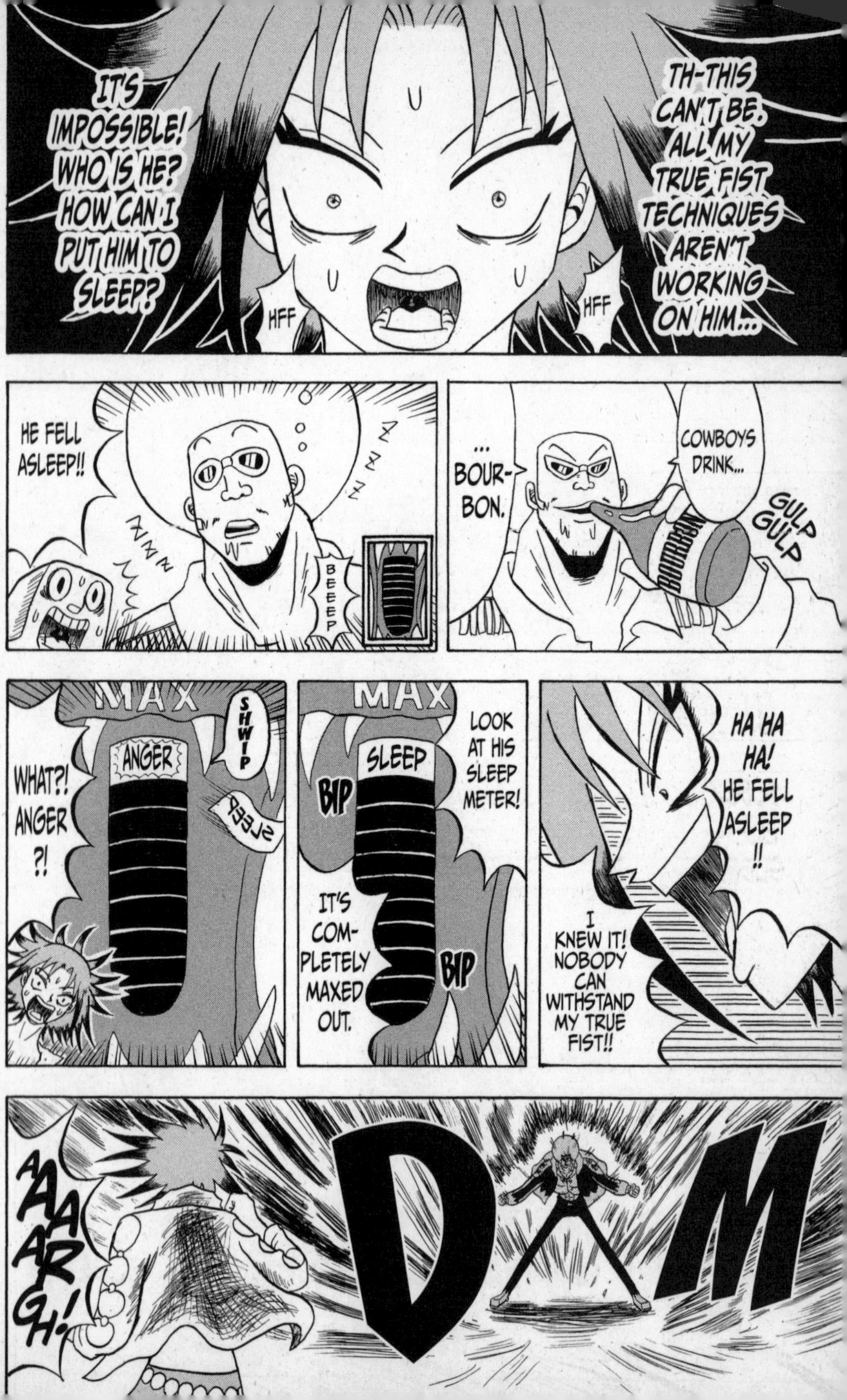
TH-THIS CAN'T BE. ALL MY TRUE FIST TECHNIQUES AREN'T WORKING ON HIM...
HFF
HFF
IT'S IMPOSSIBLE! WHO IS HE? HOW CAN I PUT HIM TO SLEEP?
COWBOYS DRINK...
...BOURBON.
GULP GULP
BOURBON
HE FELL ASLEEP!!
BEEEEP
HA HA HA! HE FELL ASLEEP!!
I KNEW IT! NOBODY CAN WITHSTAND MY TRUE FIST!!
MAX
SLEEP
LOOK AT HIS SLEEP METER!
BIP
IT'S COMPLETELY MAXED OUT.
BIP
MAX
ANGER
SHWIP
SLEEP
WHAT?! ANGER ?!
D M
AAAARGH!

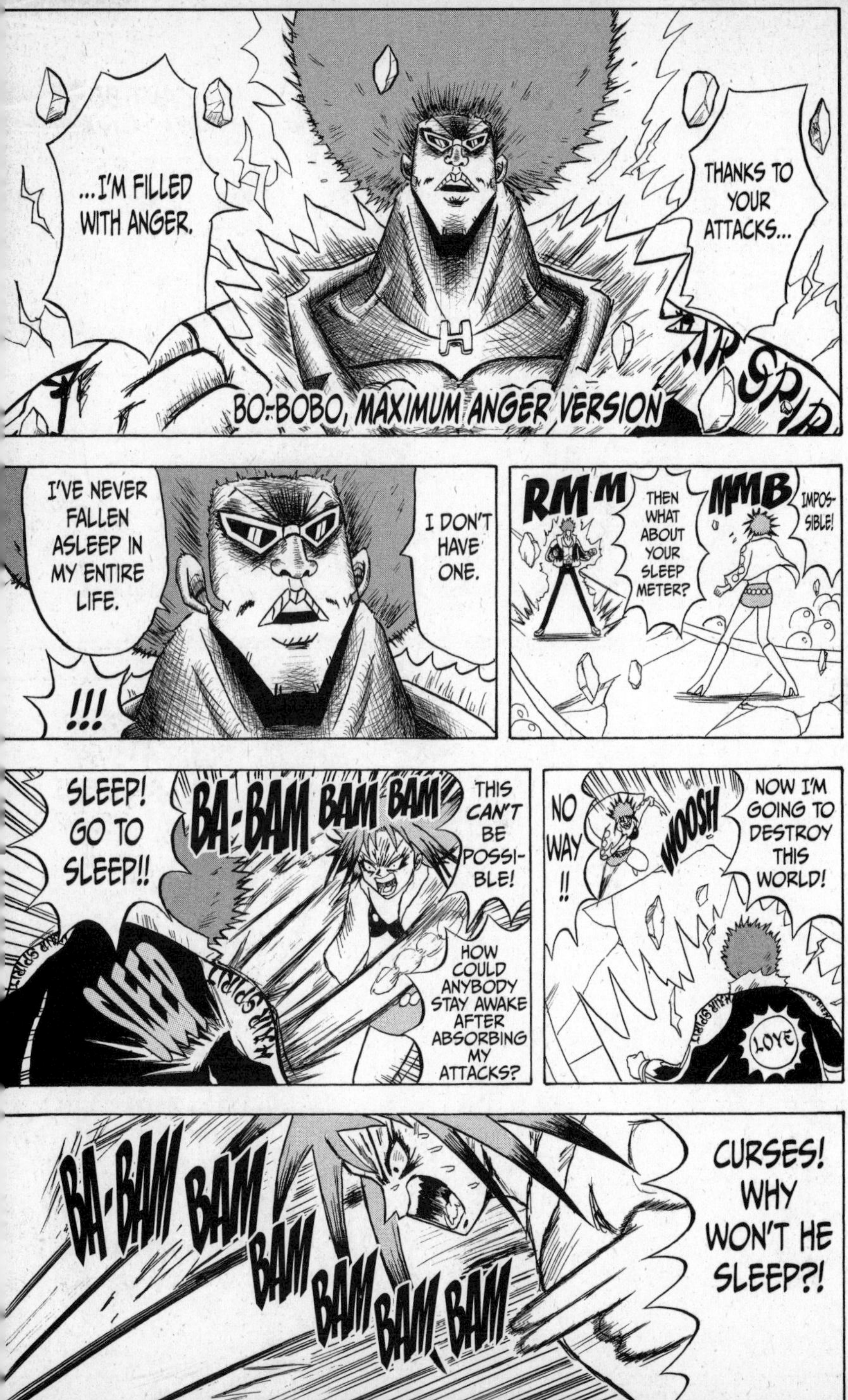
THANKS TO YOUR ATTACKS...
...I'M FILLED WITH ANGER.
BO-BOBO, MAXIMUM ANGER VERSION
IMPOS-SIBLE!
RMMMMB
THEN WHAT ABOUT YOUR SLEEP METER?
I DON'T HAVE ONE.
I'VE NEVER FALLEN ASLEEP IN MY ENTIRE LIFE.
!!!
NOW I'M GOING TO DESTROY THIS WORLD!
WOOSH
NO WAY !!
LOVE
THIS CAN'T BE POSSI-BLE!
BA-BAM BAM BAM
SLEEP! GO TO SLEEP!!
HOW COULD ANYBODY STAY AWAKE AFTER ABSORBING MY ATTACKS?
CURSES! WHY WON'T HE SLEEP?!
BA-BAM BAM BAM BAM BAM BAM

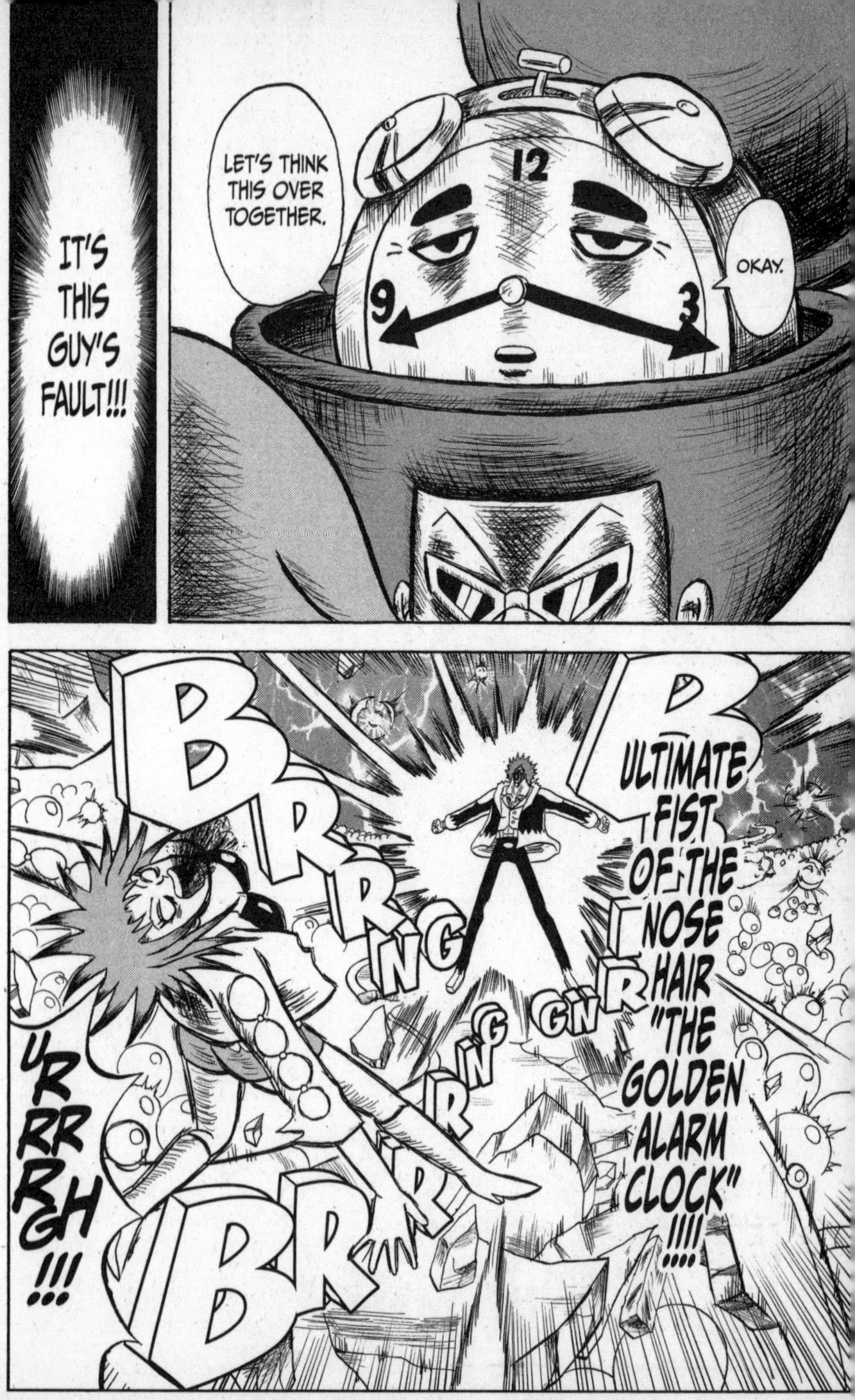
LET'S THINK THIS OVER TOGETHER.
OKAY.
IT'S THIS GUY'S FAULT!!!
BRRNG
BRRNG GNRR
ULTIMATE FIST OF THE NOSE HAIR "THE GOLDEN ALARM CLOCK"!!!!
BRRRNG
URRRRGH!!!

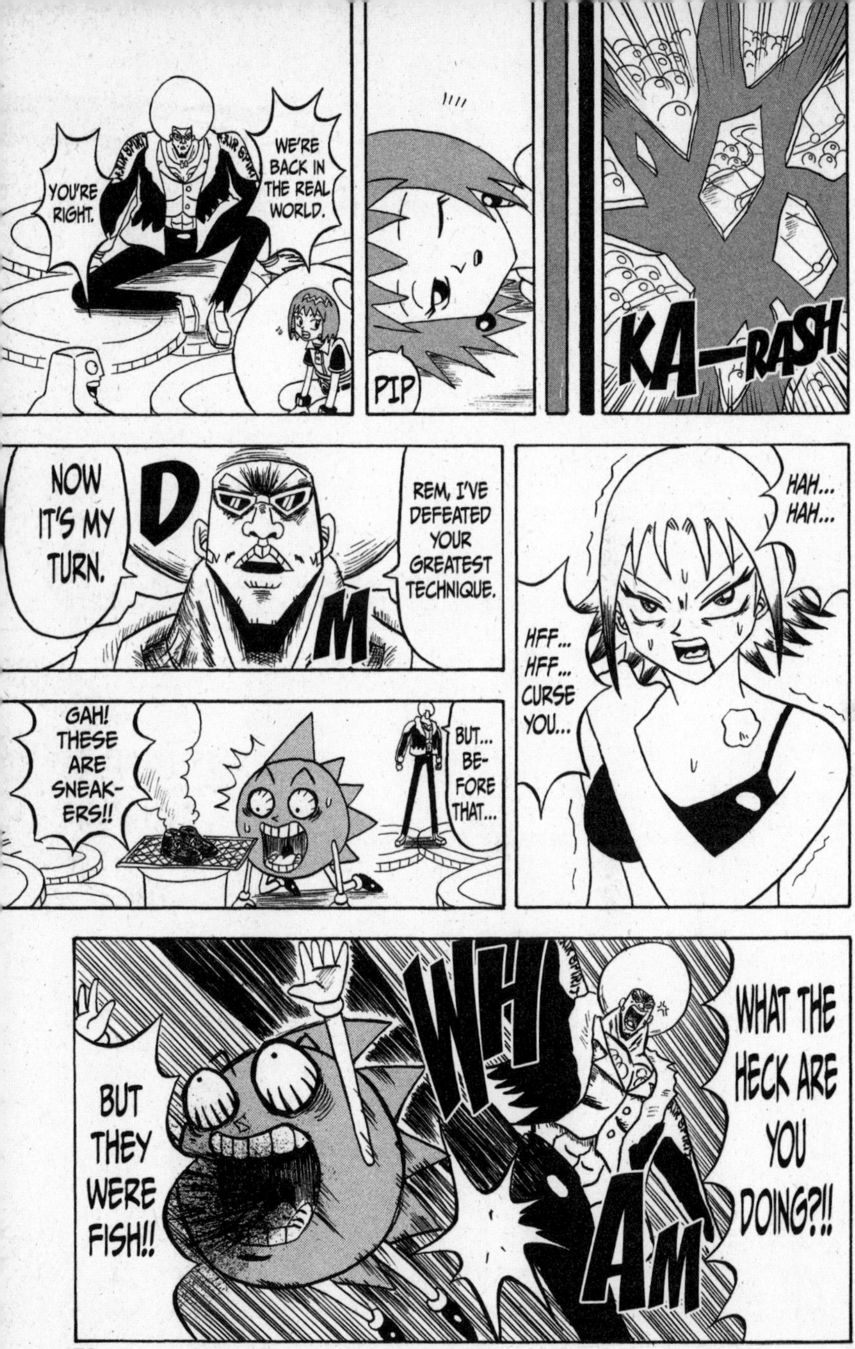
KA-RASH
PIP
WE'RE BACK IN THE REAL WORLD.
YOU'RE RIGHT.
HAH... HAH...
HFF... HFF... CURSE YOU...
REM, I'VE DEFEATED YOUR GREATEST TECHNIQUE.
D M
NOW IT'S MY TURN.
BUT... BE-FORE THAT...
GAH! THESE ARE SNEAKERS!!
WHAT THE HECK ARE YOU DOING?!!
WHAM
BUT THEY WERE FISH!!

Bo-bobo Q & A?!!

Volume 11 THIS IS AN ILLUSTRATION OF BO-BOBO AND HIS FRIENDS WHO ARE ON THEIR WAY TO SAVE GASSER FROM GIGA. GASSER HAS BEEN CAPTURED, AND HATENKO IS ACTING ALONE. ACTUALLY, THIS IS THE ONLY ILLUSTRATION WITH JELLY JIGGLER WEARING THE "NU" SUIT (NOT THAT IT REALLY MATTERS).

Volume 12 I TRIED TO DRAW BO-BOBO, POPPA ROCKS AND JELLY JIGGLER BEING HAPPY AND CHEERFUL IN THIS ONE. I LIKE THE "WHOA, IT'S NOT GOING TO FIT ON THE PAGE" LOOK ABOUT IT. WELL, TO TELL YOU THE TRUTH, I JUST ENDED UP RUNNING OUT OF SPACE TO DRAW ON...

Volume 13 THE CONCEPT IS "THE APPEARANCE OF ROCKS-BOBO." BUT I WAS WORRIED THAT PEOPLE WOULD NOT KNOW WHAT MANGA IT WAS, SO I DREW SMALL IMAGES OF BO-BOBO AND THE OTHERS. I LIKE HOW ROCKS-BOBO IS HOLDING THE POPPA ROCKS SWORD (GREEN ONION).

Volume 14 BO-BOBO LOOKING TOUGH. HE LOOKS LIKE A TRUE CHAMPION, DOESN'T HE? I'M NOT SURE WHAT HE'S A CHAMPION OF. IT'S BEEN A WHILE SINCE I DREW A COVER WITH JUST BO-BOBO ON IT. THE BACKGROUND IS SUPPOSED TO BE A JUNGLE.

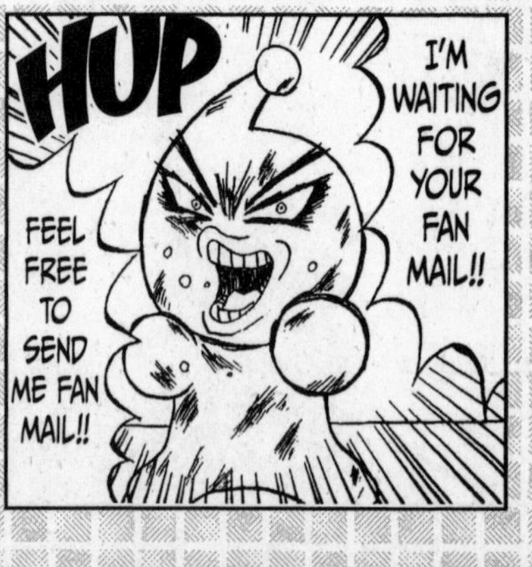
HUP
I'M WAITING FOR YOUR FAN MAIL!!
FEEL FREE TO SEND ME FAN MAIL!!

SEND DENGAKU MAN'S FAN MAIL TO DENGAKU MAN C/O VIZ MEDIA, P.O. BOX 77010, SAN FRANCISCO, CA 94107

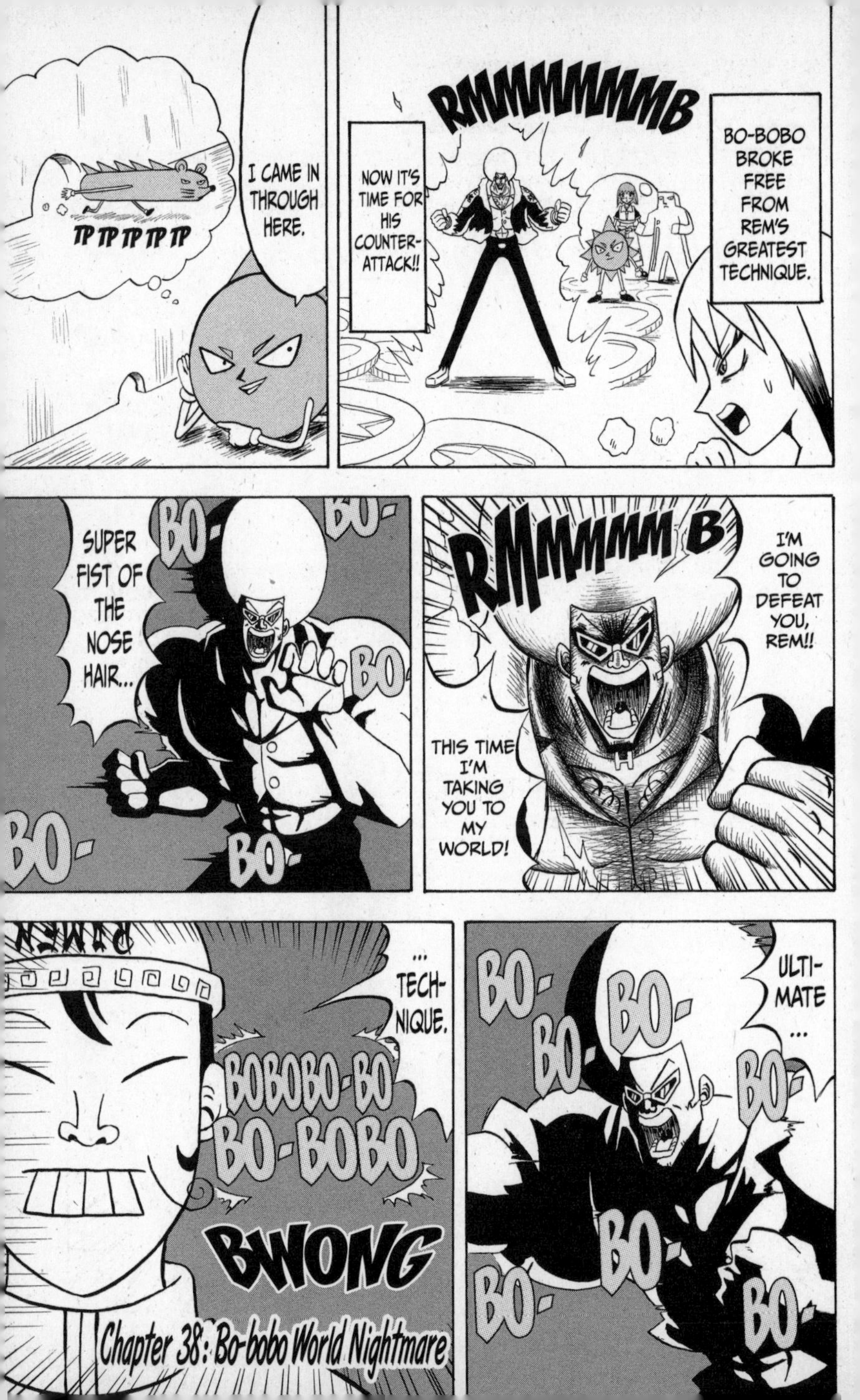
BO-BOBO BROKE FREE FROM REM'S GREATEST TECHNIQUE.
RMMMMMMMB
NOW IT'S TIME FOR HIS COUNTER-ATTACK!!
I CAME IN THROUGH HERE.
TP TP TP TP TP
I'M GOING TO DEFEAT YOU, REM!!
RMMMMM B
THIS TIME I'M TAKING YOU TO MY WORLD!
SUPER FIST OF THE NOSE HAIR...
BO-
BO-
BO
BO-
BO-
ULTI-MATE ...
BO-
BO-
BO-
BO-
BO-
BO-
BO-
... TECH-NIQUE.
BOBOBO-BO BO-BOBO
BWONG

Chapter 38: Bo-bobo World Nightmare

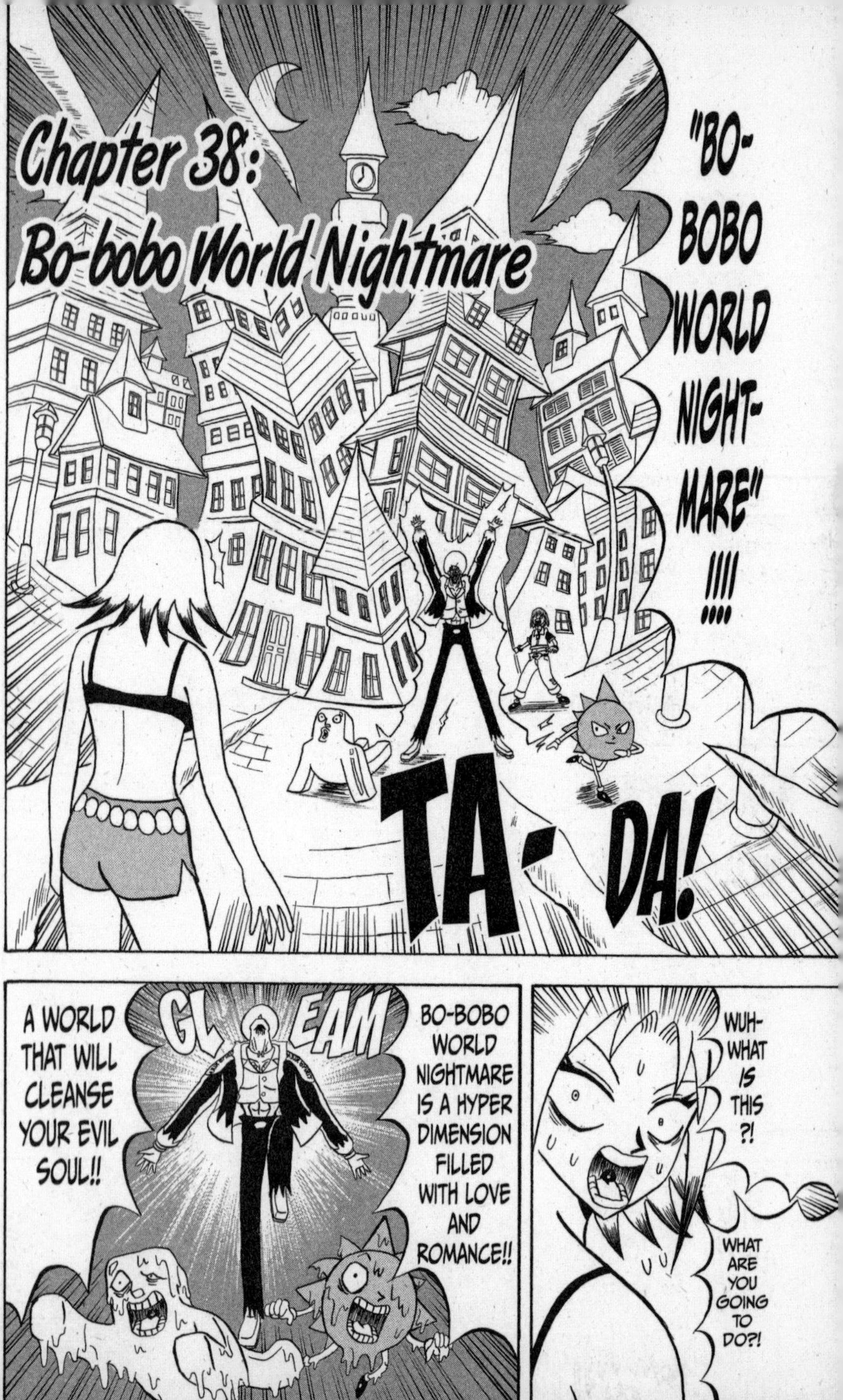
Chapter 38: Bo-bobo World Nightmare
"BO-BOBOBO WORLD NIGHT-MARE"!!!!
TA-DA!
WUH-WHAT IS THIS?!
WHAT ARE YOU GOING TO DO?!
BO-BOBO WORLD NIGHTMARE IS A HYPER DIMENSION FILLED WITH LOVE AND ROMANCE!!
GLEAM
A WORLD THAT WILL CLEANSE YOUR EVIL SOUL!!

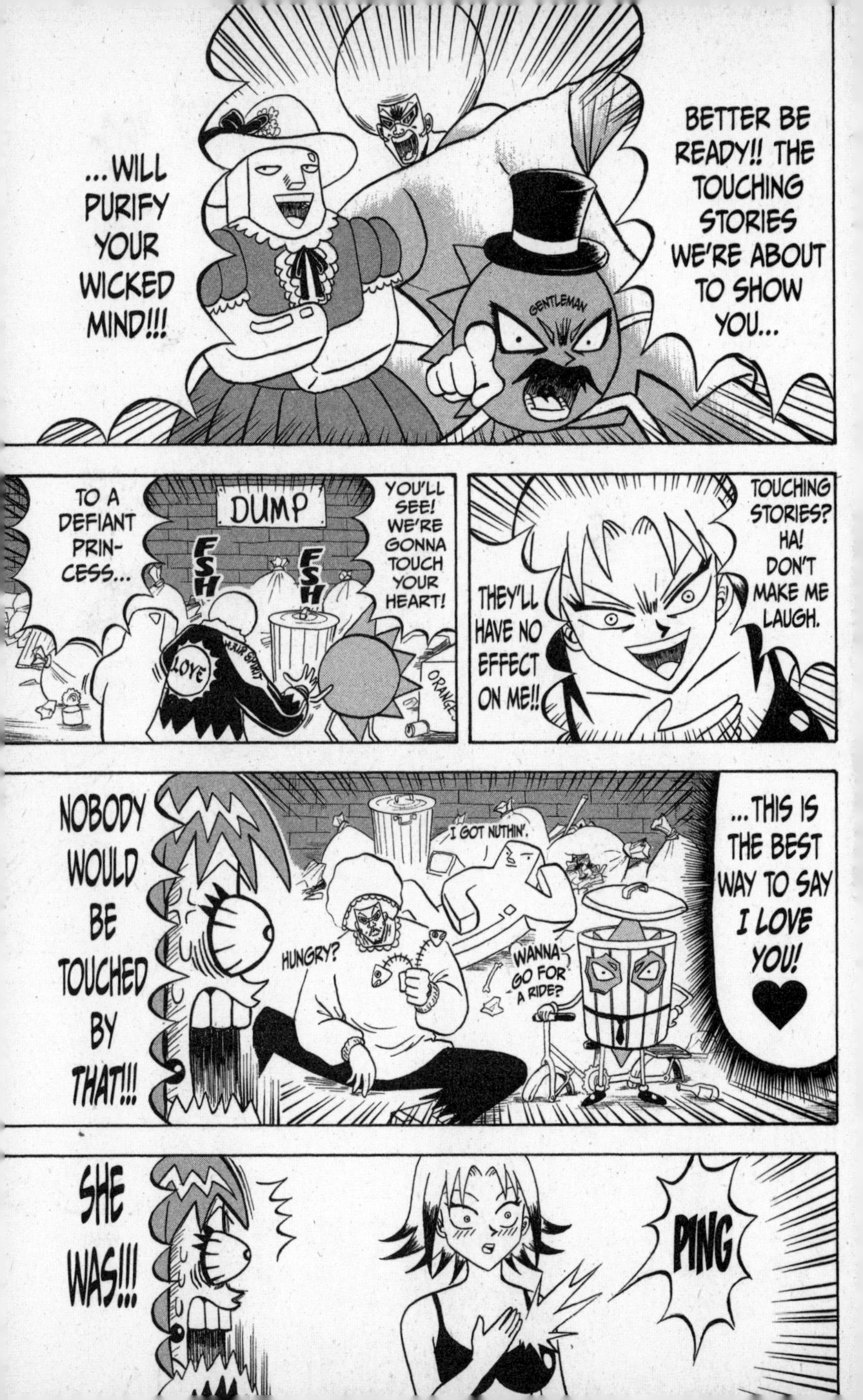
BETTER BE READY!! THE TOUCHING STORIES WE'RE ABOUT TO SHOW YOU...
GENTLEMAN
...WILL PURIFY YOUR WICKED MIND!!!
TOUCHING STORIES? HA! DON'T MAKE ME LAUGH.
THEY'LL HAVE NO EFFECT ON ME!!
YOU'LL SEE! WE'RE GONNA TOUCH YOUR HEART!
DUMP
FSH
FSH
TO A DEFIANT PRINCESS...
LOVE
ORANGE
...THIS IS THE BEST WAY TO SAY I LOVE YOU! ♥
I GOT NUTHIN'.
WANNA GO FOR A RIDE?
HUNGRY?
NOBODY WOULD BE TOUCHED BY THAT!!!
PING
SHE WAS!!!

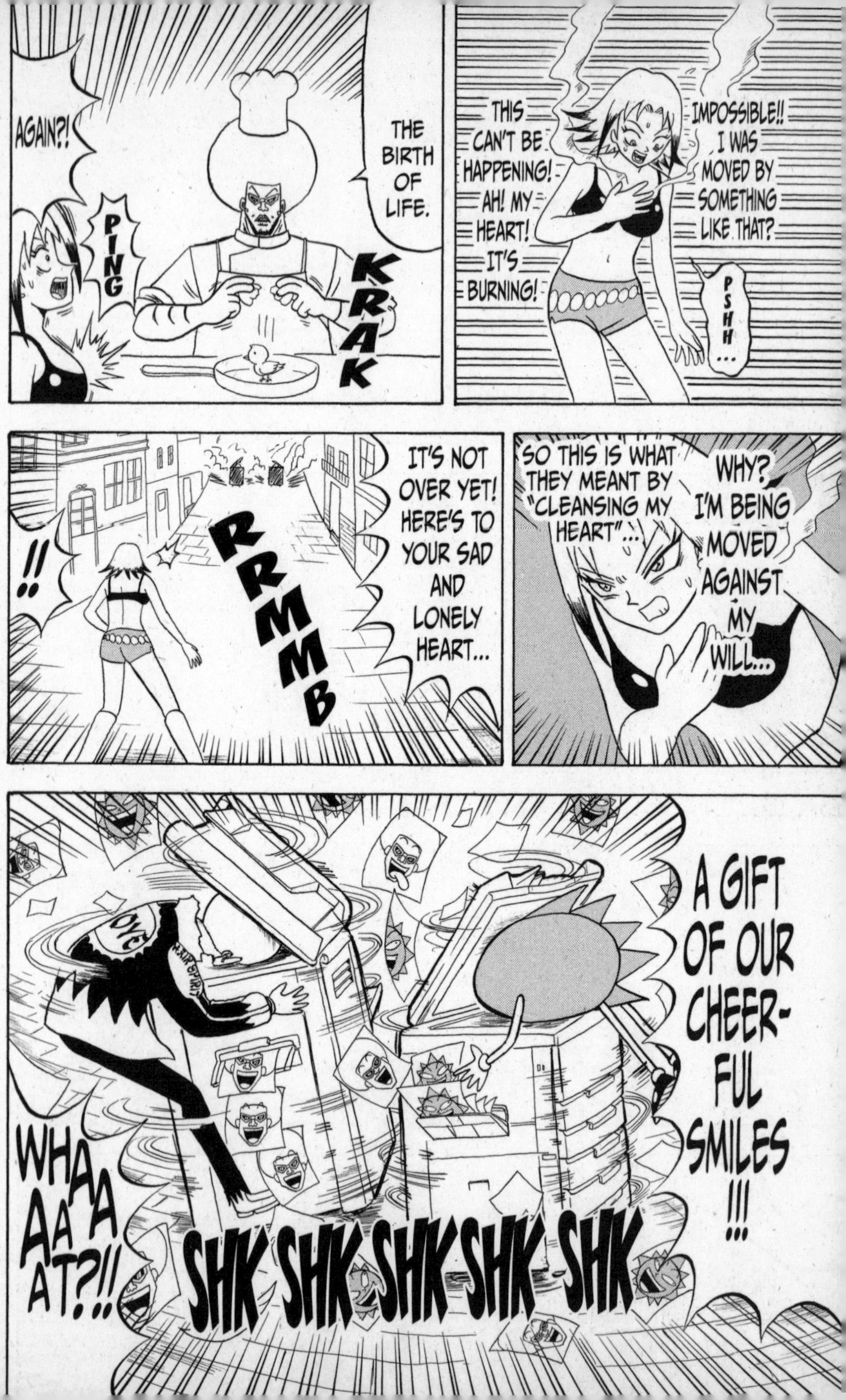
IMPOSSIBLE!! I WAS MOVED BY SOMETHING LIKE THAT?
THIS CAN'T BE HAPPENING! AH! MY HEART! IT'S BURNING!
PSHH...
THE BIRTH OF LIFE.
KRAK
AGAIN?!
PING
WHY? I'M BEING MOVED AGAINST MY WILL...
SO THIS IS WHAT THEY MEANT BY "CLEANSING MY HEART"...
IT'S NOT OVER YET! HERE'S TO YOUR SAD AND LONELY HEART...
RRMMB
!!
A GIFT OF OUR CHEER-FUL SMILES!!!
WHAAAAAT?!!
SHK SHK SHK SHK SHK

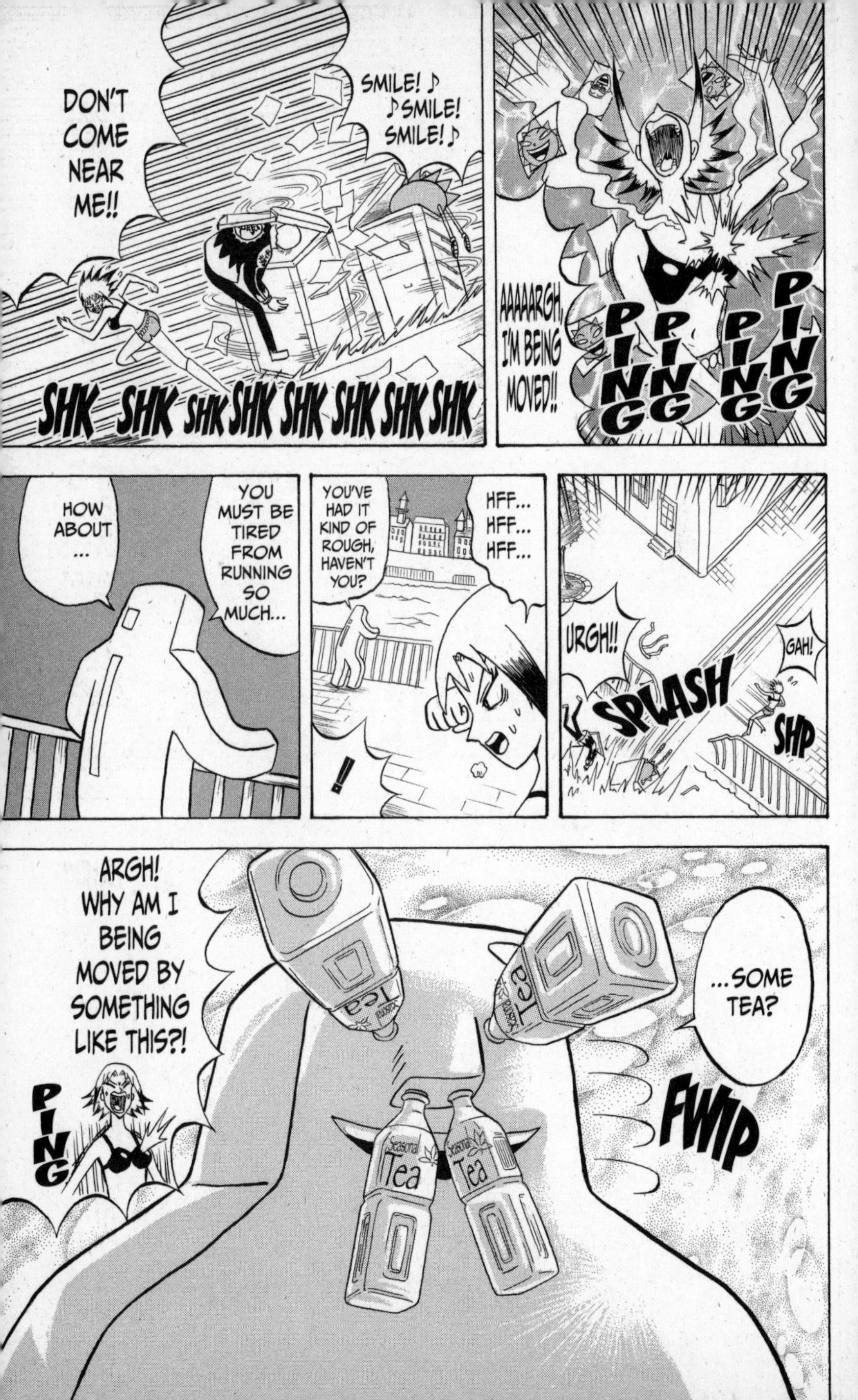
AAAAARGH, I'M BEING MOVED!!
PING PING PING PING
SMILE! ♪ ♪SMILE! SMILE!♪
DON'T COME NEAR ME!!
SHK SHK SHK SHK SHK SHK SHK SHK
GAH!
URGH!!
SPLASH
SHP
HFF... HFF... HFF...
YOU'VE HAD IT KIND OF ROUGH, HAVEN'T YOU?
!
YOU MUST BE TIRED FROM RUNNING SO MUCH...
HOW ABOUT ...
...SOME TEA?
FWIP
Seasonal Tea
Seasonal Tea
ARGH! WHY AM I BEING MOVED BY SOMETHING LIKE THIS?!
PING

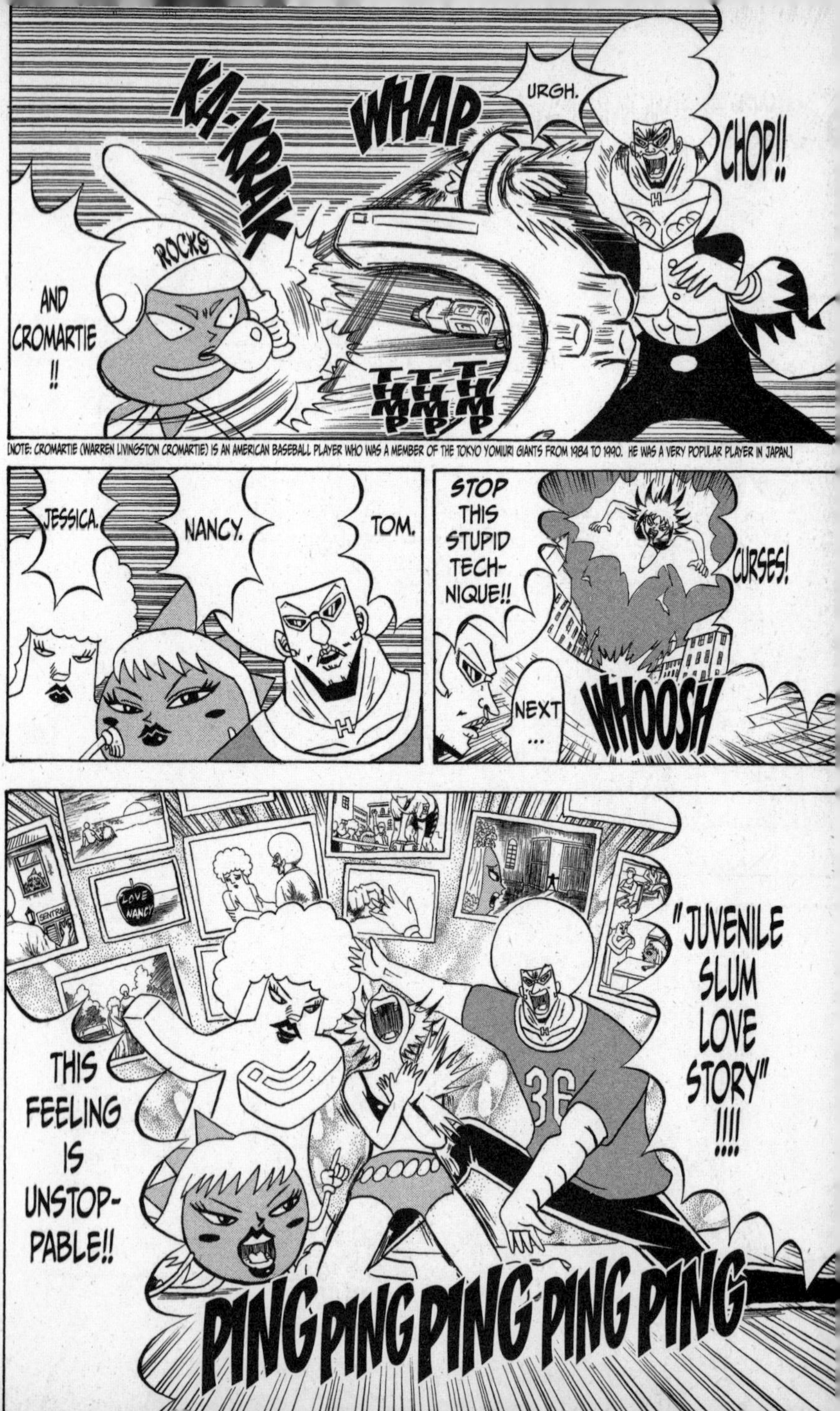
CHOP!!
URGH.
WHAP
KA-KRAK
ROCKS
AND CROMARTIE !!
THMP THMP THMP THMP
[NOTE: CROMARTIE (WARREN LIVINGSTON CROMARTIE) IS AN AMERICAN BASEBALL PLAYER WHO WAS A MEMBER OF THE TOKYO YOMIURI GIANTS FROM 1984 TO 1990. HE WAS A VERY POPULAR PLAYER IN JAPAN.]
CURSES!
STOP THIS STUPID TECH-NIQUE!!
WHOOSH
NEXT ...
TOM.
NANCY.
JESSICA.
"JUVENILE SLUM LOVE STORY" !!!!
LOVE NANCY
THIS FEELING IS UNSTOP-PABLE!!
PING PING PING PING PING PING

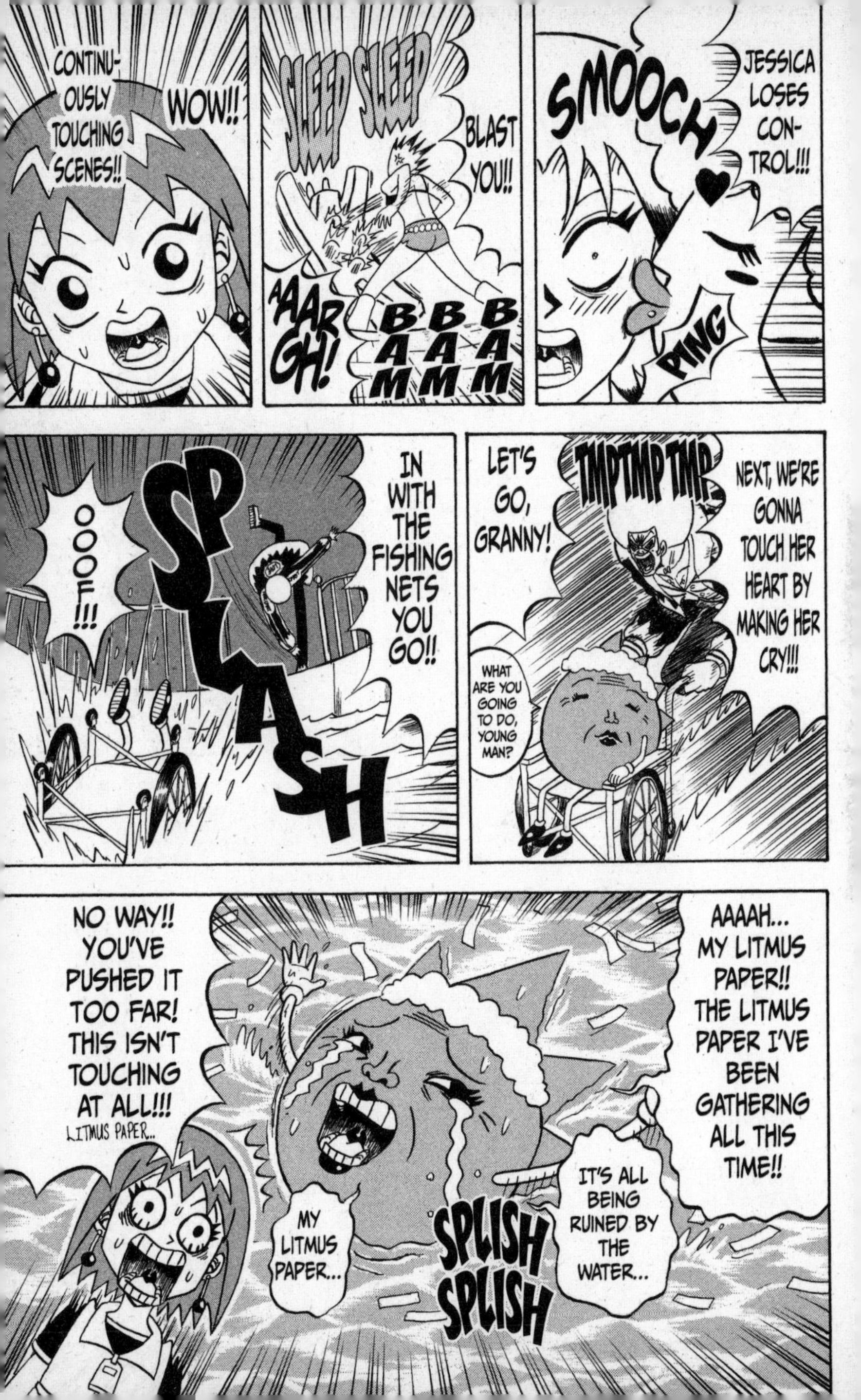
SMOOCH
JESSICA LOSES CON-TROL!!!
PING
SWEEP SWEEP
BLAST YOU!!
AAARGH!
BAM BAM BAM
CONTINU-OUSLY TOUCHING SCENES!!
WOW!!
LET'S GO, GRANNY!
TMPTMP TMP
NEXT, WE'RE GONNA TOUCH HER HEART BY MAKING HER CRY!!!
WHAT ARE YOU GOING TO DO, YOUNG MAN?
IN WITH THE FISHING NETS YOU GO!!
SPLASH
OOOF!!!
AAAAH... MY LITMUS PAPER!! THE LITMUS PAPER I'VE BEEN GATHERING ALL THIS TIME!!
IT'S ALL BEING RUINED BY THE WATER...
SPLISH SPLISH
MY LITMUS PAPER...
NO WAY!! YOU'VE PUSHED IT TOO FAR! THIS ISN'T TOUCHING AT ALL!!!
LITMUS PAPER..

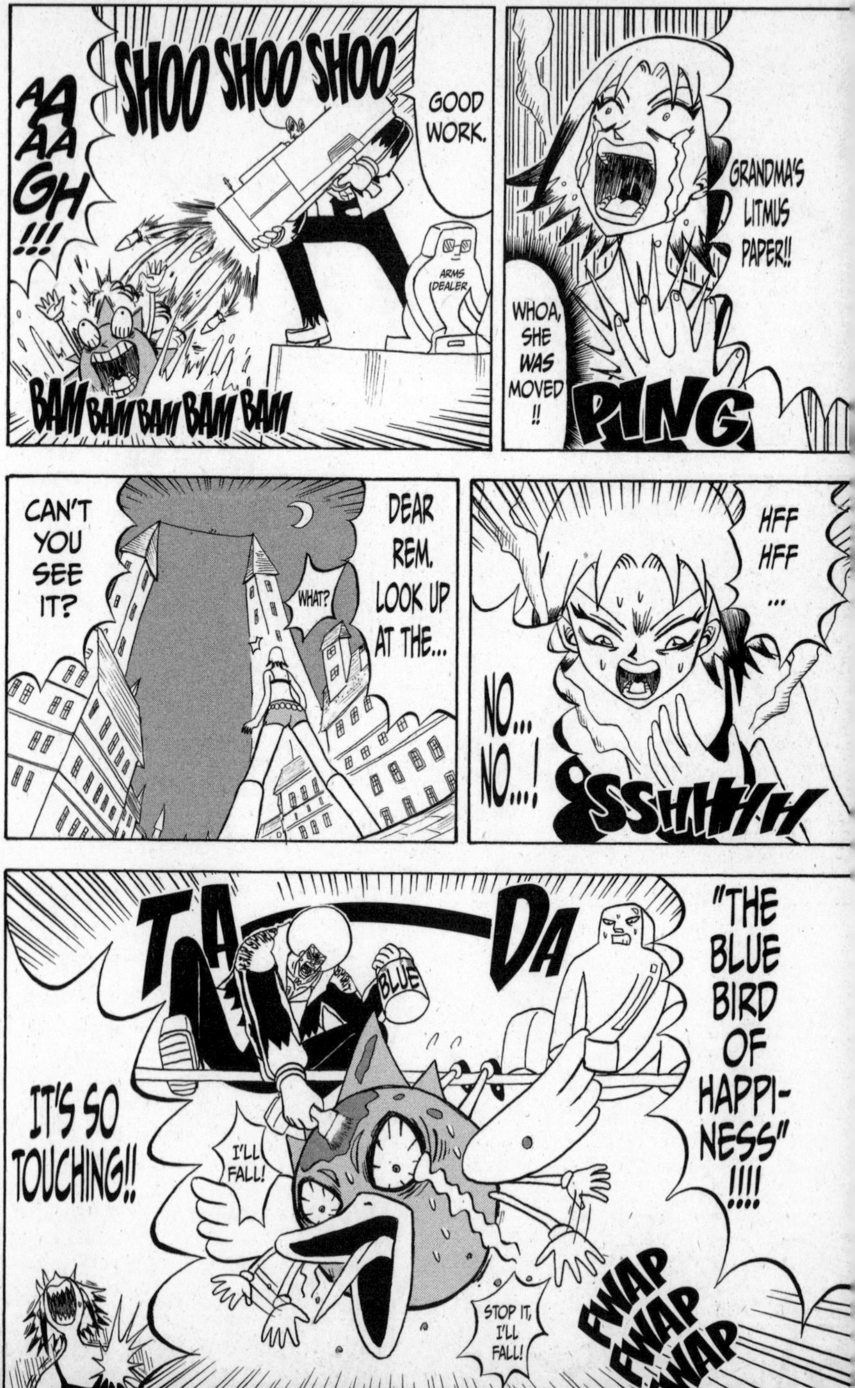
GRANDMA'S LITMUS PAPER!!
WHOA, SHE WAS MOVED!!
PING
SHOO SHOO SHOO
GOOD WORK.
AAAAGH!!!
ARMS DEALER
BAM BAM BAM BAM BAM
HFF HFF...
NO... NO...!
SSHHHH
DEAR REM. LOOK UP AT THE...
WHAT?
CAN'T YOU SEE IT?
TA DA
"THE BLUE BIRD OF HAPPI-NESS"!!!!
BLUE
IT'S SO TOUCHING!!
I'LL FALL!
STOP IT, I'LL FALL!
FWAP FWAP FWAP

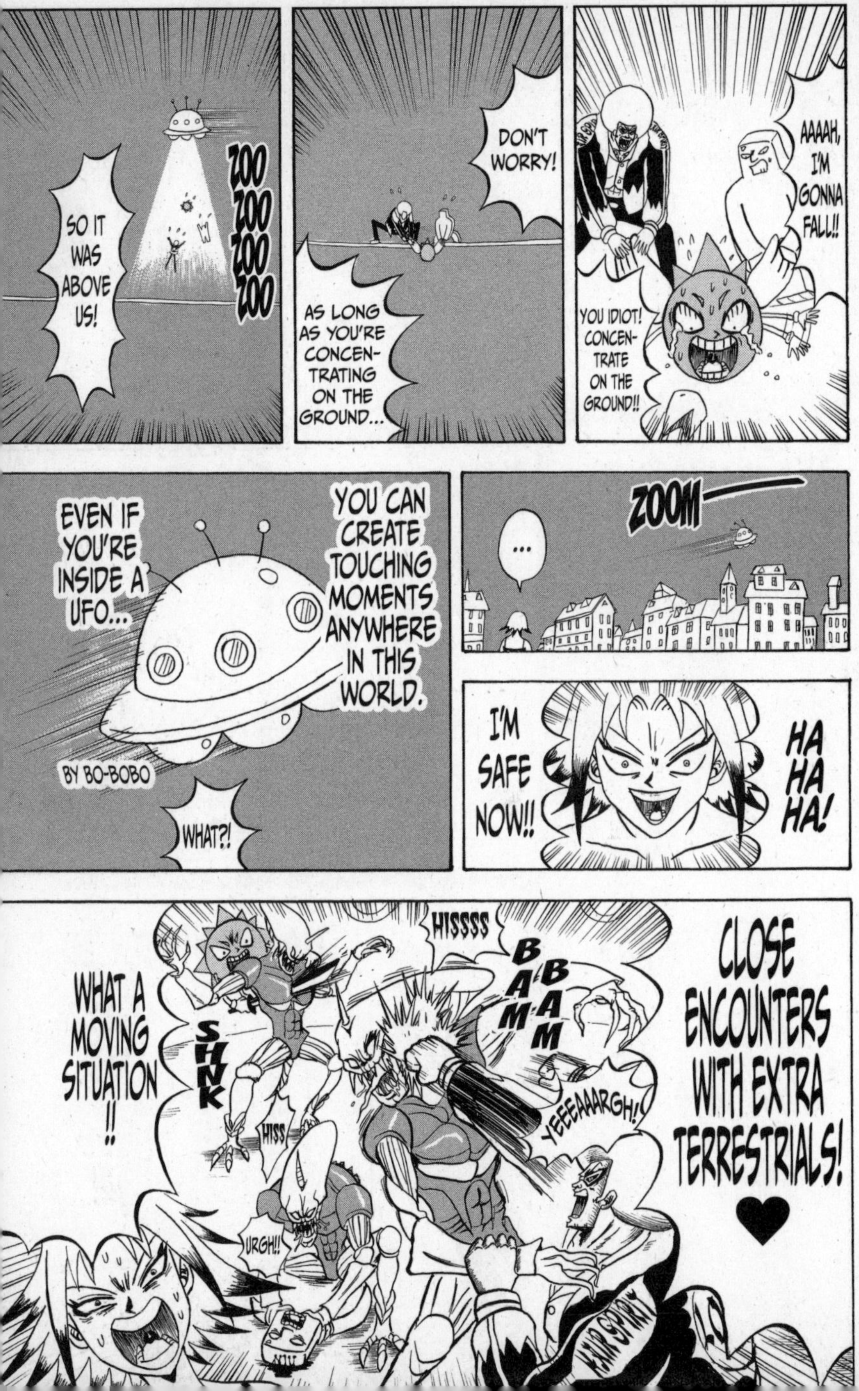
ZOO ZOO ZOO ZOO
SO IT WAS ABOVE US!
DON'T WORRY!
AS LONG AS YOU'RE CONCEN-TRATING ON THE GROUND...
AAAAH, I'M GONNA FALL!!
YOU IDIOT! CONCEN-TRATE ON THE GROUND!!
EVEN IF YOU'RE INSIDE A UFO...
YOU CAN CREATE TOUCHING MOMENTS ANYWHERE IN THIS WORLD.
BY BO-BOBO
WHAT?!
ZOOM
...
I'M SAFE NOW!!
HA HA HA!
WHAT A MOVING SITUATION!!
SHNK
HISSSS
BAM BAM
YEEEAAARGH!!
HISS
URGH!!
CLOSE ENCOUNTERS WITH EXTRA TERRESTRIALS! ♥

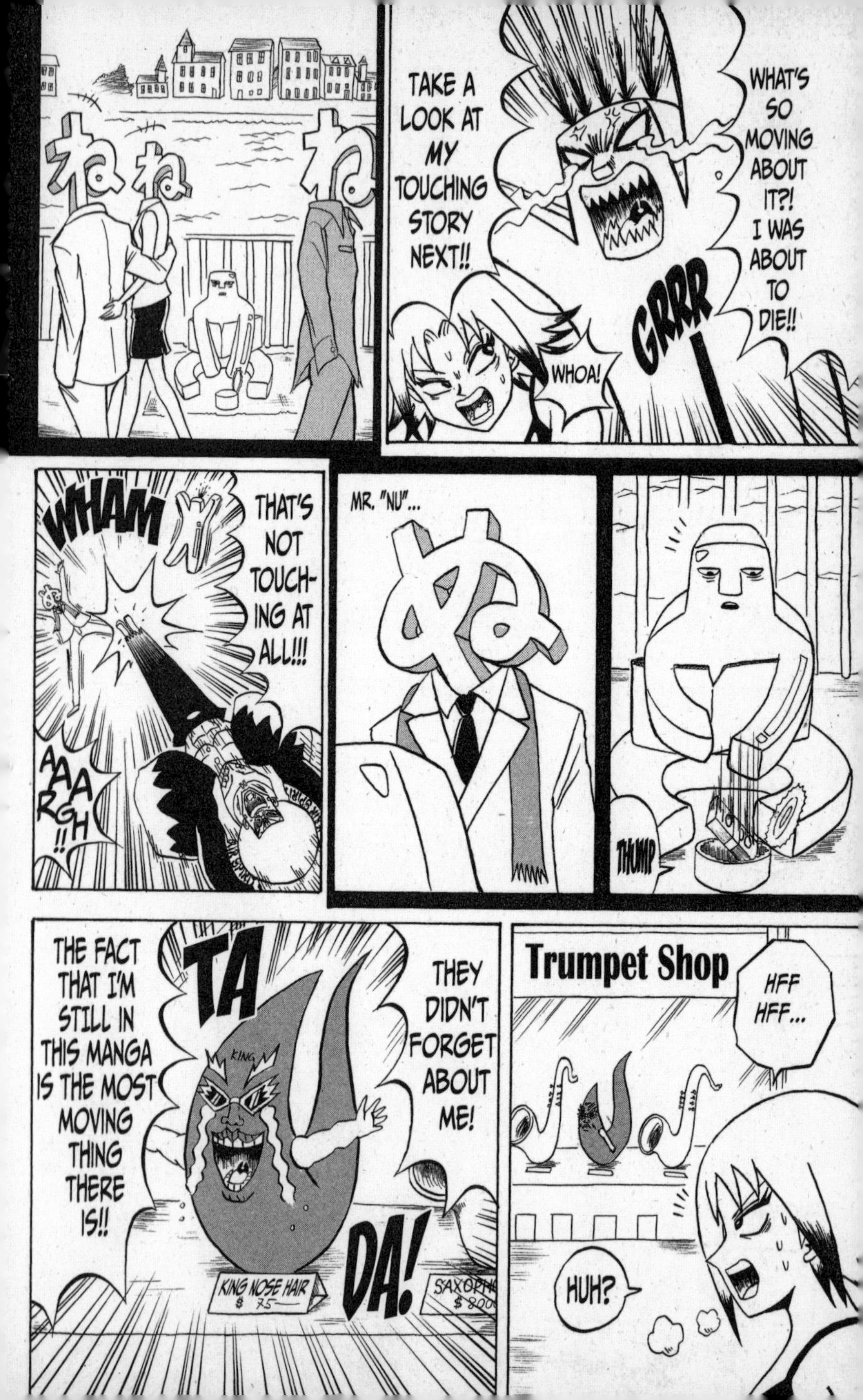
WHAT'S SO MOVING ABOUT IT?! I WAS ABOUT TO DIE!!
TAKE A LOOK AT MY TOUCHING STORY NEXT!!
GRRR
WHOA!
THUMP
MR. "NU"...
THAT'S NOT TOUCHING AT ALL!!!
WHAM
AAAARGH!!
Trumpet Shop
HFF HFF...
HUH?
THEY DIDN'T FORGET ABOUT ME!
TA
KING
THE FACT THAT I'M STILL IN THIS MANGA IS THE MOST MOVING THING THERE IS!!
DA!
KING NOSE HAIR
$ 75—

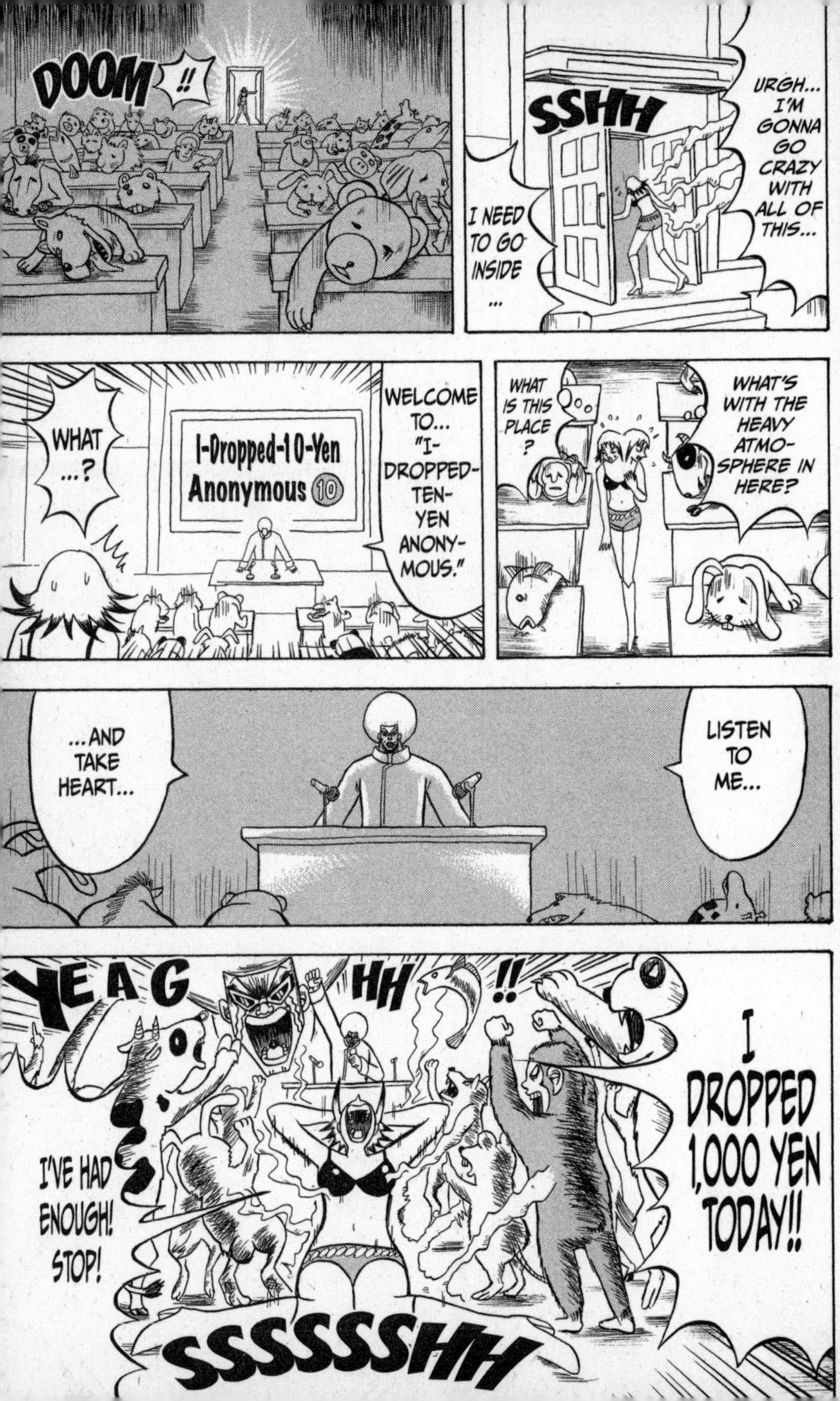
SSHH
URGH... I'M GONNA GO CRAZY WITH ALL OF THIS...
I NEED TO GO INSIDE ...
DOOM !!
WHAT'S WITH THE HEAVY ATMOSPHERE IN HERE?
WHAT IS THIS PLACE?
WELCOME TO... "I-DROPPED-TEN-YEN ANONYMOUS."
I-Dropped-10-Yen Anonymous 10
WHAT ...?
LISTEN TO ME...
...AND TAKE HEART...
YEAGHH!!
I DROPPED 1,000 YEN TODAY!!
I'VE HAD ENOUGH! STOP!
SSSSSSHH

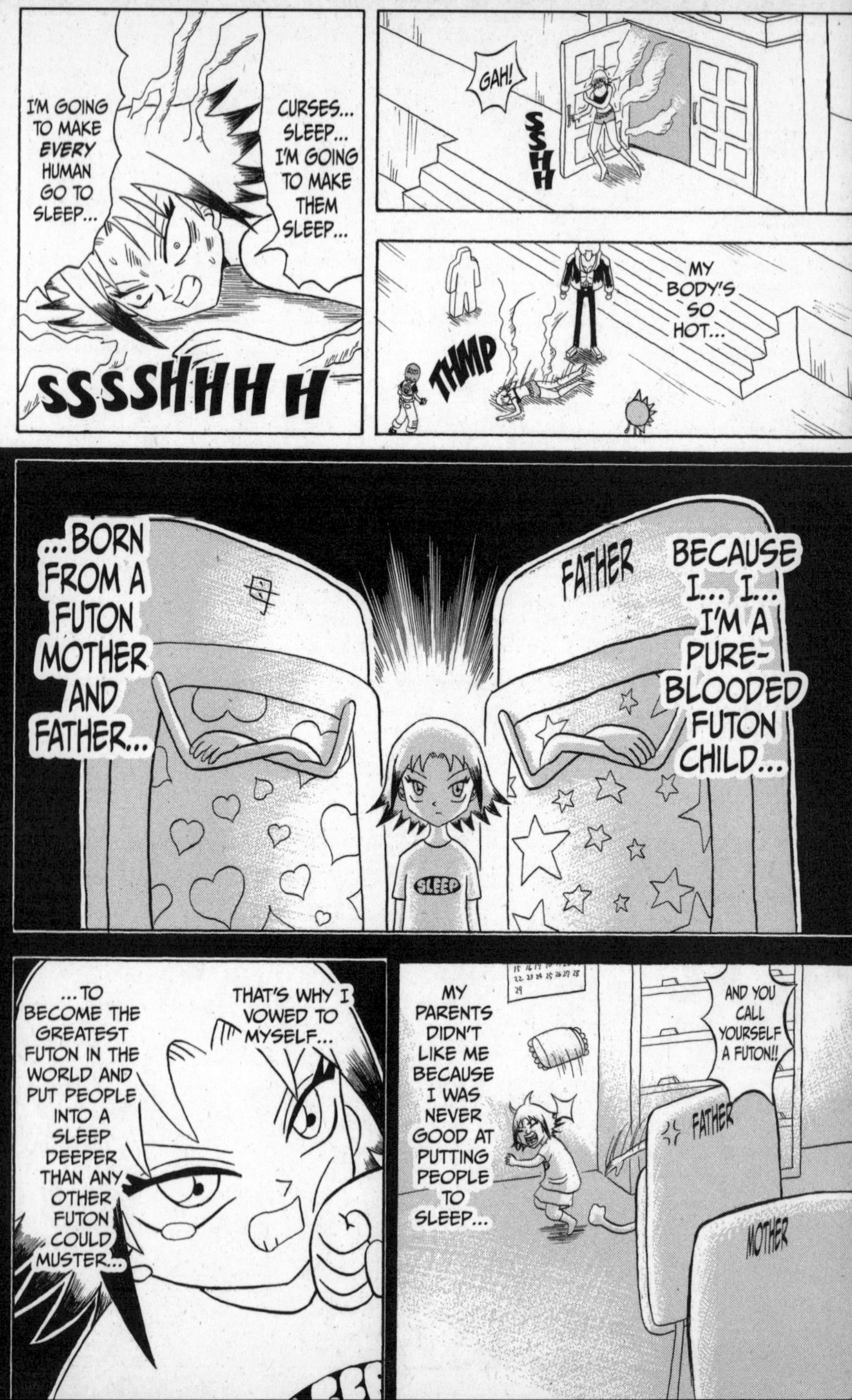
GAH!
SSHH
MY BODY'S SO HOT...
THMP
CURSES... SLEEP... I'M GOING TO MAKE THEM SLEEP...
I'M GOING TO MAKE EVERY HUMAN GO TO SLEEP...
SSSSHHHH H
BECAUSE I... I... I'M A PURE-BLOODED FUTON CHILD...
FATHER
...BORN FROM A FUTON MOTHER AND FATHER...
SLEEP
AND YOU CALL YOURSELF A FUTON!!
FATHER
MOTHER
MY PARENTS DIDN'T LIKE ME BECAUSE I WAS NEVER GOOD AT PUTTING PEOPLE TO SLEEP...
THAT'S WHY I VOWED TO MYSELF...
...TO BECOME THE GREATEST FUTON IN THE WORLD AND PUT PEOPLE INTO A SLEEP DEEPER THAN ANY OTHER FUTON COULD MUSTER...

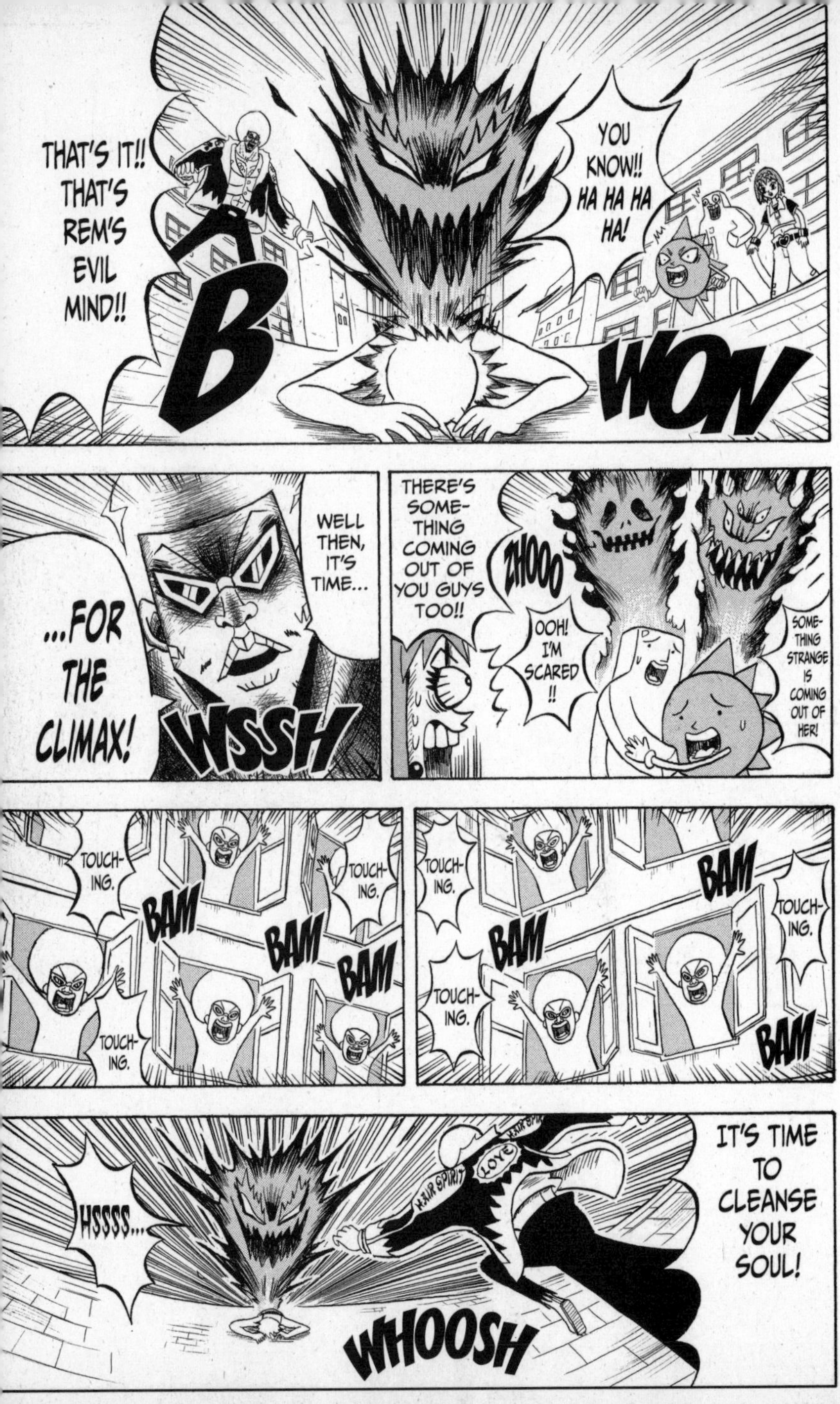
YOU KNOW!! HA HA HA HA!
THAT'S IT!! THAT'S REM'S EVIL MIND!!
B WON
THERE'S SOMETHING COMING OUT OF YOU GUYS TOO!!
ZHOOO
SOMETHING STRANGE IS COMING OUT OF HER!
OOH! I'M SCARED!!
WELL THEN, IT'S TIME...
...FOR THE CLIMAX!
WSSH
BAM
TOUCHING.
TOUCHING.
BAM
TOUCHING.
BAM
TOUCHING.
BAM
TOUCHING.
BAM
TOUCHING.
BAM
TOUCHING.
BAM
IT'S TIME TO CLEANSE YOUR SOUL!
HAIR SPIRIT
LOVE
HSSSS...
WHOOSH

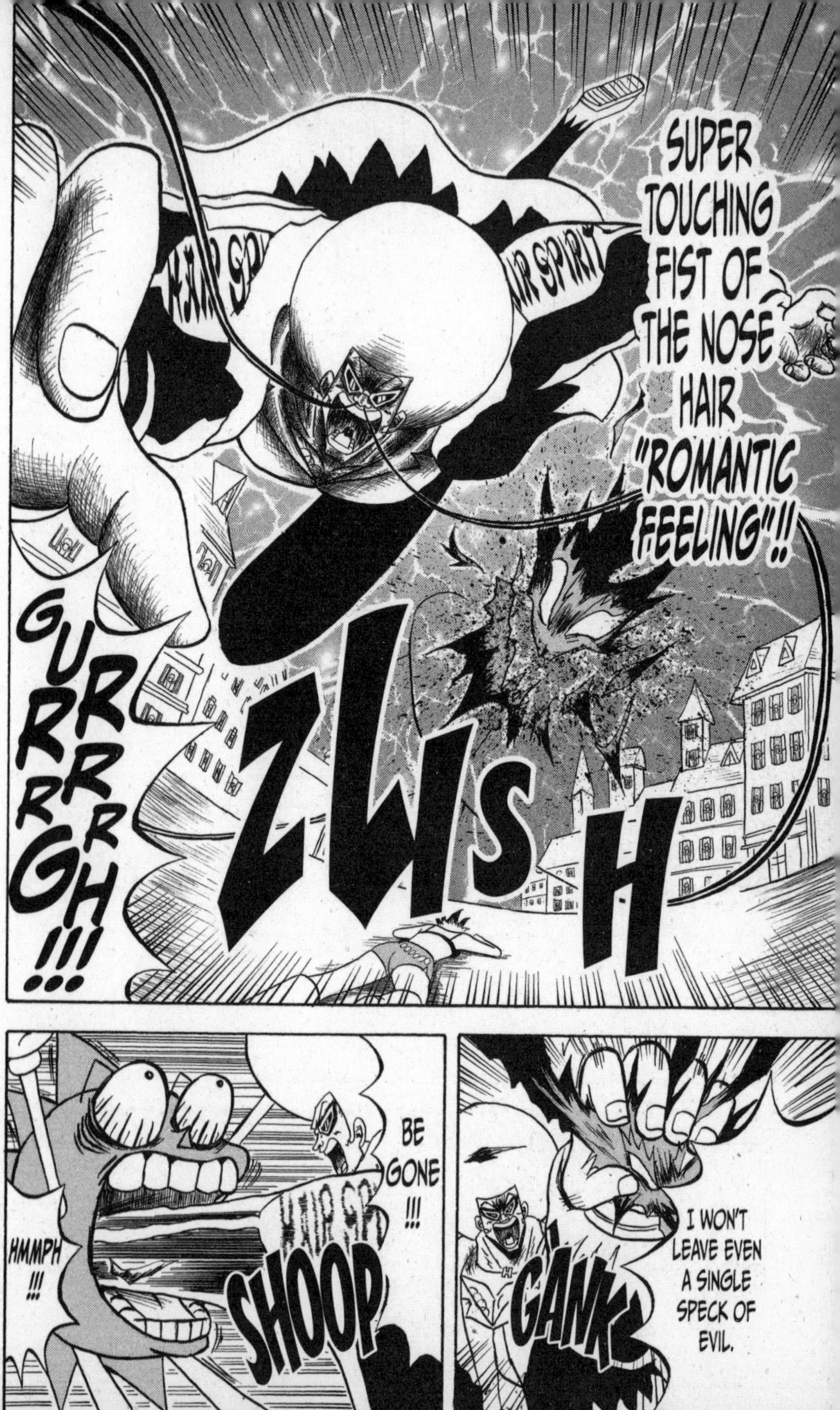

SUPER TOUCHING FIST OF THE NOSE HAIR "ROMANTIC FEELING"!!
ZWISH
GURRRRRRGH!!!
GANK
I WON'T LEAVE EVEN A SINGLE SPECK OF EVIL.
BE GONE!!!
SHOOP
HMMPH!!!

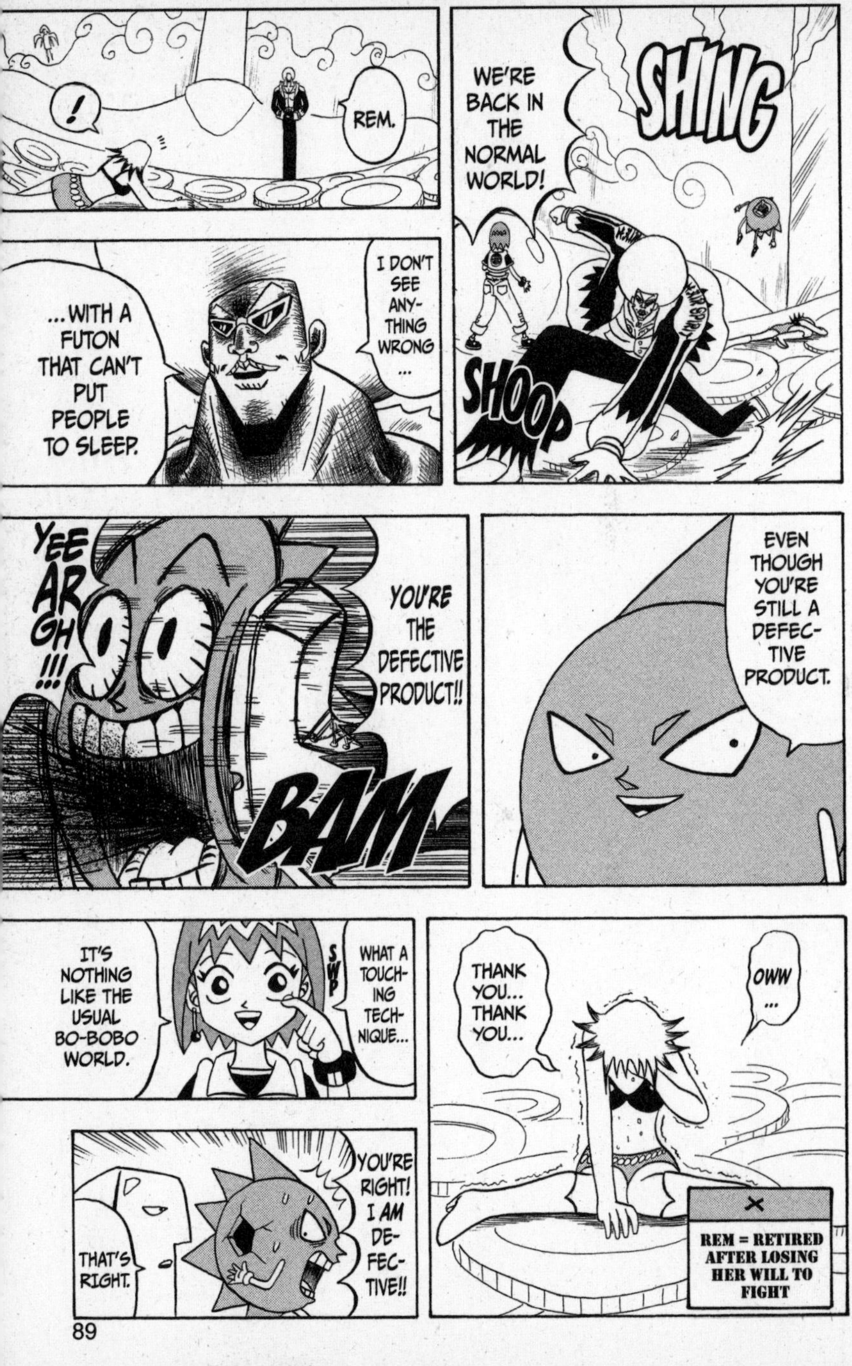
SHING
WE'RE BACK IN THE NORMAL WORLD!
SHOOP
REM.
!
I DON'T SEE ANYTHING WRONG...
...WITH A FUTON THAT CAN'T PUT PEOPLE TO SLEEP.
EVEN THOUGH YOU'RE STILL A DEFECTIVE PRODUCT.
YOU'RE THE DEFECTIVE PRODUCT!!
YEEARGH!!!
BAM
OWW...
THANK YOU... THANK YOU...
REM = RETIRED AFTER LOSING HER WILL TO FIGHT
WHAT A TOUCHING TECHNIQUE...
SWP
IT'S NOTHING LIKE THE USUAL BO-BOBO WORLD.
YOU'RE RIGHT! I AM DEFECTIVE!!
THAT'S RIGHT.

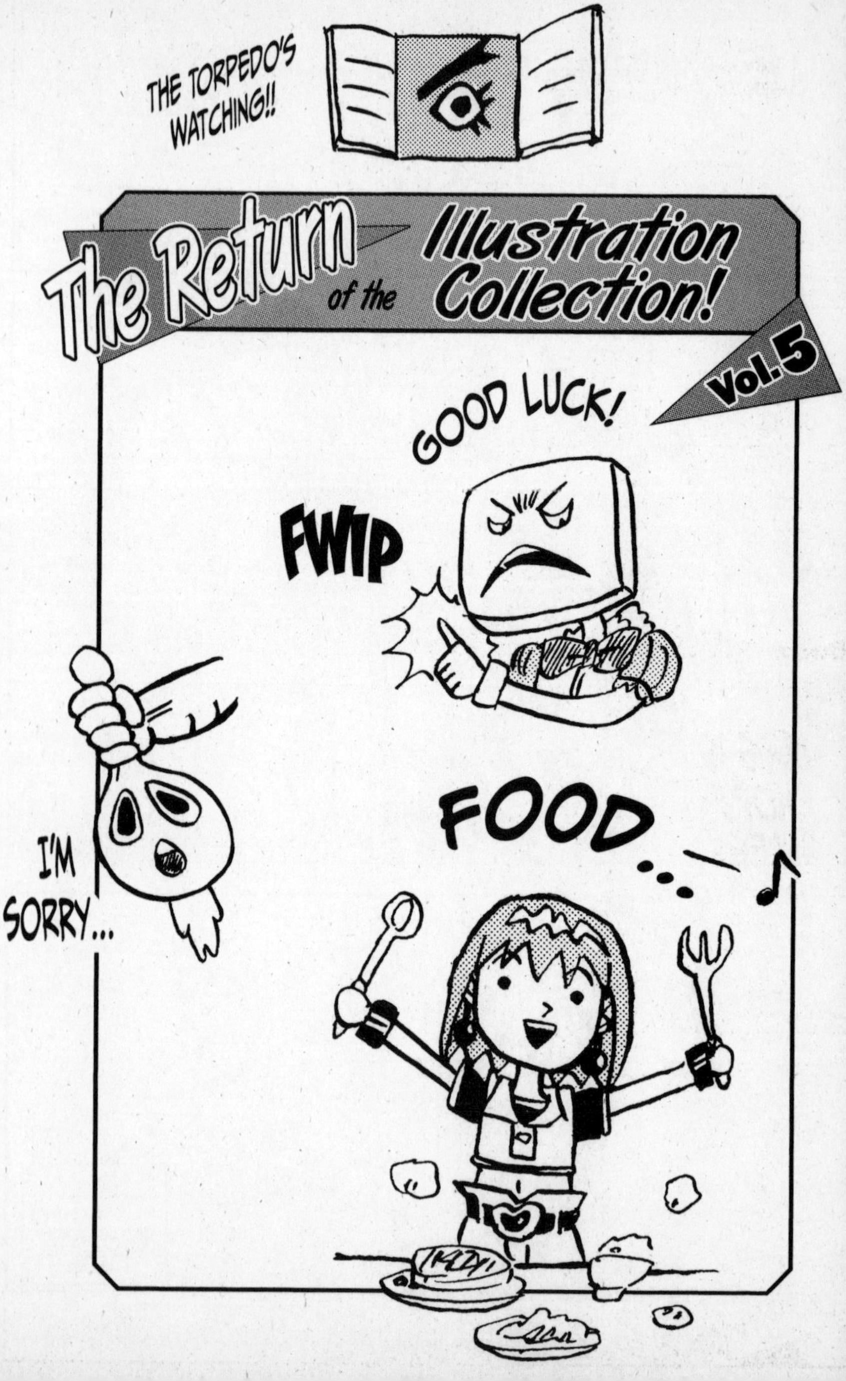
THE TORPEDO'S WATCHING!!
The Return of the Illustration Collection!
Vol. 5
GOOD LUCK!
FWIP
I'M SORRY...
FOOD...~♪

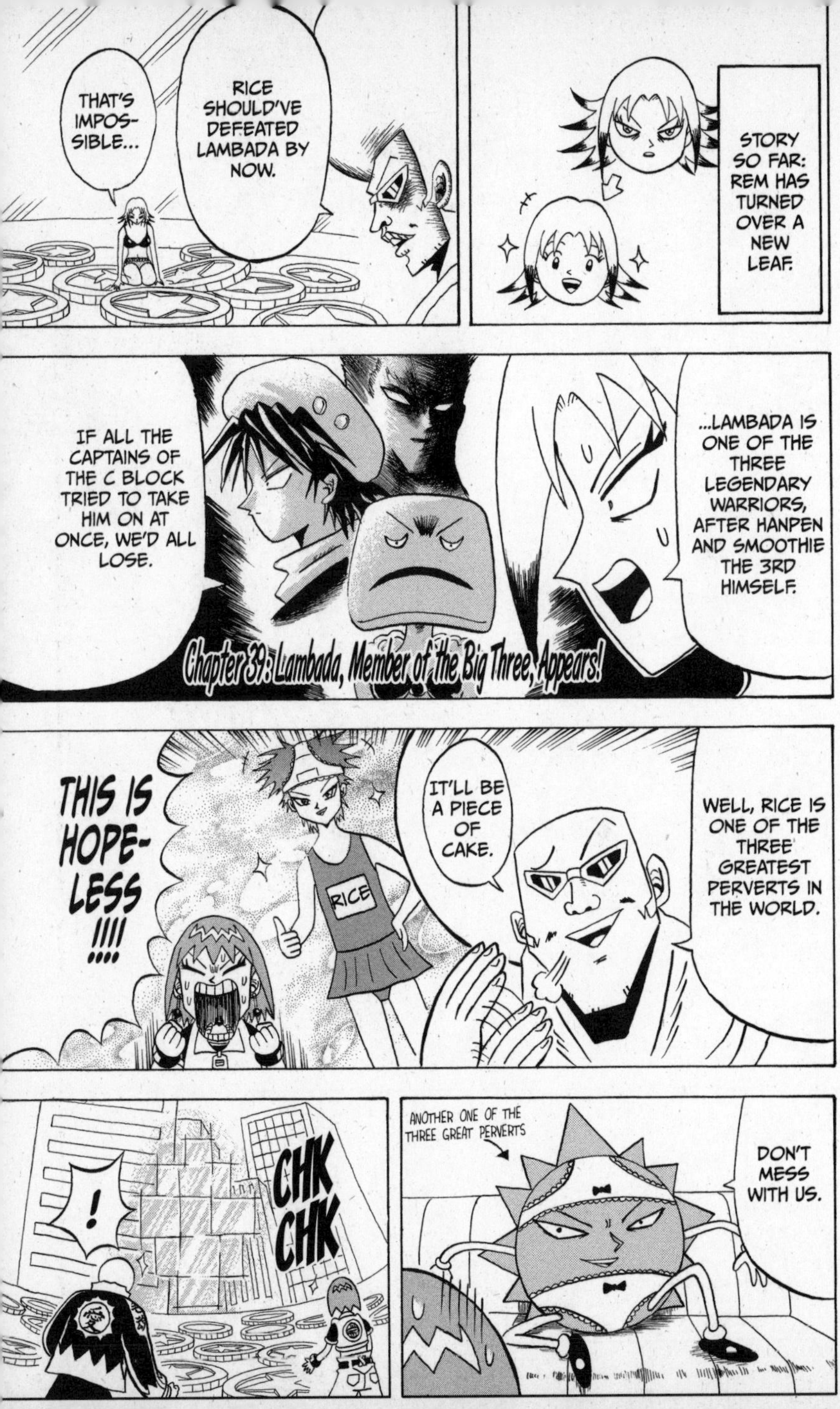
STORY SO FAR: REM HAS TURNED OVER A NEW LEAF.
RICE SHOULD'VE DEFEATED LAMBADA BY NOW.
THAT'S IMPOS-SIBLE...
...LAMBADA IS ONE OF THE THREE LEGENDARY WARRIORS, AFTER HANPEN AND SMOOTHIE THE 3RD HIMSELF.
IF ALL THE CAPTAINS OF THE C BLOCK TRIED TO TAKE HIM ON AT ONCE, WE'D ALL LOSE.
Chapter 39: Lambada, Member of the Big Three, Appears!
WELL, RICE IS ONE OF THE THREE GREATEST PERVERTS IN THE WORLD.
IT'LL BE A PIECE OF CAKE.
RICE
THIS IS HOPE-LESS!!!!
DON'T MESS WITH US.
ANOTHER ONE OF THE THREE GREAT PERVERTS
CHK CHK
!

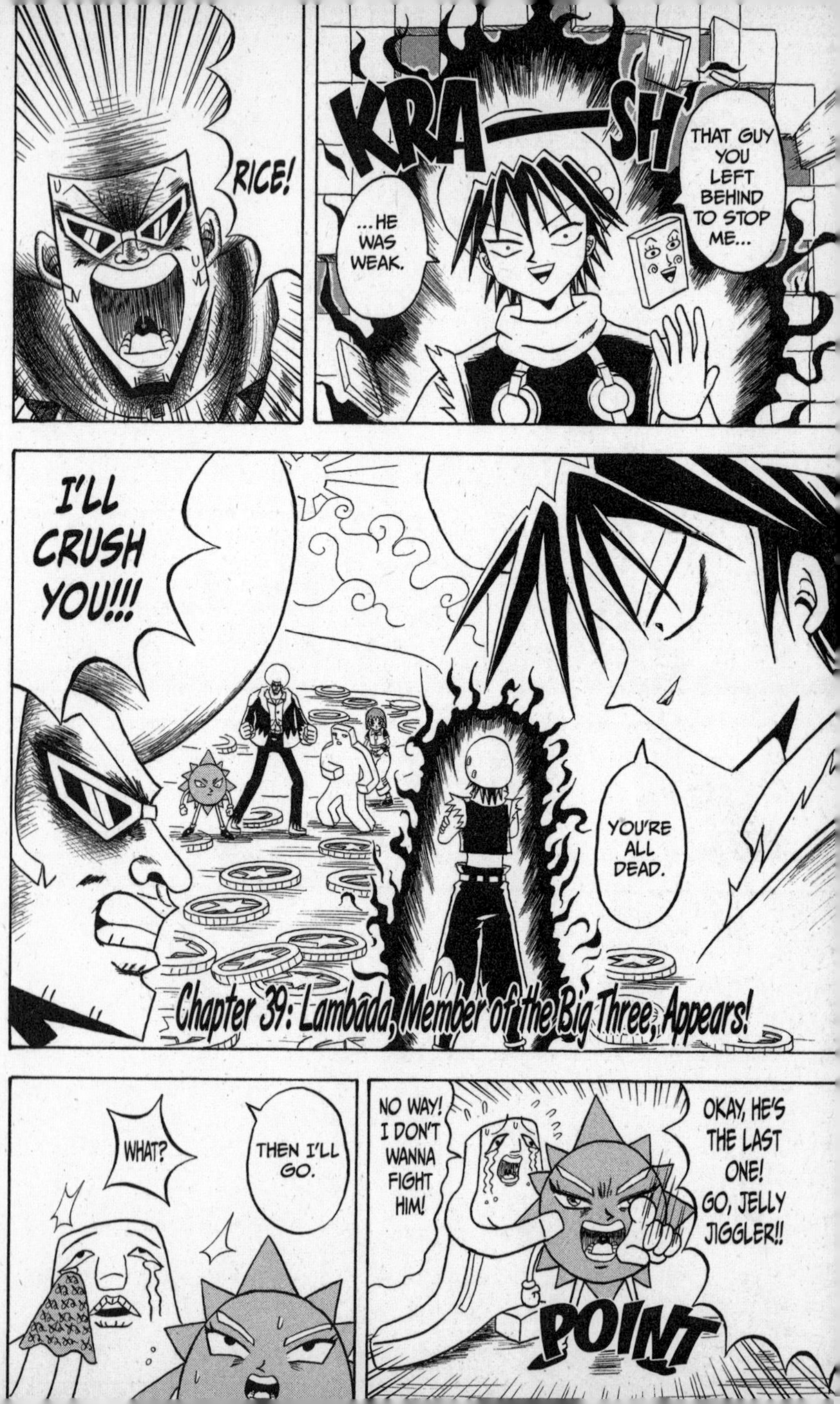
THAT GUY YOU LEFT BEHIND TO STOP ME...
KRA—SH
...HE WAS WEAK.
RICE!
YOU'RE ALL DEAD.
I'LL CRUSH YOU!!!
Chapter 39: Lambada, Member of the Big Three, Appears!
OKAY, HE'S THE LAST ONE! GO, JELLY JIGGLER!!
NO WAY! I DON'T WANNA FIGHT HIM!
POINT
THEN I'LL GO.
WHAT?

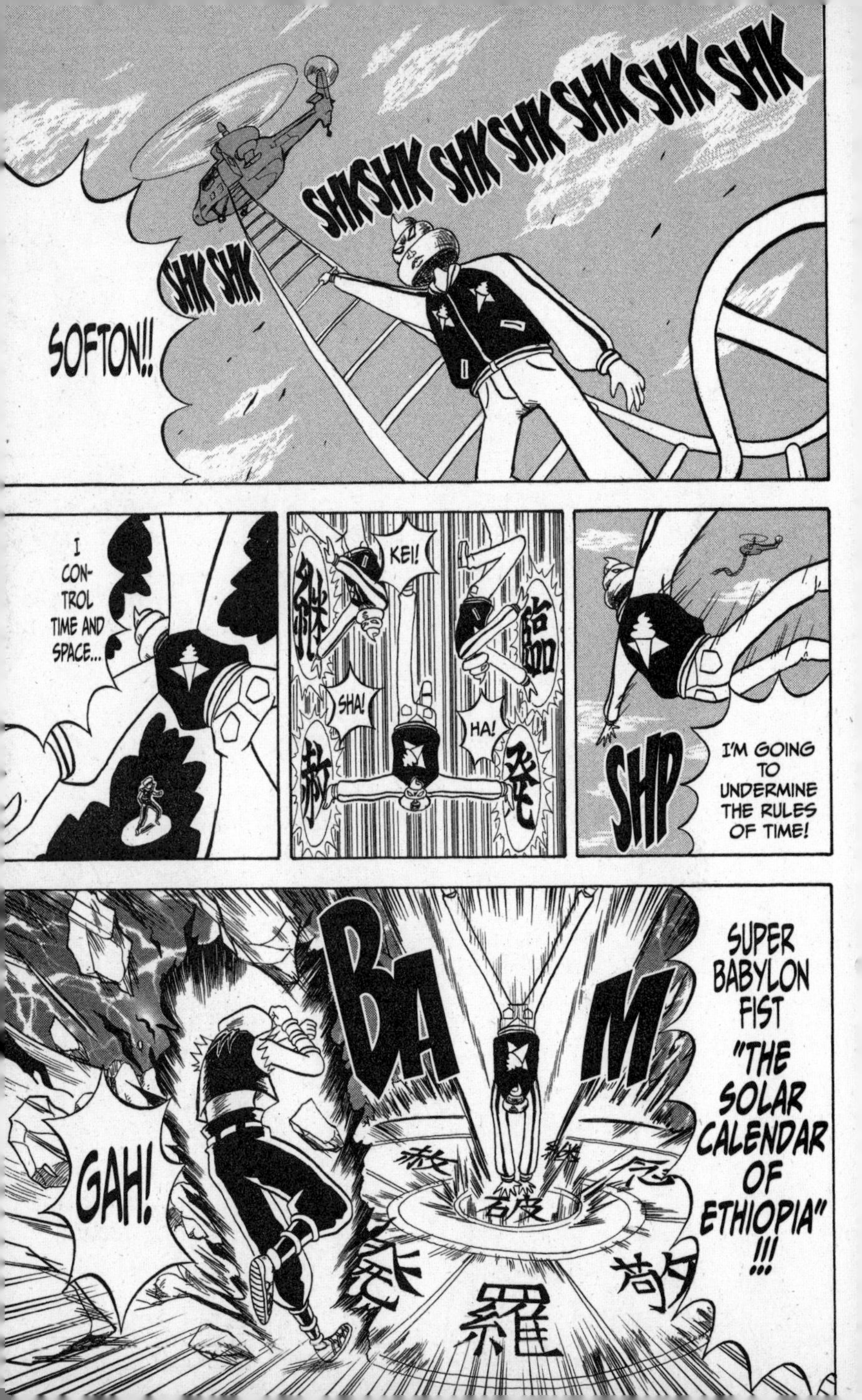
SHK SHK SHK SHK SHK SHK SHK
SHK SHK
SOFTON!!
I'M GOING TO UNDERMINE THE RULES OF TIME!
SHP
KEI!
HA!
SHA!
I CONTROL TIME AND SPACE...
SUPER BABYLON FIST "THE SOLAR CALENDAR OF ETHIOPIA"!!!
BAM
GAH!

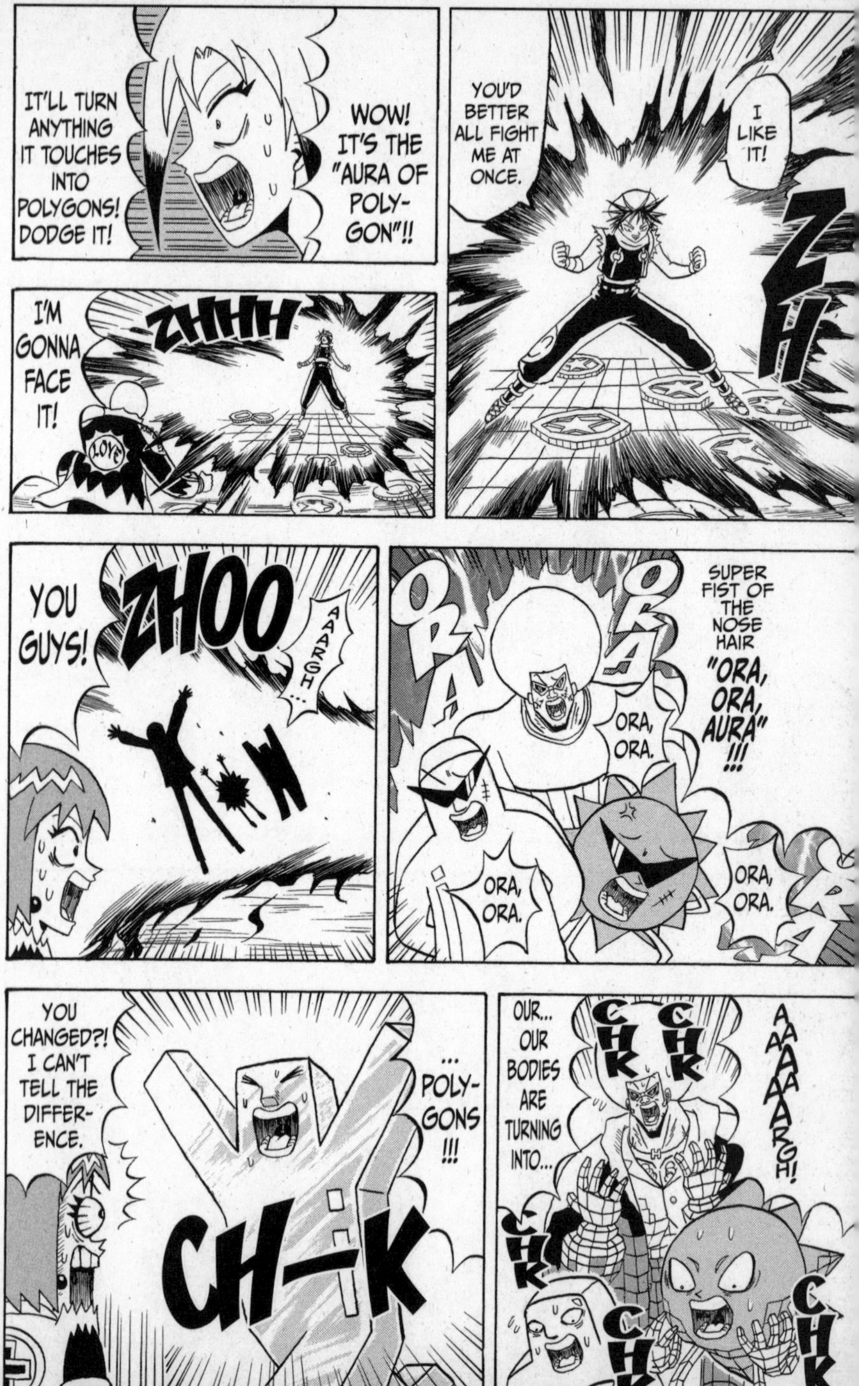

I LIKE IT!
YOU'D BETTER ALL FIGHT ME AT ONCE.
ZH
WOW! IT'S THE "AURA OF POLY-GON"!!
IT'LL TURN ANYTHING IT TOUCHES INTO POLYGONS! DODGE IT!
ZHHHH
I'M GONNA FACE IT!
SUPER FIST OF THE NOSE HAIR "ORA, ORA, AURA"!!!
ORA
ORA
ORA, ORA.
ORA, ORA.
ORA, ORA.
AAAARGH...
ZHOO
YOU GUYS!
AAAAAAARGH!
CHK
CHK
OUR... OUR BODIES ARE TURNING INTO...
CHK
CHK
CHK
... POLY-GONS!!!
YOU CHANGED?! I CAN'T TELL THE DIFFER-ENCE.
CH-K

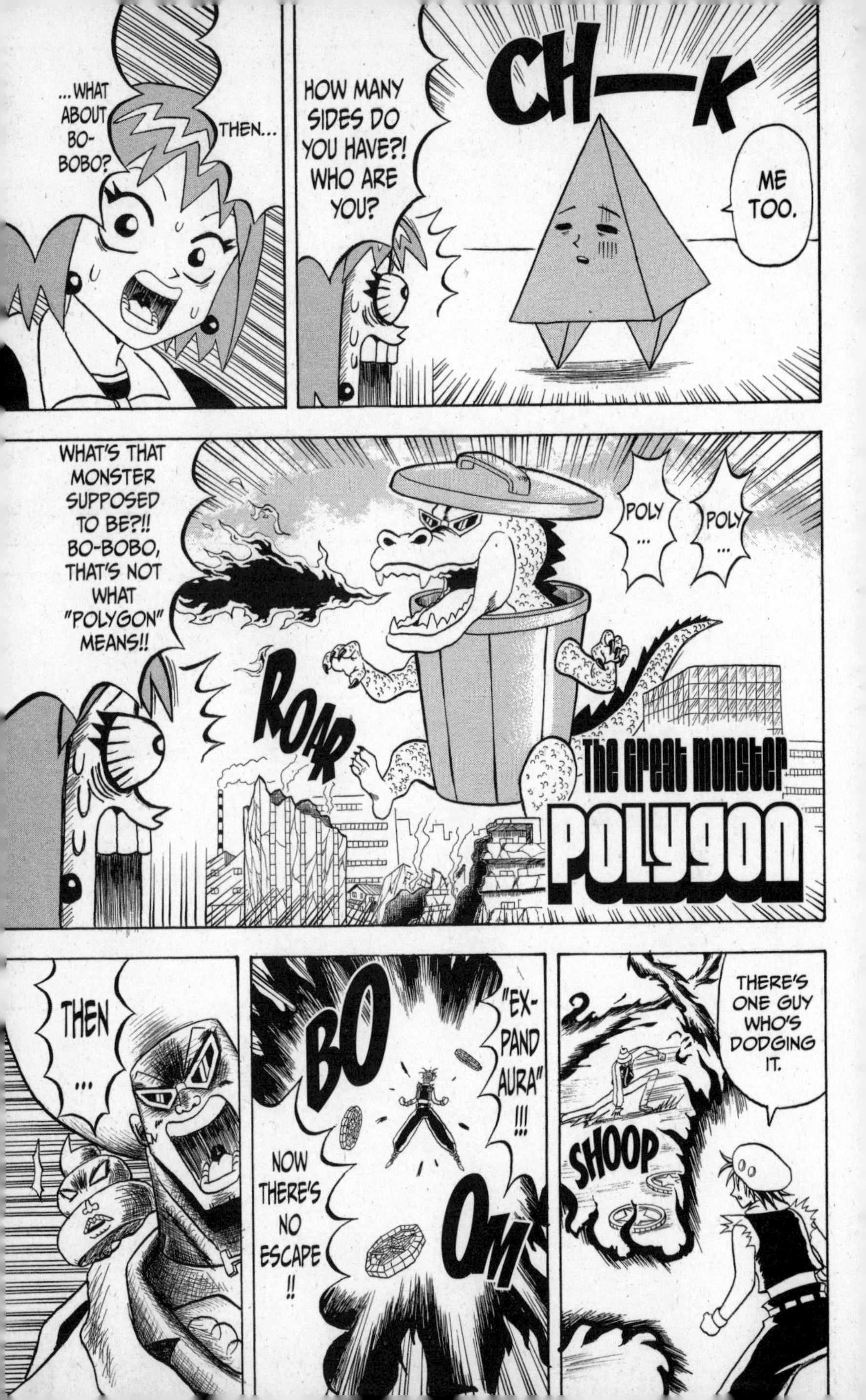
...WHAT ABOUT BO-BOBO?
THEN...
HOW MANY SIDES DO YOU HAVE?! WHO ARE YOU?
CH—K
ME TOO.
WHAT'S THAT MONSTER SUPPOSED TO BE?!! BO-BOBO, THAT'S NOT WHAT "POLYGON" MEANS!!
ROAR
POLY ...
POLY ...
The Great Monster
POLYGON
THEN ...
BO
"EX-PAND AURA" !!!
NOW THERE'S NO ESCAPE !!
OM
THERE'S ONE GUY WHO'S DODGING IT.
SHOOP

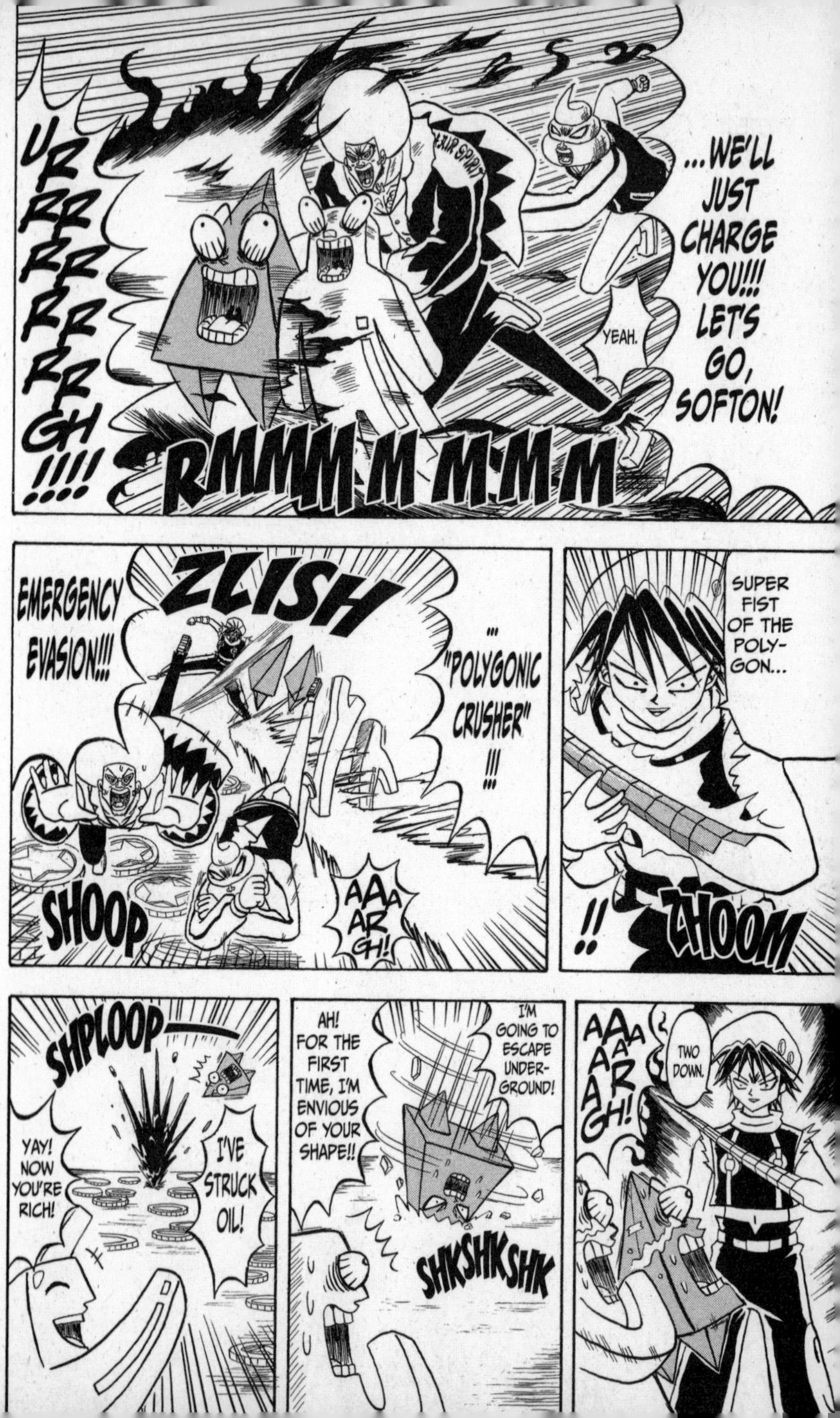
...WE'LL JUST CHARGE YOU!!! LET'S GO, SOFTON!
YEAH.
URRRRRRRRRGH!!!!
RMMMM M M M M M
HAIR SPIRIT
SUPER FIST OF THE POLY-GON...
!!
ZHOOM
..."POLYGONIC CRUSHER"!!!
ZLISH
EMERGENCY EVASION!!!
AAAARGH!
SHOOP
TWO DOWN.
AAAAARGH!
I'M GOING TO ESCAPE UNDER-GROUND!
AH! FOR THE FIRST TIME, I'M ENVIOUS OF YOUR SHAPE!!
SHKSHKSHK
SHPLOOP
I'VE STRUCK OIL!
YAY! NOW YOU'RE RICH!

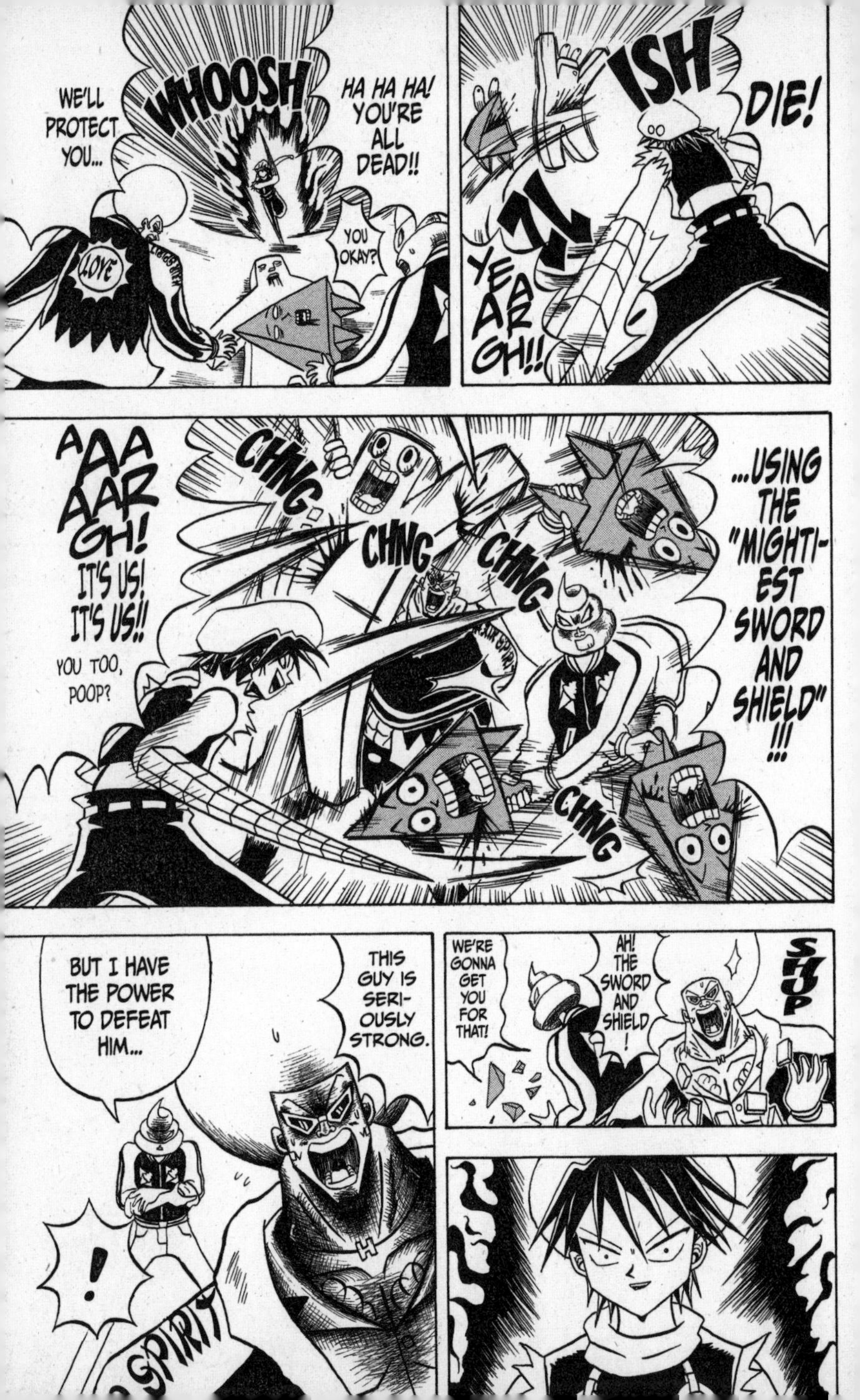
ISH
DIE!
YEAARGH!!
HA HA HA! YOU'RE ALL DEAD!!
WHOOSH
WE'LL PROTECT YOU...
YOU OKAY?
...USING THE "MIGHTIEST SWORD AND SHIELD"!!!
CHNG
CHNG
CHNG
CHNG
CHNG
AAAAARGH! IT'S US! IT'S US!!
YOU TOO, POOP?
SHUP
AH! THE SWORD AND SHIELD!
WE'RE GONNA GET YOU FOR THAT!
THIS GUY IS SERIOUSLY STRONG.
BUT I HAVE THE POWER TO DEFEAT HIM...
!
SPIRIT

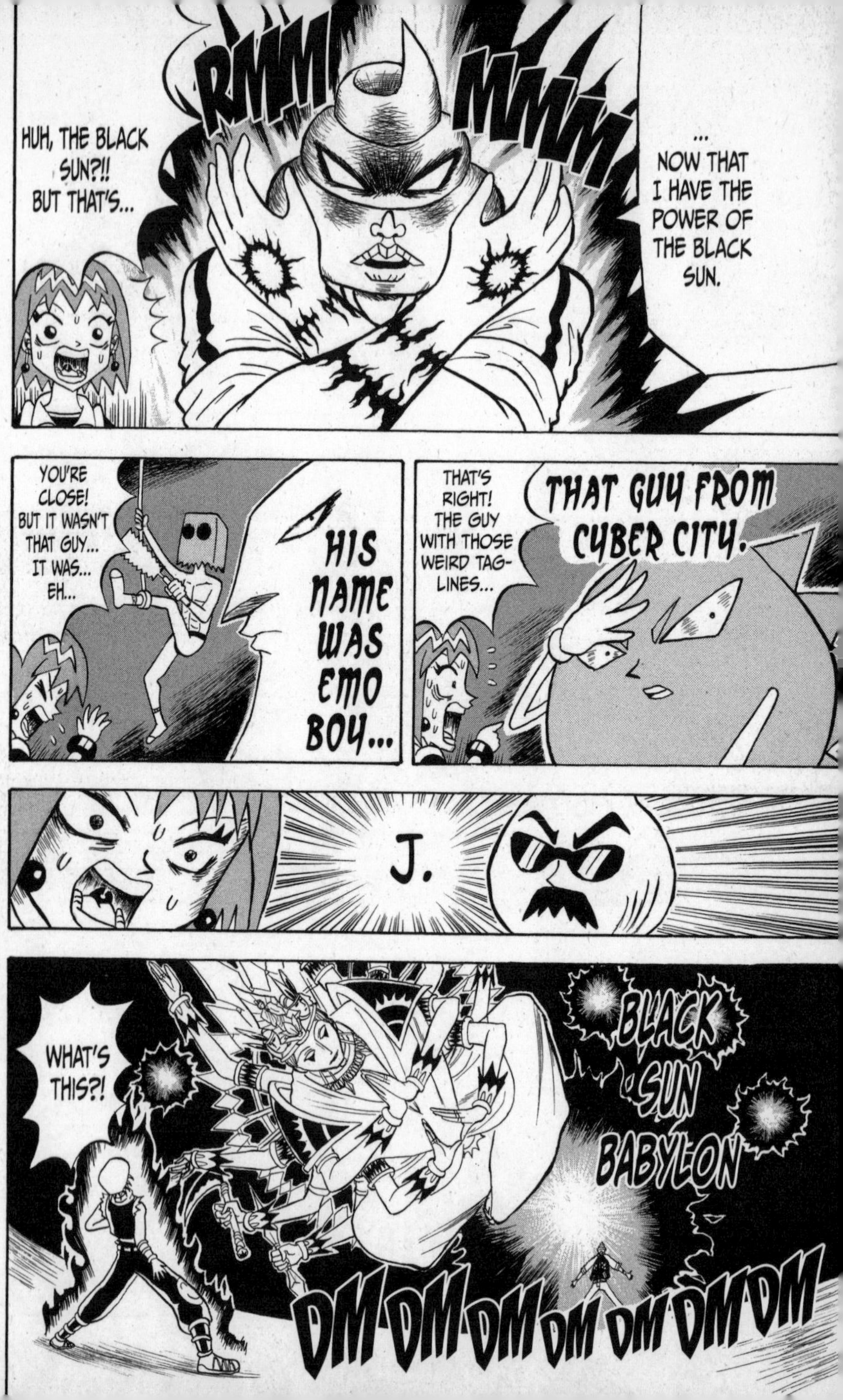
RMMM MMMM
... NOW THAT I HAVE THE POWER OF THE BLACK SUN.
HUH, THE BLACK SUN?!! BUT THAT'S...
THAT GUY FROM CYBER CITY.
THAT'S RIGHT! THE GUY WITH THOSE WEIRD TAG-LINES...
HIS NAME WAS EMO BOY...
YOU'RE CLOSE! BUT IT WASN'T THAT GUY... IT WAS... EH...
J.
BLACK SUN BABYLON
WHAT'S THIS?!
DM DM DM DM DM DM DM

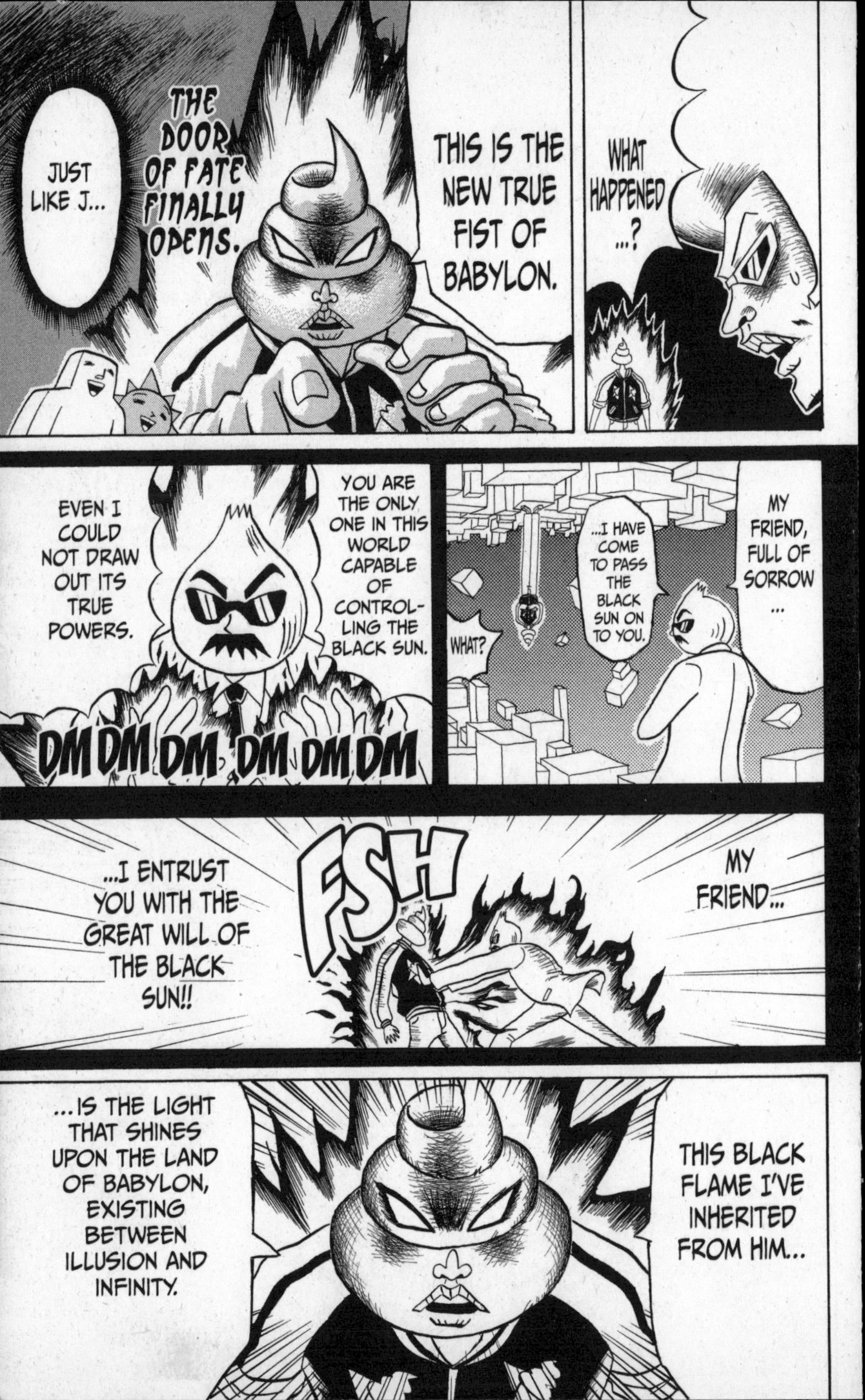
WHAT HAPPENED ...?
THIS IS THE NEW TRUE FIST OF BABYLON.
THE DOOR OF FATE FINALLY OPENS.
JUST LIKE J...
MY FRIEND, FULL OF SORROW ...
...I HAVE COME TO PASS THE BLACK SUN ON TO YOU.
WHAT?
YOU ARE THE ONLY ONE IN THIS WORLD CAPABLE OF CONTROL-LING THE BLACK SUN.
EVEN I COULD NOT DRAW OUT ITS TRUE POWERS.
DM DM DM DM DM DM
MY FRIEND...
FSH
...I ENTRUST YOU WITH THE GREAT WILL OF THE BLACK SUN!!
THIS BLACK FLAME I'VE INHERITED FROM HIM...
...IS THE LIGHT THAT SHINES UPON THE LAND OF BABYLON, EXISTING BETWEEN ILLUSION AND INFINITY.

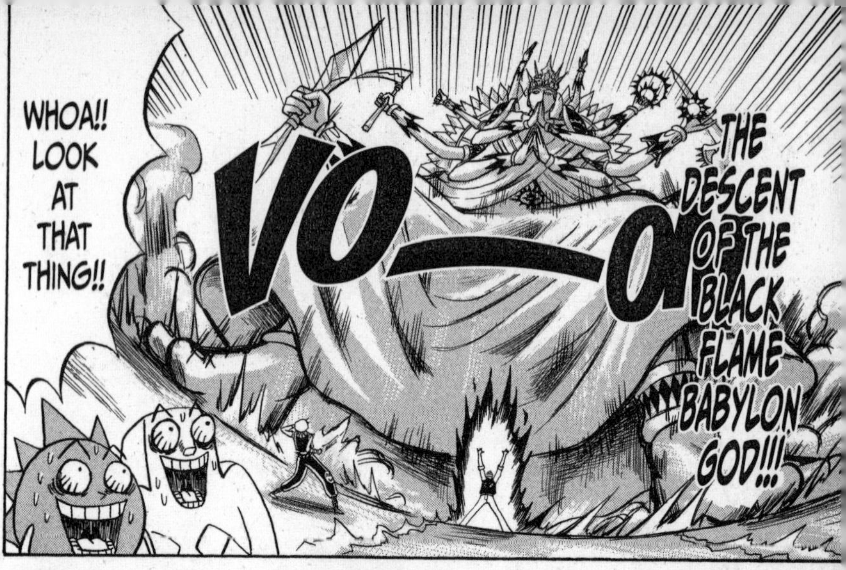
THE DESCENT OF THE BLACK FLAME BABYLON GOD!!!
VO—A
WHOA!! LOOK AT THAT THING!!

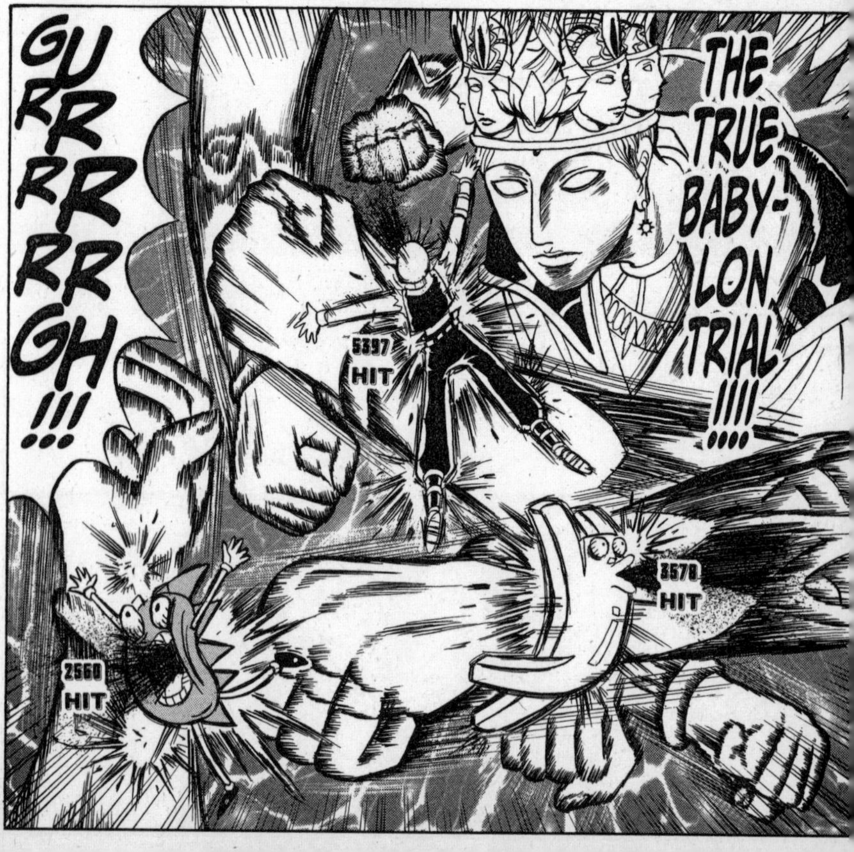
THE TRUE BABY-LON TRIAL!!!!
5397 HIT
3578 HIT
GURRRRRRRGH!!!
2560 HIT

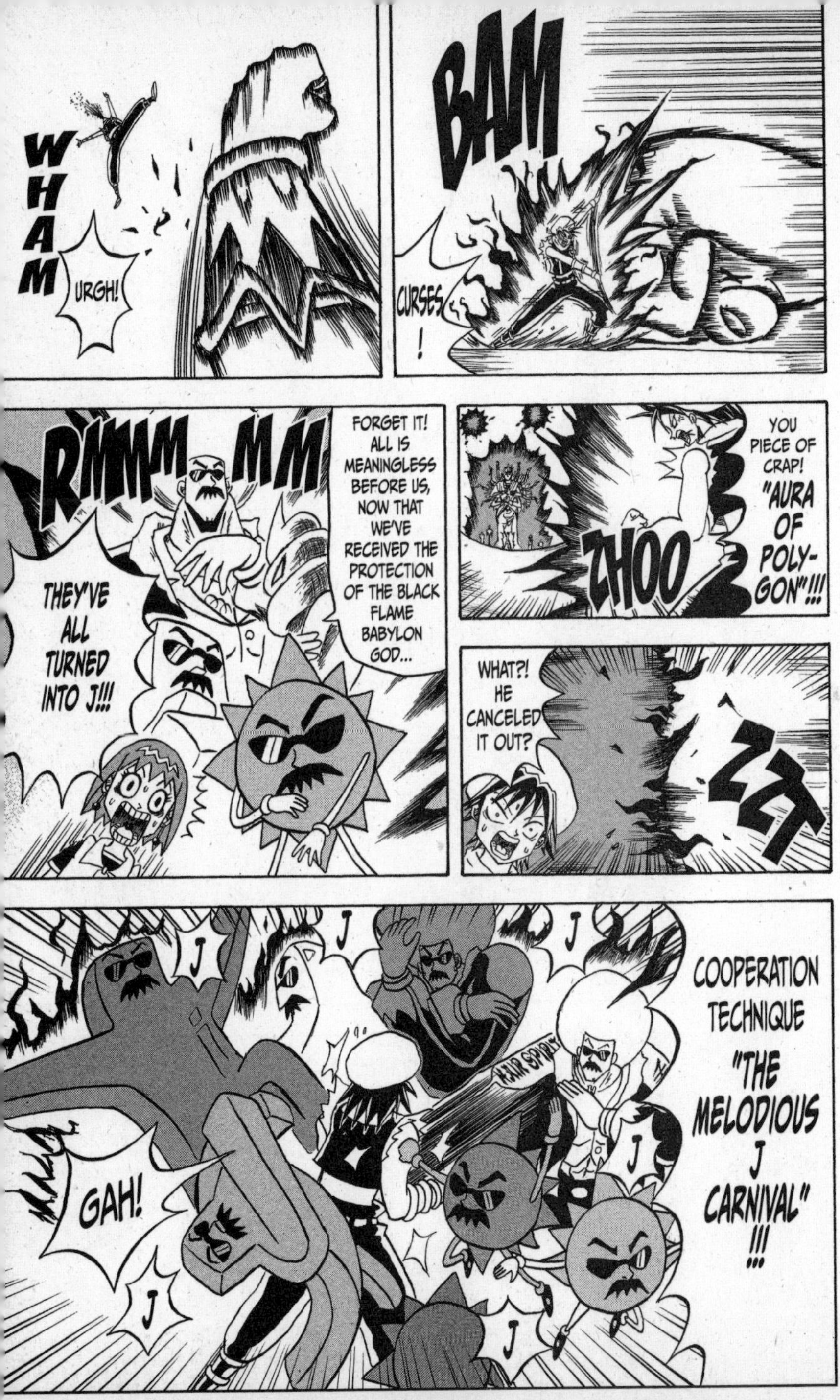
BAM
CURSES!
WHAM
URGH!
YOU PIECE OF CRAP! "AURA OF POLYGON"!!!
ZHOO
WHAT?! HE CANCELED IT OUT?
ZZT
RMMMM MM
FORGET IT! ALL IS MEANINGLESS BEFORE US, NOW THAT WE'VE RECEIVED THE PROTECTION OF THE BLACK FLAME BABYLON GOD...
THEY'VE ALL TURNED INTO J!!!
COOPERATION TECHNIQUE "THE MELODIOUS J CARNIVAL"!!!
J
J
J
J
GAH!
J
J

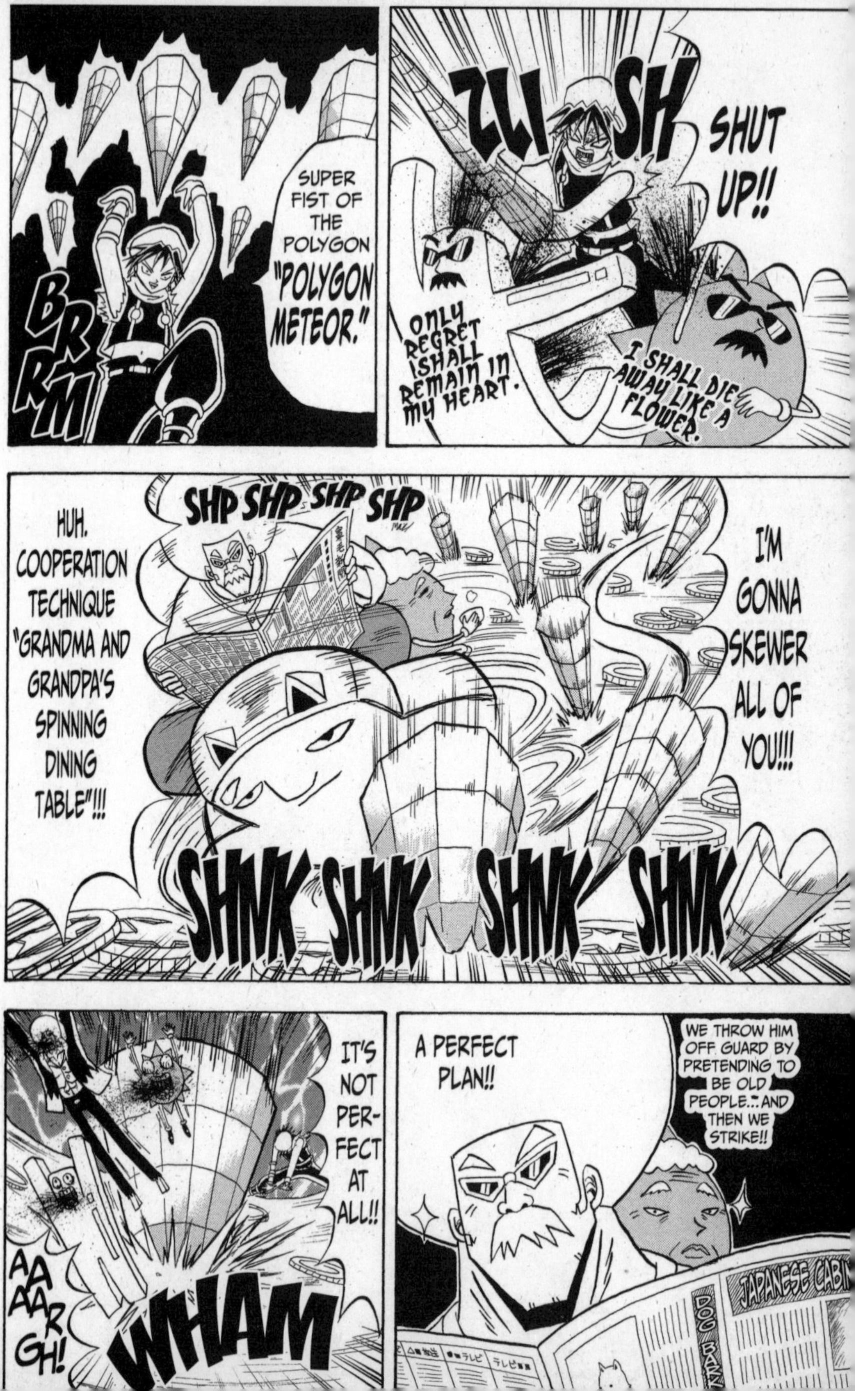
ZLLISH
SHUT UP!!
I SHALL DIE AWAY LIKE A FLOWER.
ONLY REGRET I SHALL REMAIN IN MY HEART.
SUPER FIST OF THE POLYGON "POLYGON METEOR."
BRRM
SHP SHP SHP SHP
I'M GONNA SKEWER ALL OF YOU!!!
HUH. COOPERATION TECHNIQUE "GRANDMA AND GRANDPA'S SPINNING DINING TABLE"!!!
SHNK SHNK SHNK SHNK
WE THROW HIM OFF GUARD BY PRETENDING TO BE OLD PEOPLE... AND THEN WE STRIKE!!
A PERFECT PLAN!!
IT'S NOT PER-FECT AT ALL!!
AAAARGH!
WHAM

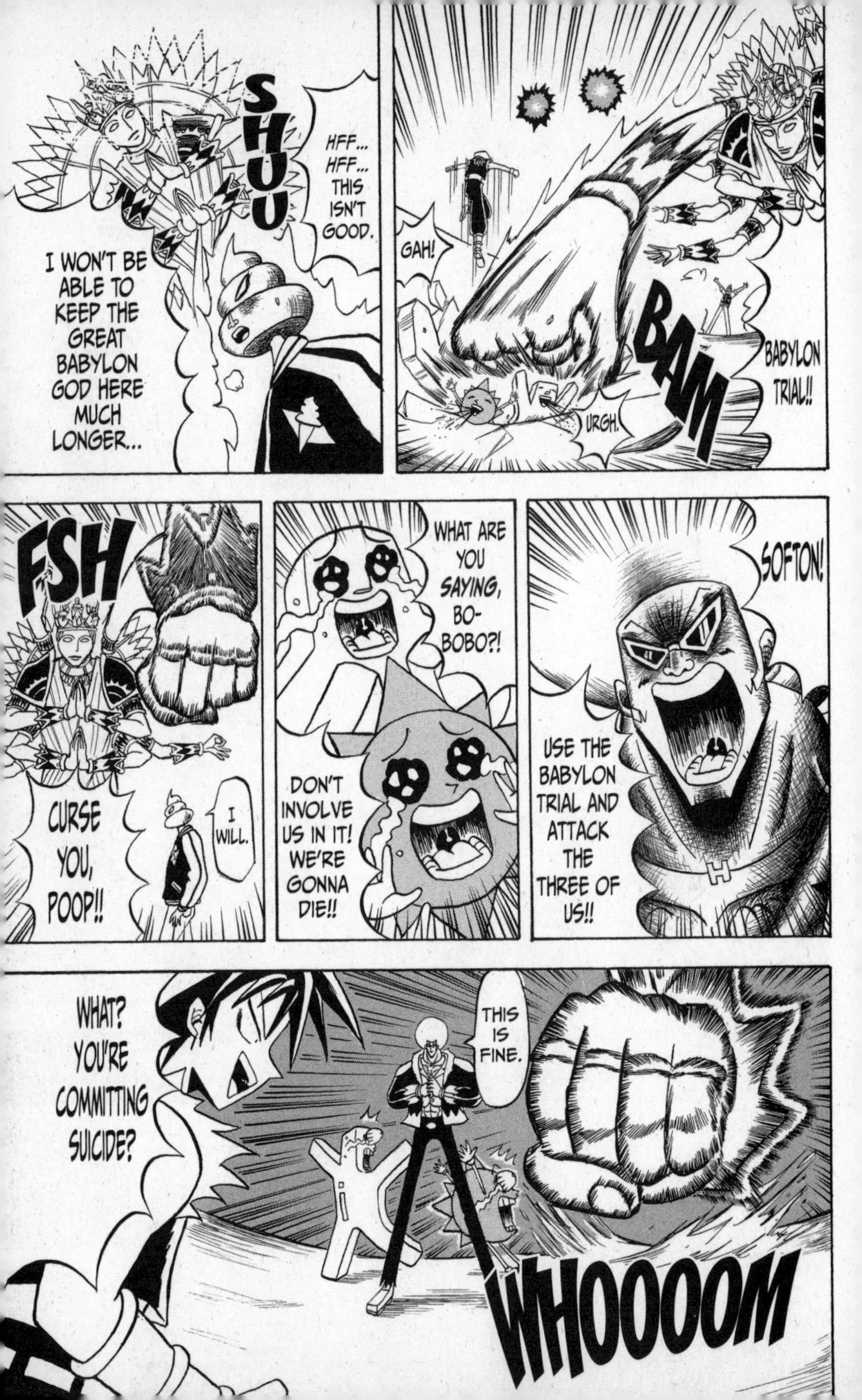
BABYLON TRIAL!!
BAM
GAH!
URGH.
SHUU
HFF... HFF... THIS ISN'T GOOD.
I WON'T BE ABLE TO KEEP THE GREAT BABYLON GOD HERE MUCH LONGER...
SOFTON!
USE THE BABYLON TRIAL AND ATTACK THE THREE OF US!!
WHAT ARE YOU SAYING, BO-BOBO?!
DON'T INVOLVE US IN IT! WE'RE GONNA DIE!!
FSH
I WILL.
CURSE YOU, POOP!!
THIS IS FINE.
WHAT? YOU'RE COMMITTING SUICIDE?
WHOOOOM

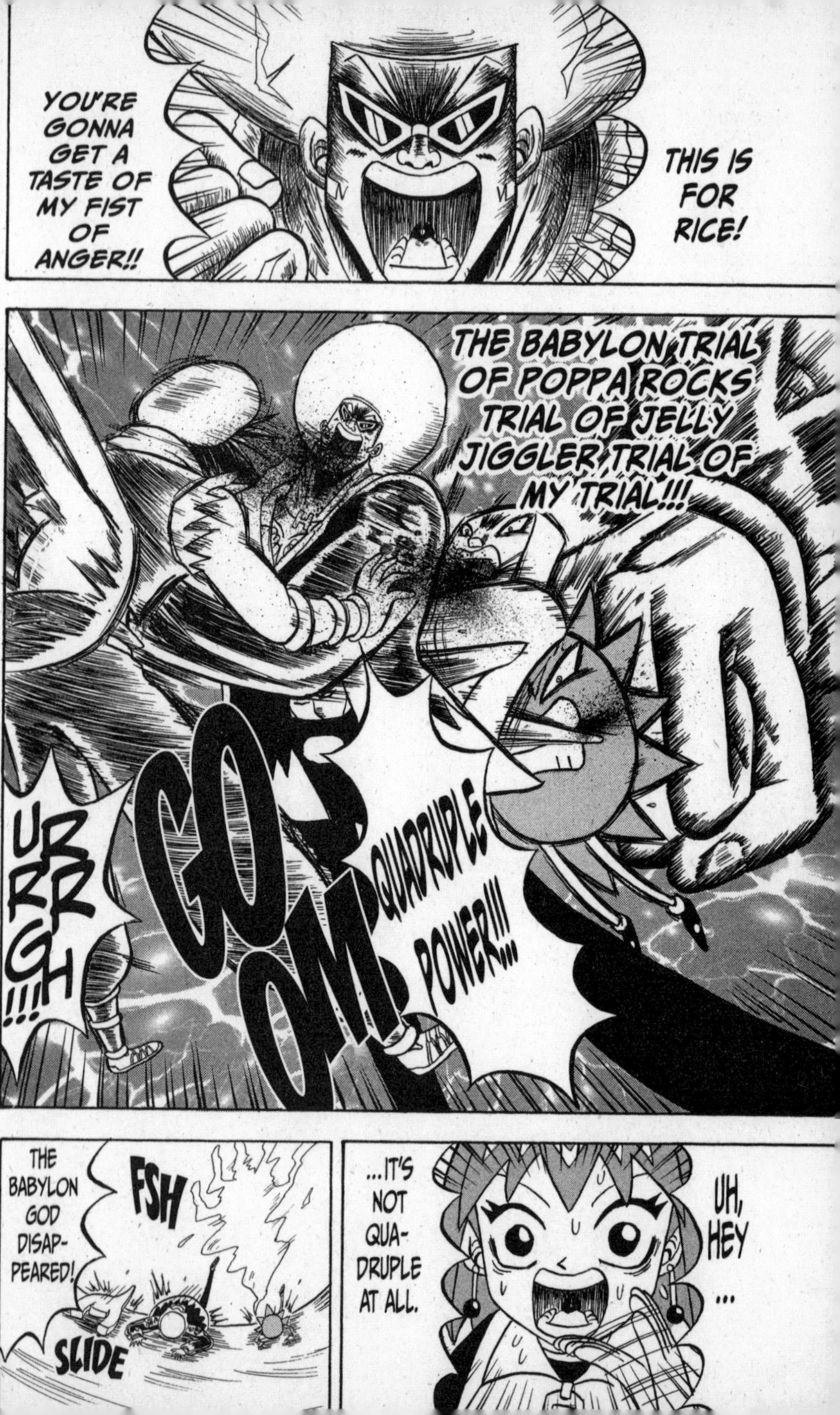
THIS IS FOR RICE!
YOU'RE GONNA GET A TASTE OF MY FIST OF ANGER!!
THE BABYLON TRIAL OF POPPA ROCKS TRIAL OF JELLY JIGGLER TRIAL OF MY TRIAL!!!
QUADRUPLE POWER!!!
GO OM
URRRGH!!!
UH, HEY ...
...IT'S NOT QUA-DRUPLE AT ALL.
FSH
THE BABYLON GOD DISAP-PEARED!
SLIDE

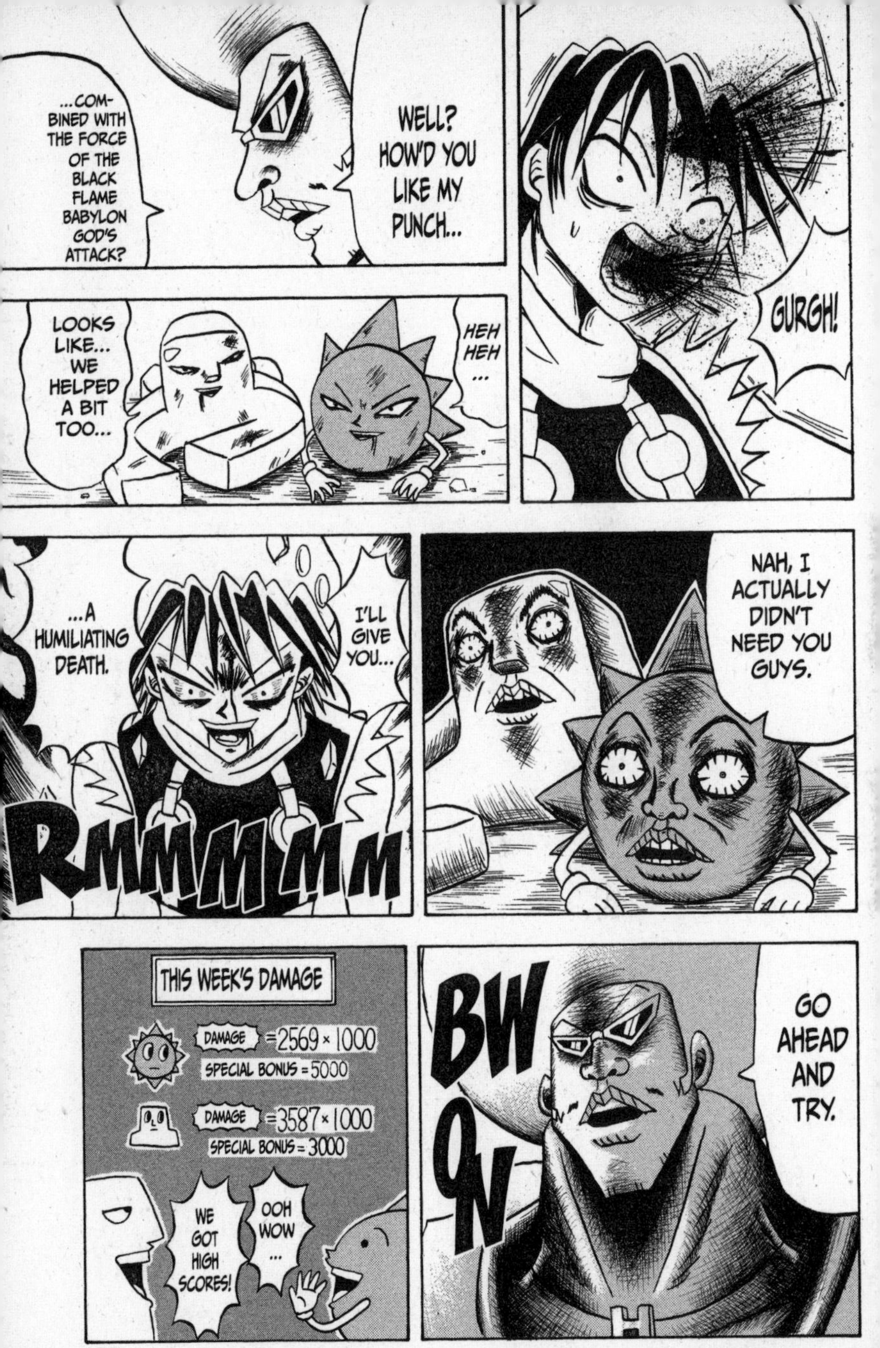
GURGH!
WELL? HOW'D YOU LIKE MY PUNCH...
...COM-BINED WITH THE FORCE OF THE BLACK FLAME BABYLON GOD'S ATTACK?
HEH HEH ...
LOOKS LIKE... WE HELPED A BIT TOO...
NAH, I ACTUALLY DIDN'T NEED YOU GUYS.
I'LL GIVE YOU...
...A HUMILIATING DEATH.
RMMMMMM
BWOON
GO AHEAD AND TRY.
THIS WEEK'S DAMAGE
DAMAGE = 2569 × 1000
SPECIAL BONUS = 5000
DAMAGE = 3587 × 1000
SPECIAL BONUS = 3000
OOH WOW ...
WE GOT HIGH SCORES!

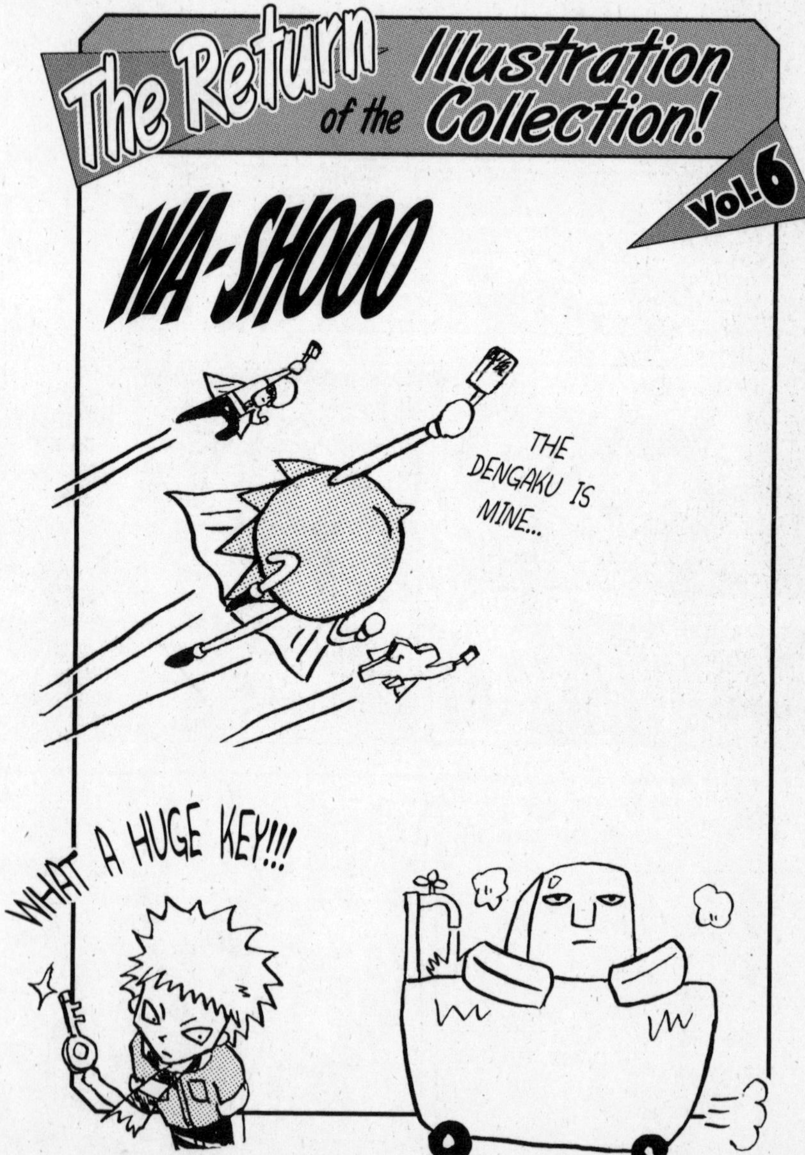
The Return of the Illustration Collection!
Vol.6
WA-SHOOO
THE DENGAKU IS MINE...
WHAT A HUGE KEY!!!

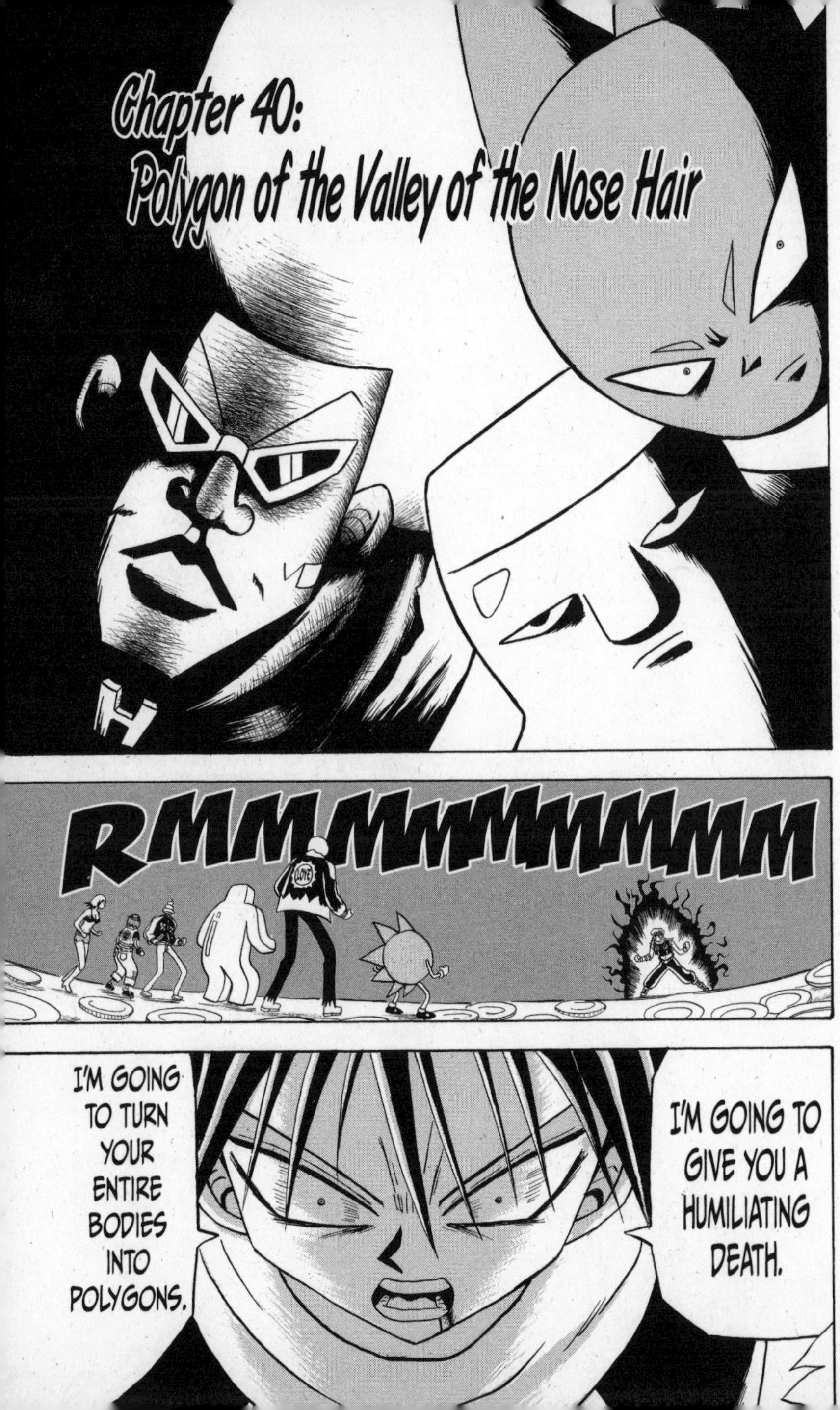
Chapter 40:
Polygon of the Valley of the Nose Hair
RMMMMMMMMMMM
LOVE
I'M GOING TO GIVE YOU A HUMILIATING DEATH.
I'M GOING TO TURN YOUR ENTIRE BODIES INTO POLYGONS.

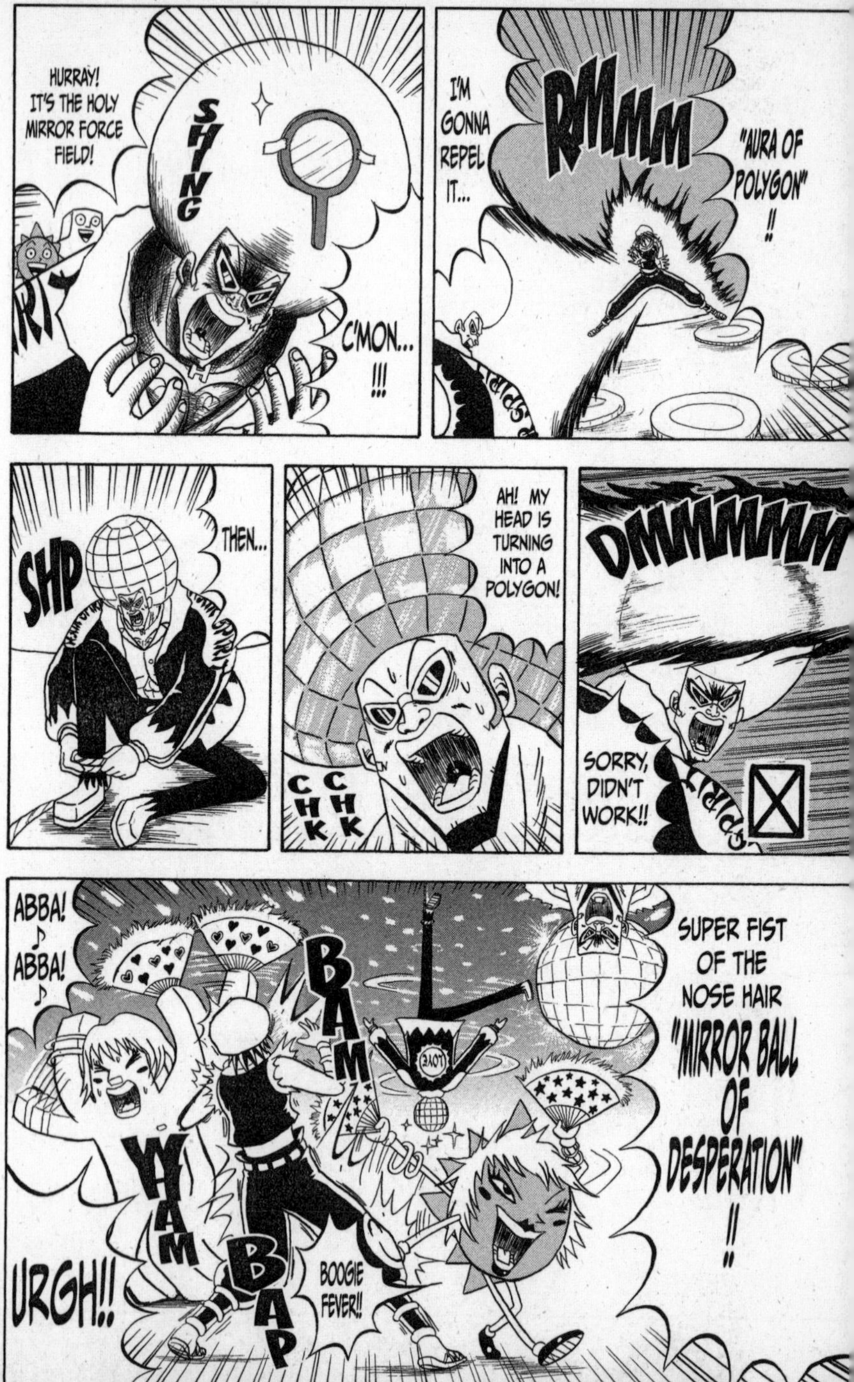
I'M GONNA REPEL IT...
RMMM
"AURA OF POLYGON" !!
HURRAY! IT'S THE HOLY MIRROR FORCE FIELD!
SHING
C'MON... !!!
DMMMMMM
SORRY, DIDN'T WORK!!
AH! MY HEAD IS TURNING INTO A POLYGON!
CHK CHK
THEN...
SHP
SUPER FIST OF THE NOSE HAIR "MIRROR BALL OF DESPERATION" !!
BAM
ABBA! ♪ ABBA! ♪
WHAM
BAP
BOOGIE FEVER!!
URGH!!

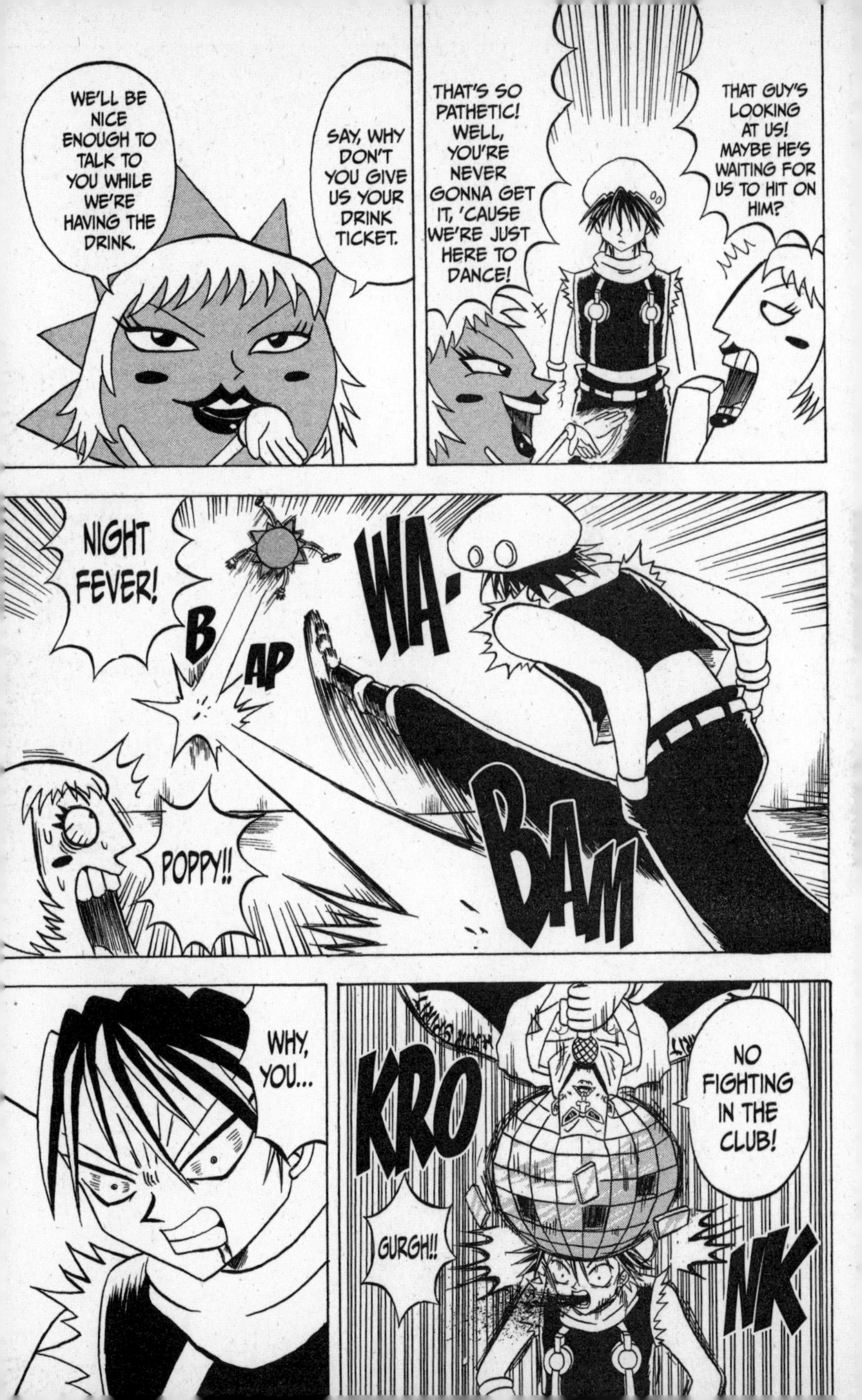
THAT GUY'S LOOKING AT US! MAYBE HE'S WAITING FOR US TO HIT ON HIM?
THAT'S SO PATHETIC! WELL, YOU'RE NEVER GONNA GET IT, 'CAUSE WE'RE JUST HERE TO DANCE!
SAY, WHY DON'T YOU GIVE US YOUR DRINK TICKET.
WE'LL BE NICE ENOUGH TO TALK TO YOU WHILE WE'RE HAVING THE DRINK.
WA-
NIGHT FEVER!
BAP
BAM
POPPY!!
NO FIGHTING IN THE CLUB!
KRONK
GURGH!!
WHY, YOU...

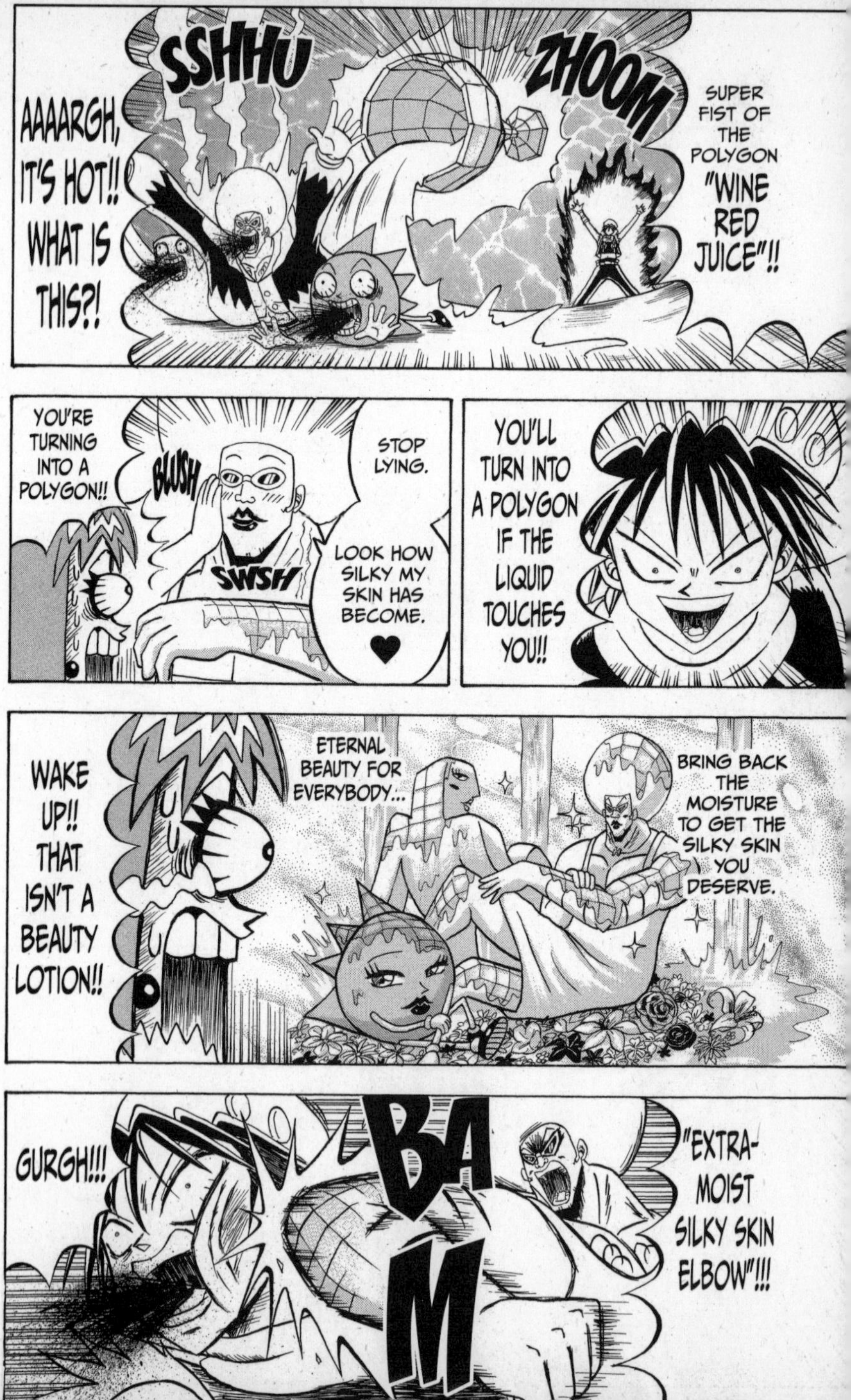
SUPER FIST OF THE POLYGON "WINE RED JUICE"!!
ZHOOM
SSHHU
AAAARGH, IT'S HOT!! WHAT IS THIS?!
YOU'LL TURN INTO A POLYGON IF THE LIQUID TOUCHES YOU!!
STOP LYING.
LOOK HOW SILKY MY SKIN HAS BECOME. ♥
BLUSH
SWSH
YOU'RE TURNING INTO A POLYGON!!
BRING BACK THE MOISTURE TO GET THE SILKY SKIN YOU DESERVE.
ETERNAL BEAUTY FOR EVERYBODY...
WAKE UP!! THAT ISN'T A BEAUTY LOTION!!
"EXTRA-MOIST SILKY SKIN ELBOW"!!!
BAM
GURGH!!!

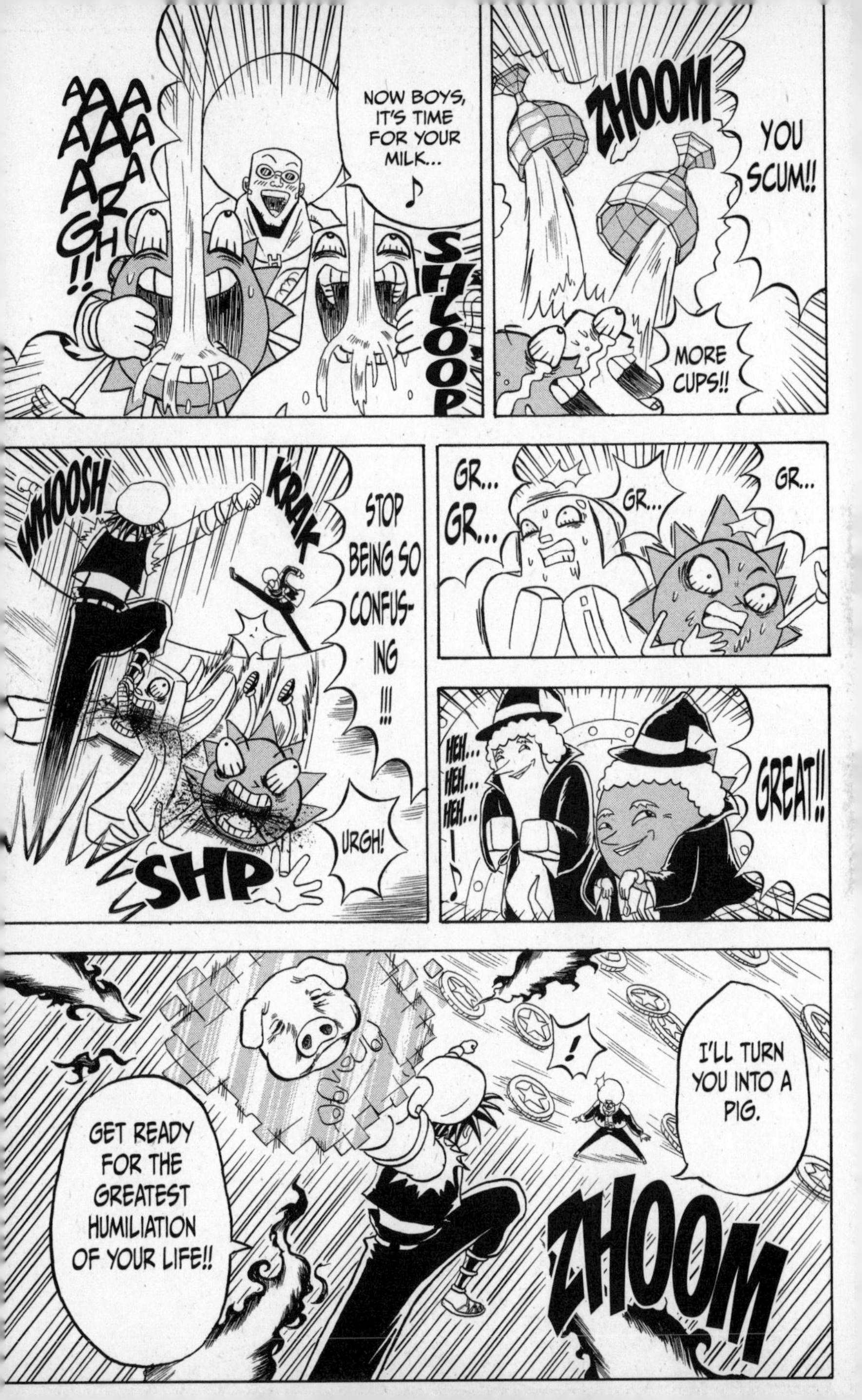
ZHOOM
YOU SCUM!!
MORE CUPS!!
NOW BOYS, IT'S TIME FOR YOUR MILK... ♪
AAAAAAAAARAGH!!
SHLOOP
GR...
GR...
GR...
GR...
HEH... HEH... HEH... ♪
GREAT!!
KRAK
STOP BEING SO CONFUSING!!
WHOOSH
URGH!
SHP
I'LL TURN YOU INTO A PIG.
!
GET READY FOR THE GREATEST HUMILIATION OF YOUR LIFE!!
ZHOOM

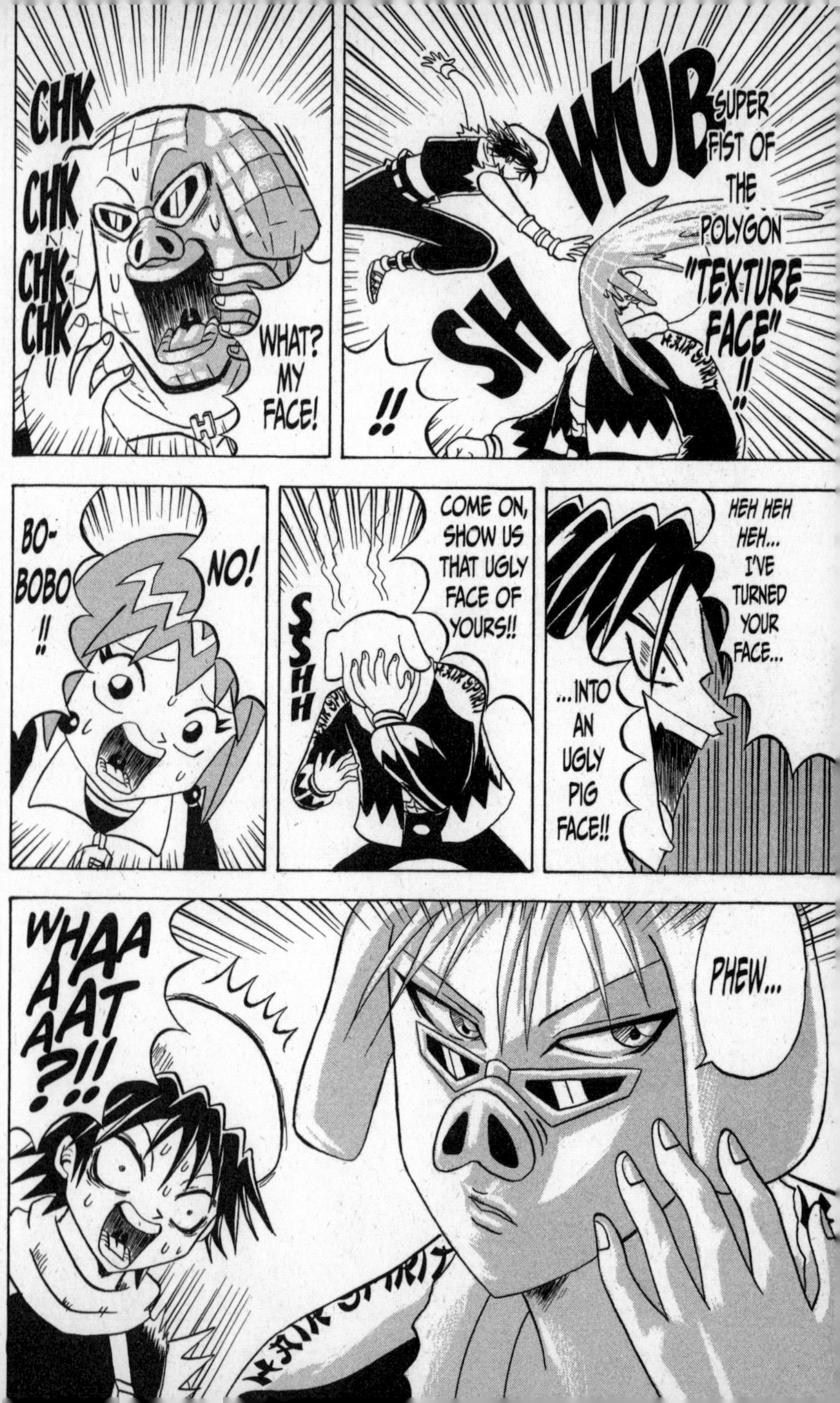
SUPER FIST OF THE POLYGON "TEXTURE FACE"!!
WUB
SH
!!
CHK CHK CHK-CHK
WHAT? MY FACE!
HEH HEH HEH... I'VE TURNED YOUR FACE...
...INTO AN UGLY PIG FACE!!
COME ON, SHOW US THAT UGLY FACE OF YOURS!!
SSHH
NO!
BO-BOBO!!
PHEW...
WHAAAAATA?!!

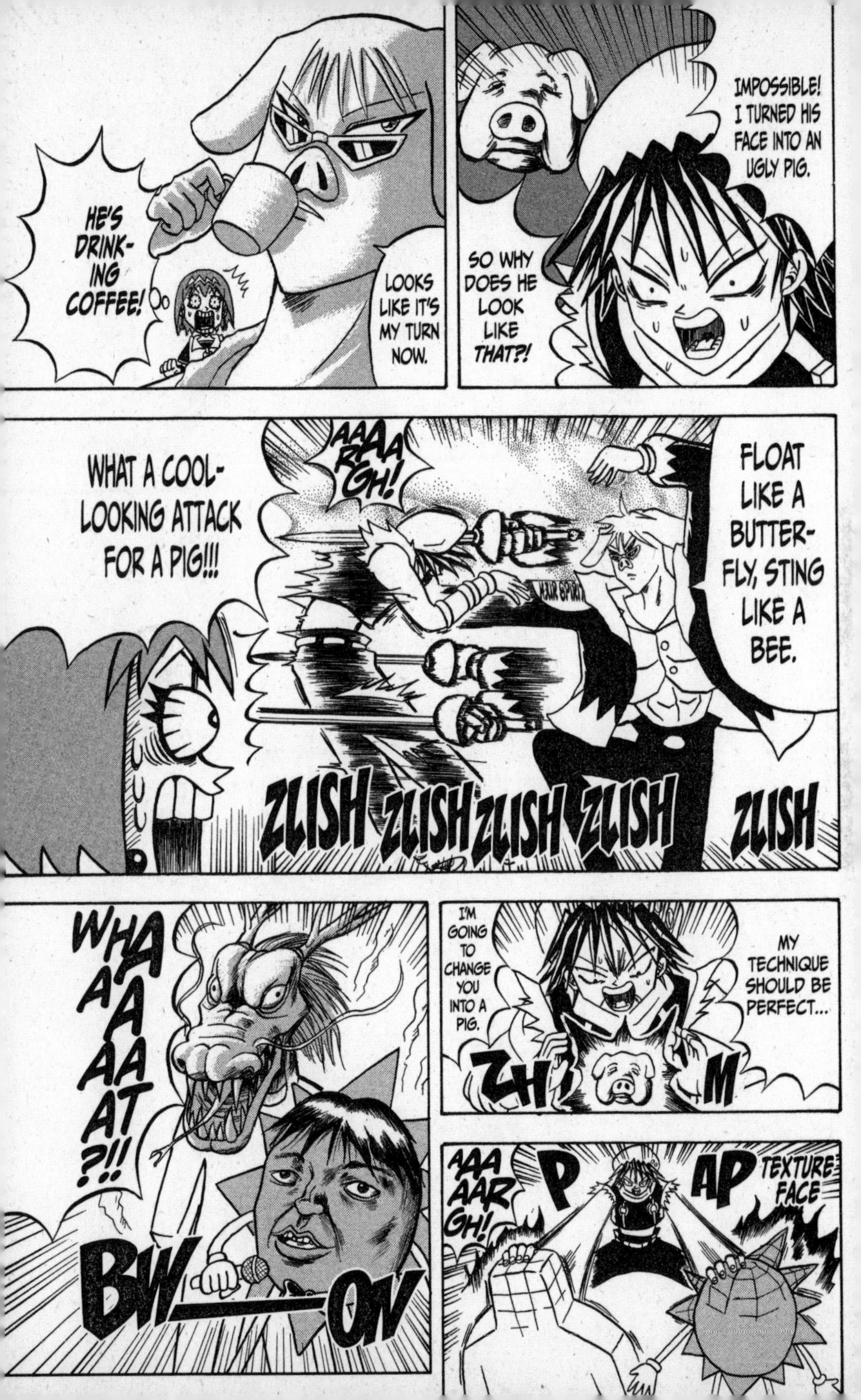
IMPOSSIBLE! I TURNED HIS FACE INTO AN UGLY PIG.
SO WHY DOES HE LOOK LIKE THAT?!
LOOKS LIKE IT'S MY TURN NOW.
HE'S DRINK-ING COFFEE!
FLOAT LIKE A BUTTER-FLY, STING LIKE A BEE.
AAAARGH!
ZLISH ZLISH ZLISH ZLISH ZLISH
WHAT A COOL-LOOKING ATTACK FOR A PIG!!!
MY TECHNIQUE SHOULD BE PERFECT...
I'M GOING TO CHANGE YOU INTO A PIG.
ZH M
TEXTURE FACE
P AP
AAAAARGH!
WHAAAAAAAT?!!
BW—OV

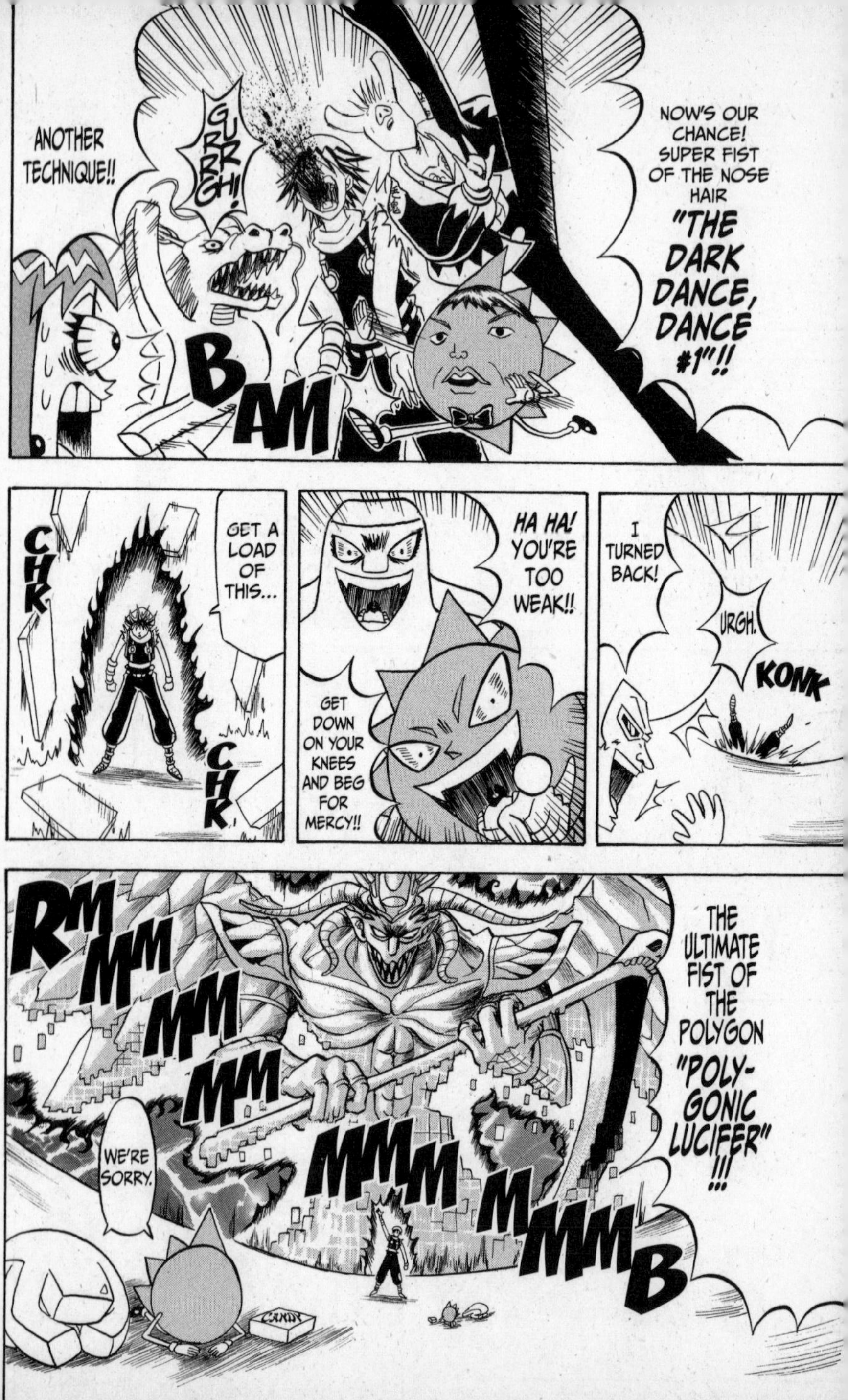
NOW'S OUR CHANCE! SUPER FIST OF THE NOSE HAIR "THE DARK DANCE, DANCE #1"!!
GURRGH!
BAM
ANOTHER TECHNIQUE!!
I TURNED BACK!
URGH.
KONK
HA HA! YOU'RE TOO WEAK!!
GET DOWN ON YOUR KNEES AND BEG FOR MERCY!!
GET A LOAD OF THIS...
CHK
CHK
THE ULTIMATE FIST OF THE POLYGON "POLY-GONIC LUCIFER"!!!
RMMMMMMMMMMMMMB
WE'RE SORRY.

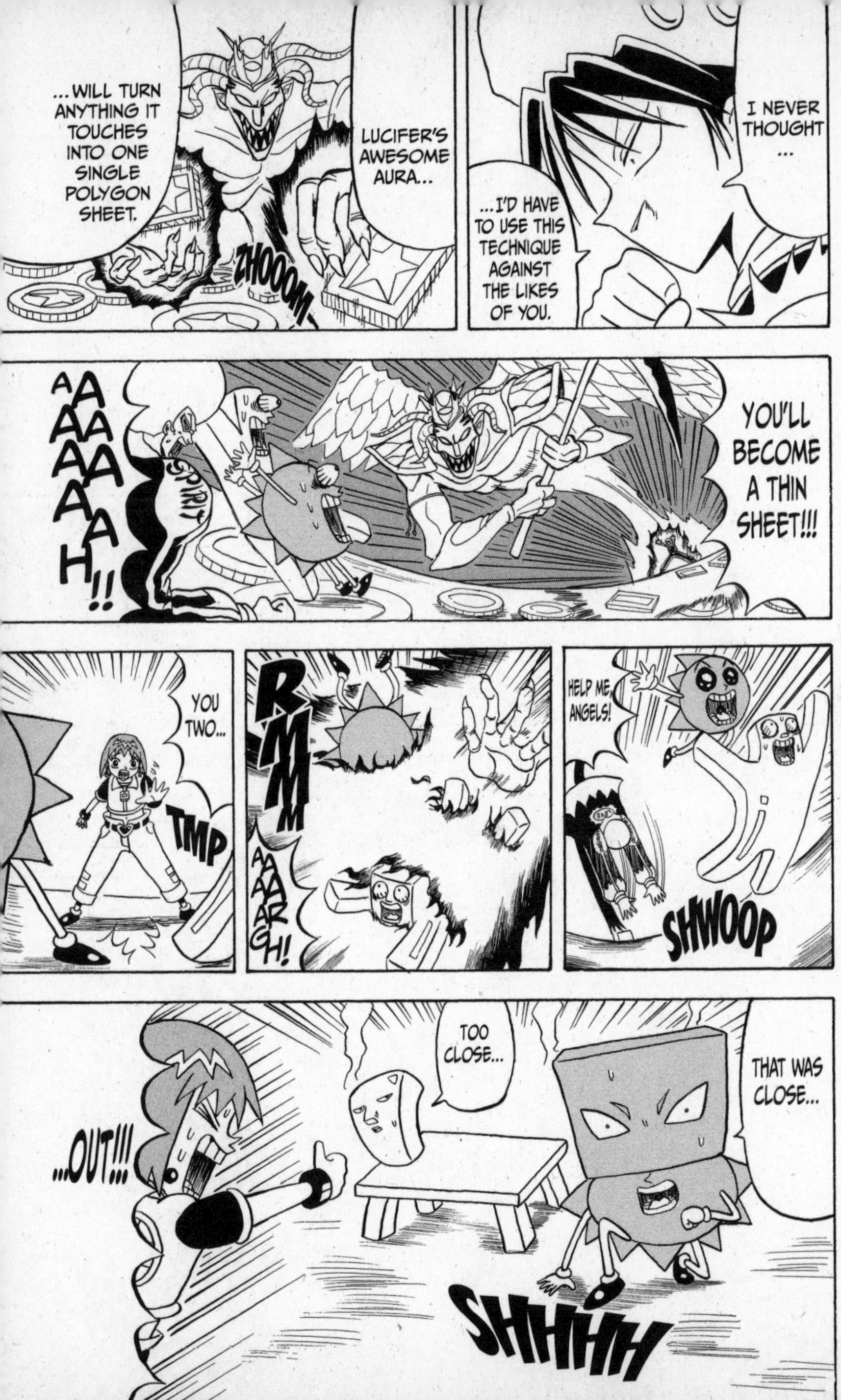
I NEVER THOUGHT...
...I'D HAVE TO USE THIS TECHNIQUE AGAINST THE LIKES OF YOU.
LUCIFER'S AWESOME AURA...
...WILL TURN ANYTHING IT TOUCHES INTO ONE SINGLE POLYGON SHEET.
ZHOOOM
YOU'LL BECOME A THIN SHEET!!!
SPIRIT
AAAAAAAAH!!
HELP ME, ANGELS!
SHWOOP
RMMM
AAAARGH!
YOU TWO...
TMP
THAT WAS CLOSE...
TOO CLOSE...
...OUT!!!
SHHHHH

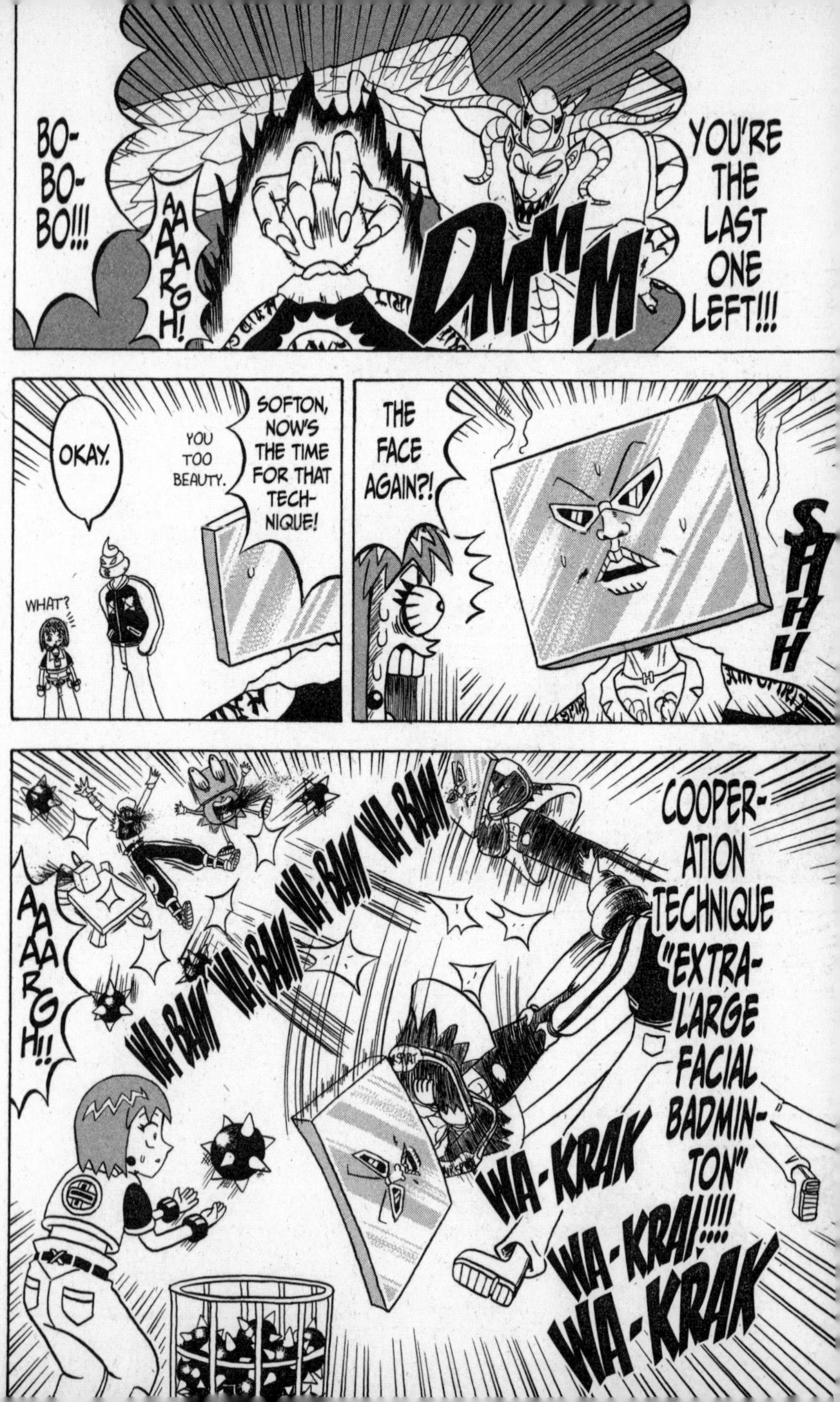

YOU'RE THE LAST ONE LEFT!!!
DMMM
BO-BO-BO!!!
AAAARGH!
SHHH
THE FACE AGAIN?!
SOFTON, NOW'S THE TIME FOR THAT TECH-NIQUE!
YOU TOO BEAUTY.
OKAY.
WHAT?
COOPER-ATION TECHNIQUE "EXTRA-LARGE FACIAL BADMIN-TON"!!!!
WA-BAM WA-BAM WA-BAM WA-BAM WA-BAM WA-BAM
WA-KRAK
WA-KRAK
WA-KRAK
AAAARGH!!

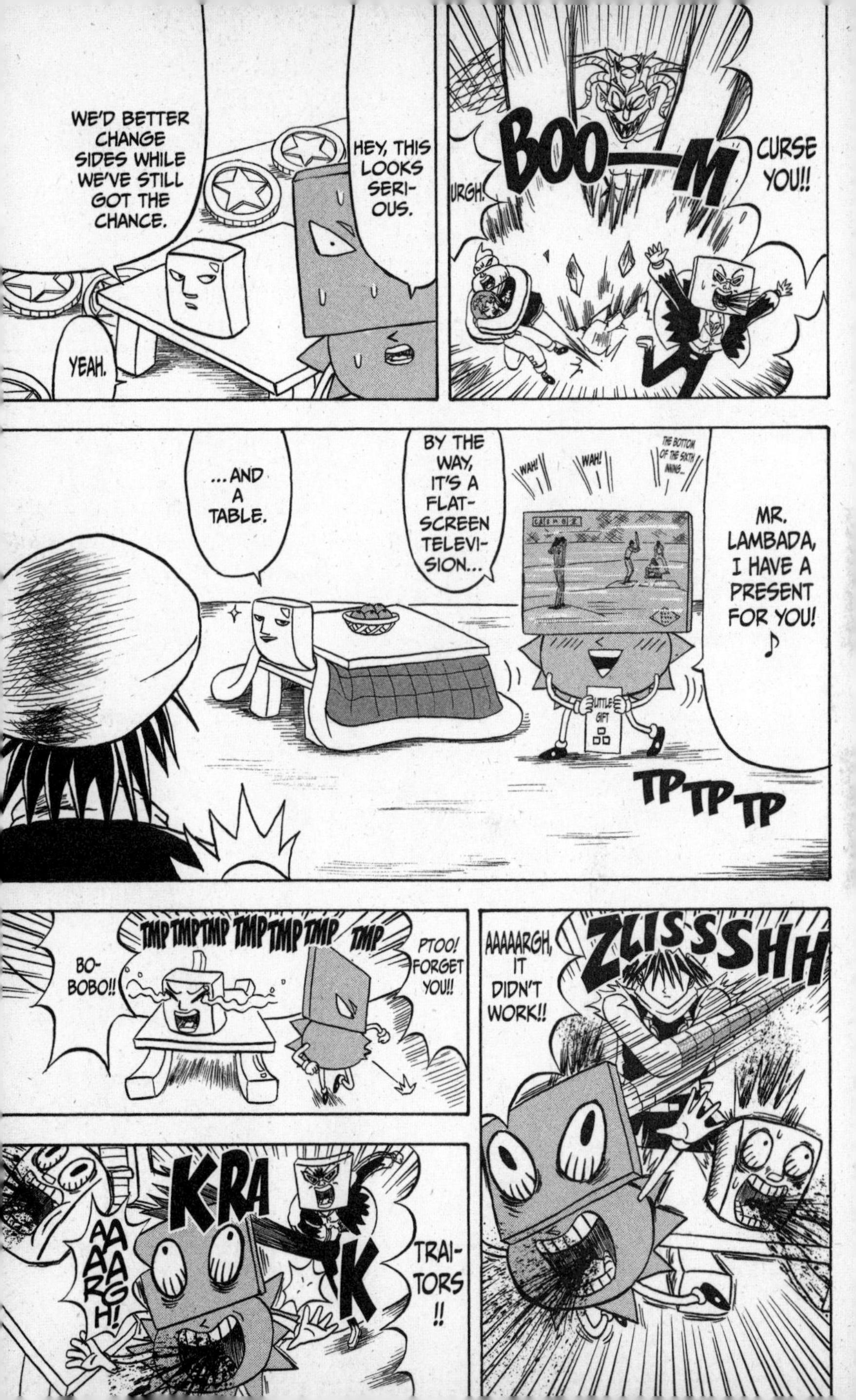
CURSE YOU!!
BOO—M
URGH!
HEY, THIS LOOKS SERIOUS.
WE'D BETTER CHANGE SIDES WHILE WE'VE STILL GOT THE CHANCE.
YEAH.
MR. LAMBADA, I HAVE A PRESENT FOR YOU! ♪
THE BOTTOM OF THE SIXTH INNING...
WAH!
WAH!
LITTLE GIFT
TP TP TP
BY THE WAY, IT'S A FLAT-SCREEN TELEVISION...
...AND A TABLE.
ZLISSSHH
AAAAARGH, IT DIDN'T WORK!!
PTOO! FORGET YOU!!
TMP TMP TMP TMP TMP TMP TMP
BO-BOBO!!
TRAITORS!!
KRAK
AAAARGH!

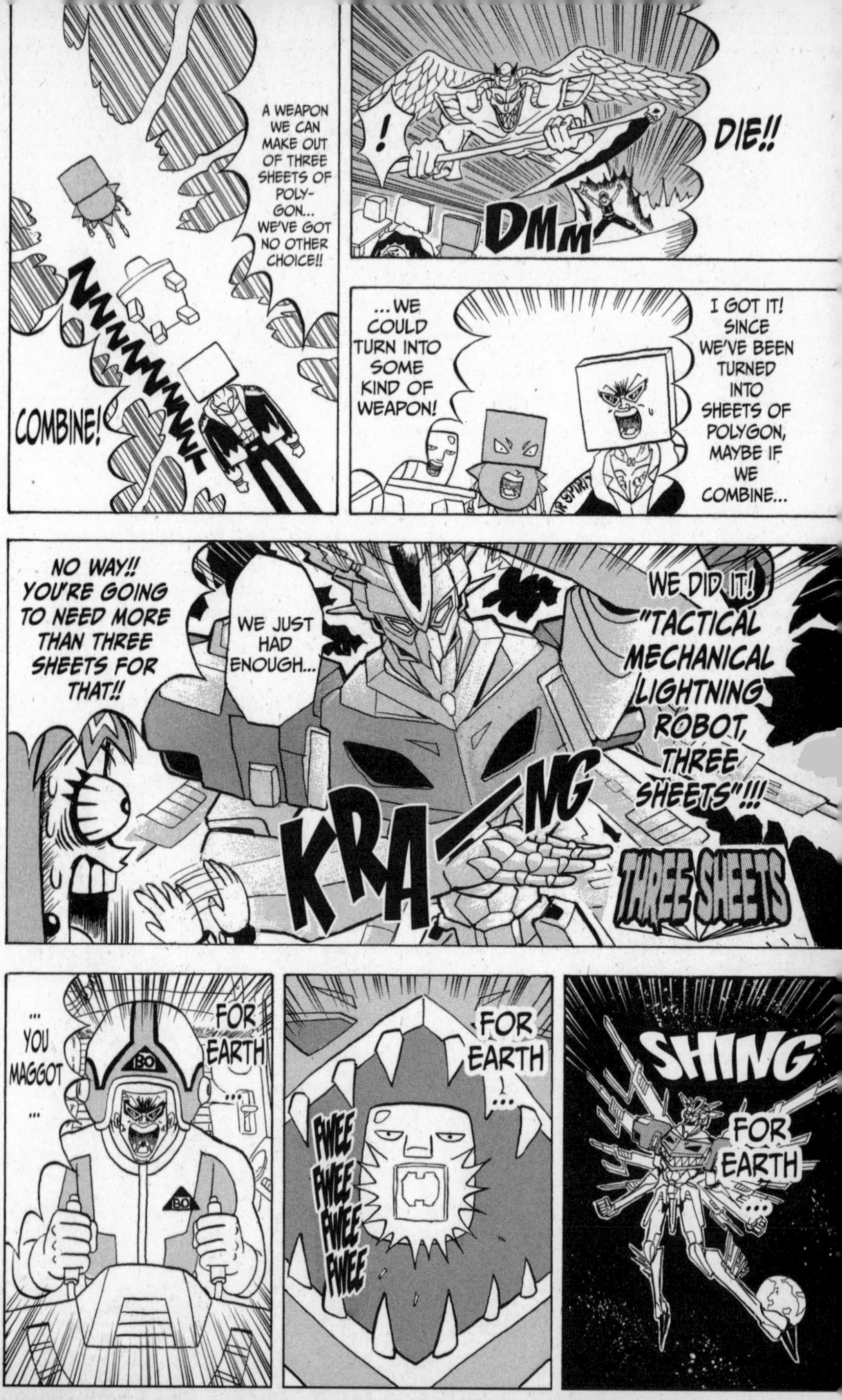
!
DIE!!
DMM
I GOT IT! SINCE WE'VE BEEN TURNED INTO SHEETS OF POLYGON, MAYBE IF WE COMBINE...
...WE COULD TURN INTO SOME KIND OF WEAPON!
A WEAPON WE CAN MAKE OUT OF THREE SHEETS OF POLY-GON... WE'VE GOT NO OTHER CHOICE!!
ZNNNNNNNNNT
COMBINE!
WE DID IT! "TACTICAL MECHANICAL LIGHTNING ROBOT, THREE SHEETS"!!!
THREE SHEETS
KRA—NG
WE JUST HAD ENOUGH...
NO WAY!! YOU'RE GOING TO NEED MORE THAN THREE SHEETS FOR THAT!!
SHING
FOR EARTH...
FOR EARTH...
FWEE FWEE FWEE FWEE
FOR EARTH...
... YOU MAGGOT ...

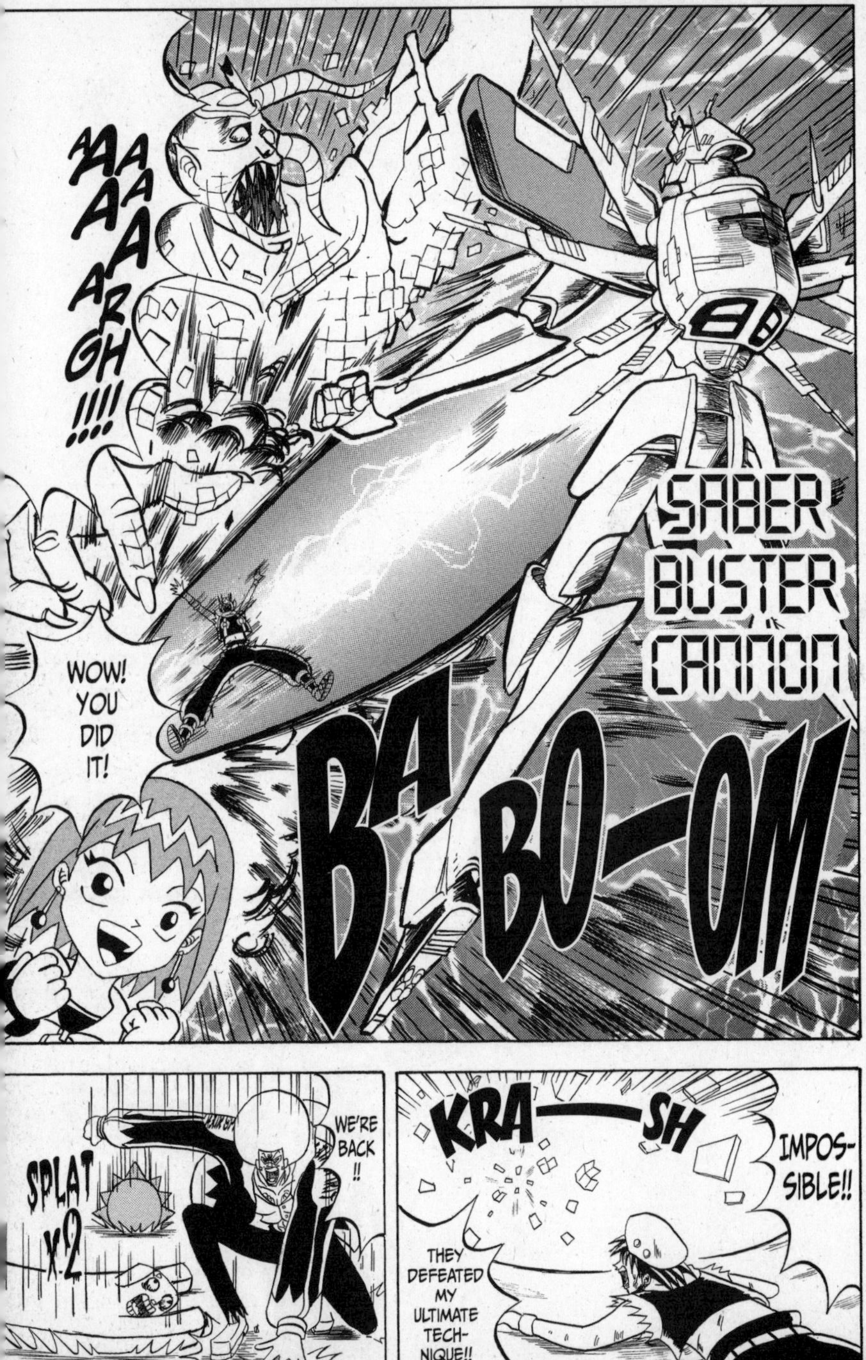
SABER BUSTER CANNON
AAAAAARGH!!!!
BA-BO-OM
WOW! YOU DID IT!
KRA—SH
IMPOSSIBLE!!
THEY DEFEATED MY ULTIMATE TECHNIQUE!!
WE'RE BACK!!
SPLAT X2

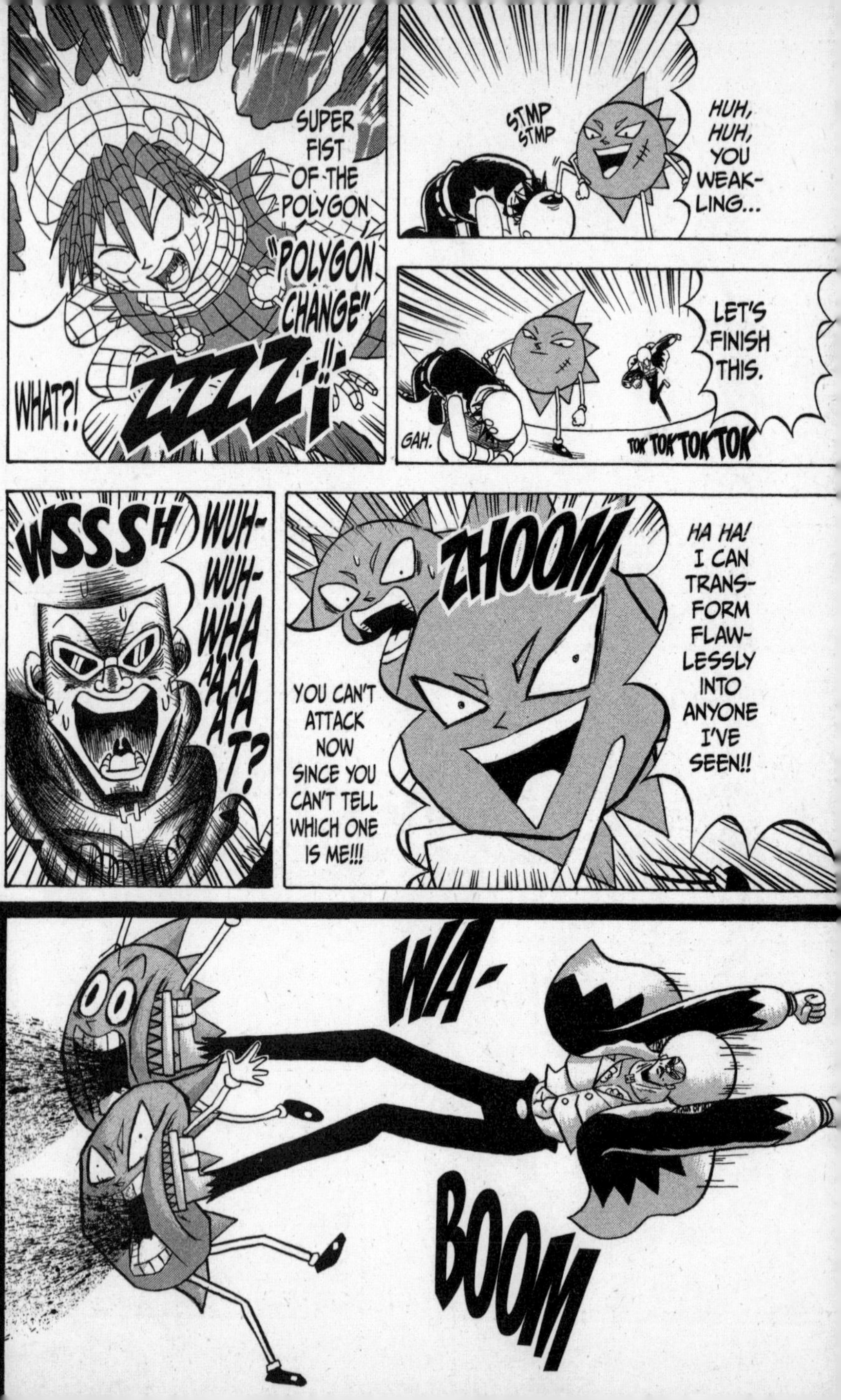
STMP STMP
HUH, HUH, YOU WEAK-LING...
LET'S FINISH THIS.
GAH.
TOK TOK TOK TOK
SUPER FIST OF THE POLYGON
"POLYGON CHANGE"!!
ZZZZ
WHAT?!
HA HA! I CAN TRANS-FORM FLAW-LESSLY INTO ANYONE I'VE SEEN!!
ZHOOM
YOU CAN'T ATTACK NOW SINCE YOU CAN'T TELL WHICH ONE IS ME!!!
WSSSH
WUH-WUH-WHAAAAAT?
WA-
BOOM

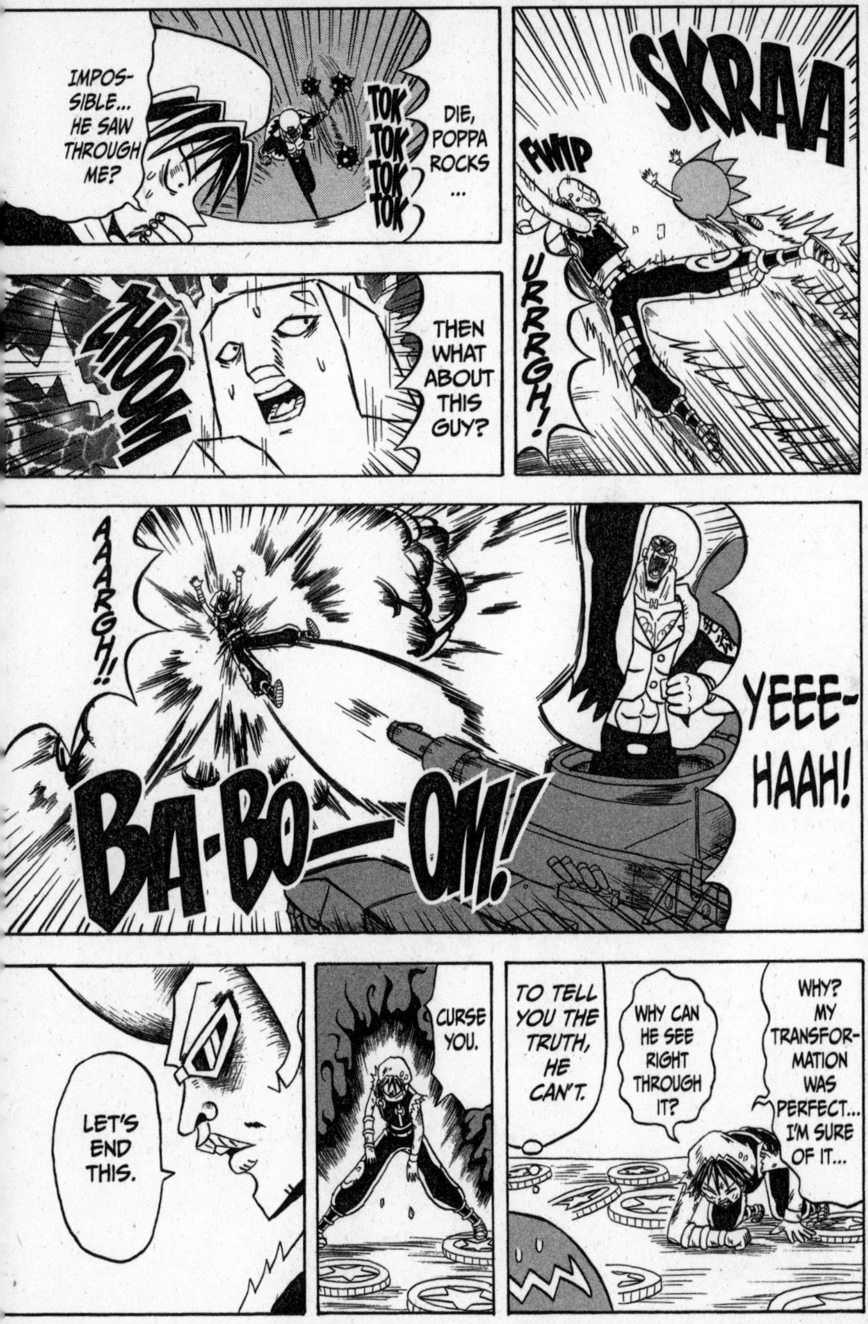
SKRAA
FWIP
URRRGH!
DIE, POPPA ROCKS ...
TOK TOK TOK TOK
IMPOS-SIBLE... HE SAW THROUGH ME?
THEN WHAT ABOUT THIS GUY?
THOOM!
YEEE-HAAH!
AAARGH!!
BA-BO—OM!
WHY? MY TRANSFOR-MATION WAS PERFECT... I'M SURE OF IT...
WHY CAN HE SEE RIGHT THROUGH IT?
TO TELL YOU THE TRUTH, HE CAN'T.
CURSE YOU.
LET'S END THIS.

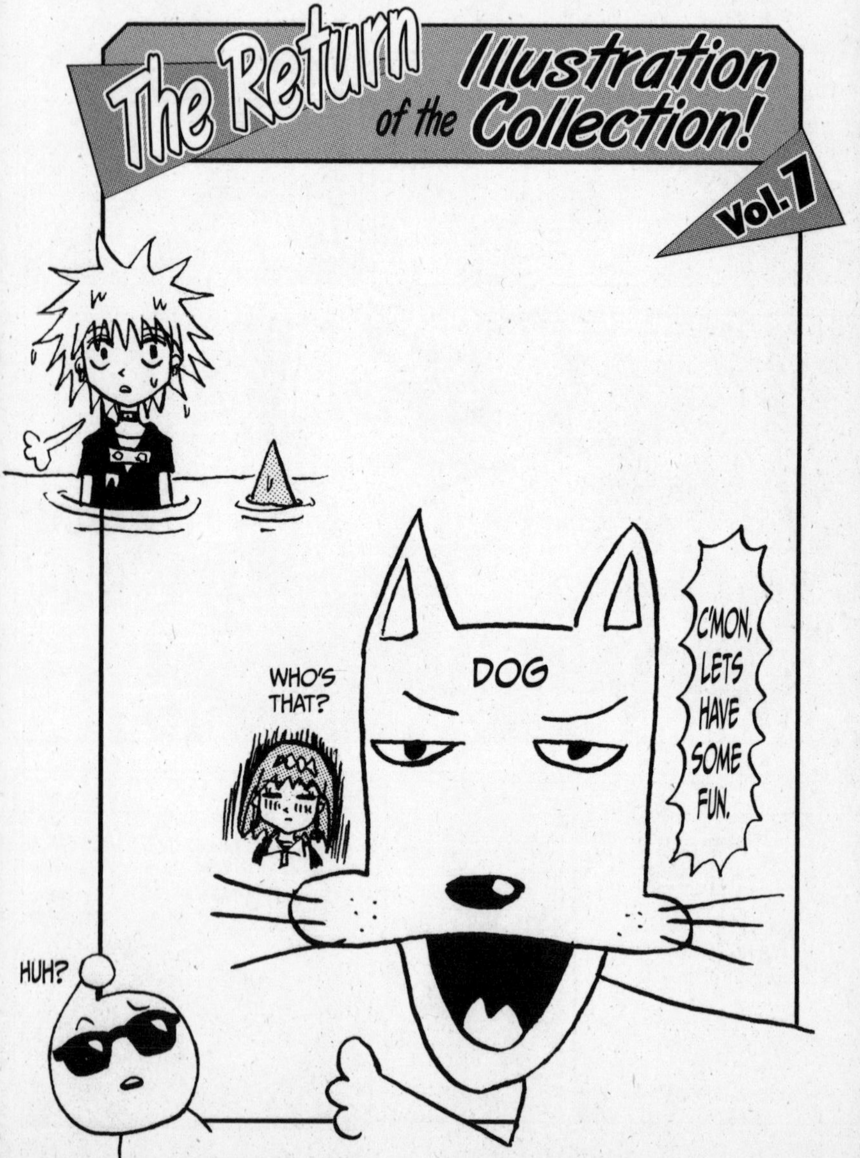
The Return of the Illustration Collection!
Vol. 7
C'MON, LETS HAVE SOME FUN.
DOG
WHO'S THAT?
HUH?

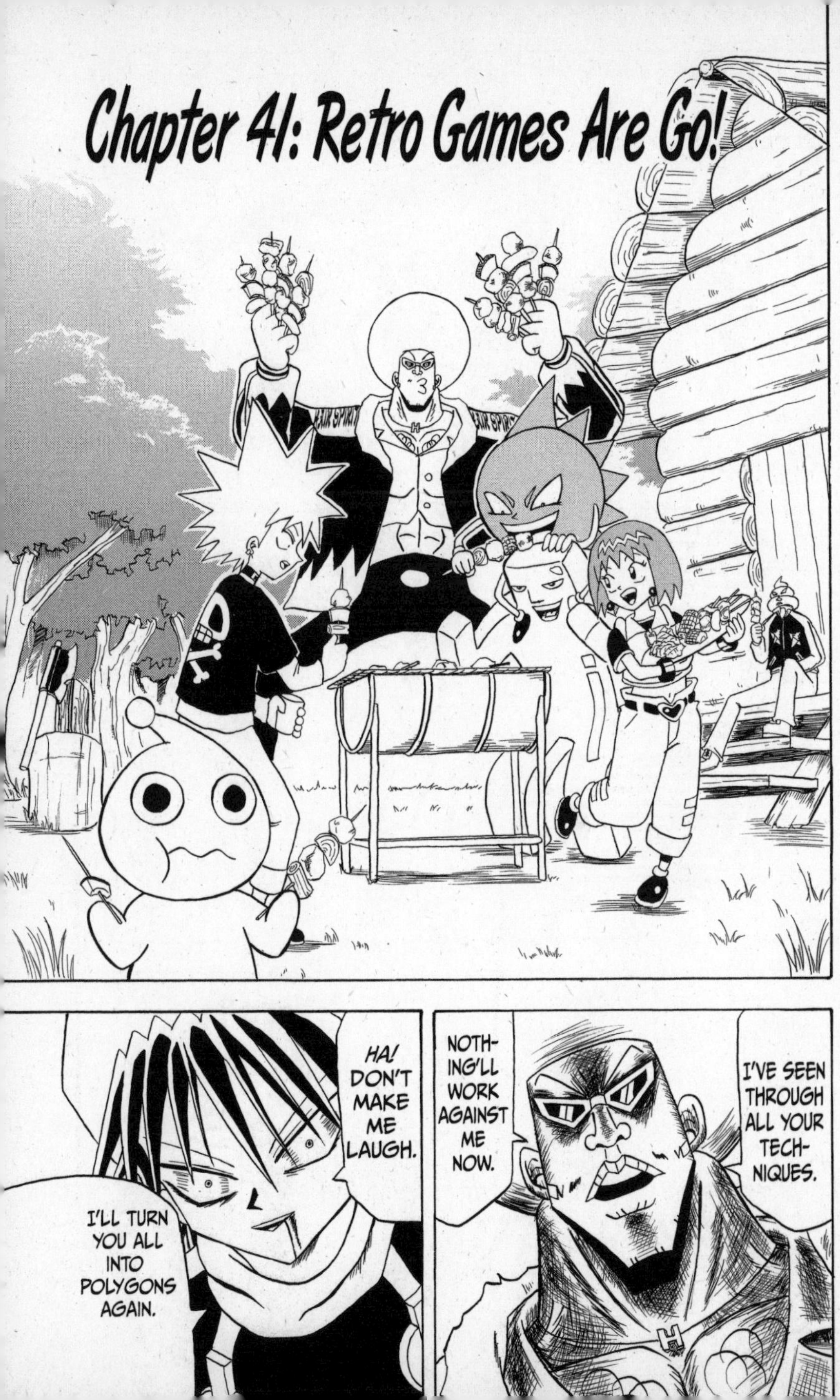
Chapter 41: Retro Games Are Go!
I'VE SEEN THROUGH ALL YOUR TECH-NIQUES.
NOTH-ING'LL WORK AGAINST ME NOW.
HA! DON'T MAKE ME LAUGH.
I'LL TURN YOU ALL INTO POLYGONS AGAIN.

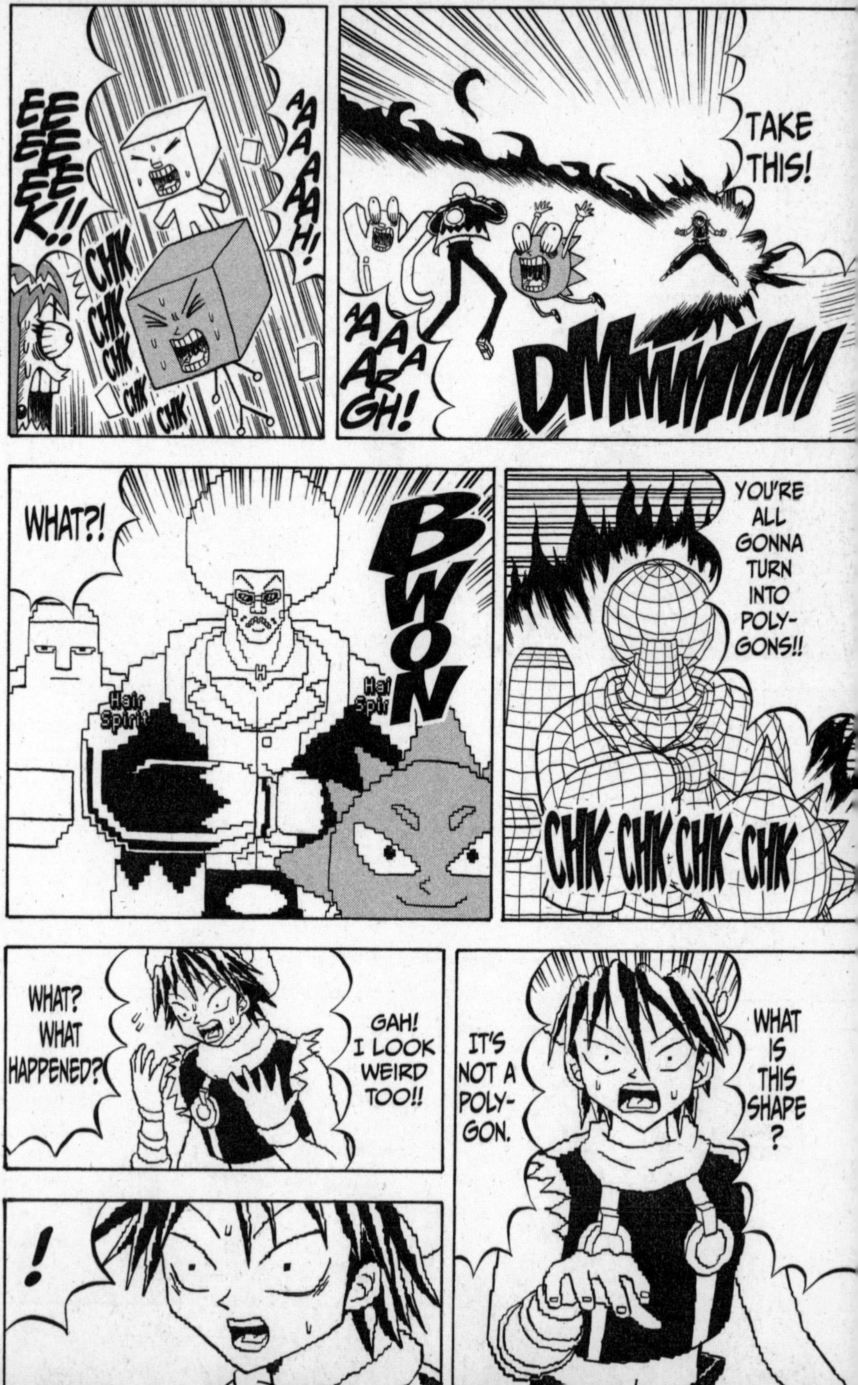
TAKE THIS!
AAAAARGH!
DMMMMMM
AAAAAAAH!
CHK CHK CHK CHK CHK CHK
EEEEEEK!!
YOU'RE ALL GONNA TURN INTO POLYGONS!!
CHK CHK CHK CHK
BWON
WHAT?!
Hair Spirit
WHAT IS THIS SHAPE?
IT'S NOT A POLYGON.
GAH! I LOOK WEIRD TOO!!
WHAT? WHAT HAPPENED?
!

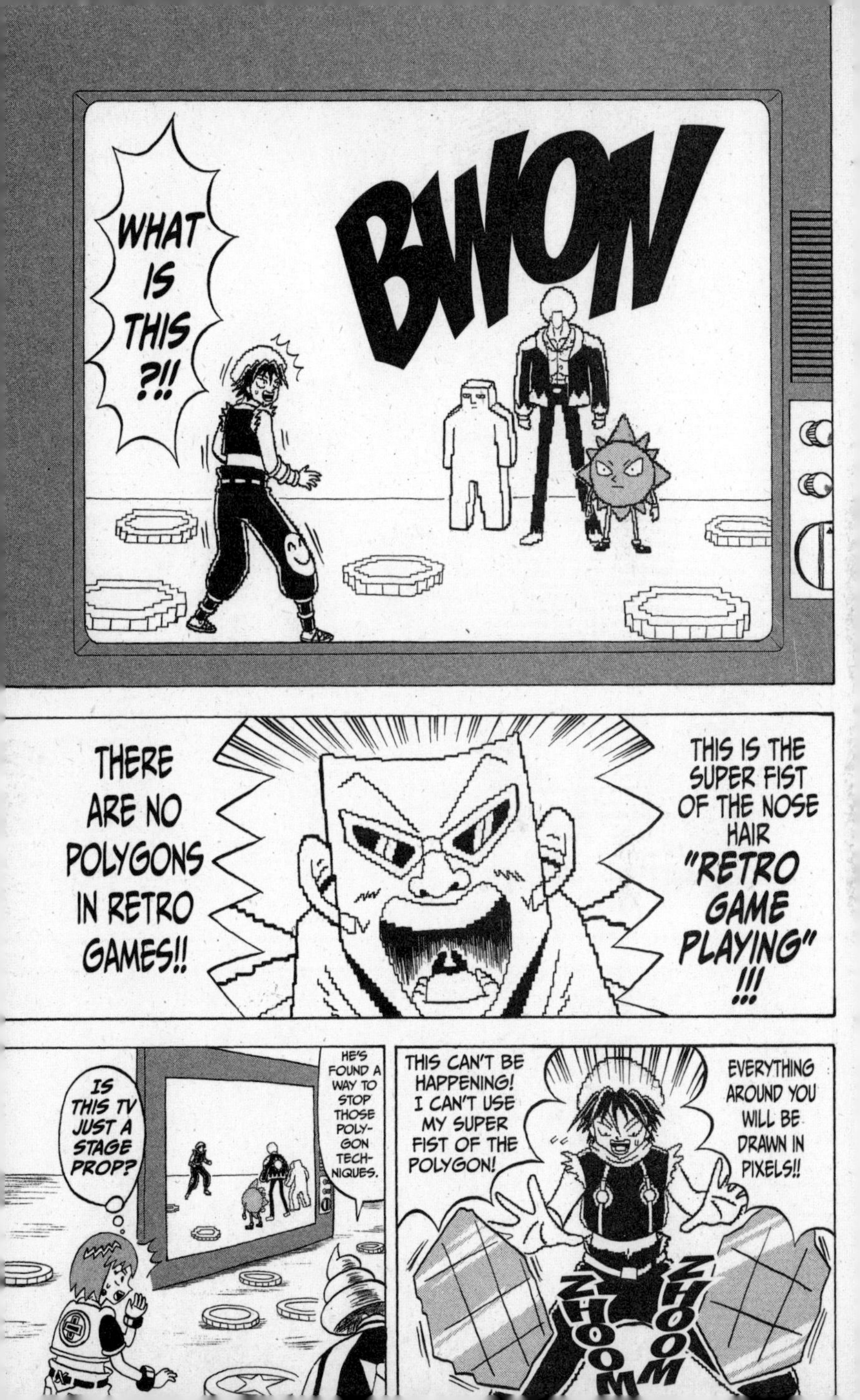
BWOW
WHAT IS THIS ?!!
THIS IS THE SUPER FIST OF THE NOSE HAIR "RETRO GAME PLAYING" !!!
THERE ARE NO POLYGONS IN RETRO GAMES!!
EVERYTHING AROUND YOU WILL BE DRAWN IN PIXELS!!
THIS CAN'T BE HAPPENING! I CAN'T USE MY SUPER FIST OF THE POLYGON!
ZHOOOM
ZHOOOM
HE'S FOUND A WAY TO STOP THOSE POLY-GON TECH-NIQUES.
IS THIS TV JUST A STAGE PROP?

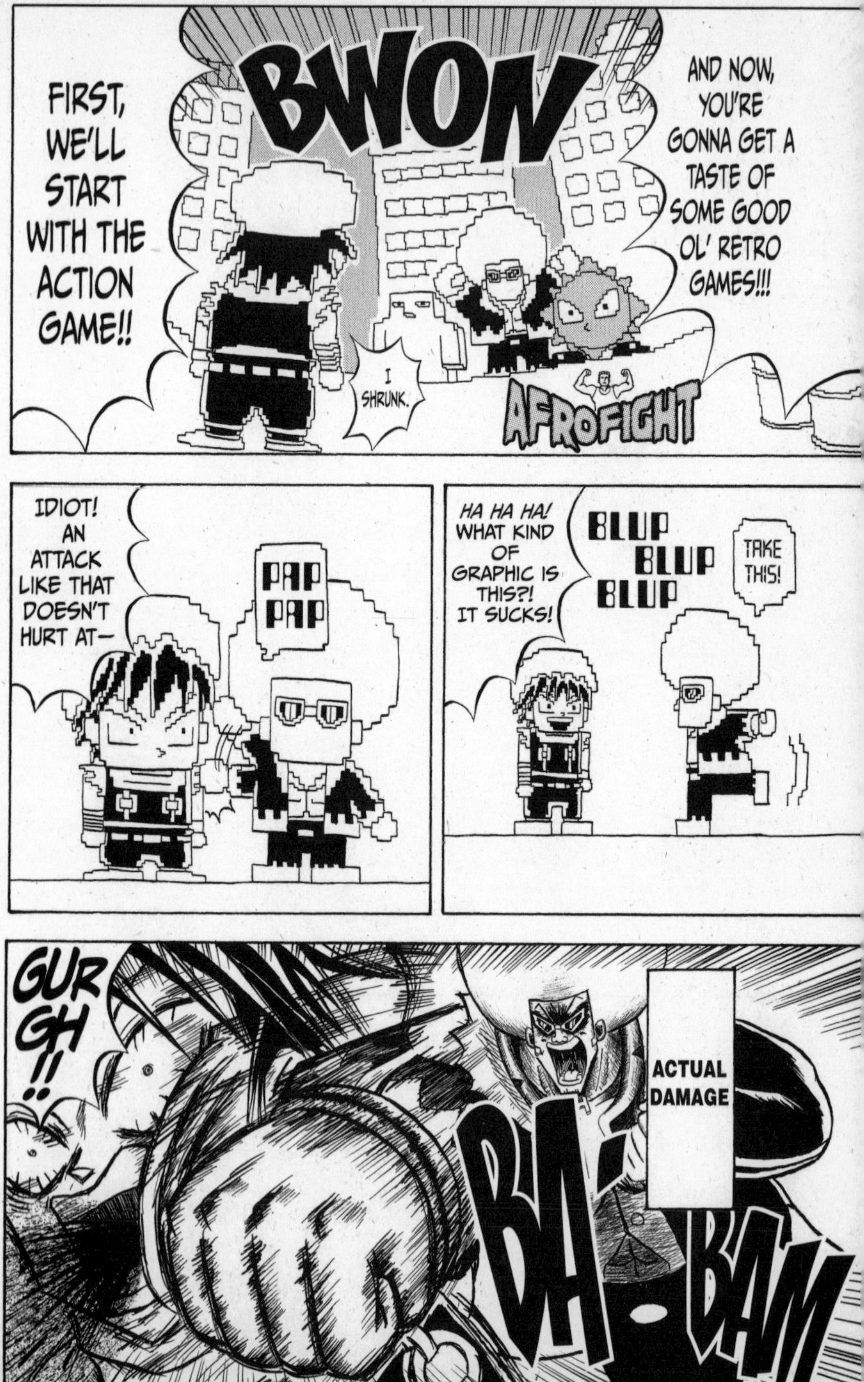
AND NOW, YOU'RE GONNA GET A TASTE OF SOME GOOD OL' RETRO GAMES!!!
BWON
FIRST, WE'LL START WITH THE ACTION GAME!!
AFROFIGHT
I SHRUNK.
TAKE THIS!
BLUP BLUP BLUP
HA HA HA! WHAT KIND OF GRAPHIC IS THIS?! IT SUCKS!
PAP PAP
IDIOT! AN ATTACK LIKE THAT DOESN'T HURT AT—
ACTUAL DAMAGE
BA-BAM
GURGH!!

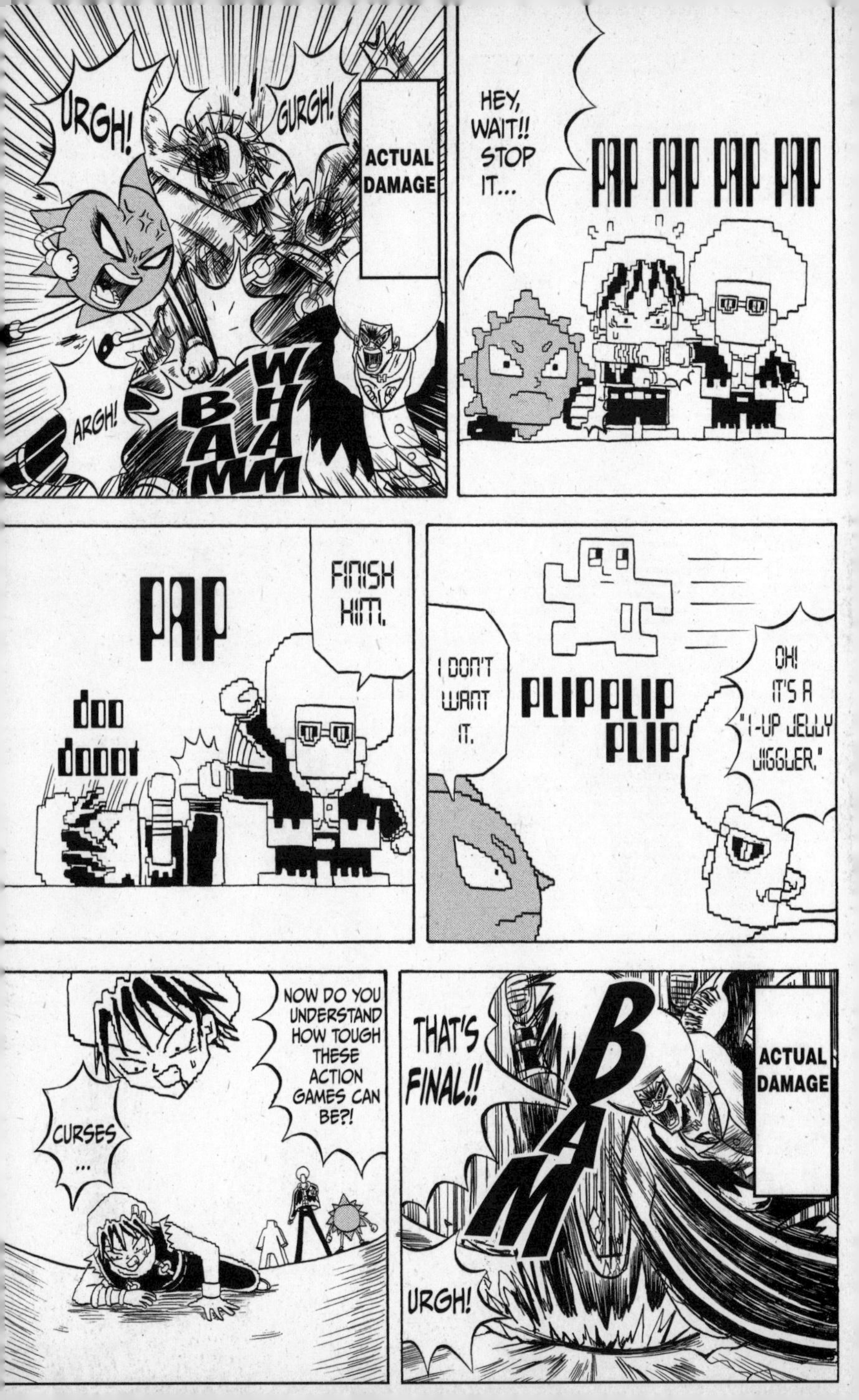
HEY, WAIT!! STOP IT...
PAP PAP PAP PAP
ACTUAL DAMAGE
GURGH!
URGH!
WHAM
BAMM
ARGH!
OH! IT'S A "1-UP JELLY JIGGLER."
PLIP PLIP PLIP
I DON'T WANT IT.
FINISH HIM.
PAP
doo dooot
ACTUAL DAMAGE
BAM
THAT'S FINAL!!
URGH!
NOW DO YOU UNDERSTAND HOW TOUGH THESE ACTION GAMES CAN BE?!
CURSES...

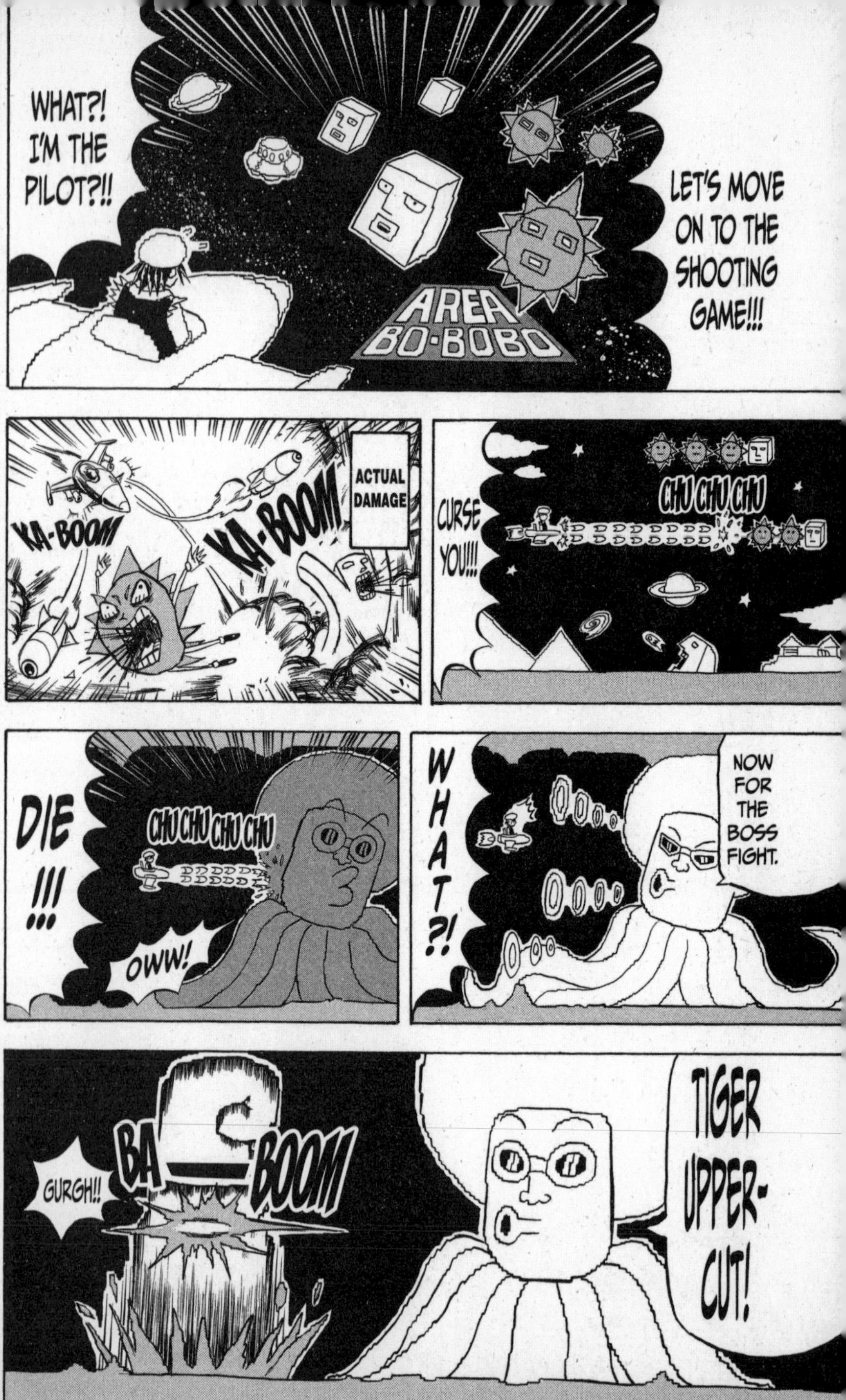
LET'S MOVE ON TO THE SHOOTING GAME!!!
AREA BO-BOBO
WHAT?! I'M THE PILOT?!!
CHU CHU CHU
CURSE YOU!!!
ACTUAL DAMAGE
KA-BOOM
KA-BOOM
NOW FOR THE BOSS FIGHT.
WHAT?!
CHU CHU CHU CHU
DIE!!!
OWW!
TIGER UPPER-CUT!
BA-BOOM
GURGH!!

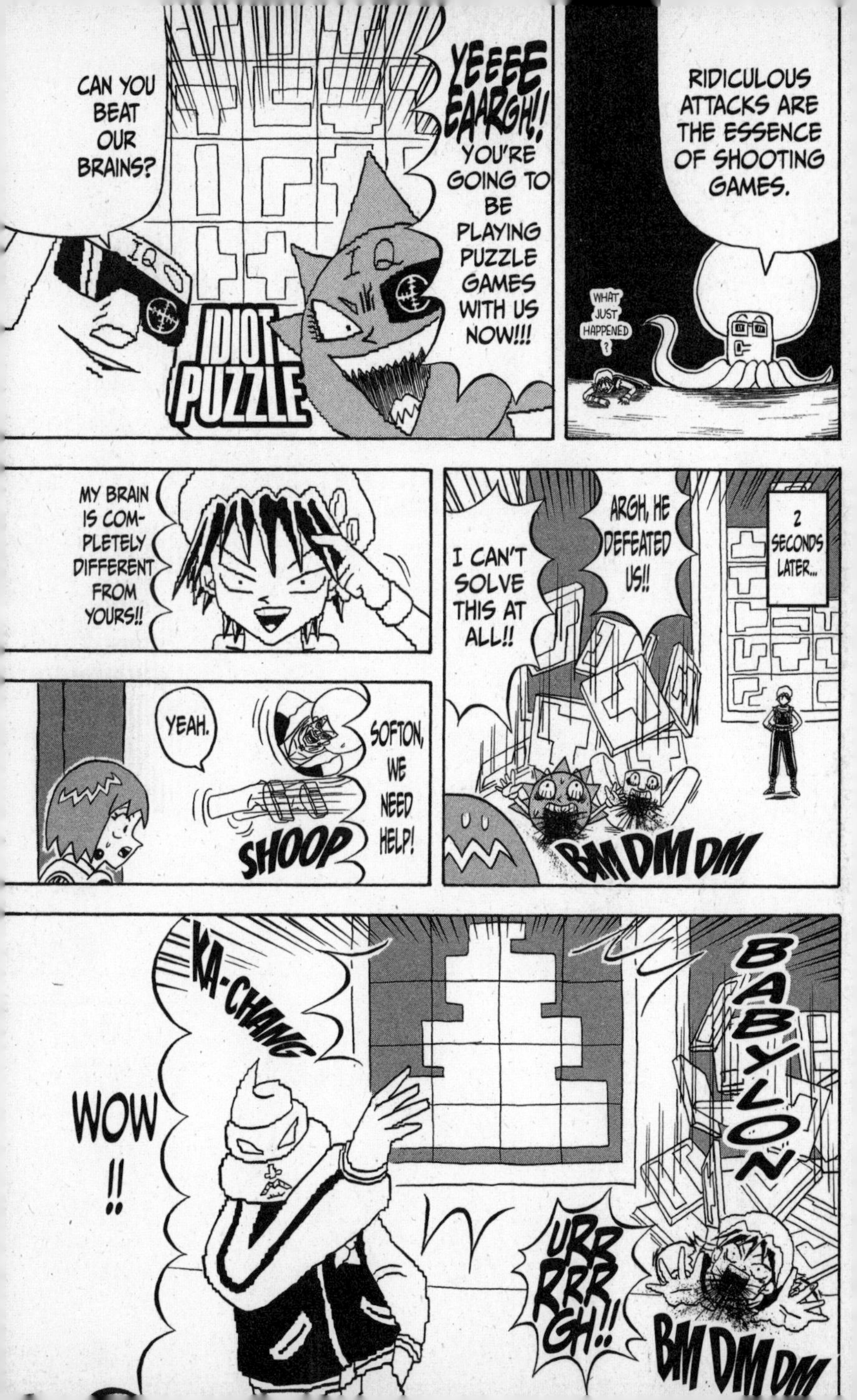
RIDICULOUS ATTACKS ARE THE ESSENCE OF SHOOTING GAMES.
WHAT JUST HAPPENED ?
YEEEE EAARGH!! YOU'RE GOING TO BE PLAYING PUZZLE GAMES WITH US NOW!!!
CAN YOU BEAT OUR BRAINS?
IQ
IDIOT PUZZLE
2 SECONDS LATER...
ARGH, HE DEFEATED US!!
I CAN'T SOLVE THIS AT ALL!!
BM DM DM
MY BRAIN IS COMPLETELY DIFFERENT FROM YOURS!!
SOFTON, WE NEED HELP!
YEAH.
SHOOP
BABYLON
KA-CHANG
WOW!!
URRRRRGH!!
BM DM DM

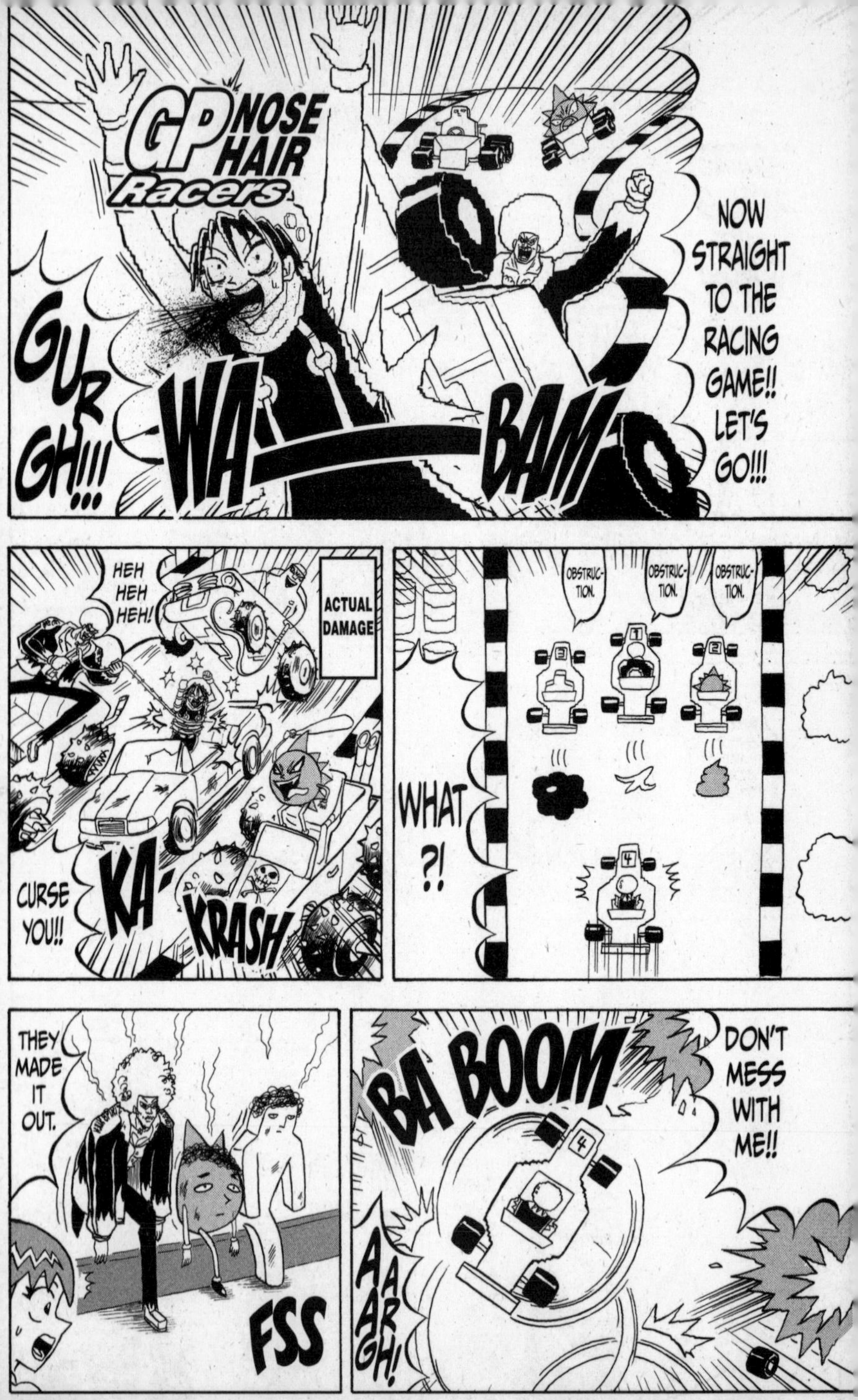
NOW STRAIGHT TO THE RACING GAME!! LET'S GO!!!
GP NOSE HAIR Racers
WA-BAM
GURGH!!!...
OBSTRUC-TION.
OBSTRUC-TION.
OBSTRUC-TION.
WHAT?!
ACTUAL DAMAGE
HEH HEH HEH!
KA-KRASH
CURSE YOU!!
DON'T MESS WITH ME!!
BA BOOM
AAARGH!
THEY MADE IT OUT.
FSS

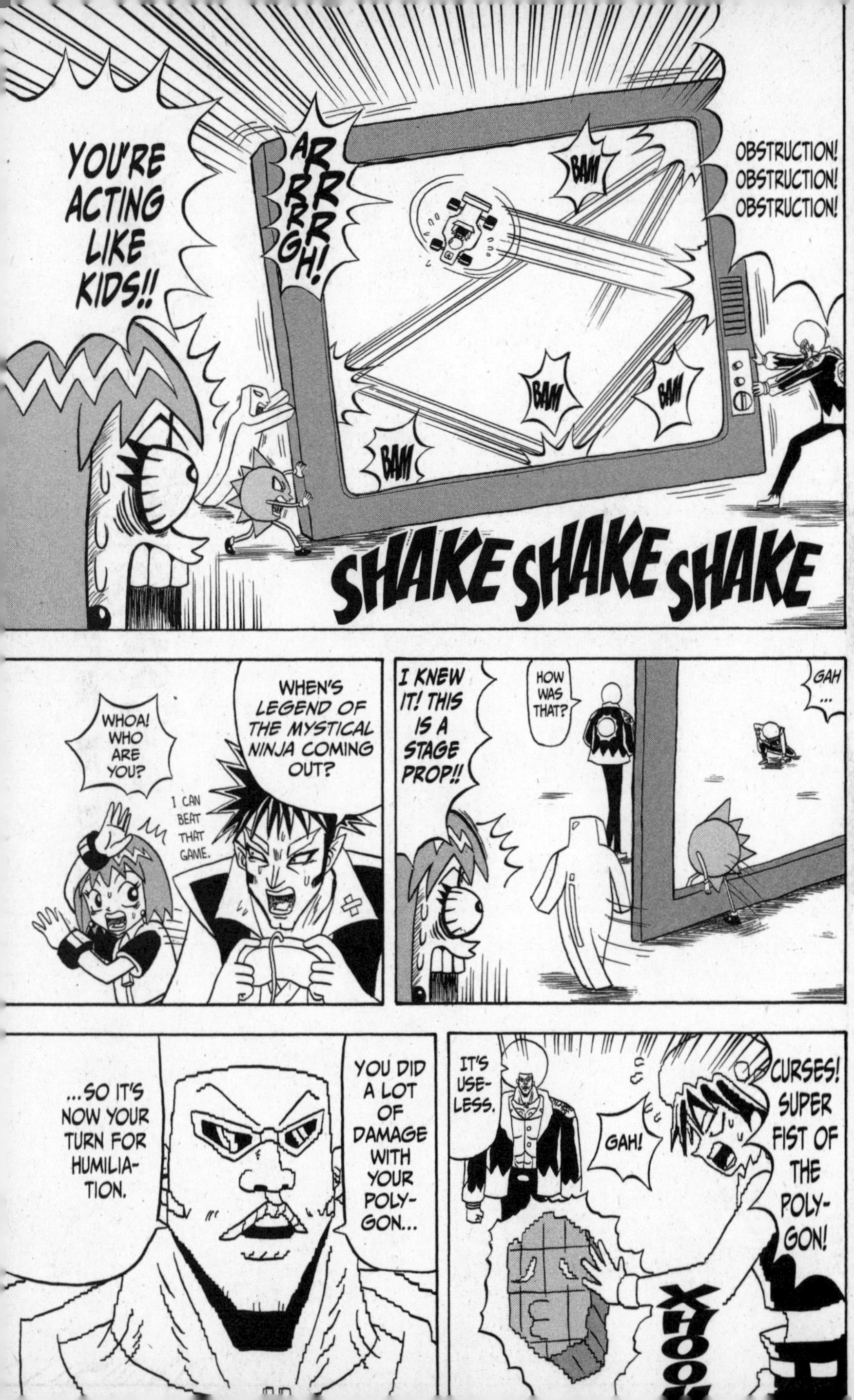
OBSTRUCTION! OBSTRUCTION! OBSTRUCTION!
BAM
ARRRRGH!
BAM
BAM
BAM
YOU'RE ACTING LIKE KIDS!!
SHAKE SHAKE SHAKE
GAH ...
HOW WAS THAT?
I KNEW IT! THIS IS A STAGE PROP!!
WHEN'S LEGEND OF THE MYSTICAL NINJA COMING OUT?
I CAN BEAT THAT GAME.
WHOA! WHO ARE YOU?
CURSES! SUPER FIST OF THE POLYGON!
GAH!
IT'S USE-LESS.
YOU DID A LOT OF DAMAGE WITH YOUR POLY-GON...
...SO IT'S NOW YOUR TURN FOR HUMILIA-TION.

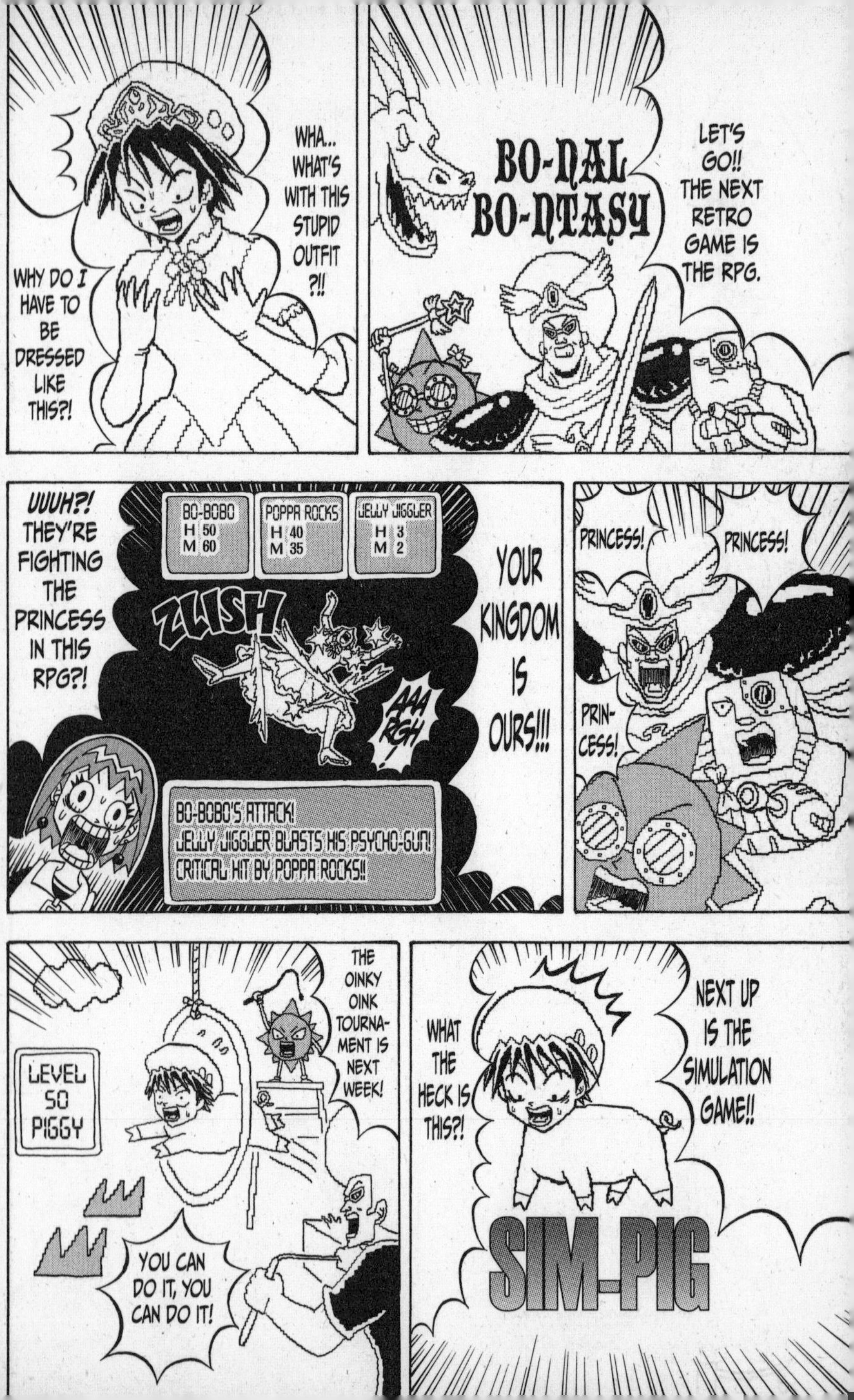
BO-NAL BO-NTASY
LET'S GO!! THE NEXT RETRO GAME IS THE RPG.
WHA... WHAT'S WITH THIS STUPID OUTFIT?!!
WHY DO I HAVE TO BE DRESSED LIKE THIS?!
PRINCESS!
PRINCESS!
PRIN-CESS!
YOUR KINGDOM IS OURS!!!
BO-BOBO H 50 M 60
POPPA ROCKS H 40 M 35
JELLY JIGGLER H 3 M 2
UUUH?! THEY'RE FIGHTING THE PRINCESS IN THIS RPG?!
ZLISH
AAARGH!
BO-BOBO'S ATTACK!
JELLY JIGGLER BLASTS HIS PSYCHO-GUN!
CRITICAL HIT BY POPPA ROCKS!!
NEXT UP IS THE SIMULATION GAME!!
WHAT THE HECK IS THIS?!
SIM-PIG
THE OINKY OINK TOURNAMENT IS NEXT WEEK!
LEVEL 50 PIGGY
YOU CAN DO IT, YOU CAN DO IT!

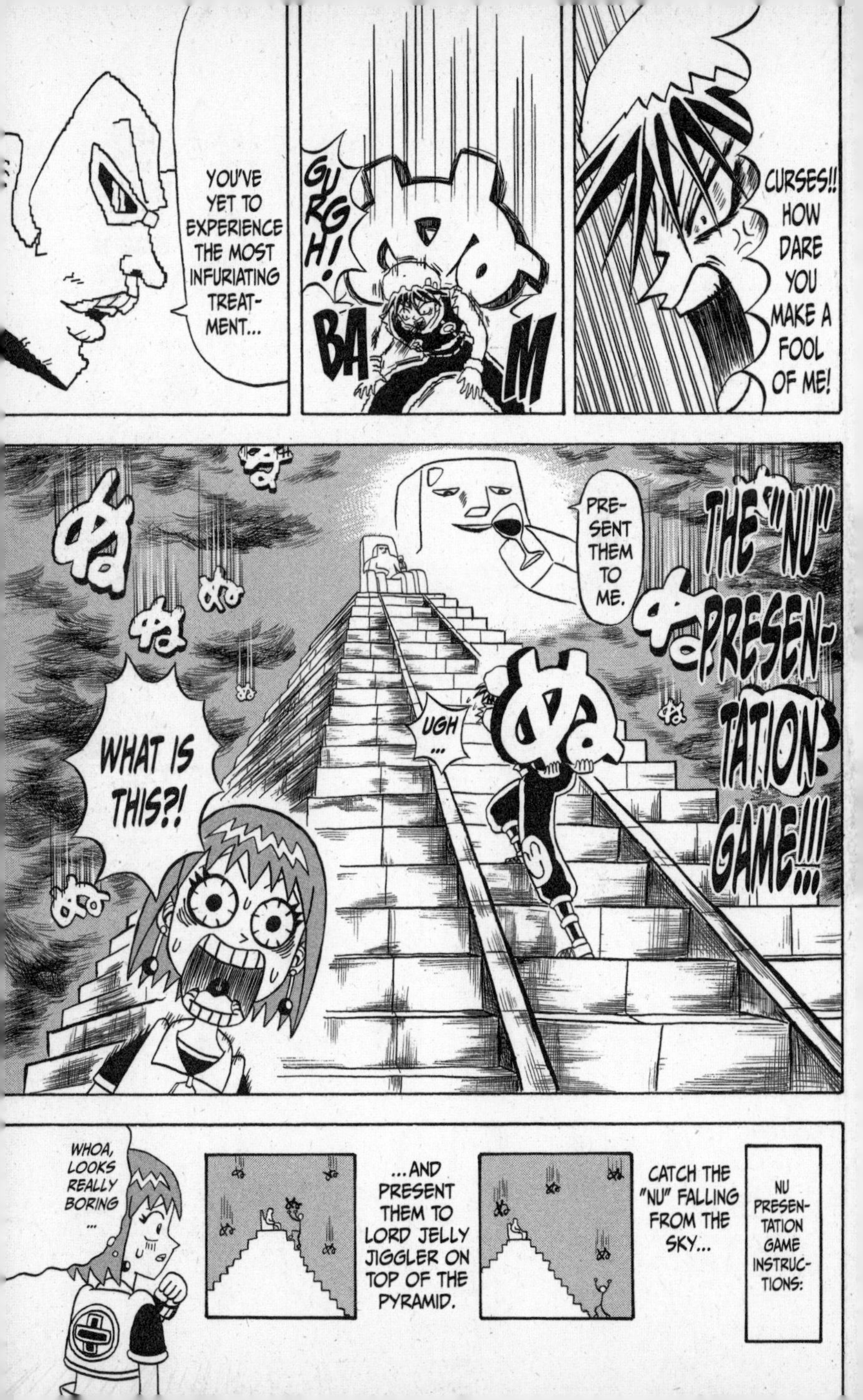
CURSES!! HOW DARE YOU MAKE A FOOL OF ME!
GURGH!
BAM
YOU'VE YET TO EXPERIENCE THE MOST INFURIATING TREAT-MENT...
THE "NU" PRESEN-TATION GAME!!!
PRE-SENT THEM TO ME.
UGH ...
WHAT IS THIS?!
NU PRESEN-TATION GAME INSTRUC-TIONS:
CATCH THE "NU" FALLING FROM THE SKY...
...AND PRESENT THEM TO LORD JELLY JIGGLER ON TOP OF THE PYRAMID.
WHOA, LOOKS REALLY BORING ...

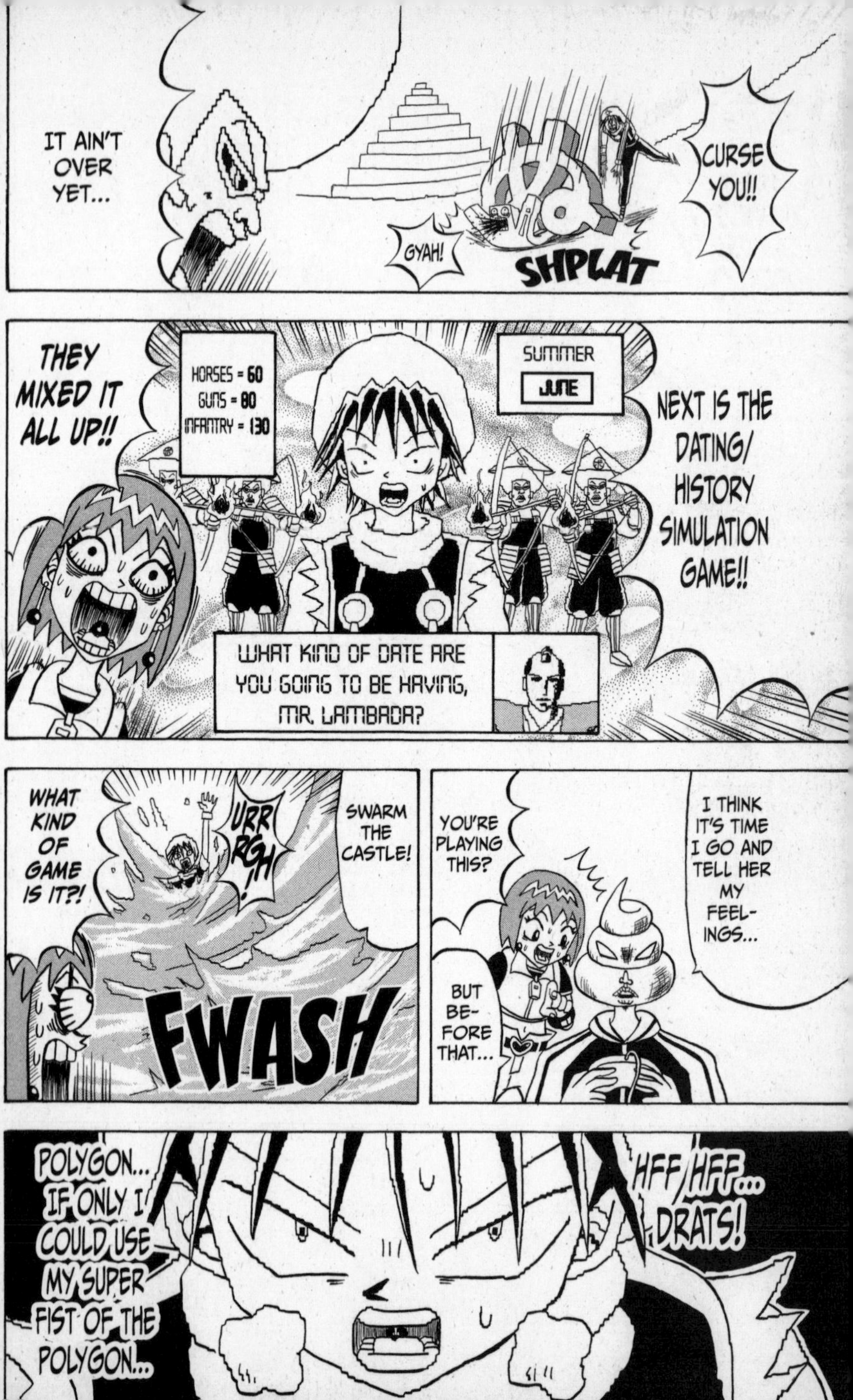
CURSE YOU!!
SHPLAT
GYAH!
IT AIN'T OVER YET...
NEXT IS THE DATING/HISTORY SIMULATION GAME!!
SUMMER
JUNE
HORSES = 60
GUNS = 80
INFANTRY = 130
WHAT KIND OF DATE ARE YOU GOING TO BE HAVING, MR. LAMBADA?
THEY MIXED IT ALL UP!!
I THINK IT'S TIME I GO AND TELL HER MY FEELINGS...
YOU'RE PLAYING THIS?
BUT BE-FORE THAT...
SWARM THE CASTLE!
URRRGH!
WHAT KIND OF GAME IS IT?!
FWASH
HFF HFF... DRATS!
POLYGON... IF ONLY I COULD USE MY SUPER FIST OF THE POLYGON...

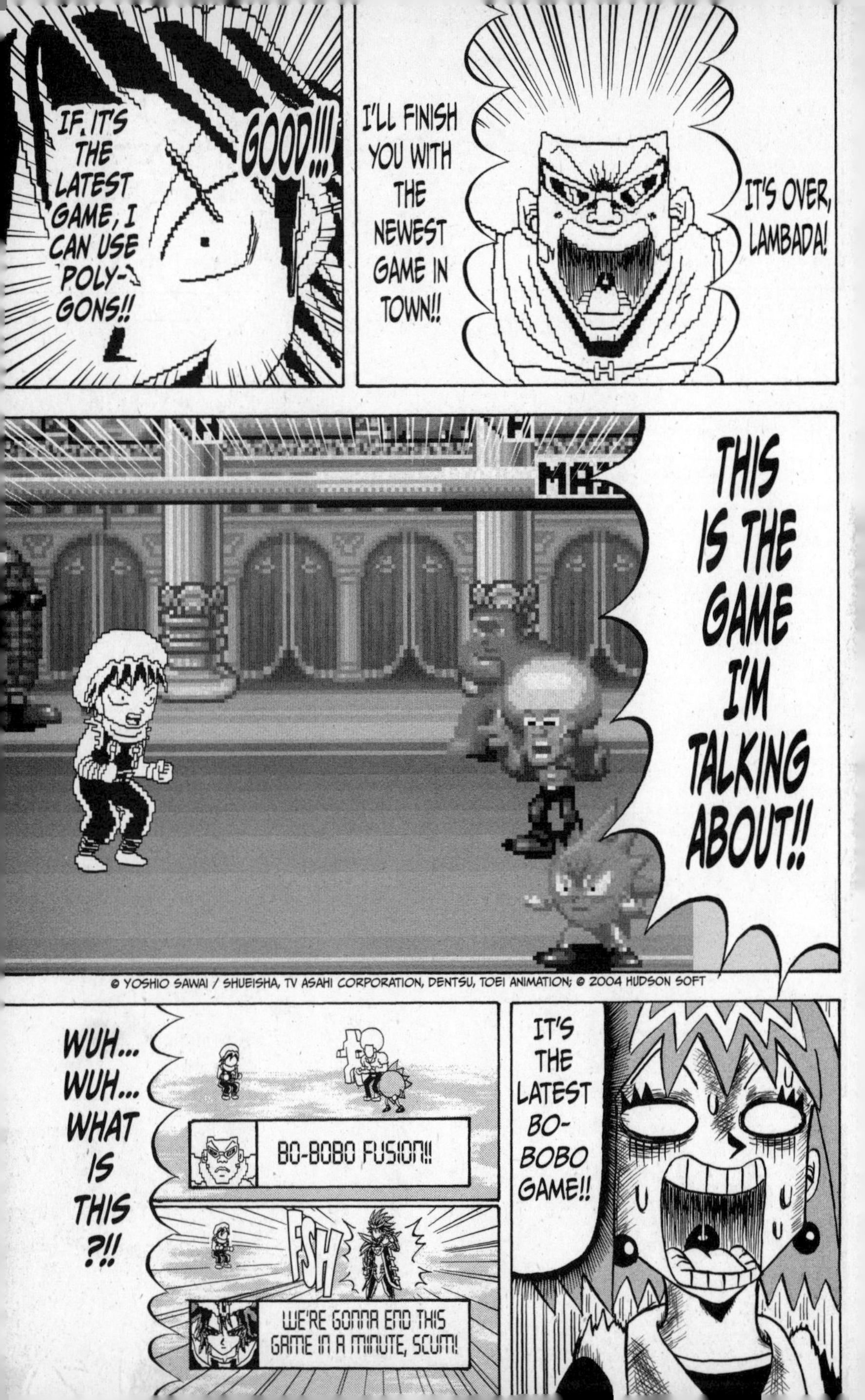
IT'S OVER, LAMBADA!
I'LL FINISH YOU WITH THE NEWEST GAME IN TOWN!!
GOOD!!!
IF IT'S THE LATEST GAME, I CAN USE POLYGONS!!
THIS IS THE GAME I'M TALKING ABOUT!!
MAX
IT'S THE LATEST BO-BOBO GAME!!
BO-BOBO FUSION!!
WUH... WUH... WHAT IS THIS?!!
FSH
WE'RE GONNA END THIS GAME IN A MINUTE, SCUM!

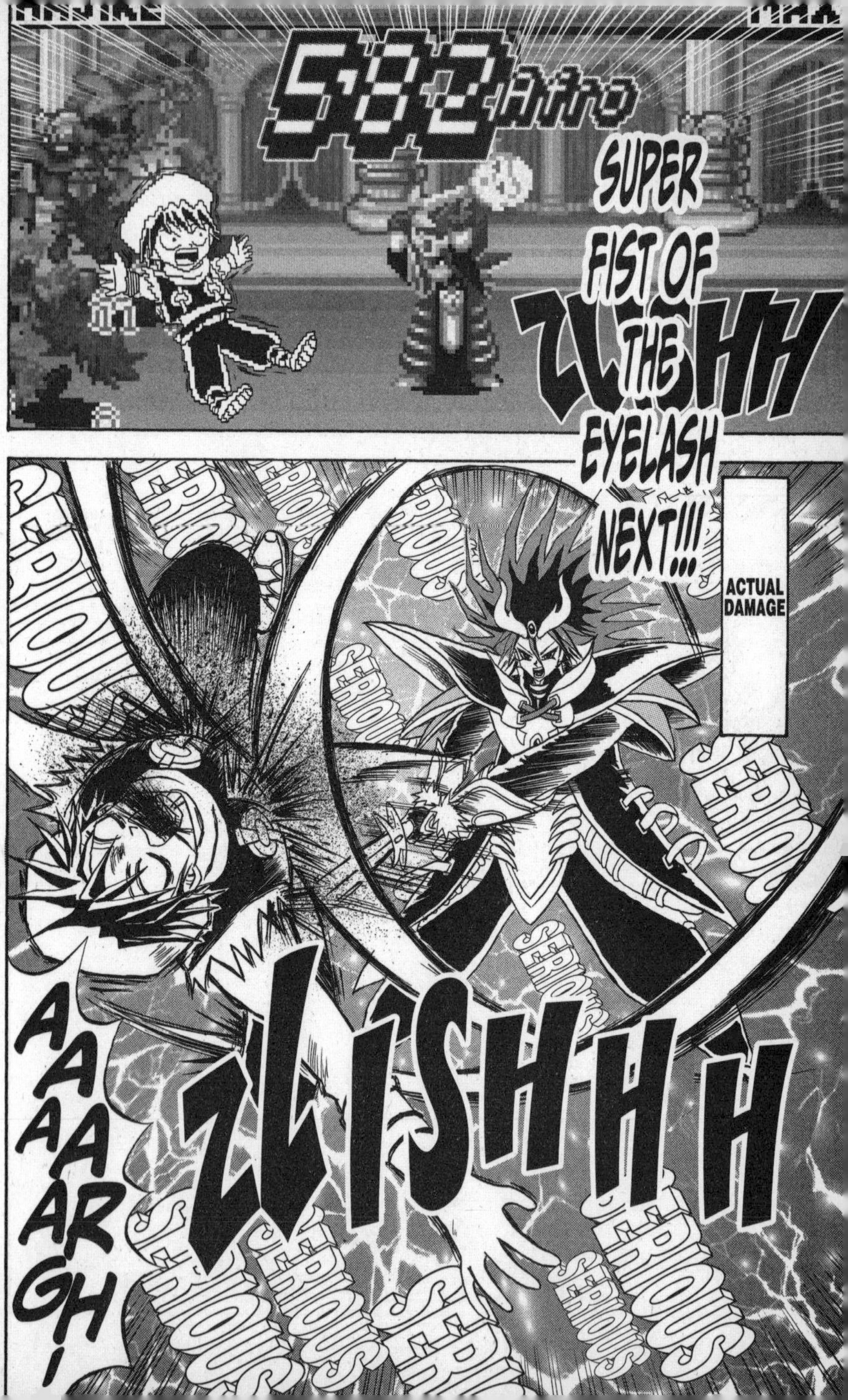
532
SUPER FIST OF THE EYELASH NEXT!!!
ZLISHH
ACTUAL DAMAGE
SERIOUS
ZLISHHH
AAAAARGH!

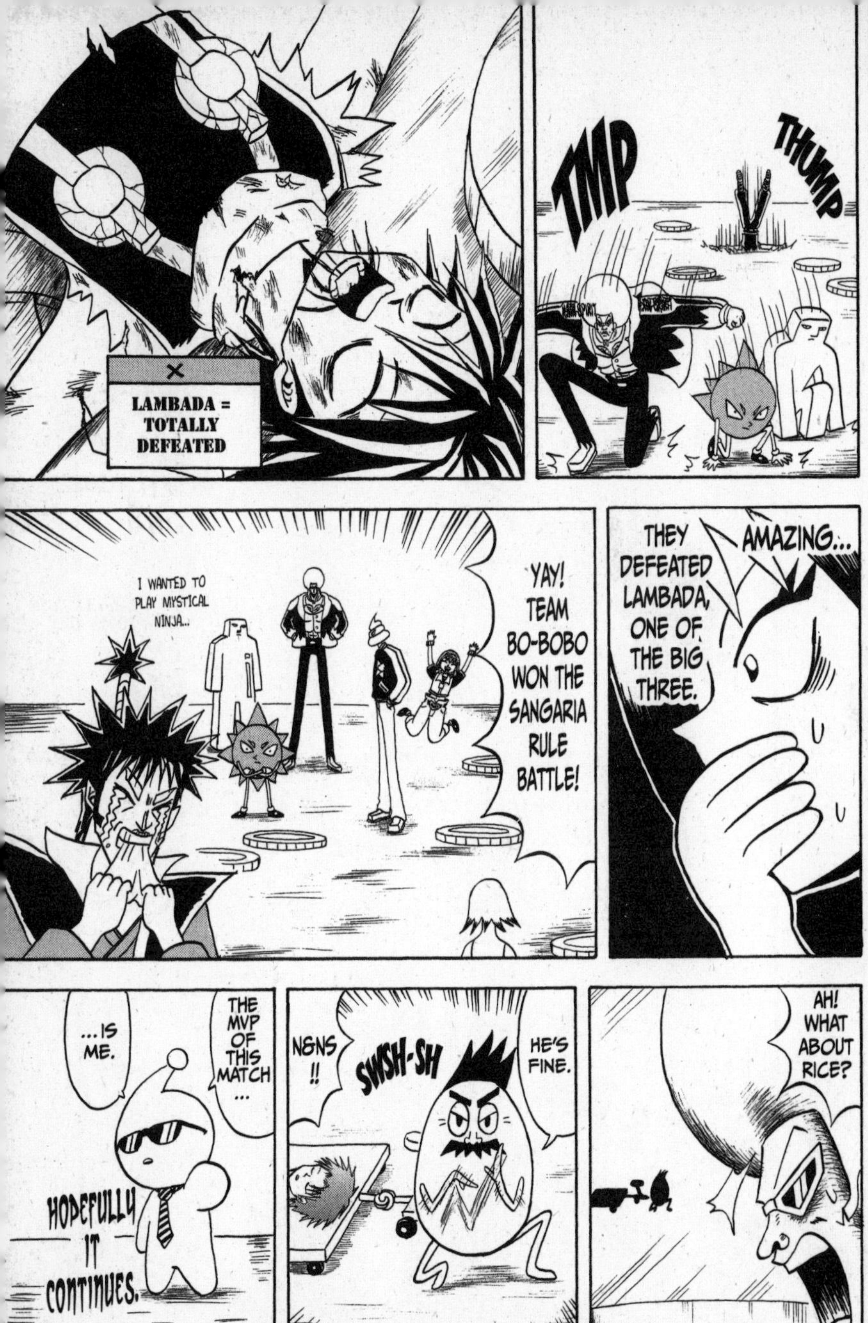
THUMP
TMP
LAMBADA = TOTALLY DEFEATED
AMAZING...
THEY DEFEATED LAMBADA, ONE OF THE BIG THREE.
YAY! TEAM BO-BOBO WON THE SANGARIA RULE BATTLE!
I WANTED TO PLAY MYSTICAL NINJA...
AH! WHAT ABOUT RICE?
HE'S FINE.
SWSH-SH
N&NS !!
THE MVP OF THIS MATCH ...
...IS ME.
HOPEFULLY IT CONTINUES.

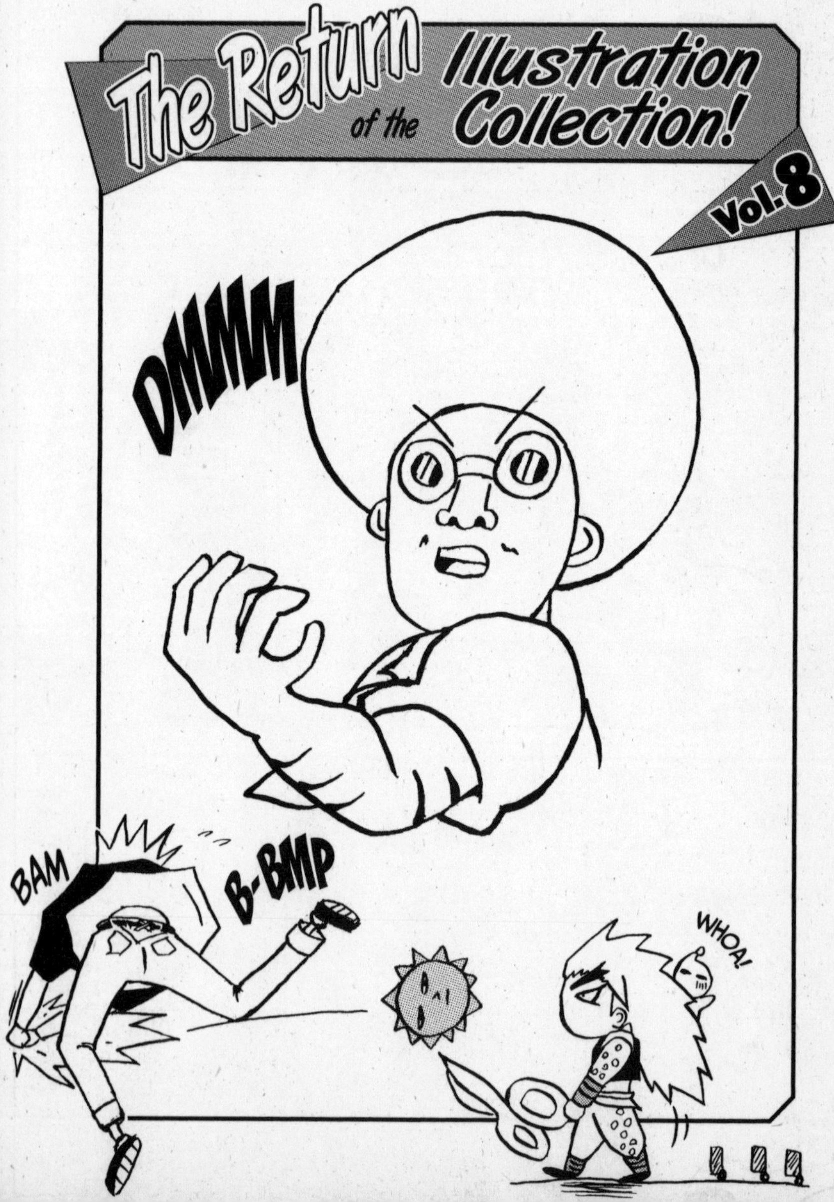
The Return of the Illustration Collection!
Vol. 8
DMMM
BAM
B-BMP
WHOA!

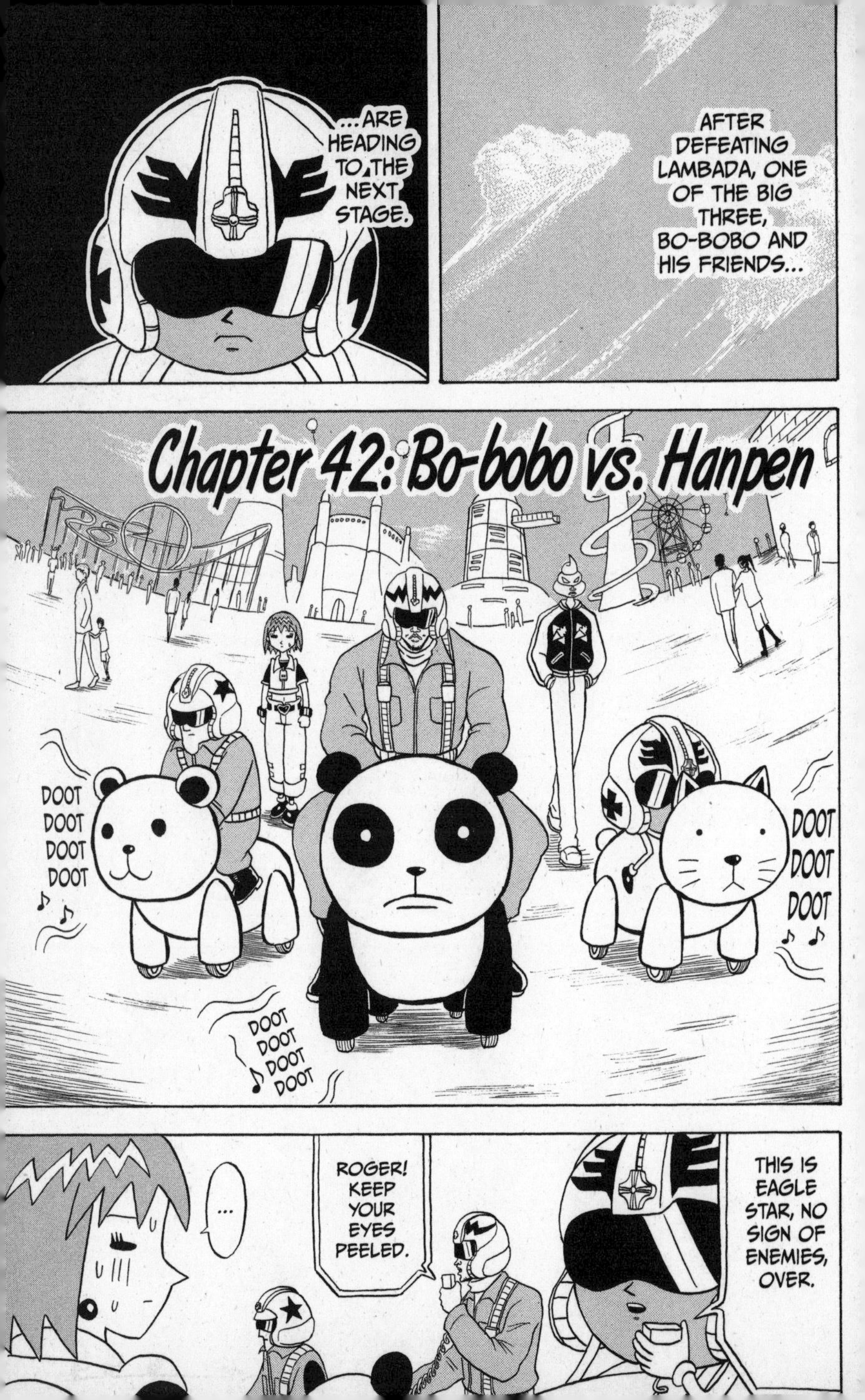
AFTER DEFEATING LAMBADA, ONE OF THE BIG THREE, BO-BOBO AND HIS FRIENDS...
...ARE HEADING TO THE NEXT STAGE.
Chapter 42: Bo-bobo vs. Hanpen
DOOT DOOT DOOT
DOOT DOOT DOOT DOOT
DOOT DOOT DOOT DOOT
THIS IS EAGLE STAR, NO SIGN OF ENEMIES, OVER.
ROGER! KEEP YOUR EYES PEELED.
...

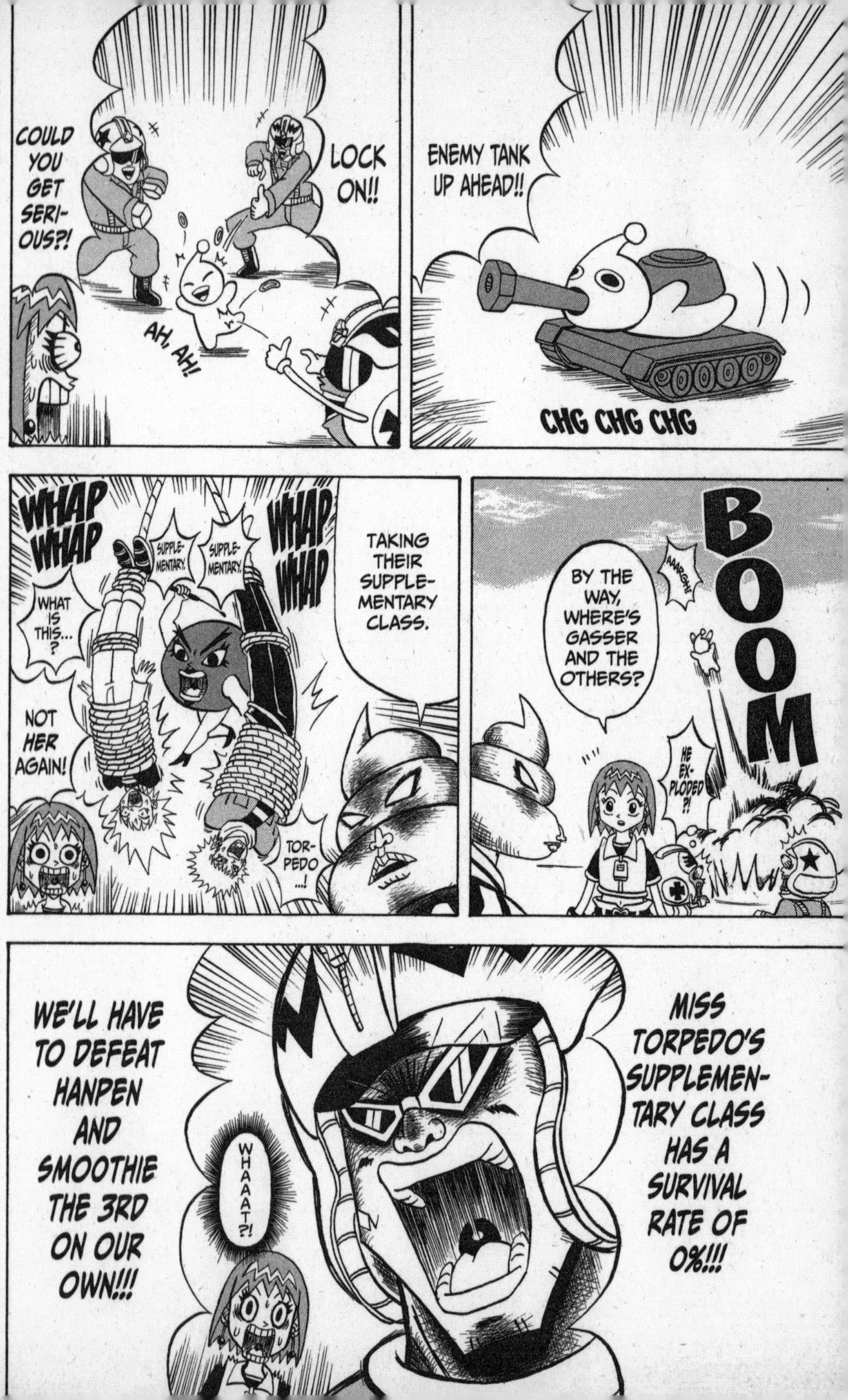
ENEMY TANK UP AHEAD!!
CHG CHG CHG
LOCK ON!!
COULD YOU GET SERI-OUS?!
AH, AH!
BOOM
AAARGH!
BY THE WAY, WHERE'S GASSER AND THE OTHERS?
HE EX-PLODED?!
TAKING THEIR SUPPLE-MENTARY CLASS.
WHAP WHAP
SUPPLE-MENTARY.
SUPPLE-MENTARY.
WHAP WHAP
WHAT IS THIS...?
NOT HER AGAIN!
TOR-PEDO...!
MISS TORPEDO'S SUPPLEMEN-TARY CLASS HAS A SURVIVAL RATE OF 0%!!!
WHAAAT?!
WE'LL HAVE TO DEFEAT HANPEN AND SMOOTHIE THE 3RD ON OUR OWN!!!

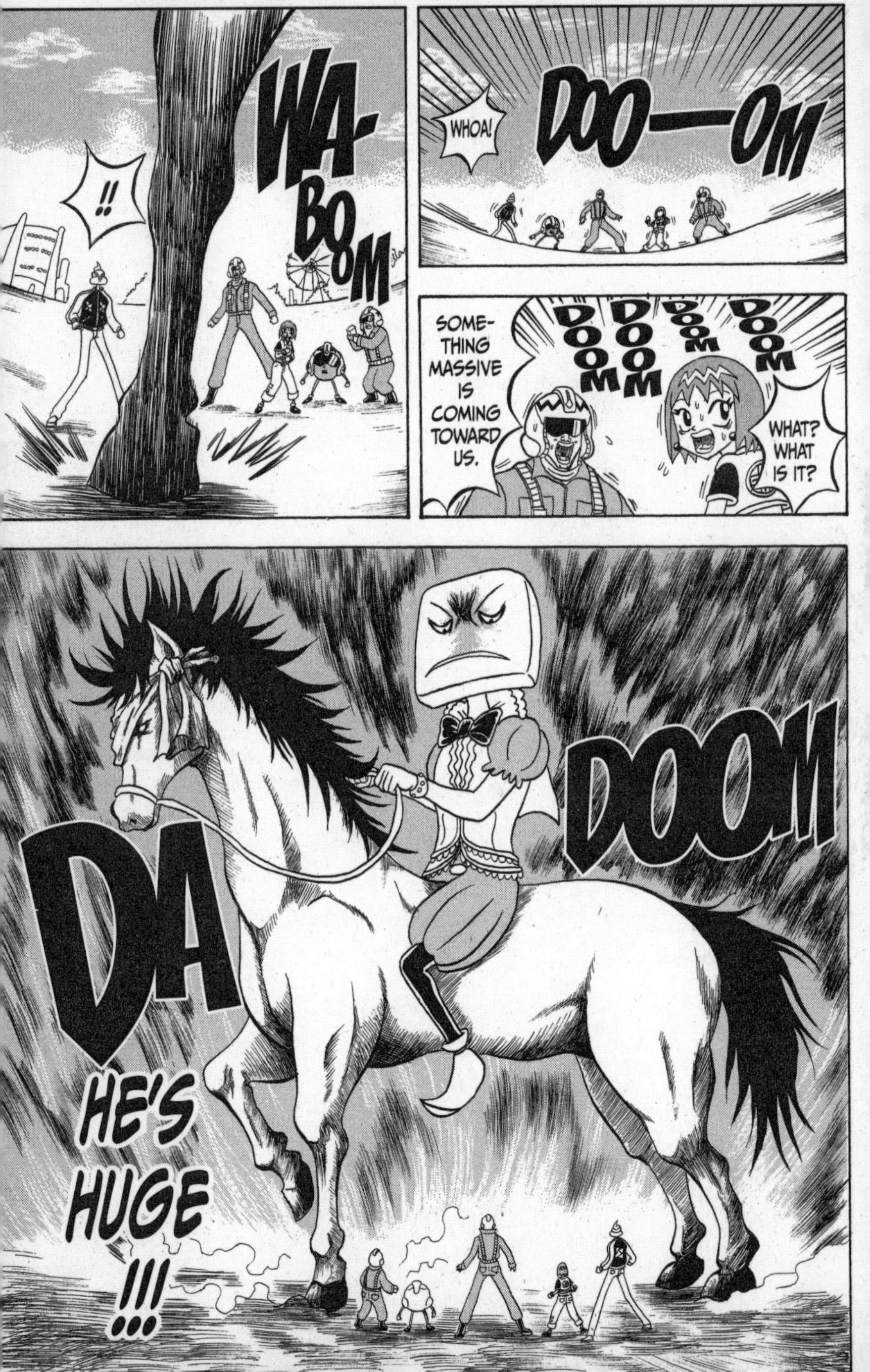
WHOA!
DOO—OM
DOOM DOOM DOOM DOOM
WHAT? WHAT IS IT?
SOME-THING MASSIVE IS COMING TOWARD US.
WA-BOOM
!!
DOOM
DA
HE'S HUGE!!!...

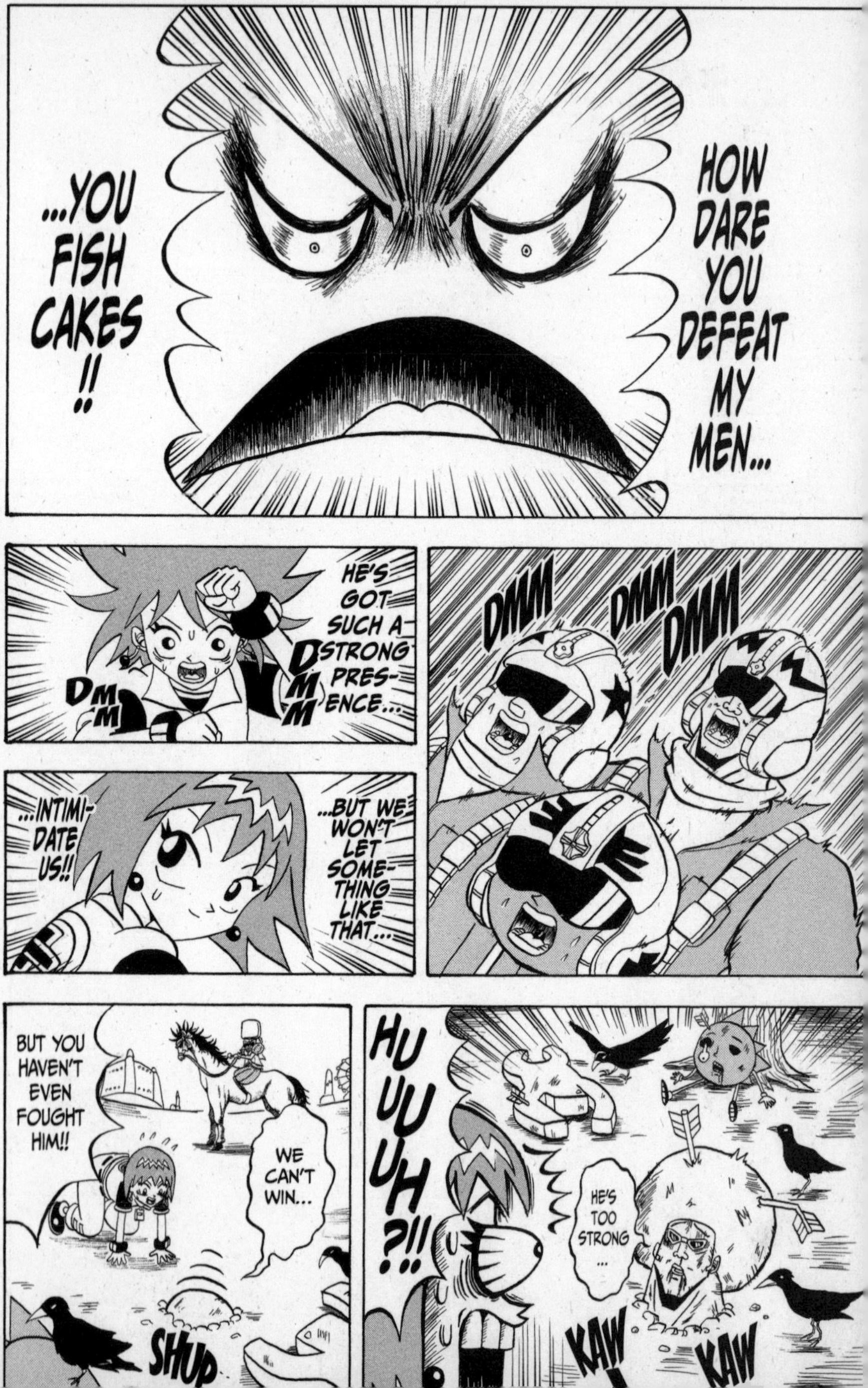
HOW DARE YOU DEFEAT MY MEN...
...YOU FISH CAKES!!
DMM
DMM
DMM
HE'S GOT SUCH A STRONG PRESENCE...
DMM
DMM
...BUT WE WON'T LET SOMETHING LIKE THAT...
...INTIMIDATE US!!
HE'S TOO STRONG ...
HUUUUH?!!
KAW
KAW
WE CAN'T WIN...
BUT YOU HAVEN'T EVEN FOUGHT HIM!!
SHUP

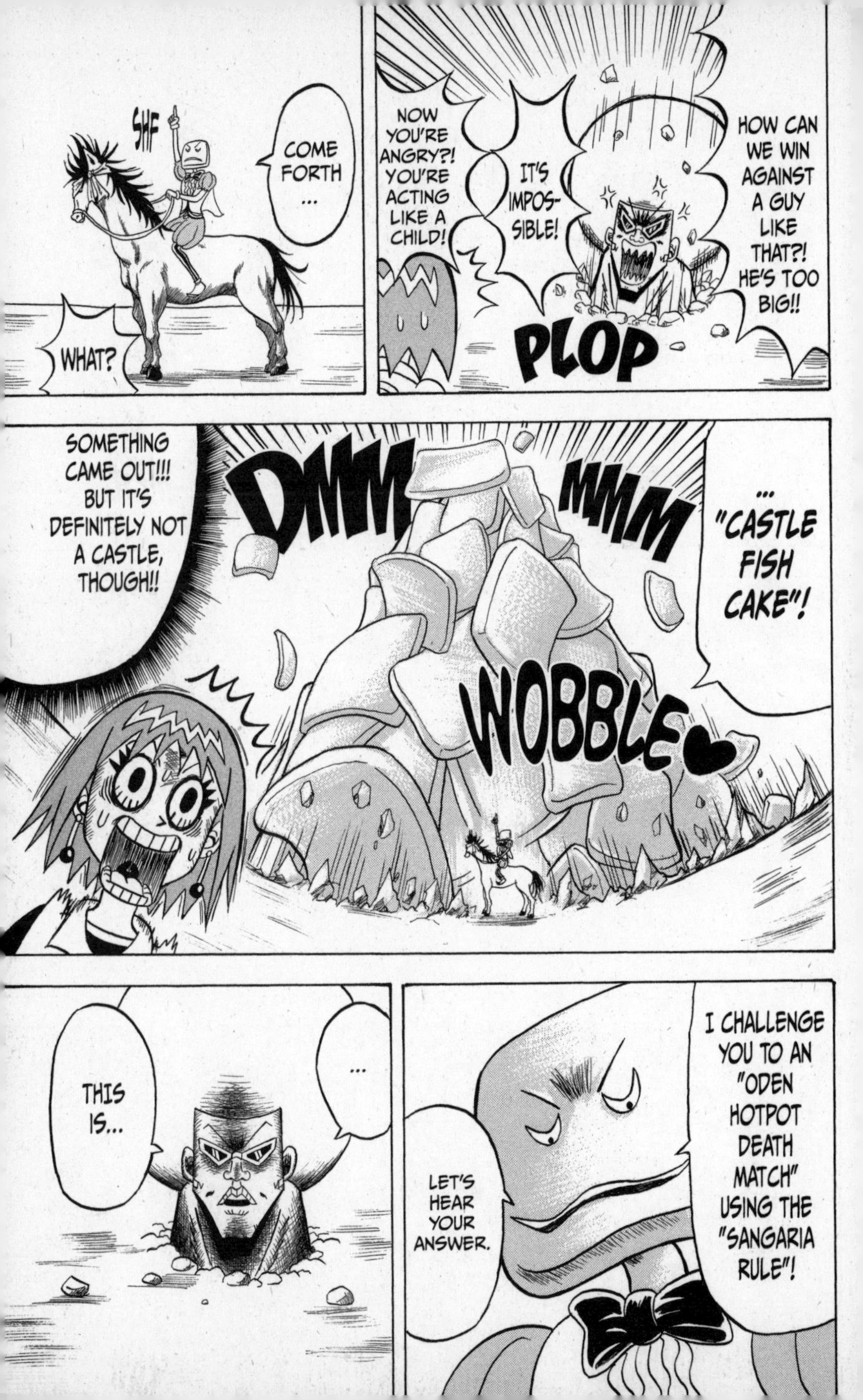
HOW CAN WE WIN AGAINST A GUY LIKE THAT?! HE'S TOO BIG!!
IT'S IMPOS-SIBLE!
NOW YOU'RE ANGRY?! YOU'RE ACTING LIKE A CHILD!
PLOP
COME FORTH ...
SHF
WHAT?
... "CASTLE FISH CAKE"!
MMM
DMM
WOBBLE
SOMETHING CAME OUT!!! BUT IT'S DEFINITELY NOT A CASTLE, THOUGH!!
I CHALLENGE YOU TO AN "ODEN HOTPOT DEATH MATCH" USING THE "SANGARIA RULE"!
LET'S HEAR YOUR ANSWER.
...
THIS IS...

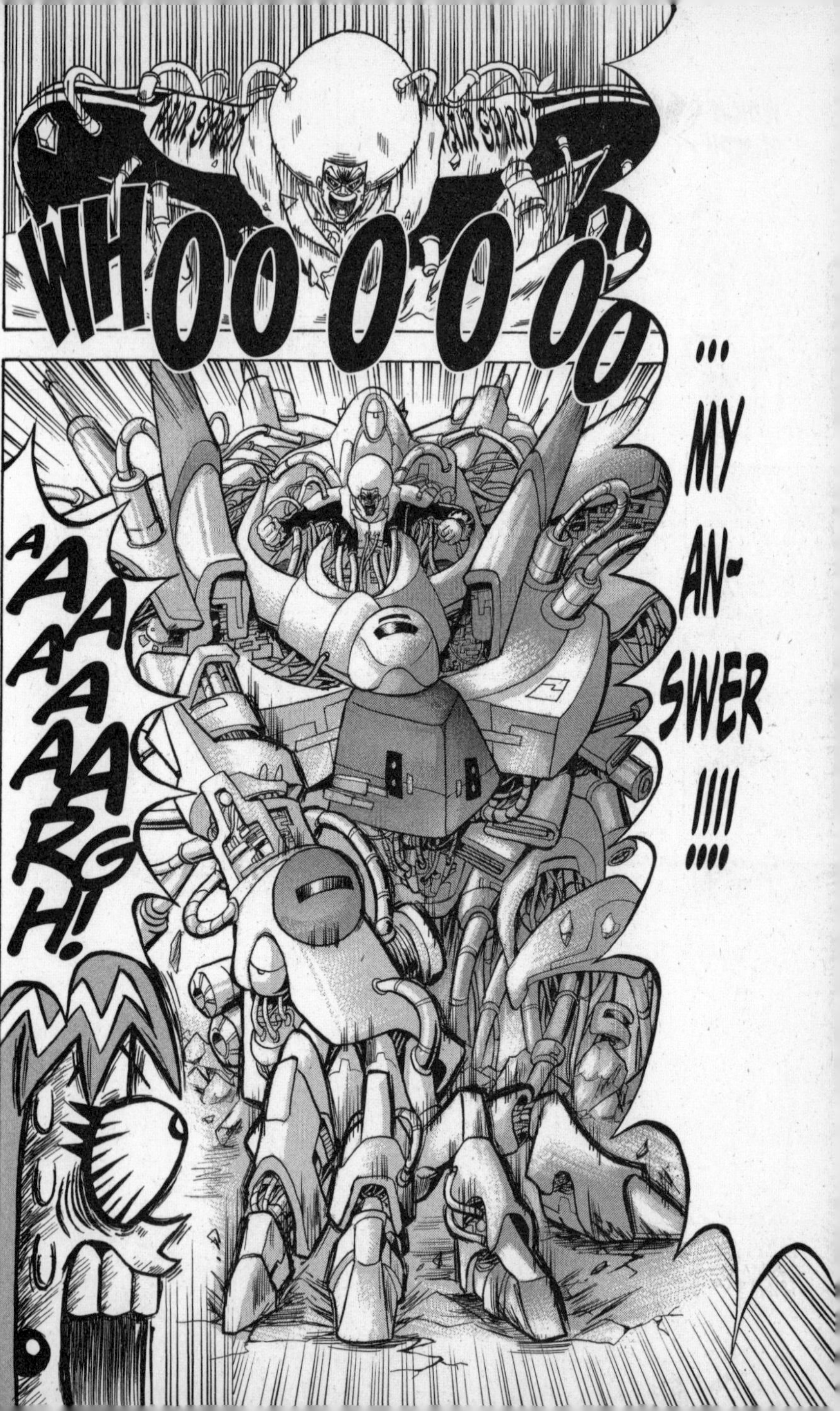
WHOOOOOO
...MY AN-SWER!!!!!
AAAAAAAARGH!

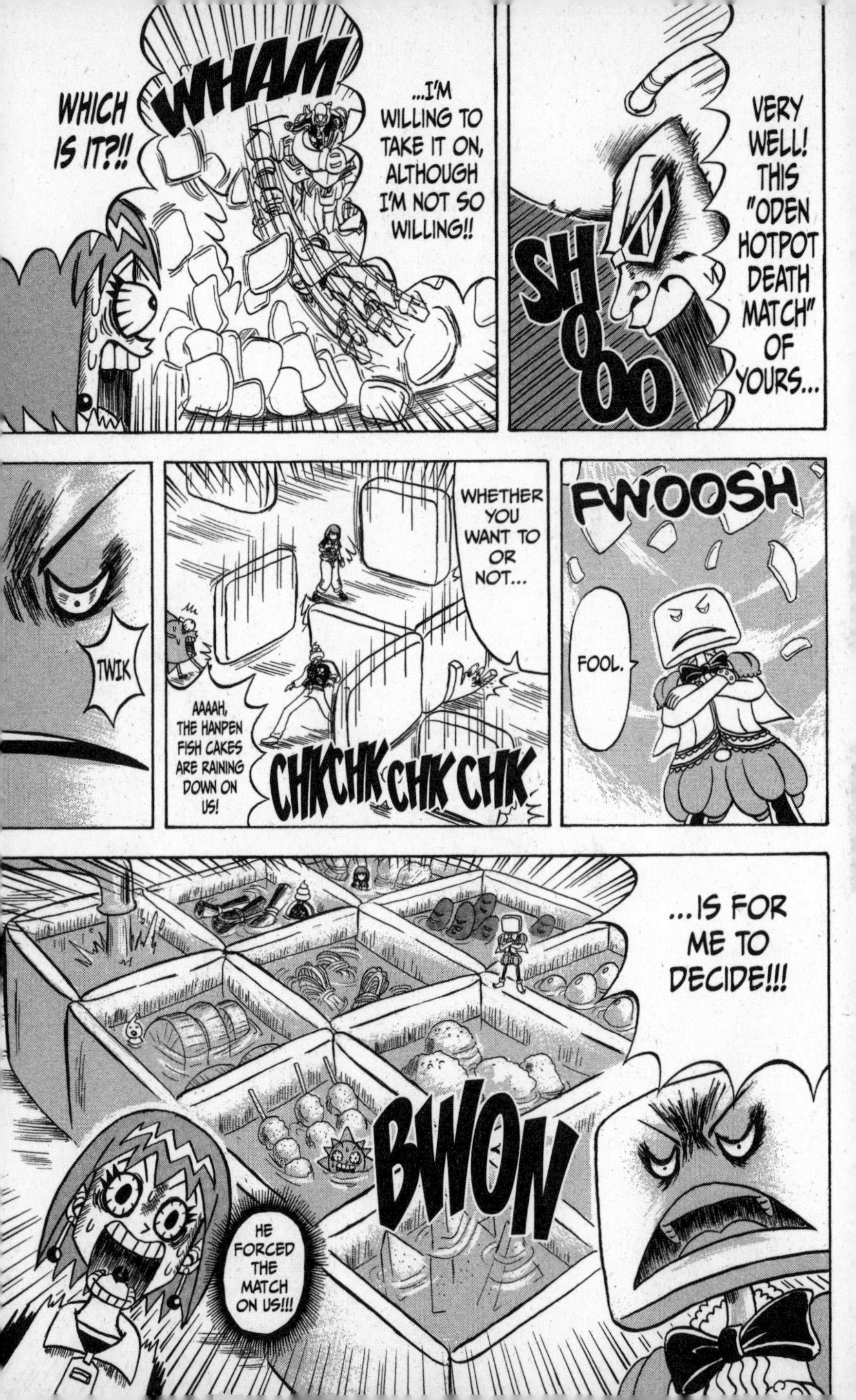
VERY WELL! THIS "ODEN HOTPOT DEATH MATCH" OF YOURS...
SHOOO
...I'M WILLING TO TAKE IT ON, ALTHOUGH I'M NOT SO WILLING!!
WHAM
WHICH IS IT?!!
FWOOSH
FOOL.
WHETHER YOU WANT TO OR NOT...
AAAAH, THE HANPEN FISH CAKES ARE RAINING DOWN ON US!
CHKCHK CHK CHK
TWIK
...IS FOR ME TO DECIDE!!!
BWON
HE FORCED THE MATCH ON US!!!

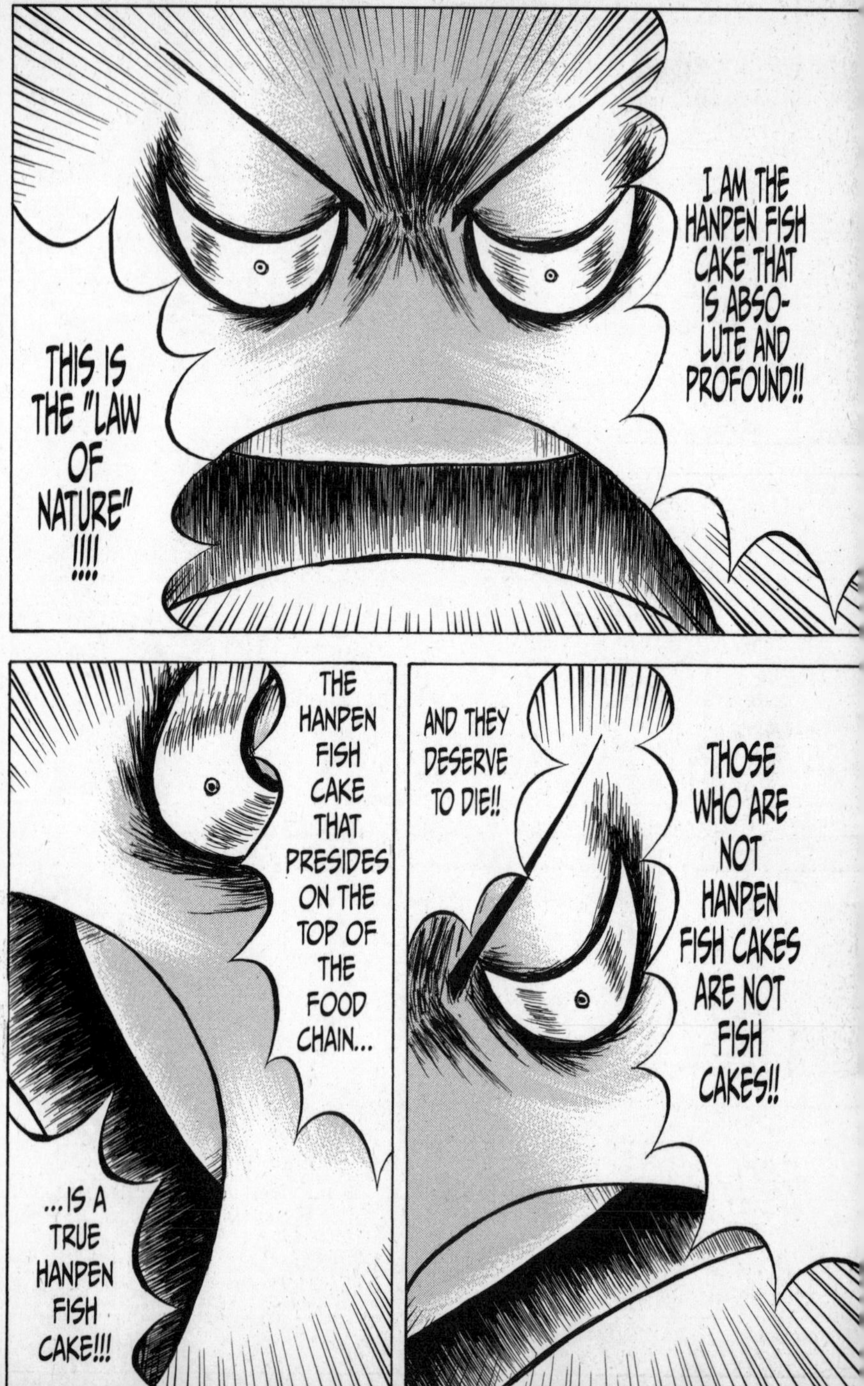
I AM THE HANPEN FISH CAKE THAT IS ABSOLUTE AND PROFOUND!!
THIS IS THE "LAW OF NATURE" !!!!
THOSE WHO ARE NOT HANPEN FISH CAKES ARE NOT FISH CAKES!!
AND THEY DESERVE TO DIE!!
THE HANPEN FISH CAKE THAT PRESIDES ON THE TOP OF THE FOOD CHAIN...
...IS A TRUE HANPEN FISH CAKE!!!

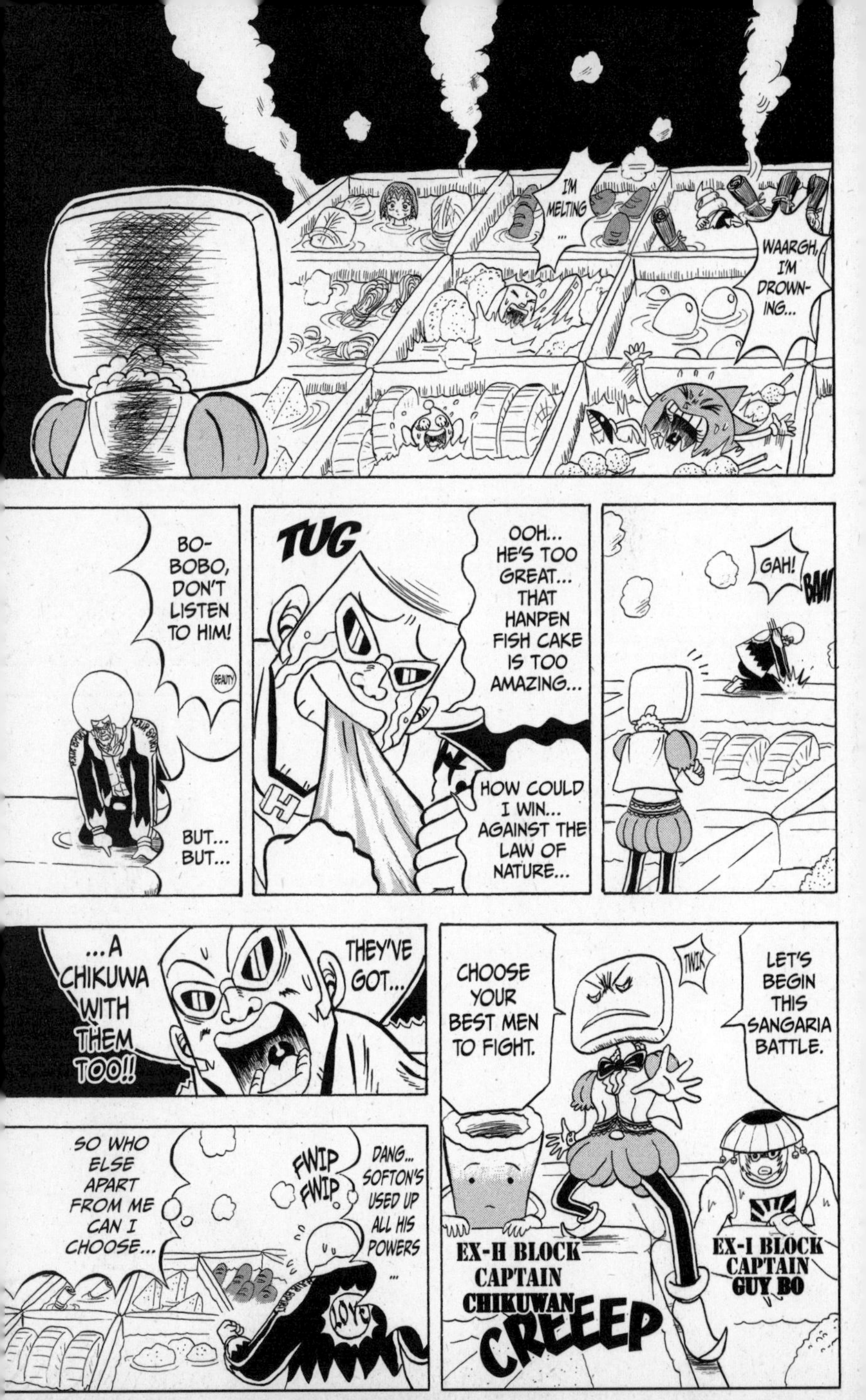
I'M MELTING...
WAARGH, I'M DROWNING...
GAH!
BAM
TUG
OOH... HE'S TOO GREAT... THAT HANPEN FISH CAKE IS TOO AMAZING...
HOW COULD I WIN... AGAINST THE LAW OF NATURE...
BO-BOBO, DON'T LISTEN TO HIM!
BEAUTY
BUT... BUT...
LET'S BEGIN THIS SANGARIA BATTLE.
TWIK
CHOOSE YOUR BEST MEN TO FIGHT.
EX-I BLOCK CAPTAIN GUY BO
EX-H BLOCK CAPTAIN CHIKUWAN
CREEEP
THEY'VE GOT...
...A CHIKUWA WITH THEM TOO!!
DANG... SOFTON'S USED UP ALL HIS POWERS...
FWIP FWIP
SO WHO ELSE APART FROM ME CAN I CHOOSE...
LOVE

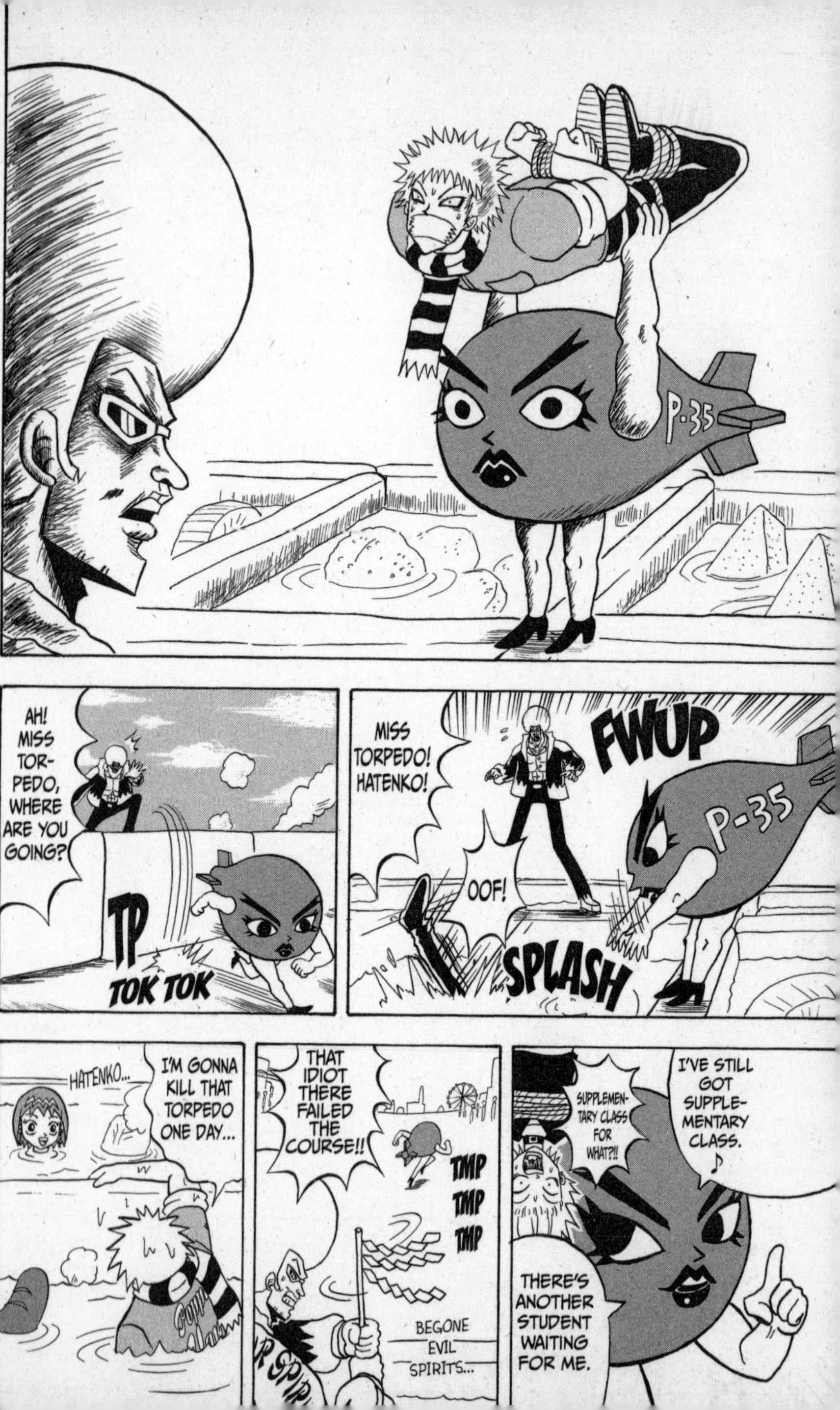
MISS TORPEDO! HATENKO!
FWUP
OOF!
SPLASH
AH! MISS TOR-PEDO, WHERE ARE YOU GOING?
TP
TOK TOK
I'VE STILL GOT SUPPLE-MENTARY CLASS. ♪
SUPPLEMEN-TARY CLASS FOR WHAT?!!
THERE'S ANOTHER STUDENT WAITING FOR ME.
THAT IDIOT THERE FAILED THE COURSE!!
TMP TMP TMP
BEGONE EVIL SPIRITS...
I'M GONNA KILL THAT TORPEDO ONE DAY...
HATENKO...

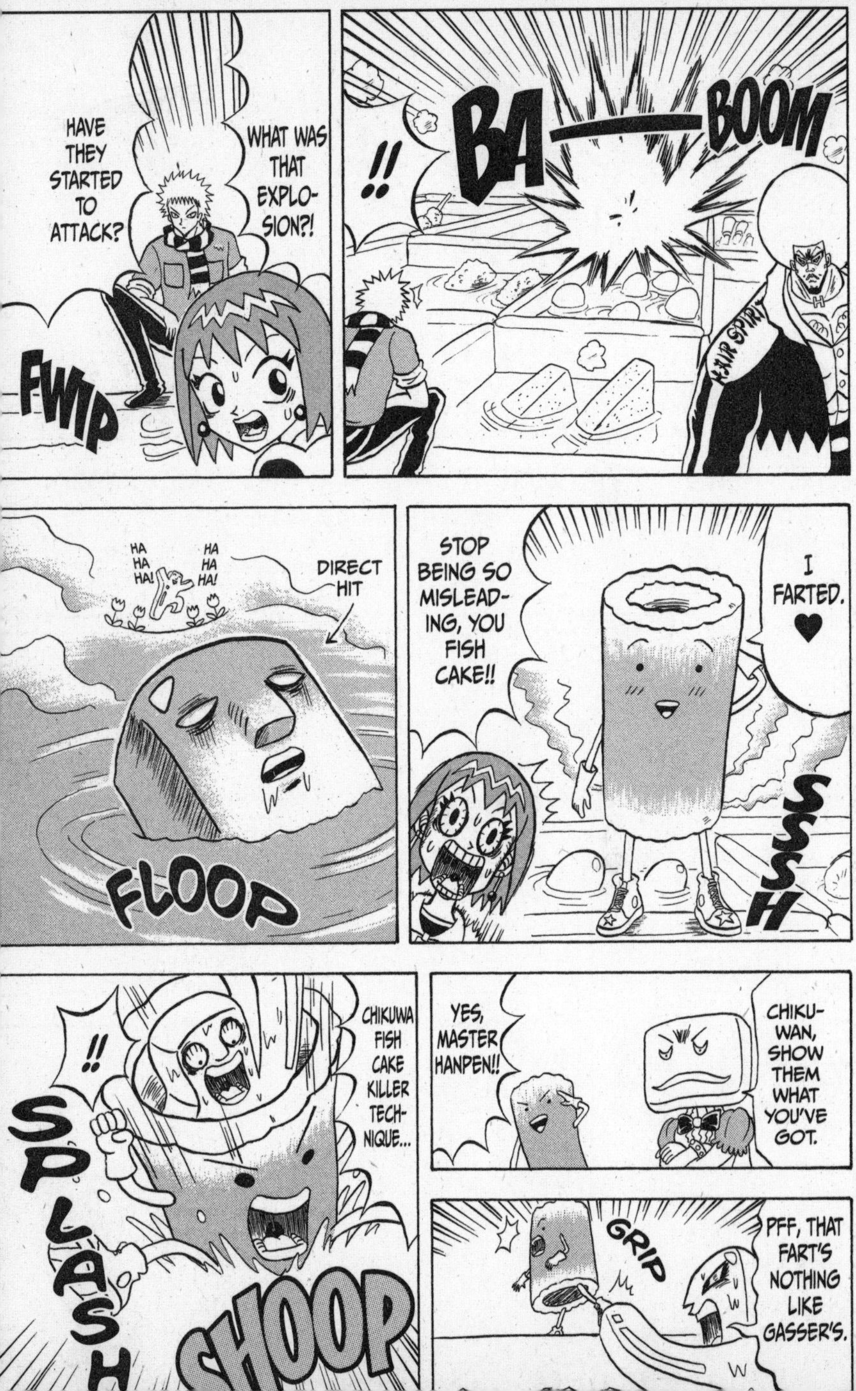

!!
BA——BOOM
HAIR SPIRIT
WHAT WAS THAT EXPLOSION?!
HAVE THEY STARTED TO ATTACK?
FWIP
I FARTED. ♥
STOP BEING SO MISLEADING, YOU FISH CAKE!!
SSSH
DIRECT HIT
HA HA HA!
HA HA HA!
FLOOP
CHIKUWAN, SHOW THEM WHAT YOU'VE GOT.
YES, MASTER HANPEN!!
PFF, THAT FART'S NOTHING LIKE GASSER'S.
GRIP
CHIKUWA FISH CAKE KILLER TECHNIQUE...
!!
SPLASH
SHOOP

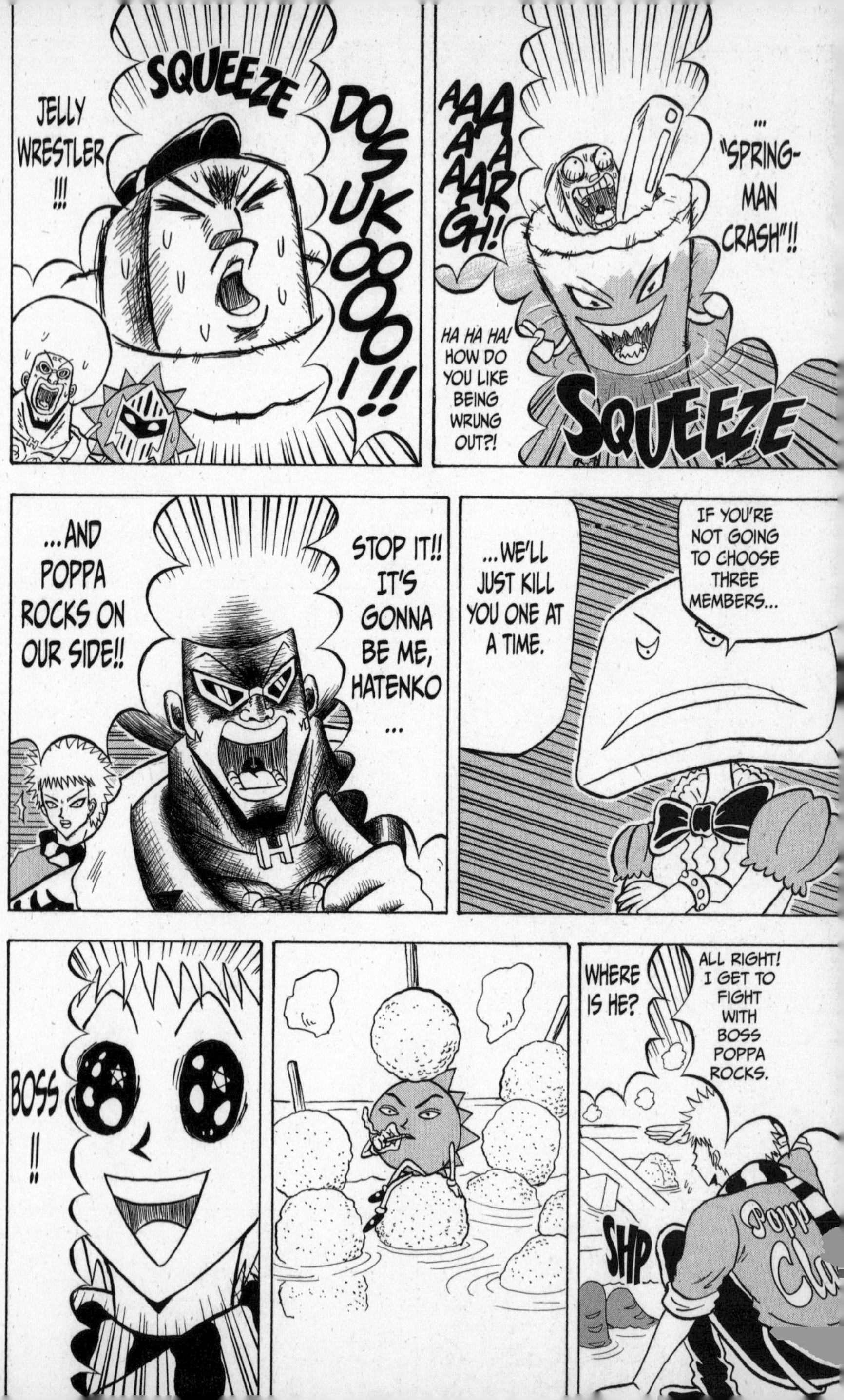

..."SPRING-MAN CRASH"!!
AAAAAAARGH!
HA HA HA! HOW DO YOU LIKE BEING WRUNG OUT?!
SQUEEZE
SQUEEZE
DOSUKOOOOO!!
JELLY WRESTLER!!!
IF YOU'RE NOT GOING TO CHOOSE THREE MEMBERS...
...WE'LL JUST KILL YOU ONE AT A TIME.
STOP IT!! IT'S GONNA BE ME, HATENKO...
...AND POPPA ROCKS ON OUR SIDE!!
ALL RIGHT! I GET TO FIGHT WITH BOSS POPPA ROCKS.
WHERE IS HE?
SHP
BOSS!!

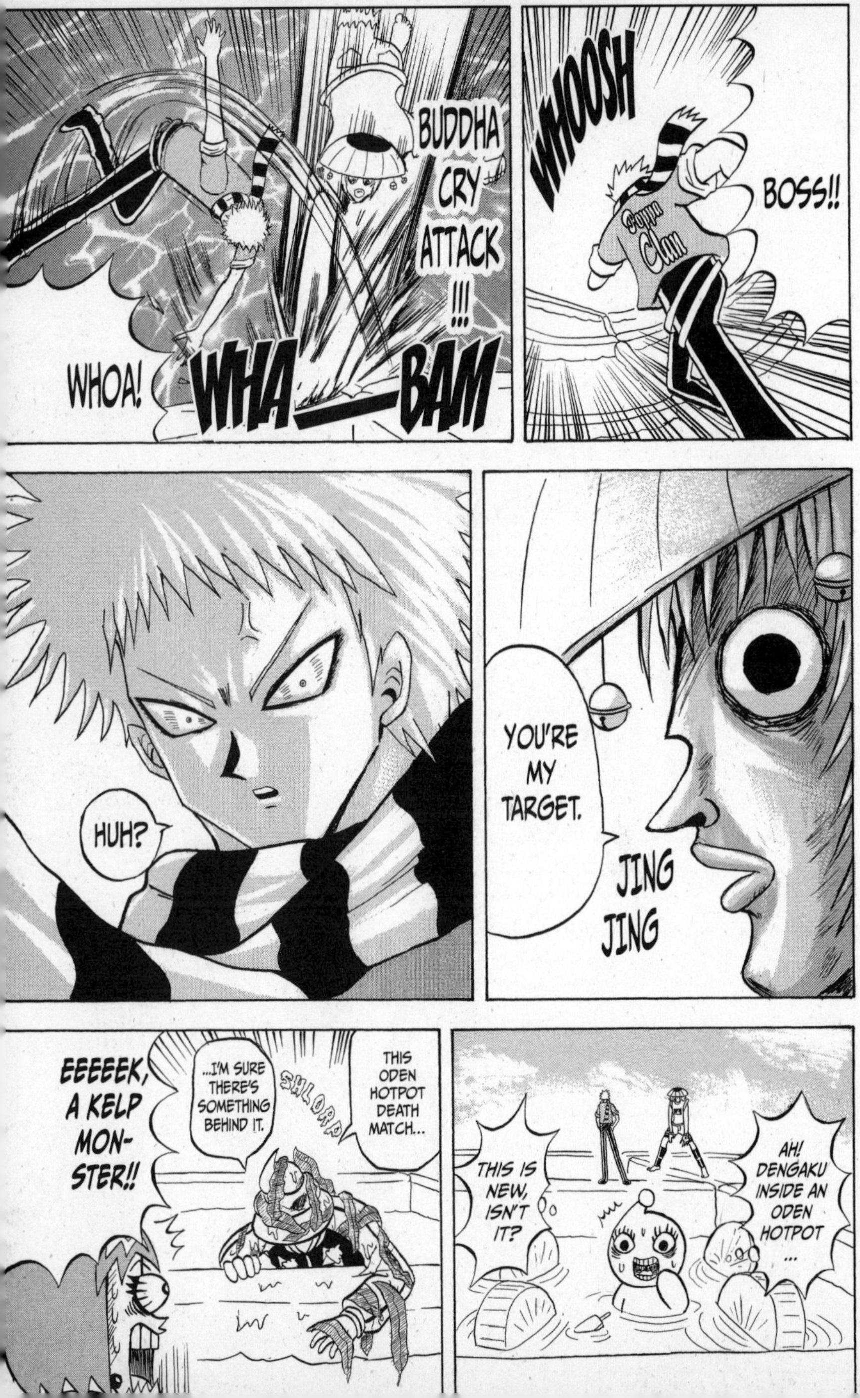
WHOOSH
BOSS!!
BUDDHA CRY ATTACK!!!
WHOA!
WHA—BAM
YOU'RE MY TARGET.
JING JING
HUH?
AH! DENGAKU INSIDE AN ODEN HOTPOT ...
THIS IS NEW, ISN'T IT?
THIS ODEN HOTPOT DEATH MATCH...
...I'M SURE THERE'S SOMETHING BEHIND IT.
SHLORP
EEEEEK, A KELP MONSTER!!

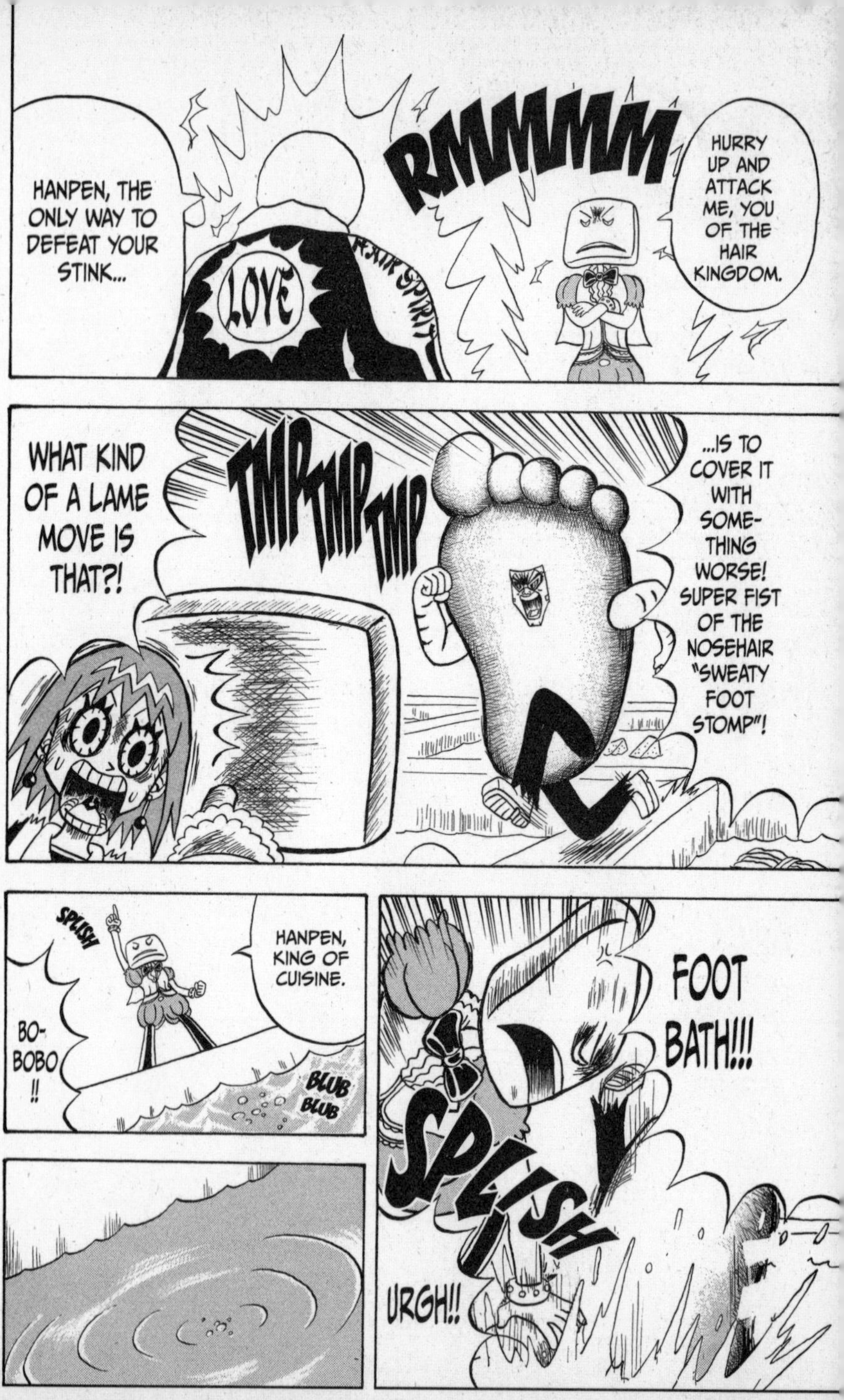
HURRY UP AND ATTACK ME, YOU OF THE HAIR KINGDOM.
RMMMMM
HAIR SPIRIT
LOVE
HANPEN, THE ONLY WAY TO DEFEAT YOUR STINK...
...IS TO COVER IT WITH SOME-THING WORSE! SUPER FIST OF THE NOSEHAIR "SWEATY FOOT STOMP"!
TMP TMP TMP
WHAT KIND OF A LAME MOVE IS THAT?!
FOOT BATH!!!
SPLISH
URGH!!
HANPEN, KING OF CUISINE.
SPLISH
BO-BOBO !!
BLUB BLUB

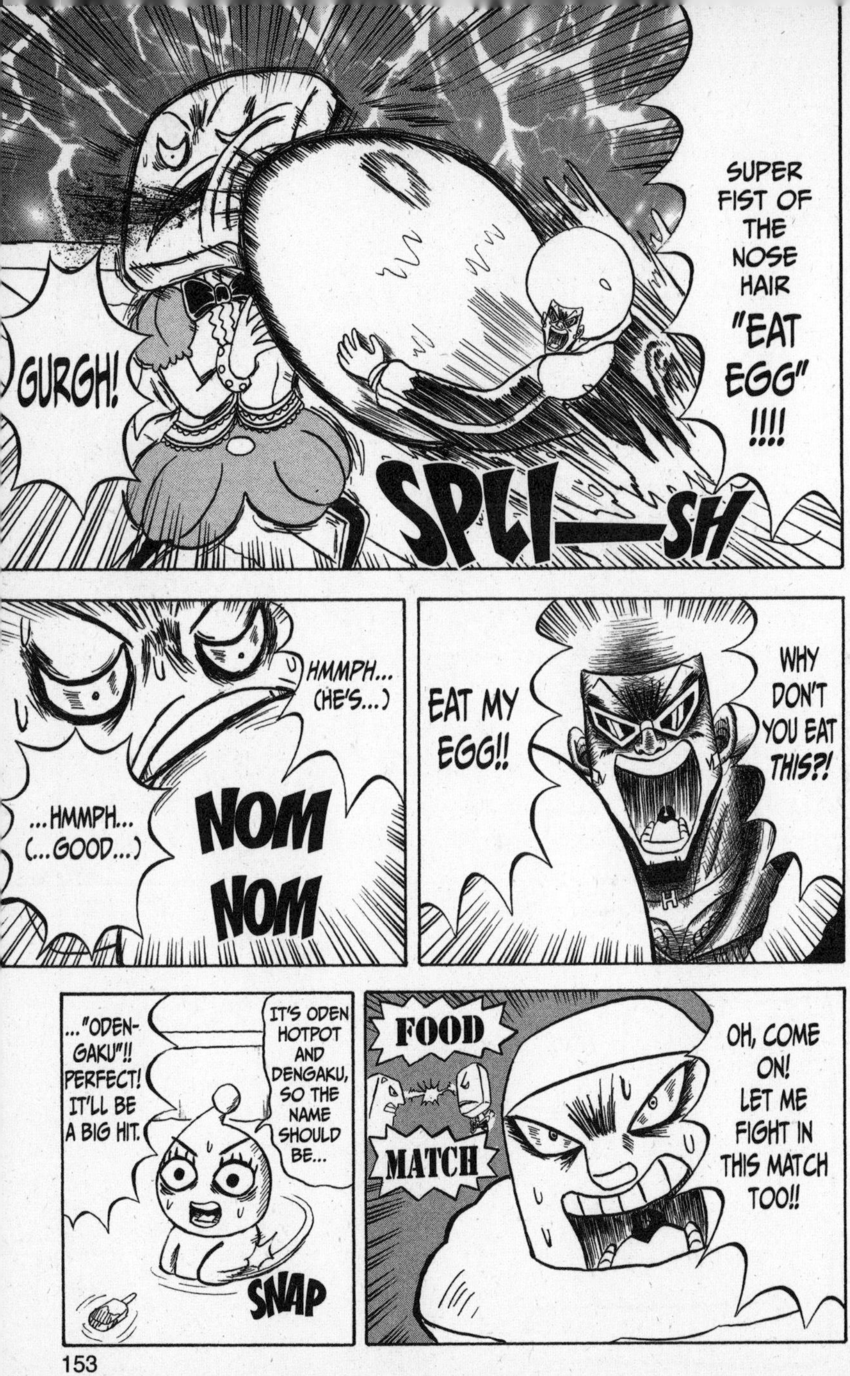
SUPER FIST OF THE NOSE HAIR "EAT EGG" !!!!
GURGH!
SPLI—SH
WHY DON'T YOU EAT THIS?!
EAT MY EGG!!
HMMPH... (HE'S...)
NOM NOM
...HMMPH... (...GOOD...)
OH, COME ON! LET ME FIGHT IN THIS MATCH TOO!!
FOOD
MATCH
IT'S ODEN HOTPOT AND DENGAKU, SO THE NAME SHOULD BE...
..."ODEN-GAKU"!! PERFECT! IT'LL BE A BIG HIT.
SNAP

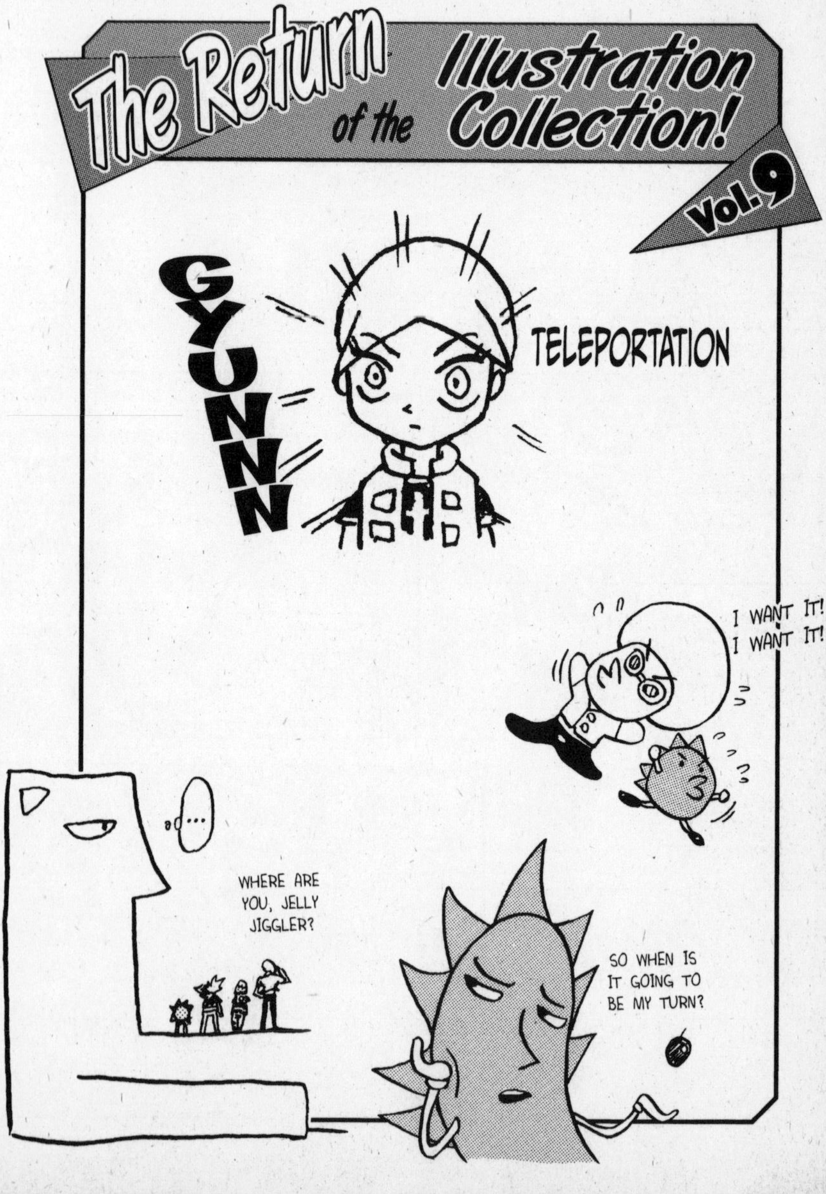
The Return of the Illustration Collection!
Vol. 9
GYUNNN
TELEPORTATION
I WANT IT! I WANT IT!
SO WHEN IS IT GOING TO BE MY TURN?
....
WHERE ARE YOU, JELLY JIGGLER?

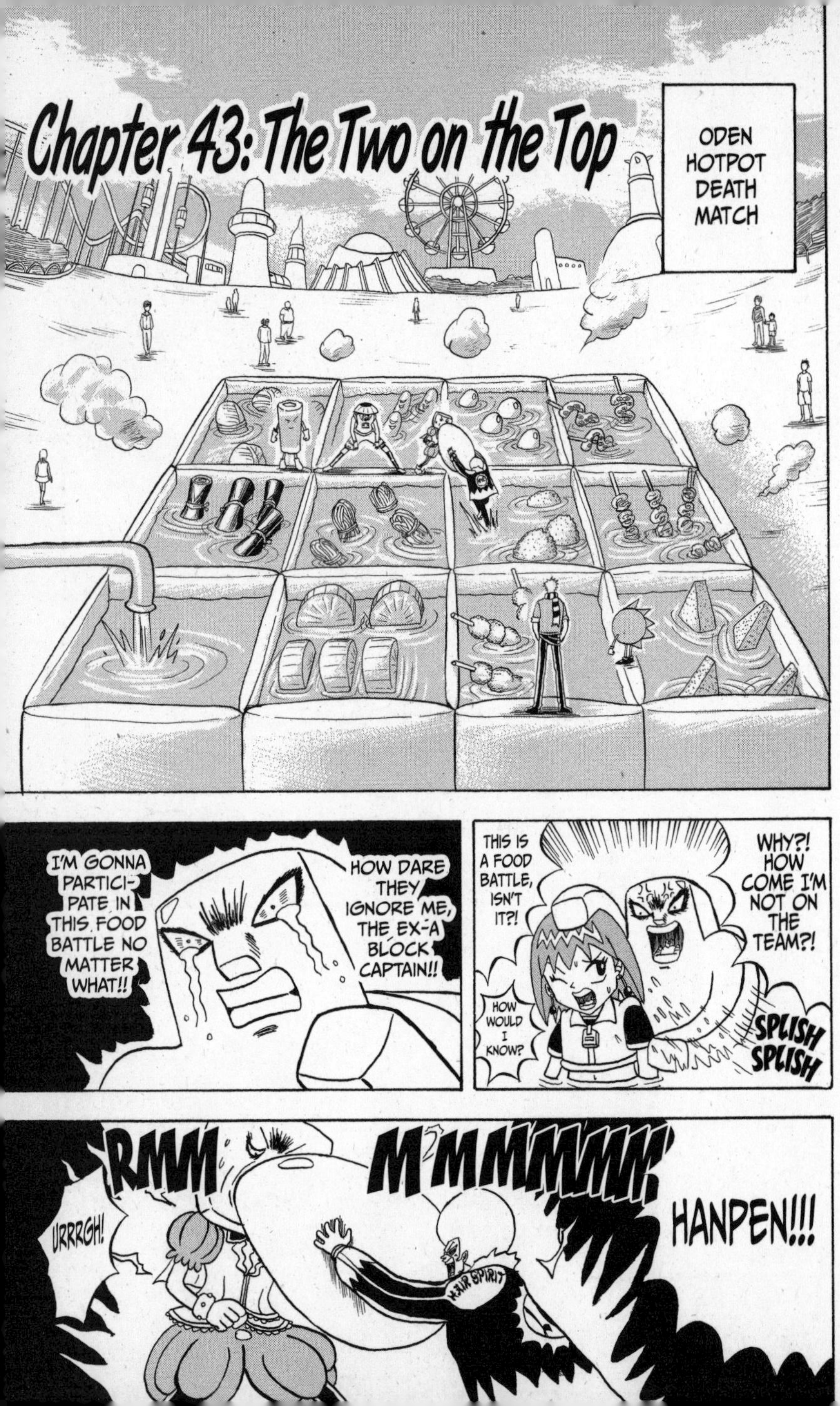
ODEN HOTPOT DEATH MATCH
Chapter 43: The Two on the Top
WHY?! HOW COME I'M NOT ON THE TEAM?!
THIS IS A FOOD BATTLE, ISN'T IT?!
HOW WOULD I KNOW?
SPLISH SPLISH
HOW DARE THEY IGNORE ME, THE EX-A BLOCK CAPTAIN!!
I'M GONNA PARTICIPATE IN THIS FOOD BATTLE NO MATTER WHAT!!
HANPEN!!!
RMMM MMMMMMM
URRRGH!
HAIR SPIRIT

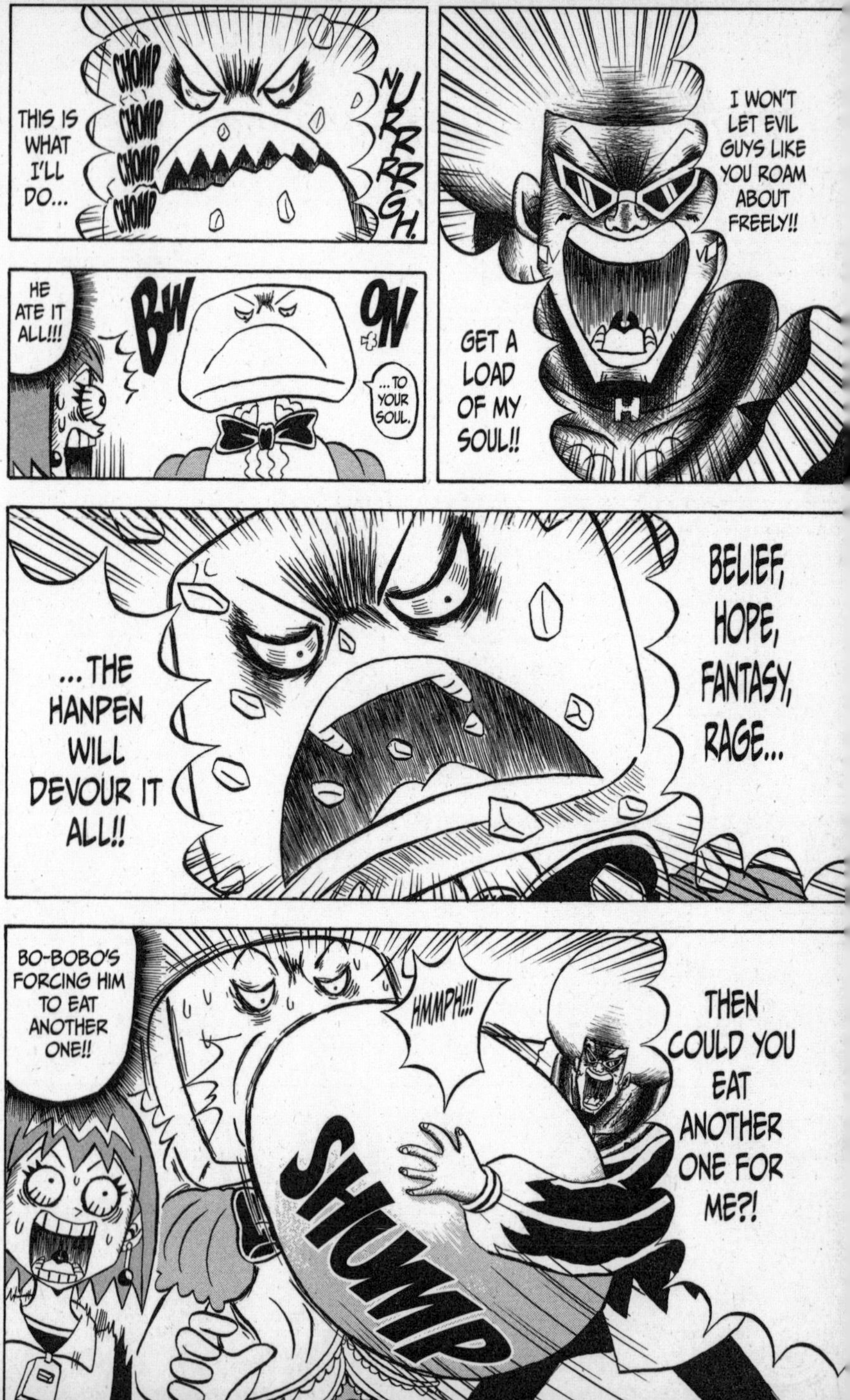
I WON'T LET EVIL GUYS LIKE YOU ROAM ABOUT FREELY!!
GET A LOAD OF MY SOUL!!
NURRRGH.
CHOMP CHOMP CHOMP CHOMP
THIS IS WHAT I'LL DO...
ON
...TO YOUR SOUL.
BW
HE ATE IT ALL!!!
BELIEF, HOPE, FANTASY, RAGE...
...THE HANPEN WILL DEVOUR IT ALL!!
THEN COULD YOU EAT ANOTHER ONE FOR ME?!
HMMPH!!!
SHUMP
BO-BOBO'S FORCING HIM TO EAT ANOTHER ONE!!

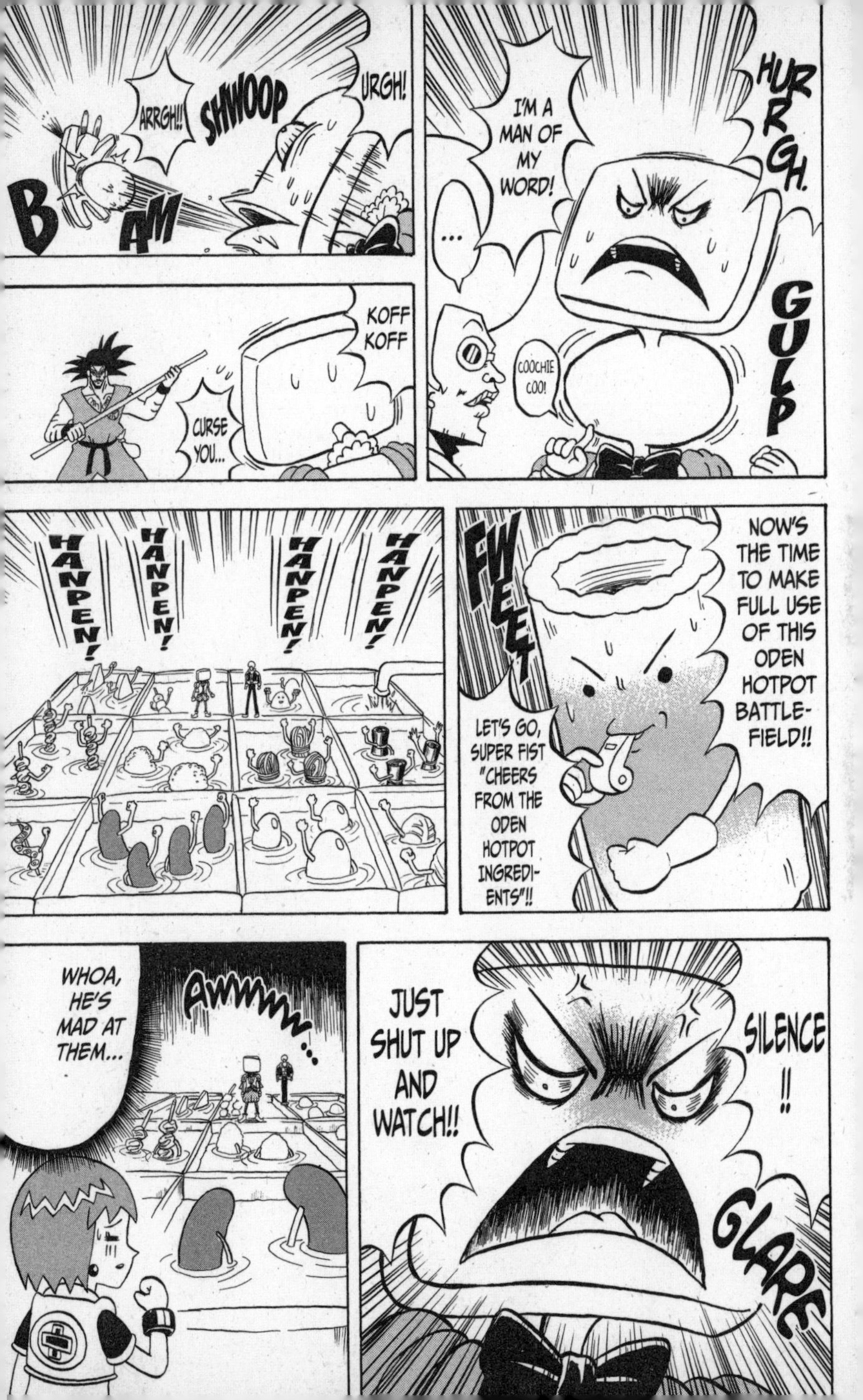
HURRGH.
I'M A MAN OF MY WORD!
...
URGH!
SHWOOP
ARRGH!!
BAM
GULP
COOCHIE COO!
KOFF KOFF
CURSE YOU...
FWEET
NOW'S THE TIME TO MAKE FULL USE OF THIS ODEN HOTPOT BATTLE-FIELD!!
LET'S GO, SUPER FIST "CHEERS FROM THE ODEN HOTPOT INGREDI-ENTS"!!
HANPEN!
HANPEN!
HANPEN!
HANPEN!
SILENCE!!
JUST SHUT UP AND WATCH!!
GLARE
AWWWW...
WHOA, HE'S MAD AT THEM...

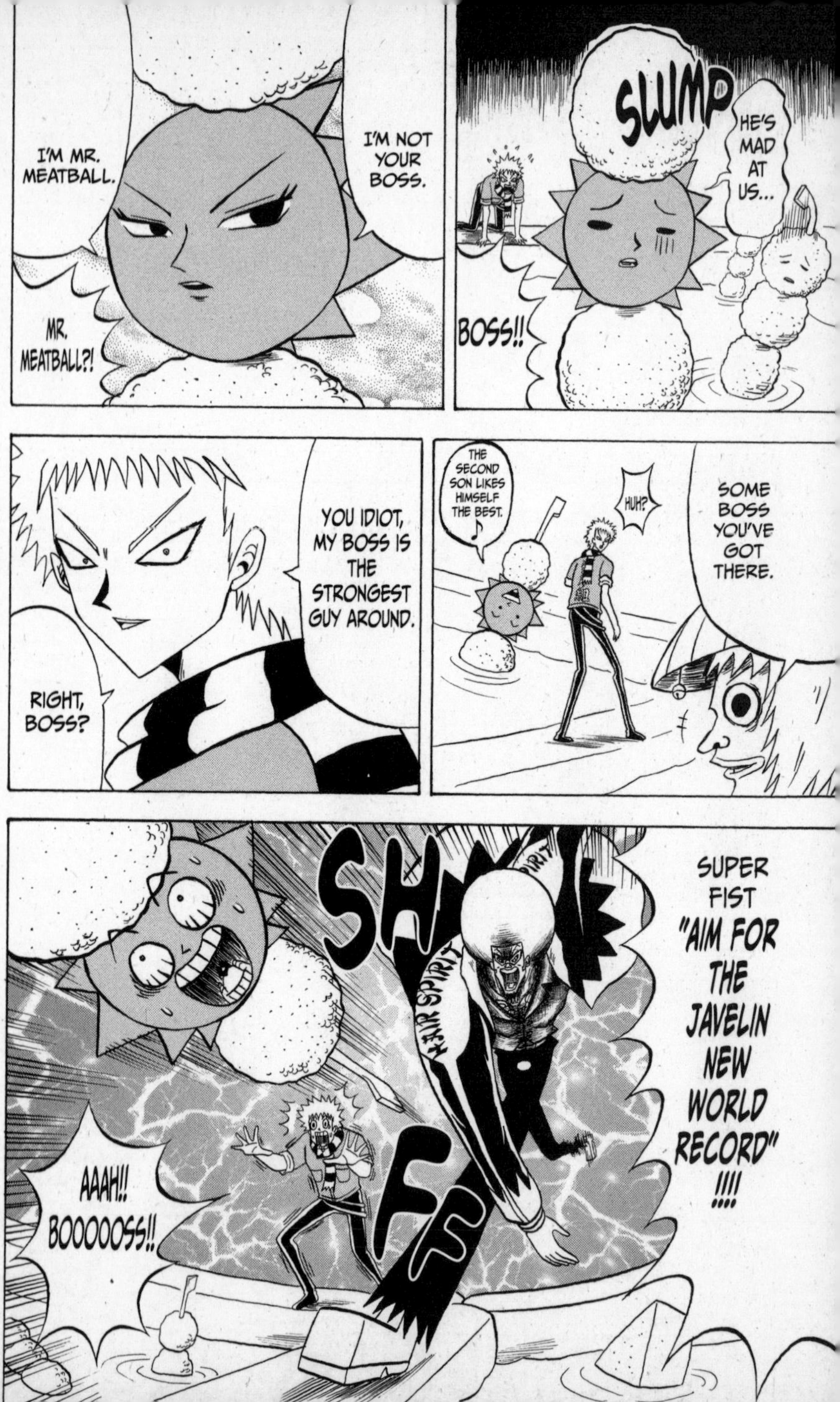
HE'S MAD AT US...
SLUMP
BOSS!!
I'M NOT YOUR BOSS.
I'M MR. MEATBALL.
MR. MEATBALL?!
SOME BOSS YOU'VE GOT THERE.
HUH?
THE SECOND SON LIKES HIMSELF THE BEST. ♪
YOU IDIOT, MY BOSS IS THE STRONGEST GUY AROUND.
RIGHT, BOSS?
SUPER FIST "AIM FOR THE JAVELIN NEW WORLD RECORD"!!!!
SH
HAIR SPIRIT
FF
AAAH!! BOOOOOSS!!

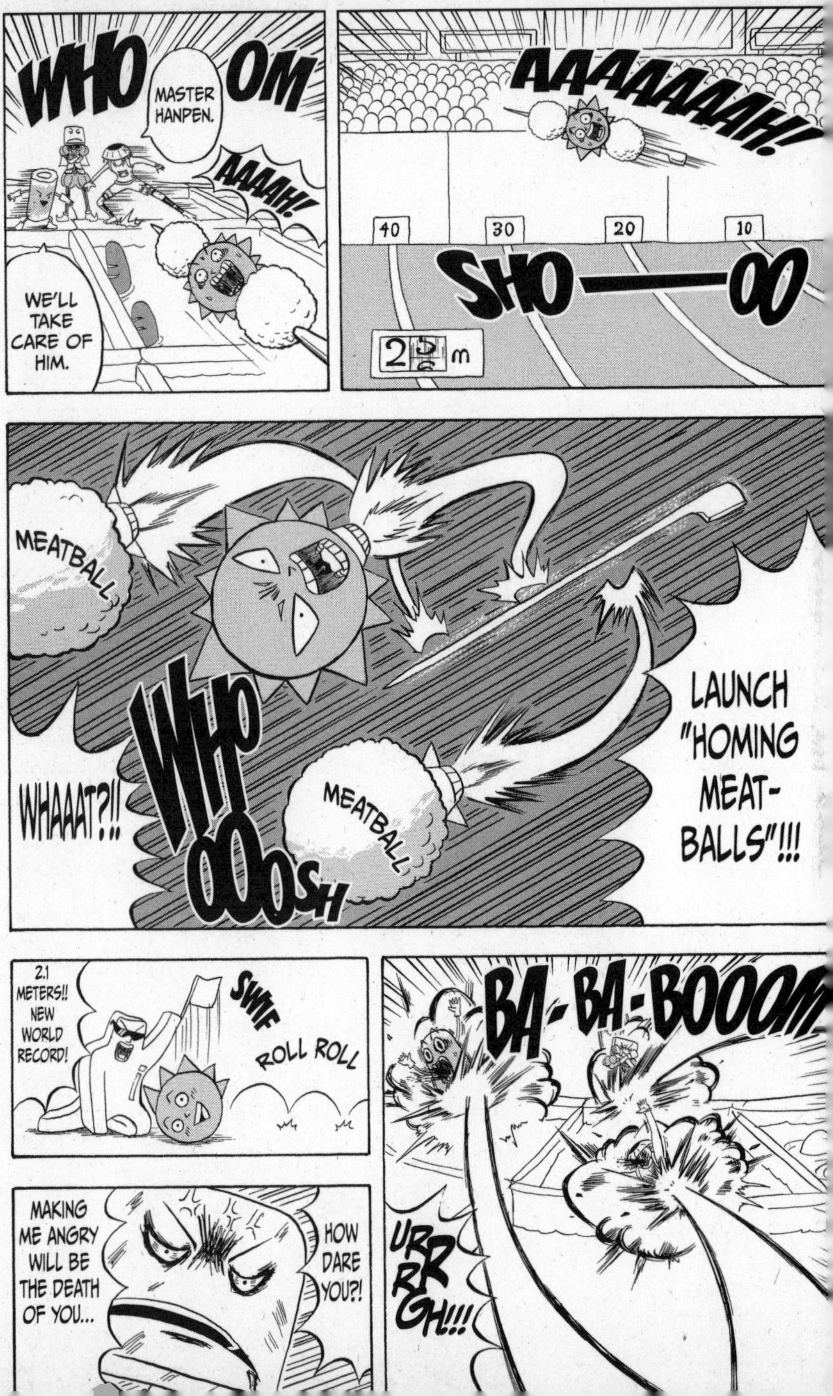
AAAAAAAAH!
40
30
20
10
SHO—OO
WHO OM
MASTER HANPEN.
AAAAH!
WE'LL TAKE CARE OF HIM.
LAUNCH "HOMING MEAT-BALLS"!!!
MEATBALL
WHOOOOSH
MEATBALL
WHAAAT?!!
BA-BA-BOOOM
URRRGH!!!
2.1 METERS!! NEW WORLD RECORD!
SWIF
ROLL ROLL
HOW DARE YOU?!
MAKING ME ANGRY WILL BE THE DEATH OF YOU...

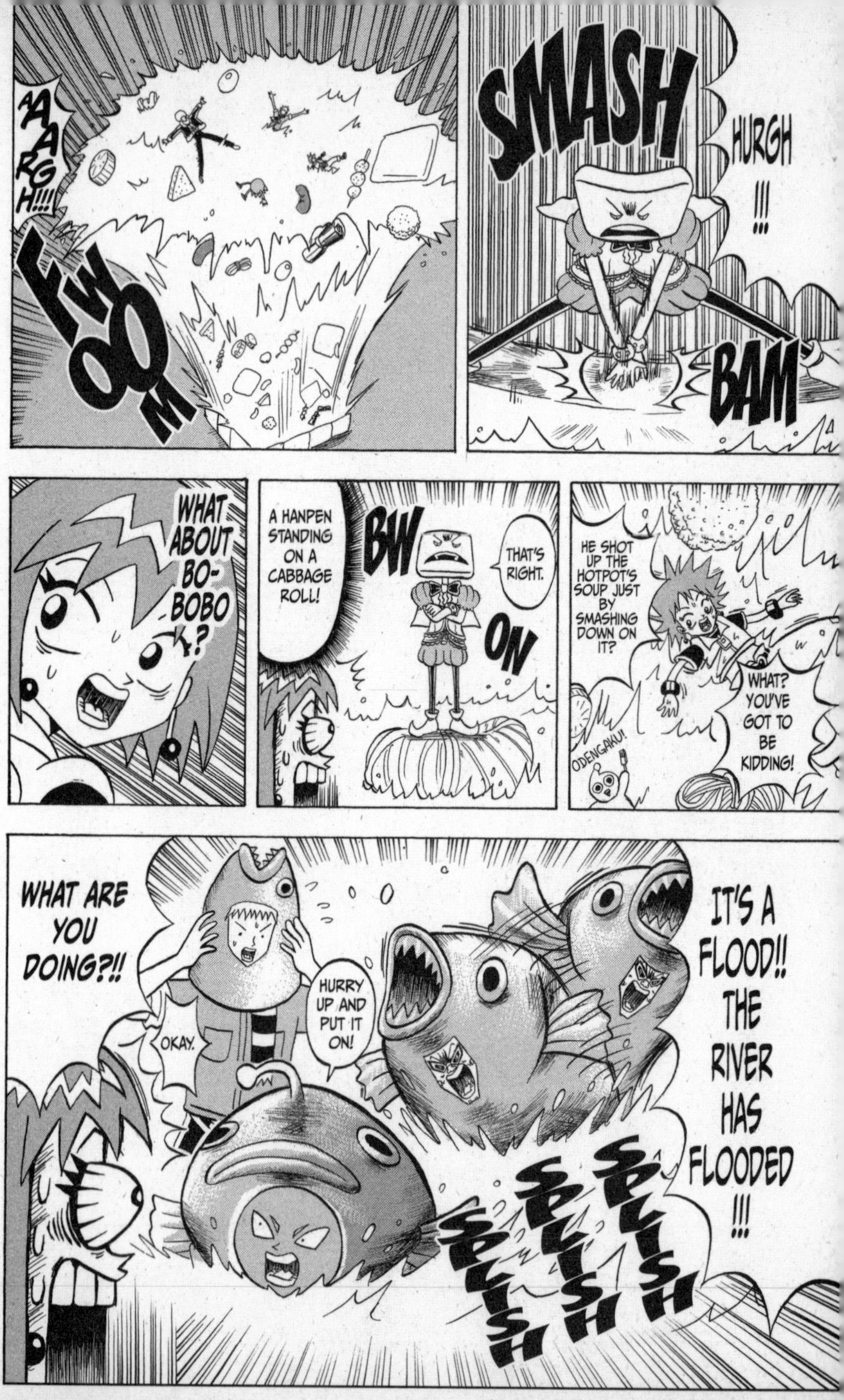
SMASH
HURGH!!!
BAM
AAARGH!!!
FWOOOM
WHAT? YOU'VE GOT TO BE KIDDING!
HE SHOT UP THE HOTPOT'S SOUP JUST BY SMASHING DOWN ON IT?
ODENGAKU!
THAT'S RIGHT.
BWON
A HANPEN STANDING ON A CABBAGE ROLL!
WHAT ABOUT BO-BOBOBO?
IT'S A FLOOD!! THE RIVER HAS FLOODED!!!
SPLISH
SPLISH
SPLISH
HURRY UP AND PUT IT ON!
WHAT ARE YOU DOING?!!
OKAY.

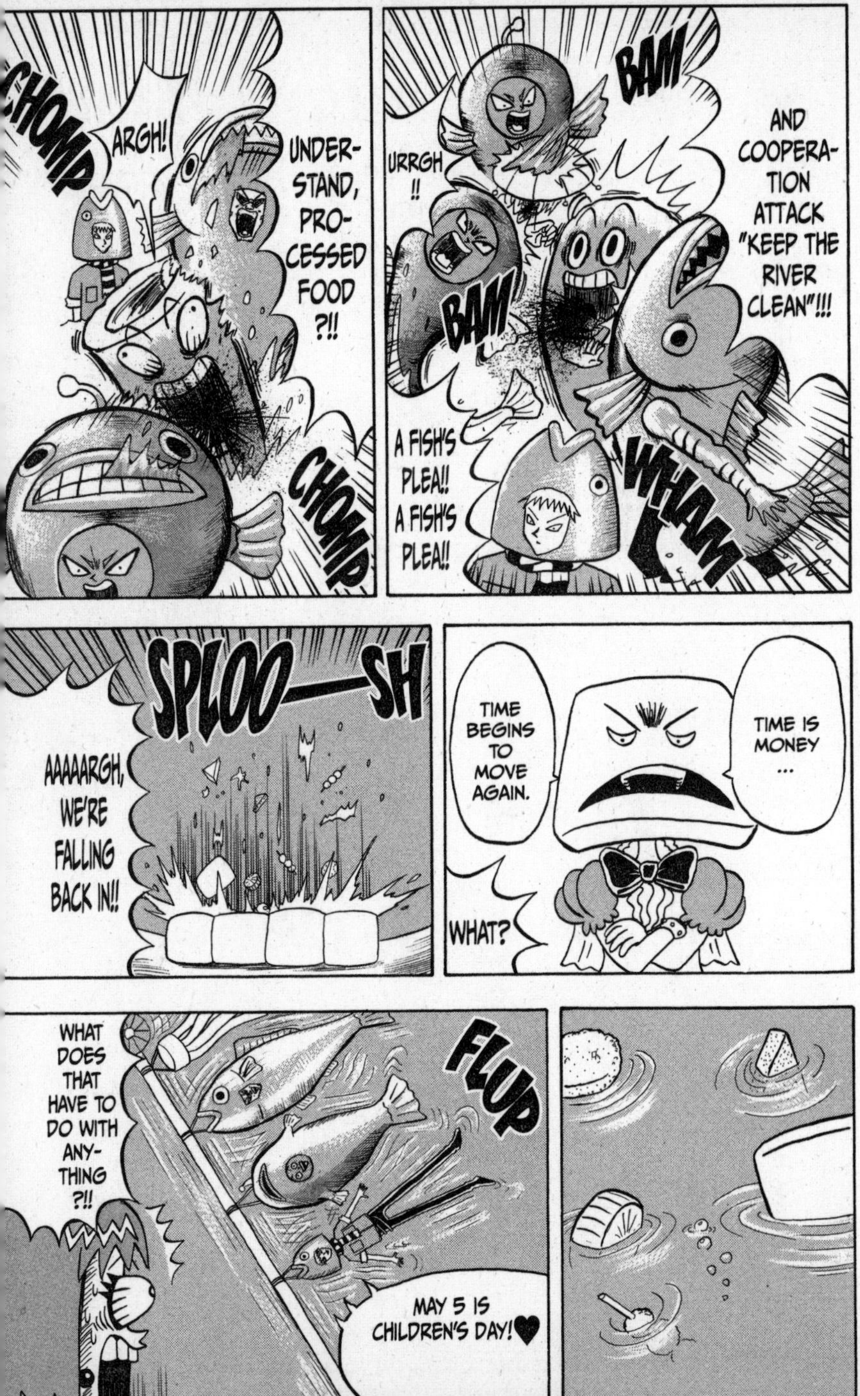
BAM
AND COOPERATION ATTACK "KEEP THE RIVER CLEAN"!!!
URRGH!!
BAM
WHAM
A FISH'S PLEA!! A FISH'S PLEA!!
UNDERSTAND, PROCESSED FOOD?!!
ARGH!
CHOMP
CHOMP
TIME IS MONEY...
TIME BEGINS TO MOVE AGAIN.
WHAT?
SPLOO—SH
AAAAARGH, WE'RE FALLING BACK IN!!
FLUP
WHAT DOES THAT HAVE TO DO WITH ANYTHING?!!
MAY 5 IS CHILDREN'S DAY!♥

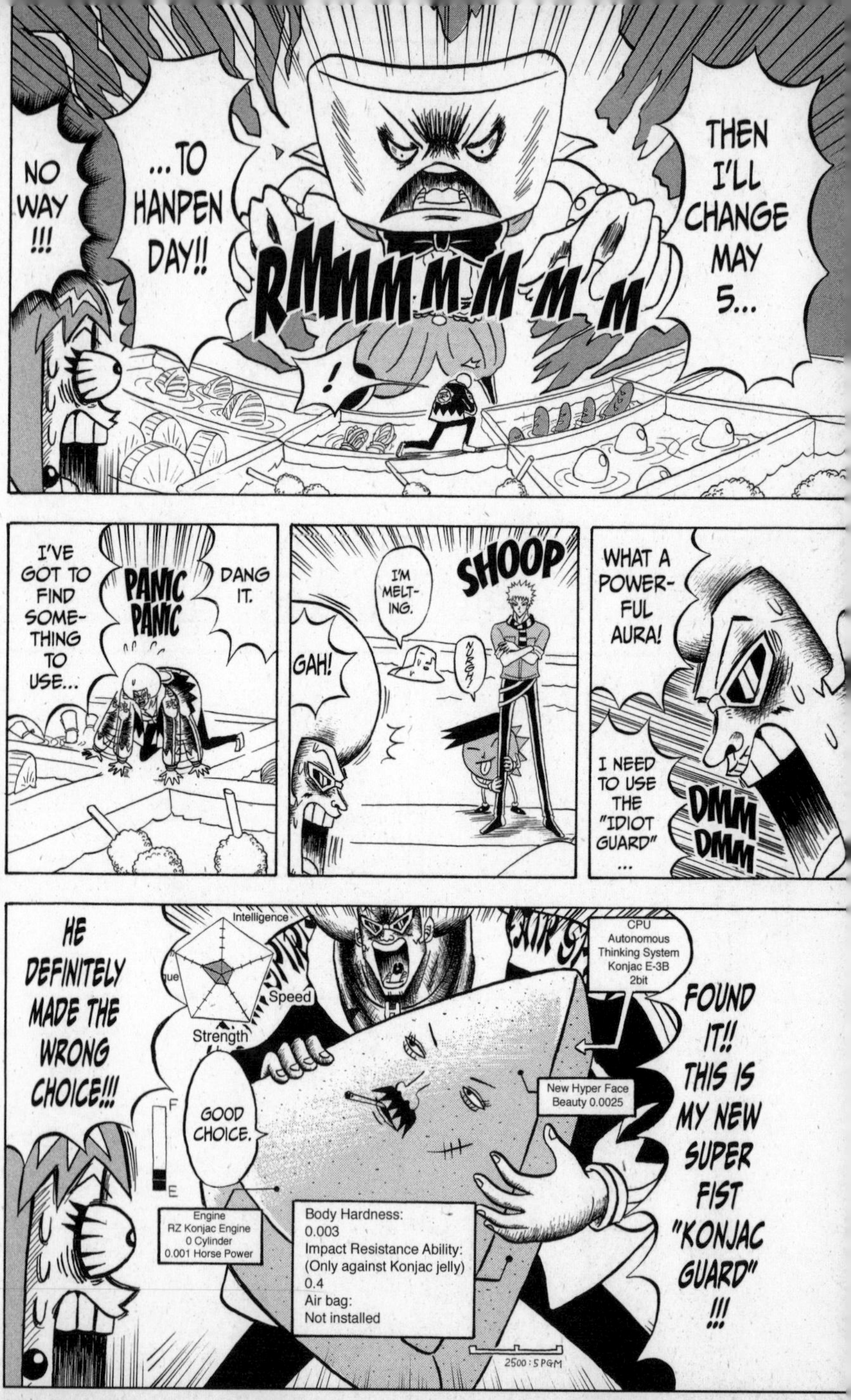
THEN I'LL CHANGE MAY 5...
RMMMMMMMMM
...TO HANPEN DAY!!
NO WAY!!!
WHAT A POWER-FUL AURA!
I NEED TO USE THE "IDIOT GUARD"...
DMM DMM
SHOOP
I'M MELT-ING.
NURGH!
GAH!
DANG IT.
PANIC PANIC
I'VE GOT TO FIND SOME-THING TO USE...
FOUND IT!! THIS IS MY NEW SUPER FIST "KONJAC GUARD"!!!
CPU Autonomous Thinking System Konjac E-3B 2bit
New Hyper Face Beauty 0.0025
Intelligence
Speed
Strength
F
E
GOOD CHOICE.
Body Hardness: 0.003
Impact Resistance Ability: (Only against Konjac jelly) 0.4
Air bag: Not installed
Engine RZ Konjac Engine 0 Cylinder 0.001 Horse Power
2500:5PGM
HE DEFINITELY MADE THE WRONG CHOICE!!!

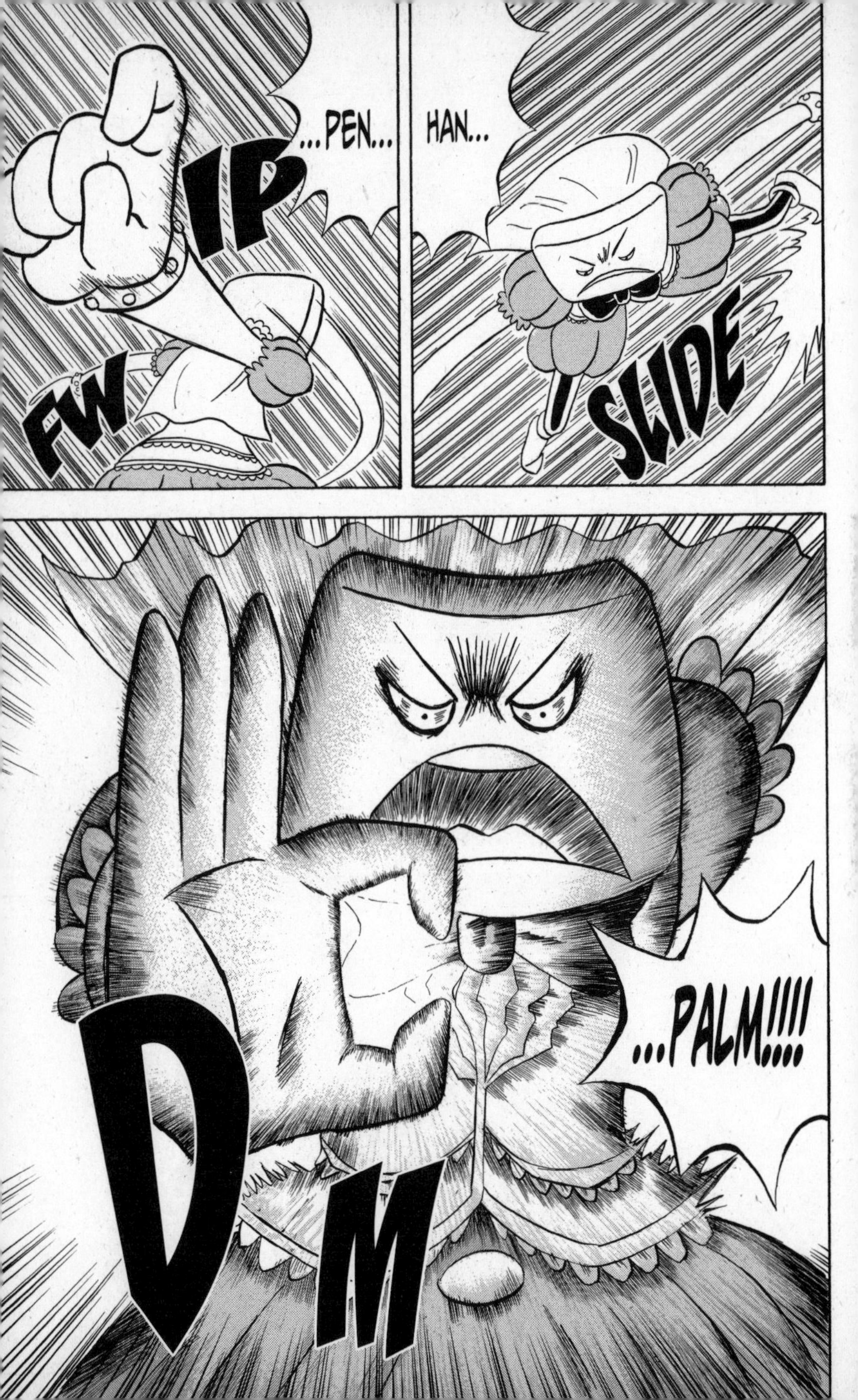

HAN...
SLIDE
DIP
...PEN...
FW
...PALM!!!!
D
M

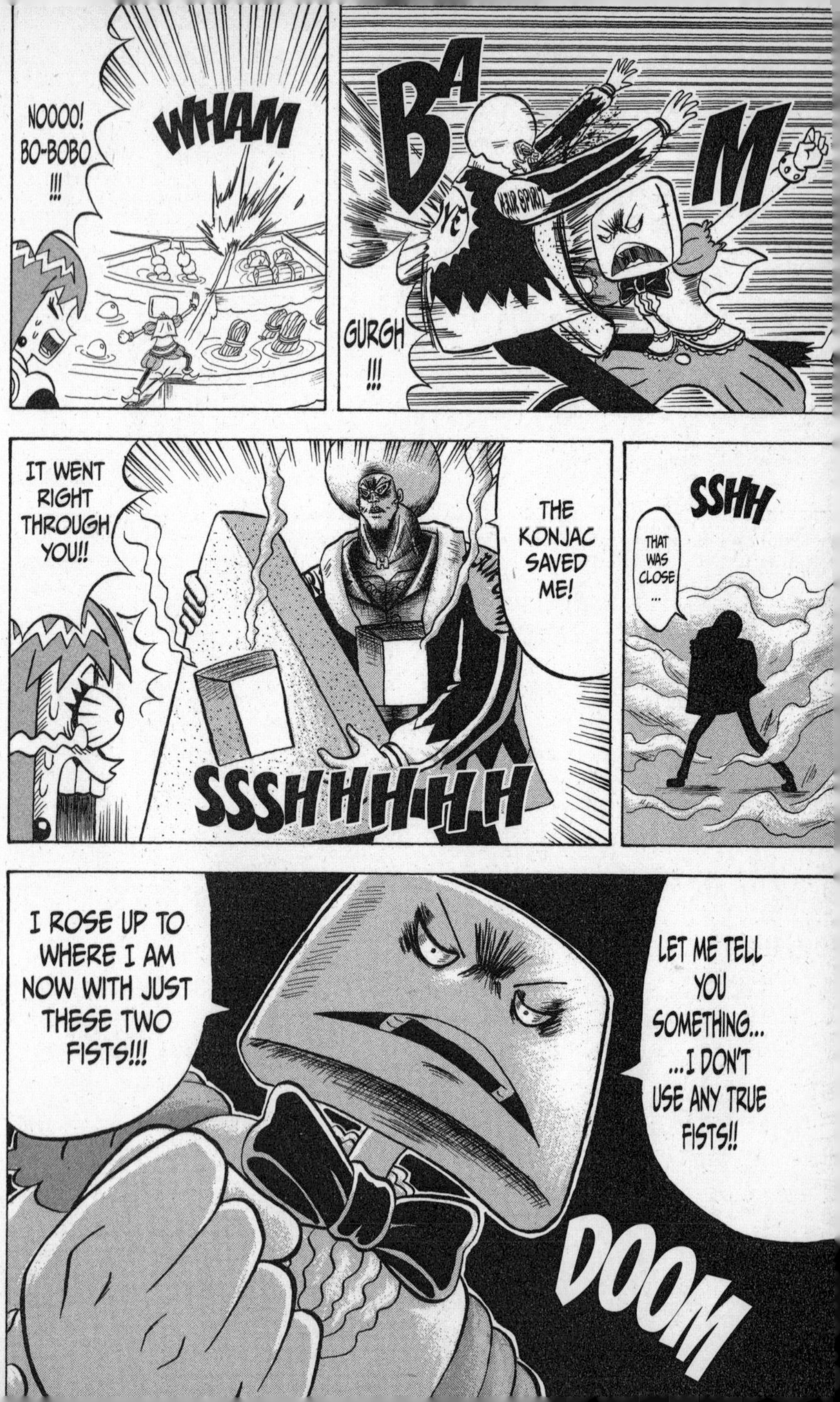
BAM
GURGH!!!
NOOOO! BO-BOBO!!!
WHAM
SSHH
THAT WAS CLOSE...
THE KONJAC SAVED ME!
IT WENT RIGHT THROUGH YOU!!
SSSHHHHHH
LET ME TELL YOU SOMETHING... ...I DON'T USE ANY TRUE FISTS!!
I ROSE UP TO WHERE I AM NOW WITH JUST THESE TWO FISTS!!!
DOOM

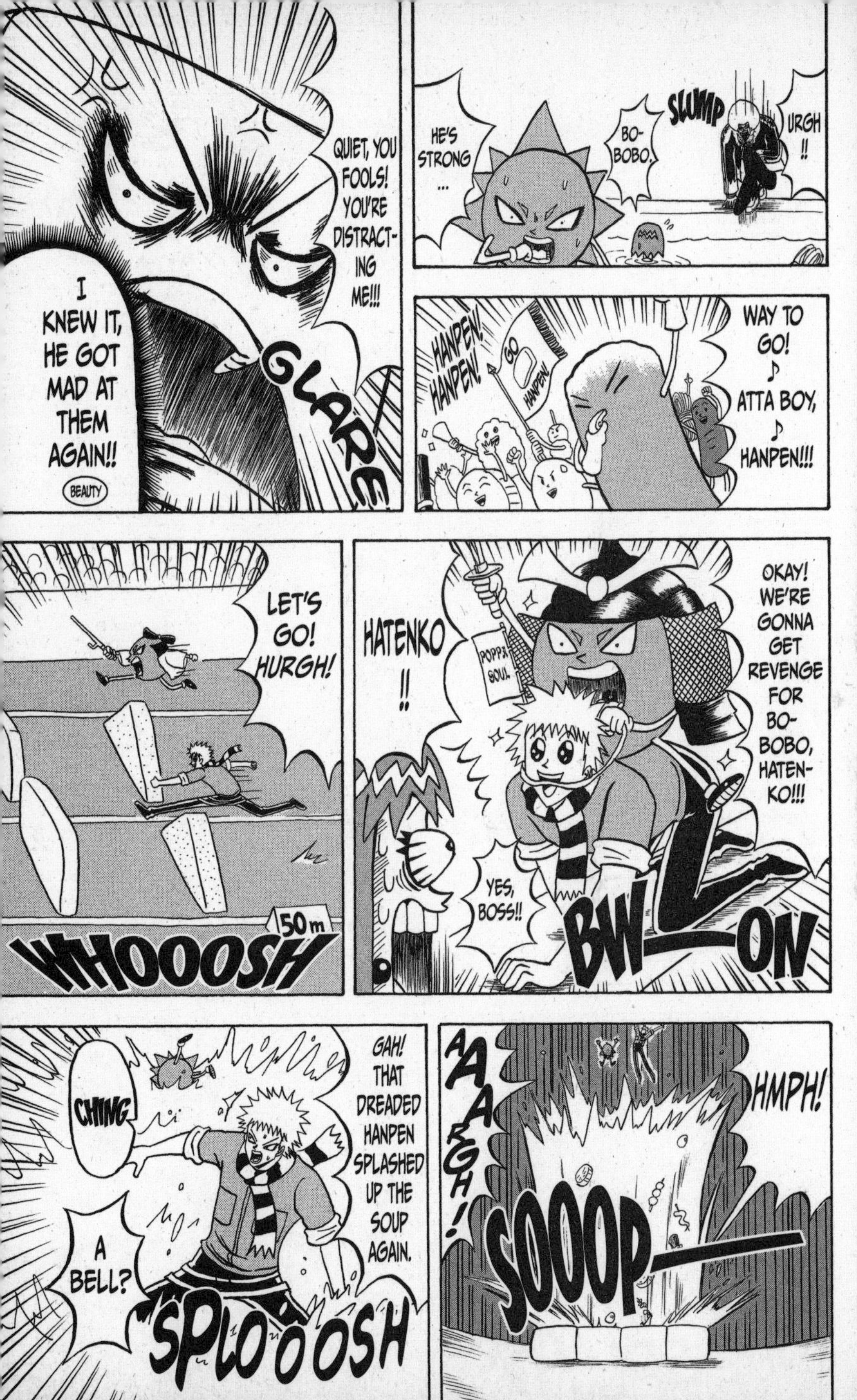
URGH !!
SLUMP
BO-BOBO.
HE'S STRONG ...
WAY TO GO! ♪ ATTA BOY, ♪ HANPEN!!!
GO HANPEN
HANPEN! HANPEN!
QUIET, YOU FOOLS! YOU'RE DISTRACT-ING ME!!!
GLARE
I KNEW IT, HE GOT MAD AT THEM AGAIN!!
BEAUTY
OKAY! WE'RE GONNA GET REVENGE FOR BO-BOBO, HATEN-KO!!!
HATENKO !!
YES, BOSS!!
BW—ON
LET'S GO! HURGH!
50m
WHOOOSH
HMPH!
AAAARGH!
SOOOP—
GAH! THAT DREADED HANPEN SPLASHED UP THE SOUP AGAIN.
CHING
A BELL?
SPLOOOOSH

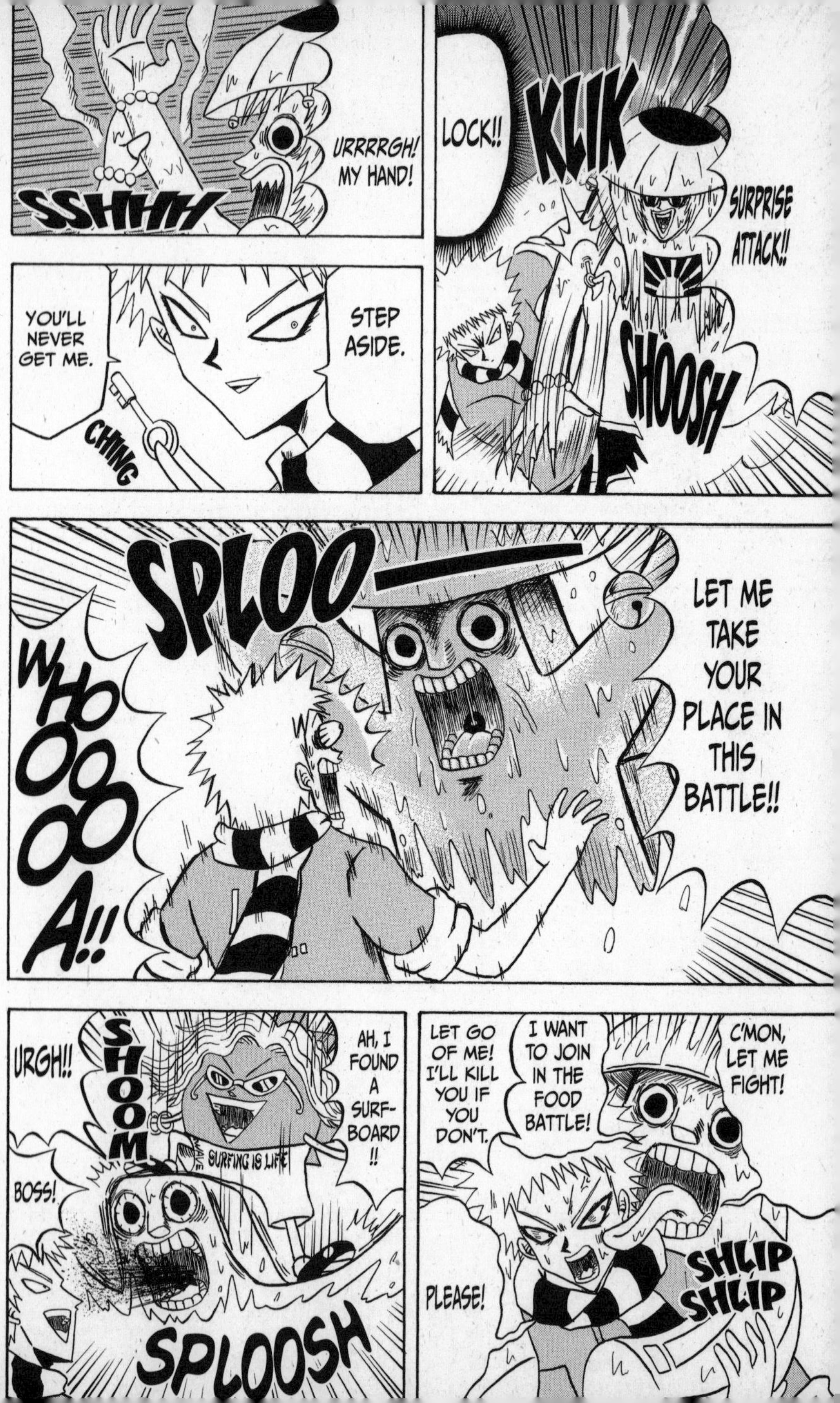
LOCK!!
KLIK
SURPRISE ATTACK!!
SHOOSH
URRRRGH! MY HAND!
SSHHHH
STEP ASIDE.
YOU'LL NEVER GET ME.
CHING
SPLOO—
LET ME TAKE YOUR PLACE IN THIS BATTLE!!
WHOOOOA!!
C'MON, LET ME FIGHT!
I WANT TO JOIN IN THE FOOD BATTLE!
LET GO OF ME! I'LL KILL YOU IF YOU DON'T.
SHLIP SHLIP
PLEASE!
AH, I FOUND A SURF-BOARD!!
SHOOOM
URGH!!
SURFING IS LIFE
BOSS!
SPLOOSH

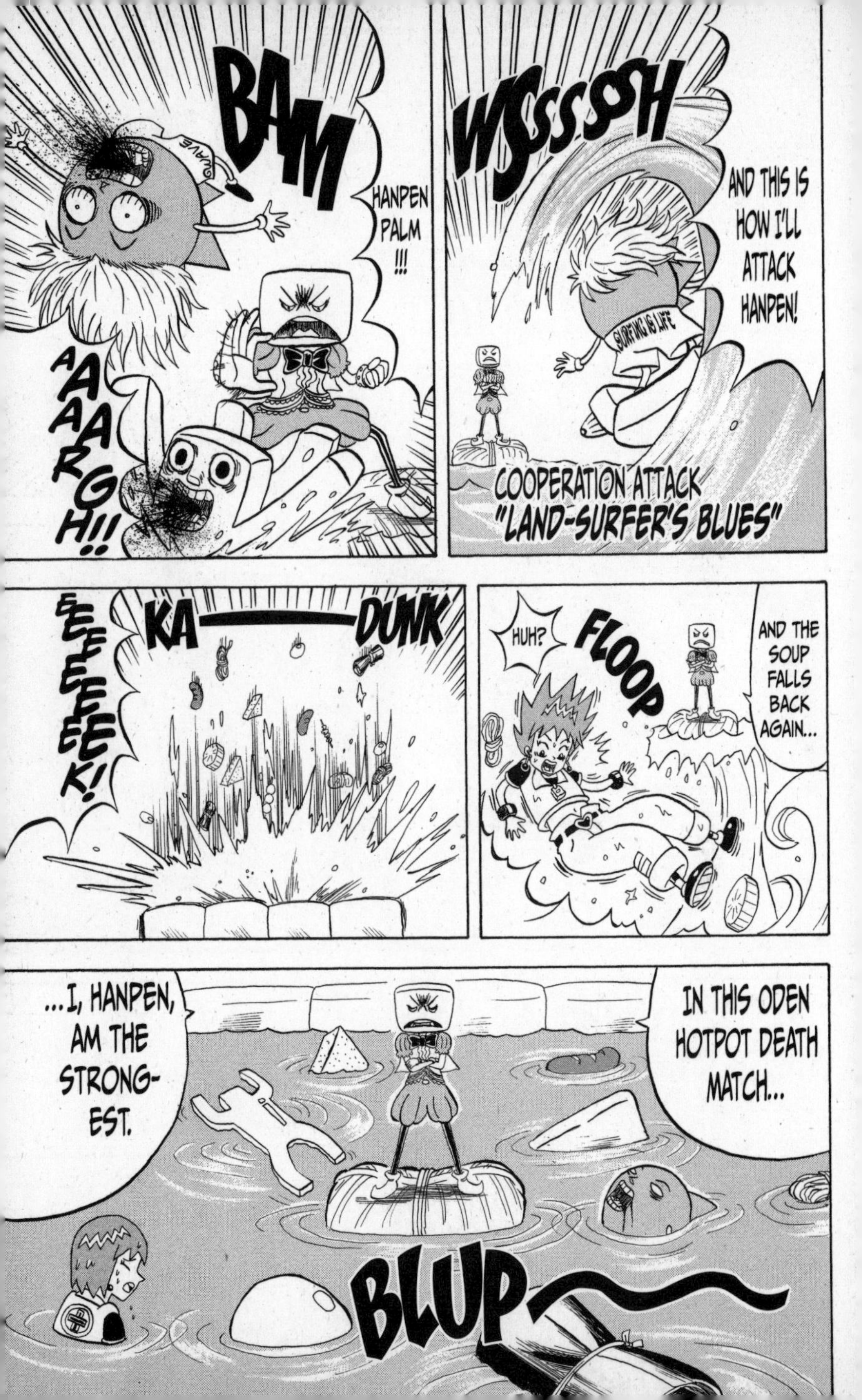
WSSSSOSH
AND THIS IS HOW I'LL ATTACK HANPEN!
SURFING IS LIFE
COOPERATION ATTACK "LAND-SURFER'S BLUES"
BAM
HANPEN PALM !!!
WAVE
AAAARGH!!
HUH?
FLOOP
AND THE SOUP FALLS BACK AGAIN...
KA——DUNK
EEEEEEEK!
IN THIS ODEN HOTPOT DEATH MATCH...
...I, HANPEN, AM THE STRONG-EST.
BLUP

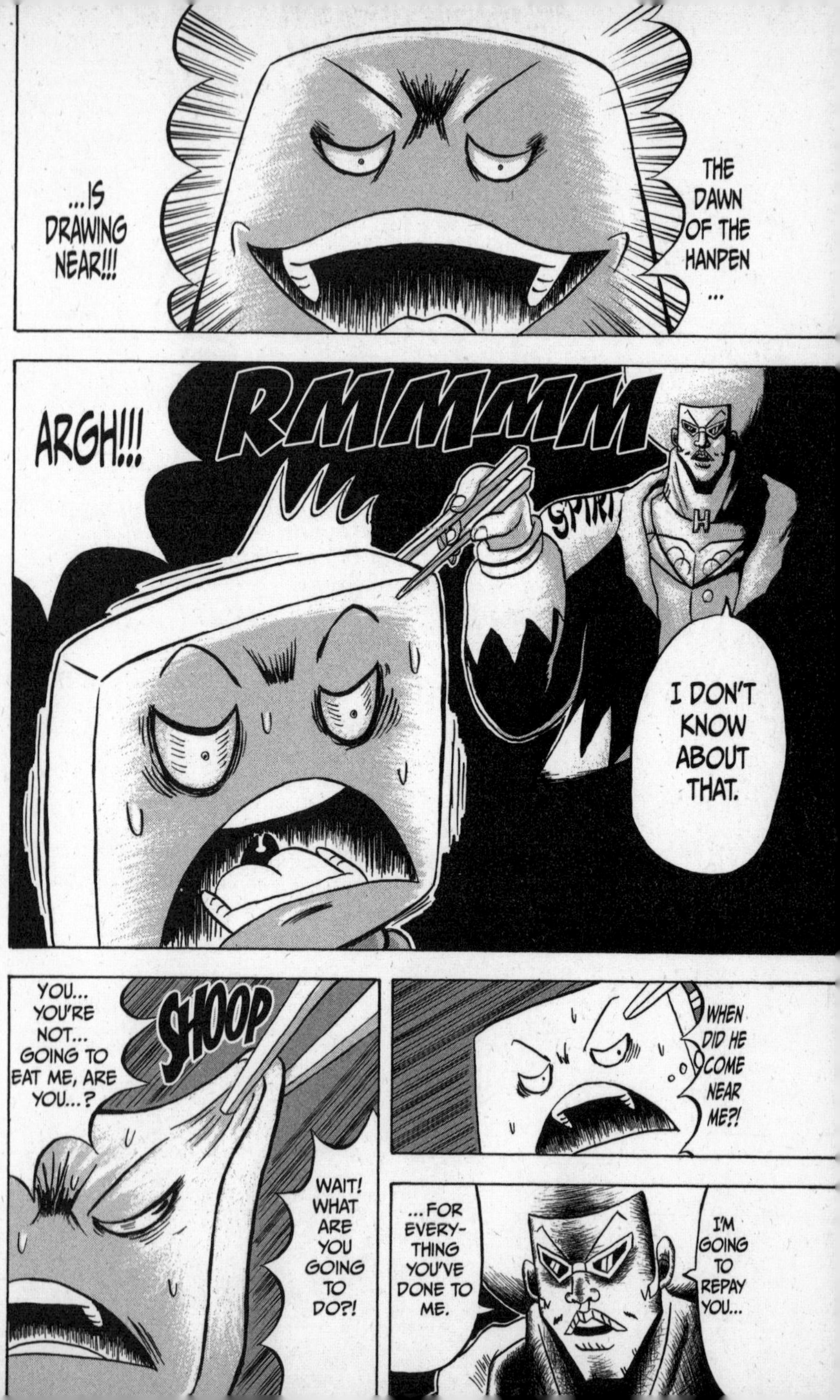
THE DAWN OF THE HANPEN ...
...IS DRAWING NEAR!!!
RMMMMM
ARGH!!!
SPIRIT
I DON'T KNOW ABOUT THAT.
WHEN DID HE COME NEAR ME?!
I'M GOING TO REPAY YOU...
...FOR EVERYTHING YOU'VE DONE TO ME.
SHOOP
YOU... YOU'RE NOT... GOING TO EAT ME, ARE YOU...?
WAIT! WHAT ARE YOU GOING TO DO?!

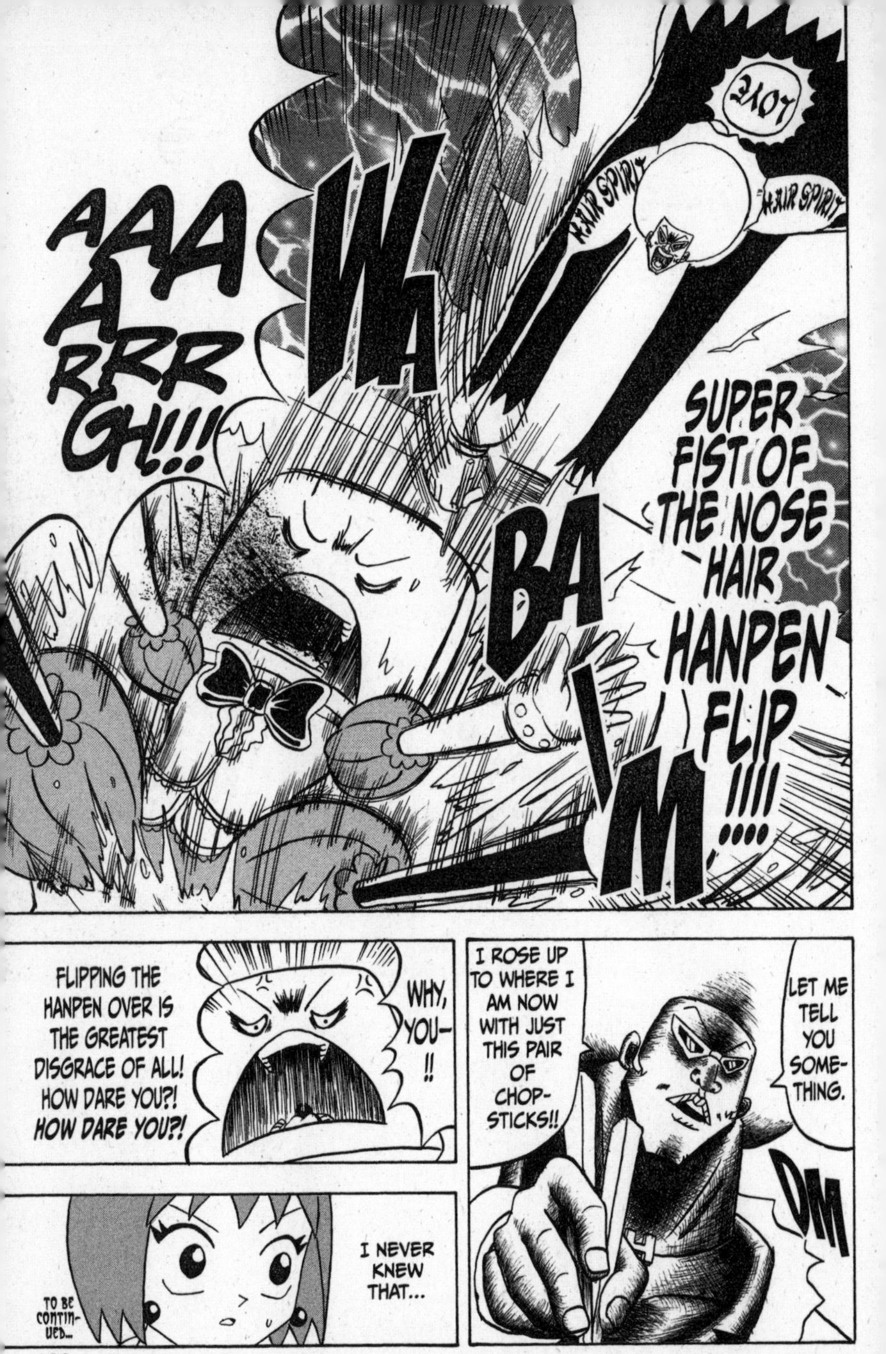
HAIR SPIRIT
HAIR SPIRIT
SUPER FIST OF THE NOSE HAIR HANPEN FLIP!!!!
BA
M
WA
AAAARRRGH!!!
LET ME TELL YOU SOME-THING.
I ROSE UP TO WHERE I AM NOW WITH JUST THIS PAIR OF CHOP-STICKS!!
DM
WHY, YOU-!!
FLIPPING THE HANPEN OVER IS THE GREATEST DISGRACE OF ALL! HOW DARE YOU?! HOW DARE YOU?!
I NEVER KNEW THAT...
TO BE CONTIN-UED...

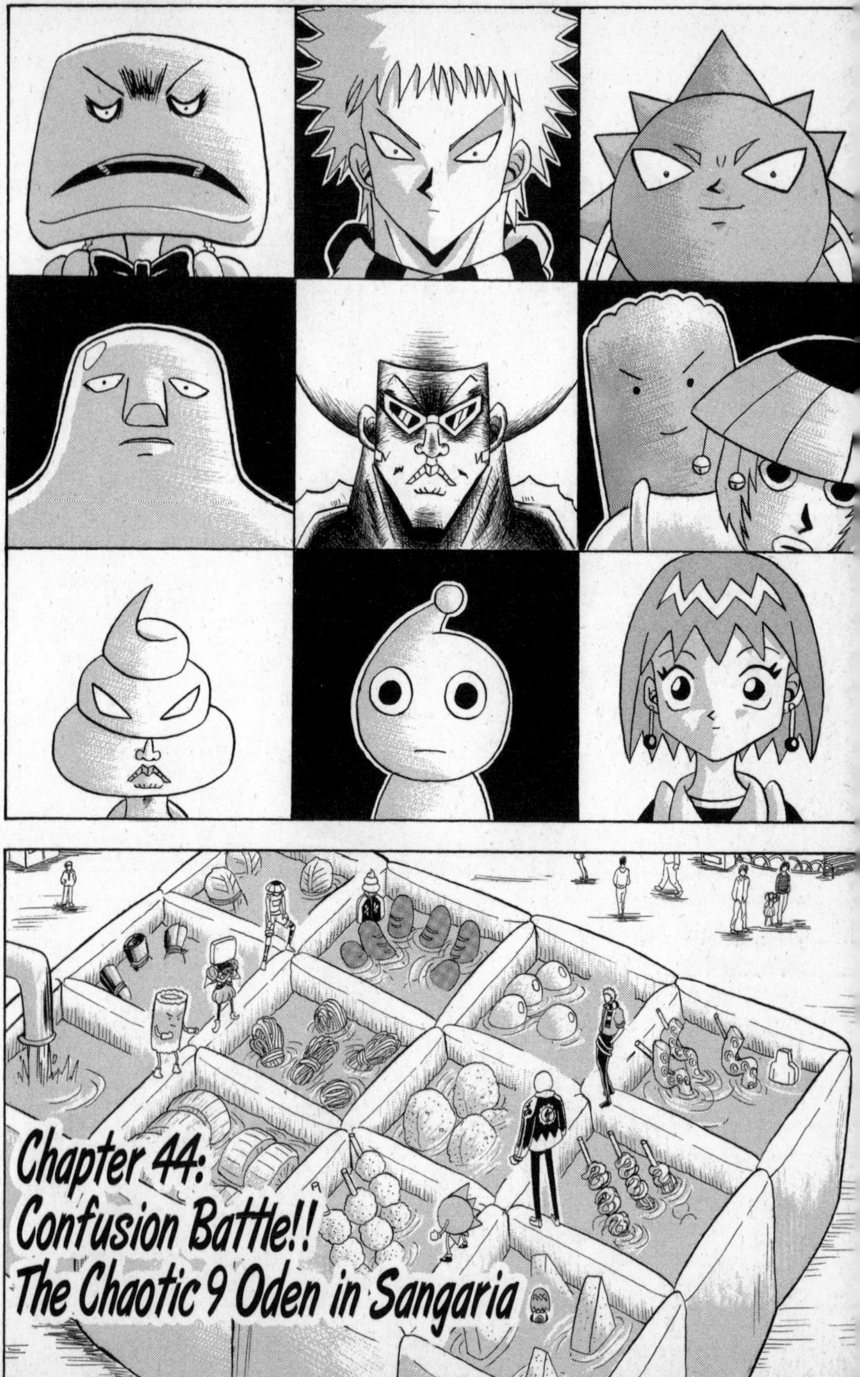
Chapter 44:
Confusion Battle!!
The Chaotic 9 Oden in Sangaria

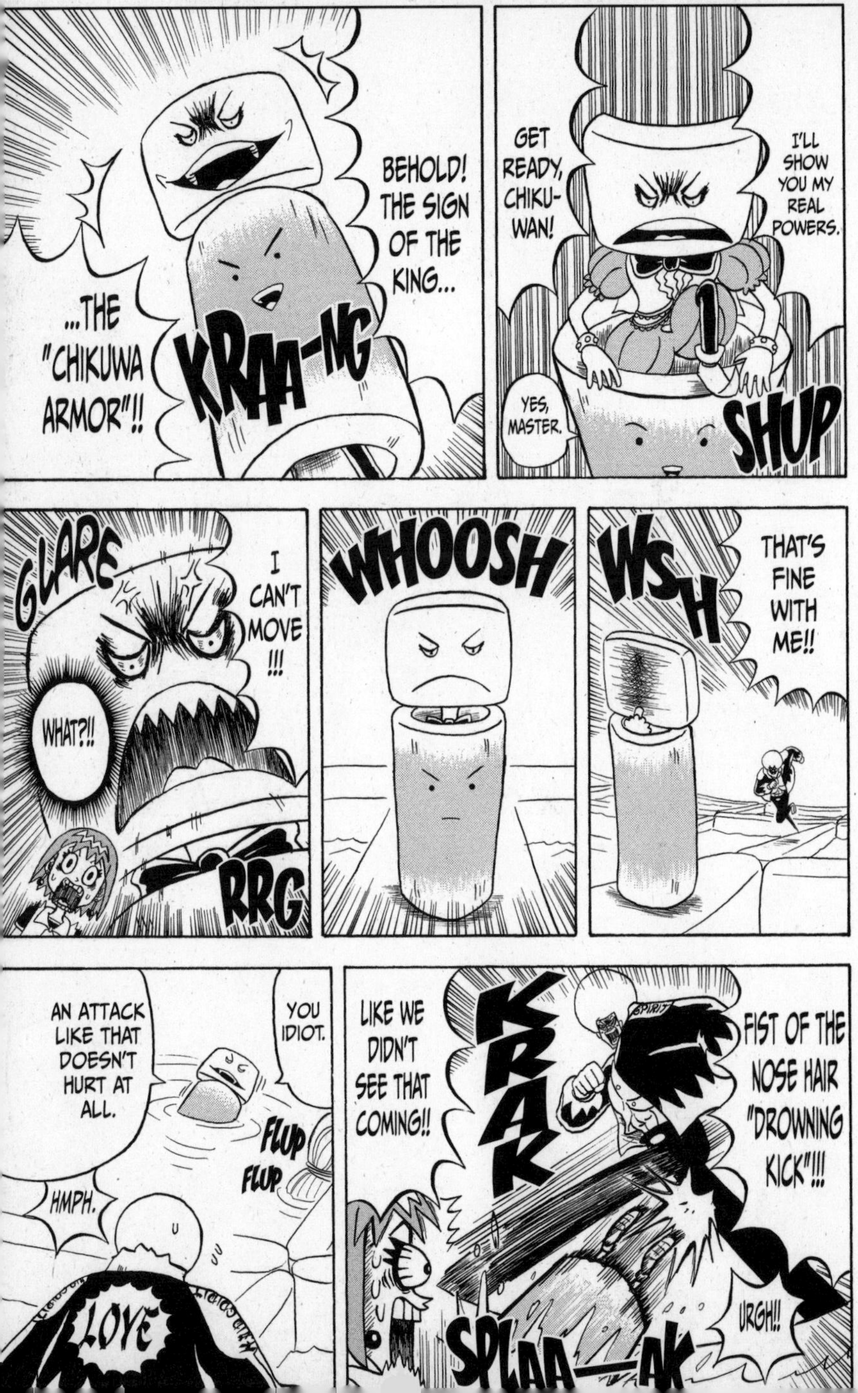
I'LL SHOW YOU MY REAL POWERS.
GET READY, CHIKU-WAN!
SHUP
YES, MASTER.
BEHOLD! THE SIGN OF THE KING...
KRAA-NG
...THE "CHIKUWA ARMOR"!!
THAT'S FINE WITH ME!!
WSH
WHOOSH
I CAN'T MOVE !!!
GLARE
WHAT?!!
RRG
FIST OF THE NOSE HAIR "DROWNING KICK"!!!
SPIRIT
KRAK
LIKE WE DIDN'T SEE THAT COMING!!
URGH!!
SPLAA-AK
YOU IDIOT.
AN ATTACK LIKE THAT DOESN'T HURT AT ALL.
FLUP
FLUP
HMPH.
LOVE

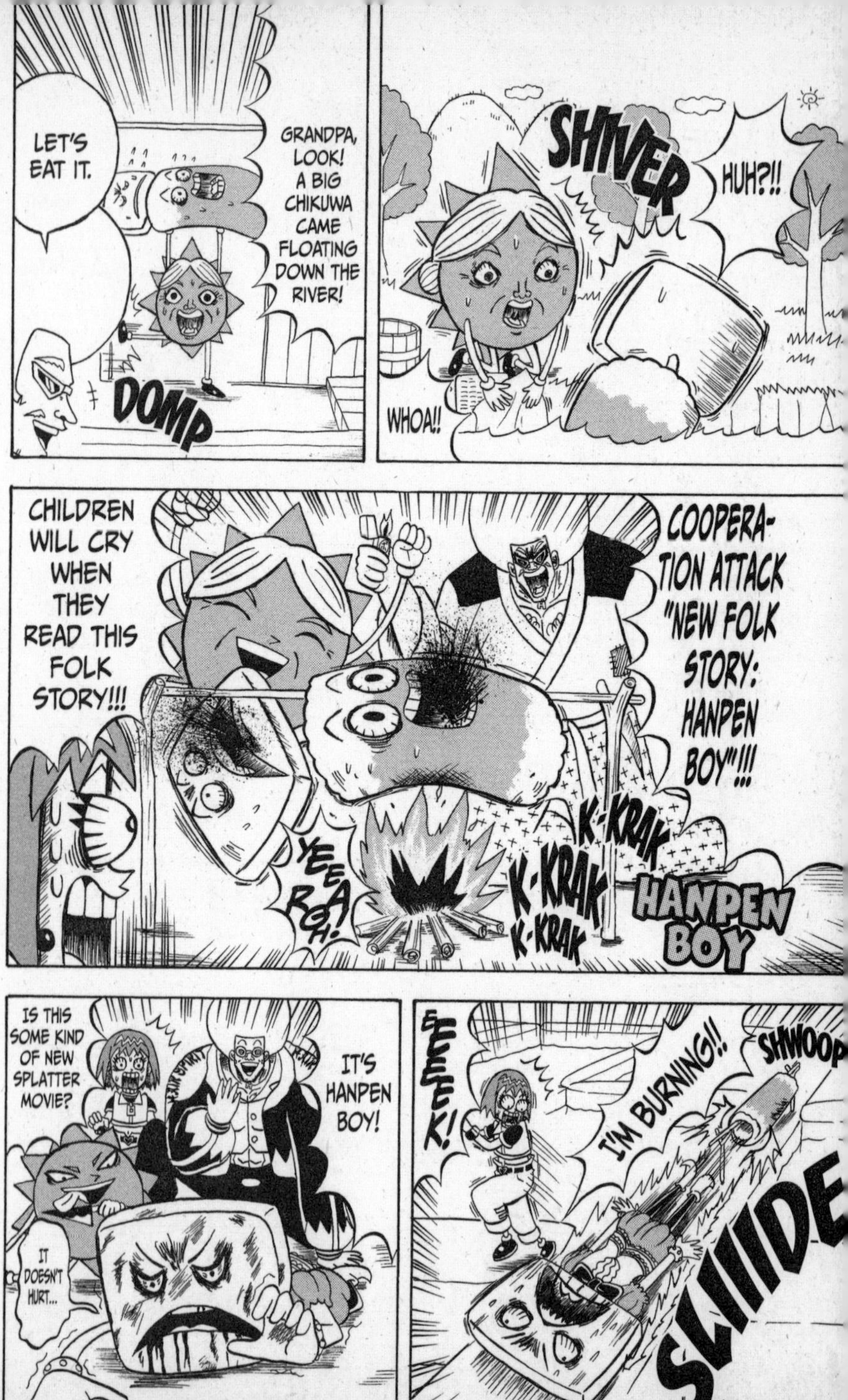
SHIVER
HUH?!!
WHOA!!
GRANDPA, LOOK! A BIG CHIKUWA CAME FLOATING DOWN THE RIVER!
LET'S EAT IT.
DOMP
COOPERA-TION ATTACK "NEW FOLK STORY: HANPEN BOY"!!!
CHILDREN WILL CRY WHEN THEY READ THIS FOLK STORY!!!
K-KRAK
YEEEARGH!
K-KRAK K-KRAK
HANPEN BOY
SHWOOP
I'M BURNING!!
EEEEEK!
SLIIIDE
IT'S HANPEN BOY!
IS THIS SOME KIND OF NEW SPLATTER MOVIE?
IT DOESN'T HURT...

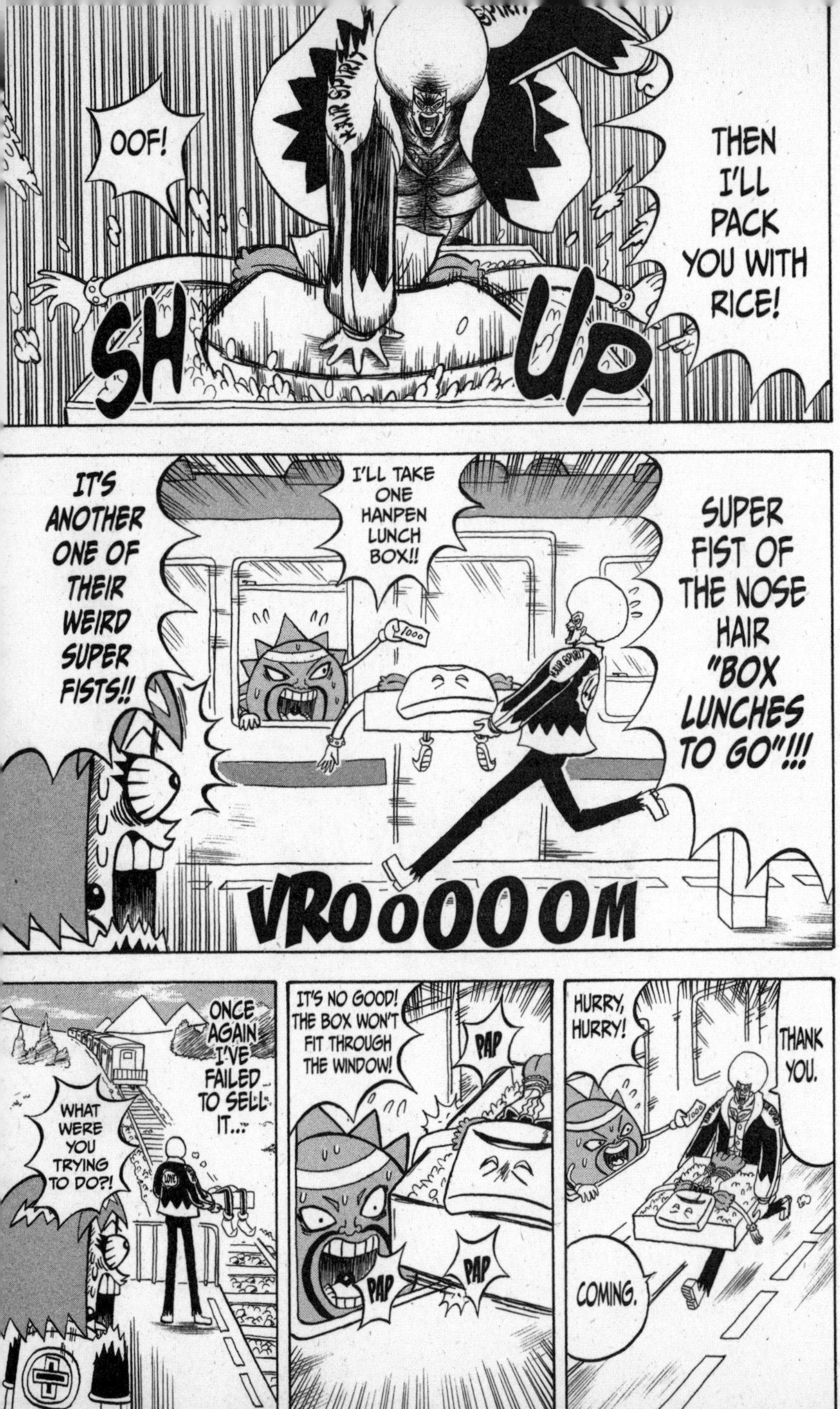
THEN I'LL PACK YOU WITH RICE!
OOF!
SH UP
SUPER FIST OF THE NOSE HAIR "BOX LUNCHES TO GO"!!!
I'LL TAKE ONE HANPEN LUNCH BOX!!
IT'S ANOTHER ONE OF THEIR WEIRD SUPER FISTS!!
VROOOOOOM
THANK YOU.
HURRY, HURRY!
COMING.
PAP
IT'S NO GOOD! THE BOX WON'T FIT THROUGH THE WINDOW!
PAP
PAP
ONCE AGAIN I'VE FAILED TO SELL IT...
WHAT WERE YOU TRYING TO DO?!

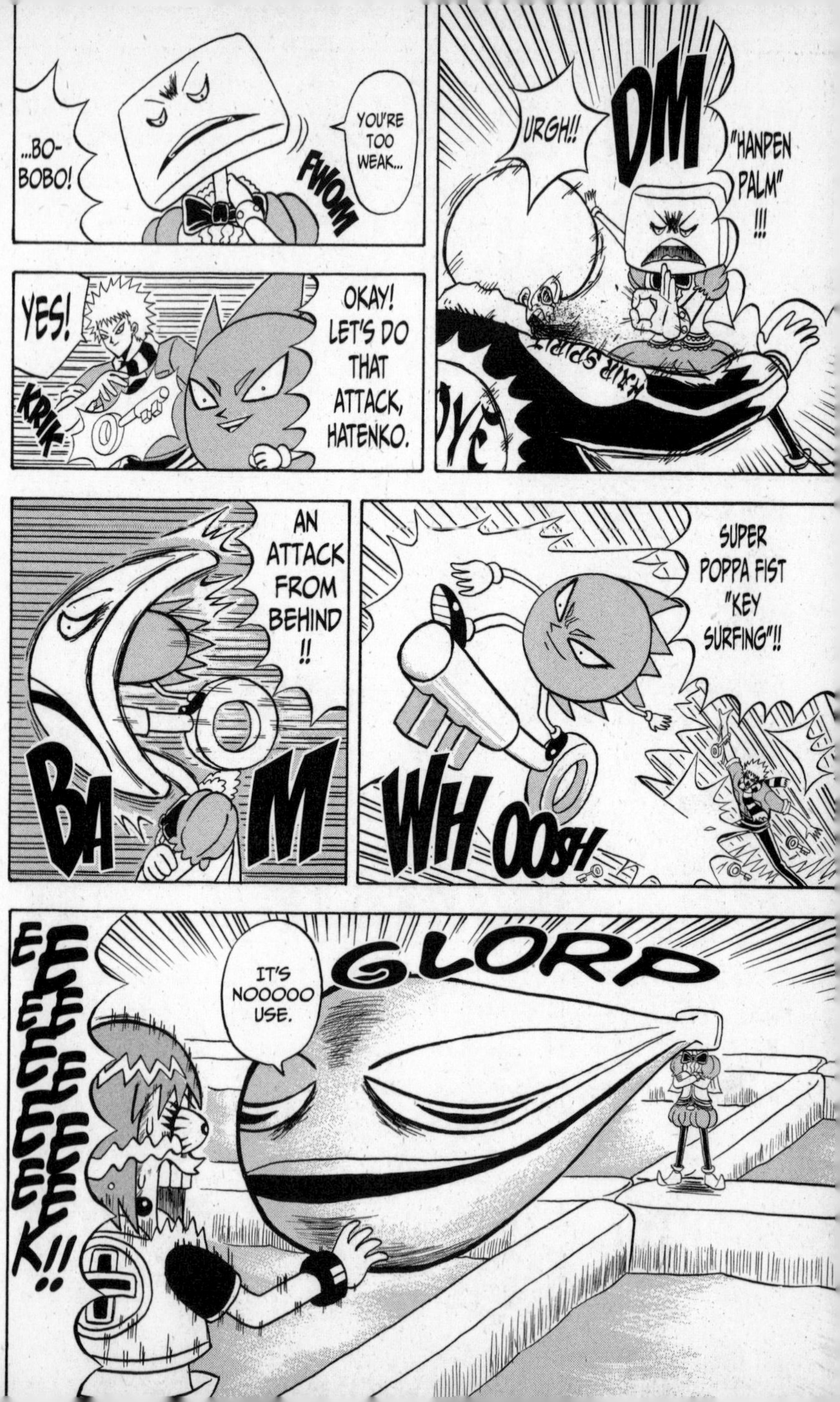
"HANPEN PALM"!!!
DM
URGH!!
YOU'RE TOO WEAK...
FWOM
...BO-BOBO!
OKAY! LET'S DO THAT ATTACK, HATENKO.
YES!
KRIK
SUPER POPPA FIST "KEY SURFING"!!
WHOOSH
AN ATTACK FROM BEHIND!!
BAM
GLORP
IT'S NOOOOO USE.
EEEEEEEEEEEEK!!

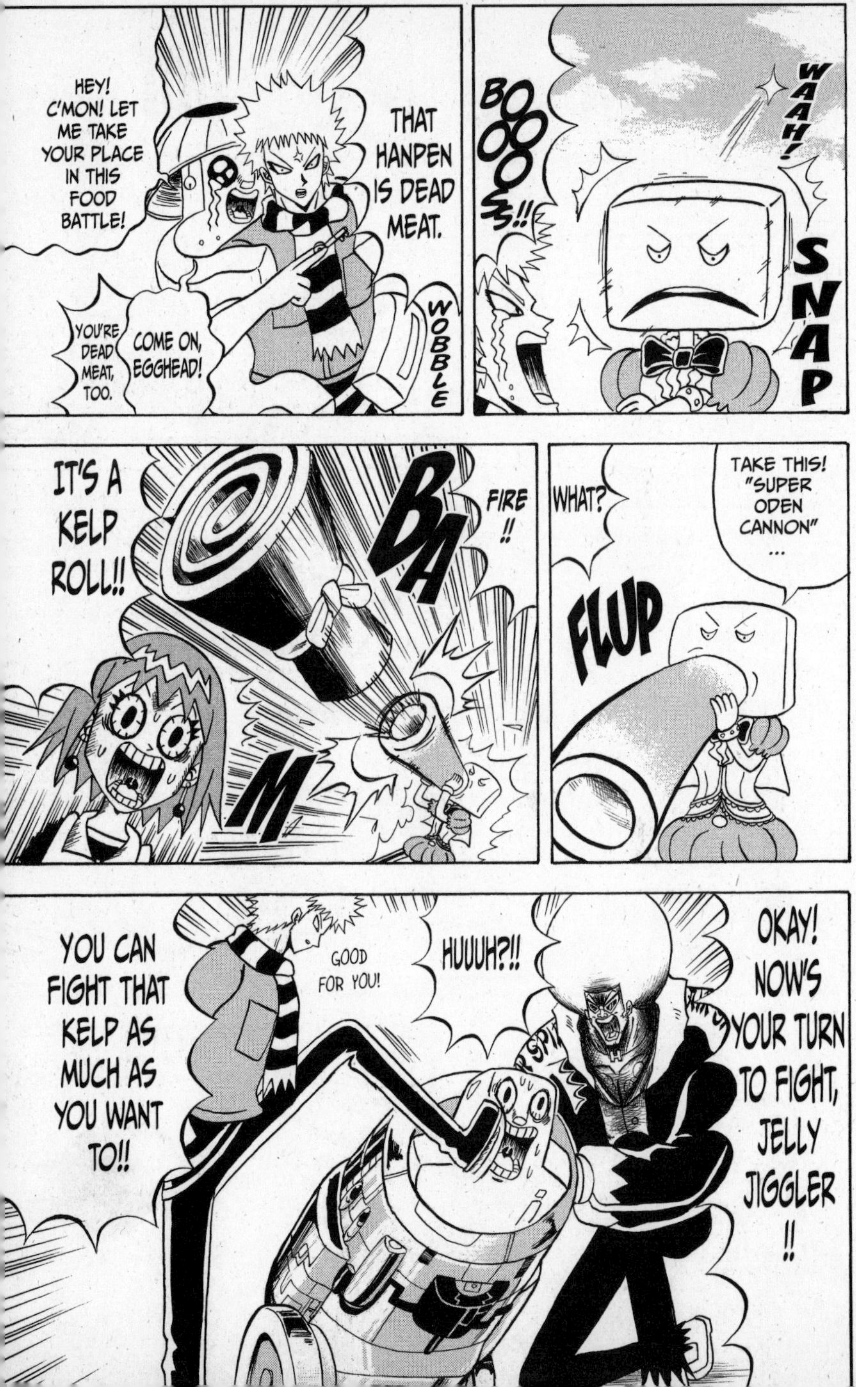
WAAH!
BOOOOOSS!!
SNAP
THAT HANPEN IS DEAD MEAT.
HEY! C'MON! LET ME TAKE YOUR PLACE IN THIS FOOD BATTLE!
WOBBLE
COME ON, EGGHEAD!
YOU'RE DEAD MEAT, TOO.
TAKE THIS! "SUPER ODEN CANNON" ...
WHAT?
FLUP
FIRE!!
BA
M
IT'S A KELP ROLL!!
OKAY! NOW'S YOUR TURN TO FIGHT, JELLY JIGGLER!!
HUUUH?!!
GOOD FOR YOU!
YOU CAN FIGHT THAT KELP AS MUCH AS YOU WANT TO!!

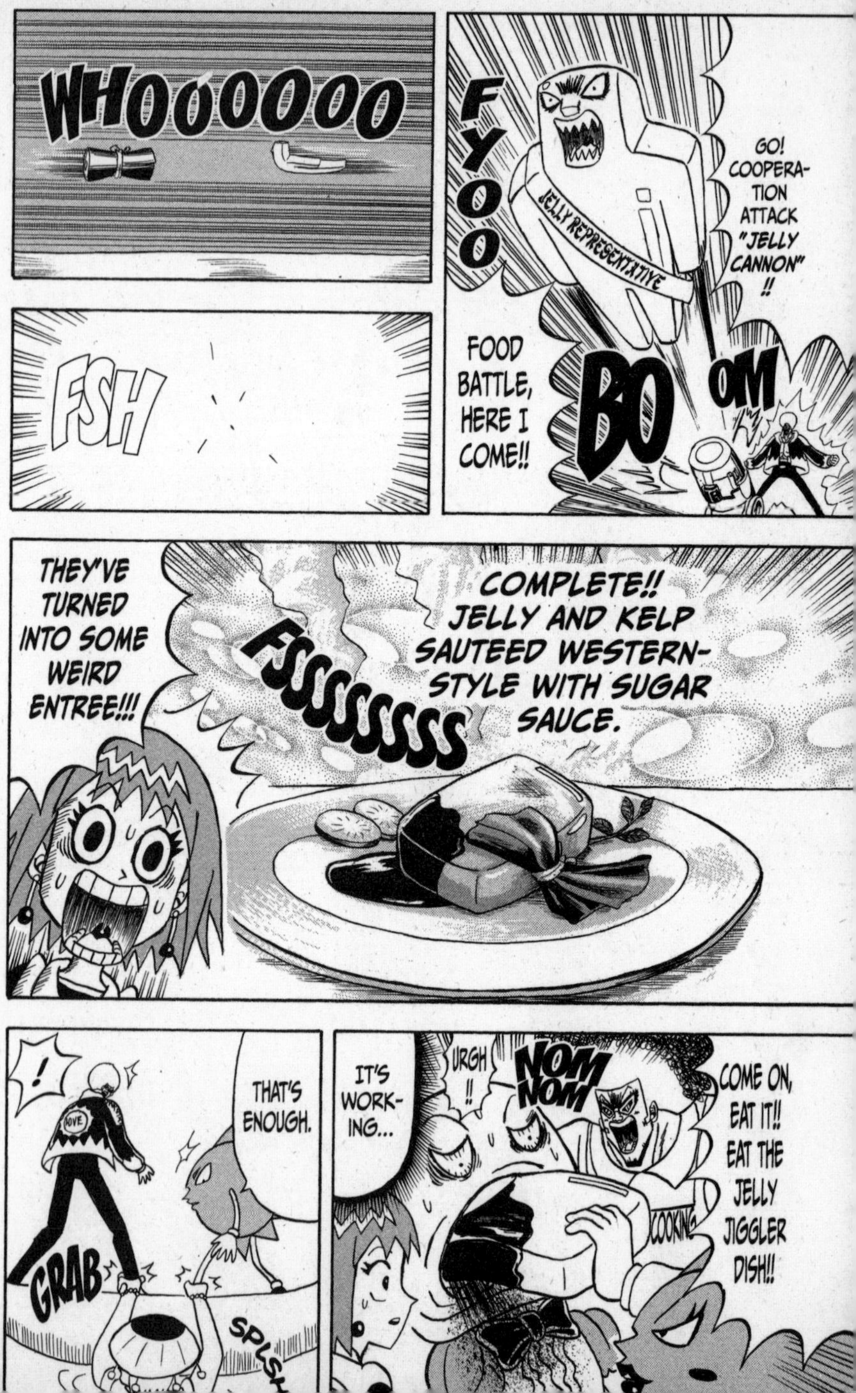
FYOO
JELLY REPRESENTATIVE
GO! COOPERATION ATTACK "JELLY CANNON" !!
BOOM
FOOD BATTLE, HERE I COME!!
WHOOOOOO
FSH
COMPLETE!! JELLY AND KELP SAUTEED WESTERN-STYLE WITH SUGAR SAUCE.
FSSSSSSSS
THEY'VE TURNED INTO SOME WEIRD ENTREE!!!
COME ON, EAT IT!! EAT THE JELLY JIGGLER DISH!!
NOM NOM
URGH !!
COOKING
IT'S WORKING...
THAT'S ENOUGH.
!
LOVE
GRAB
SPLSH

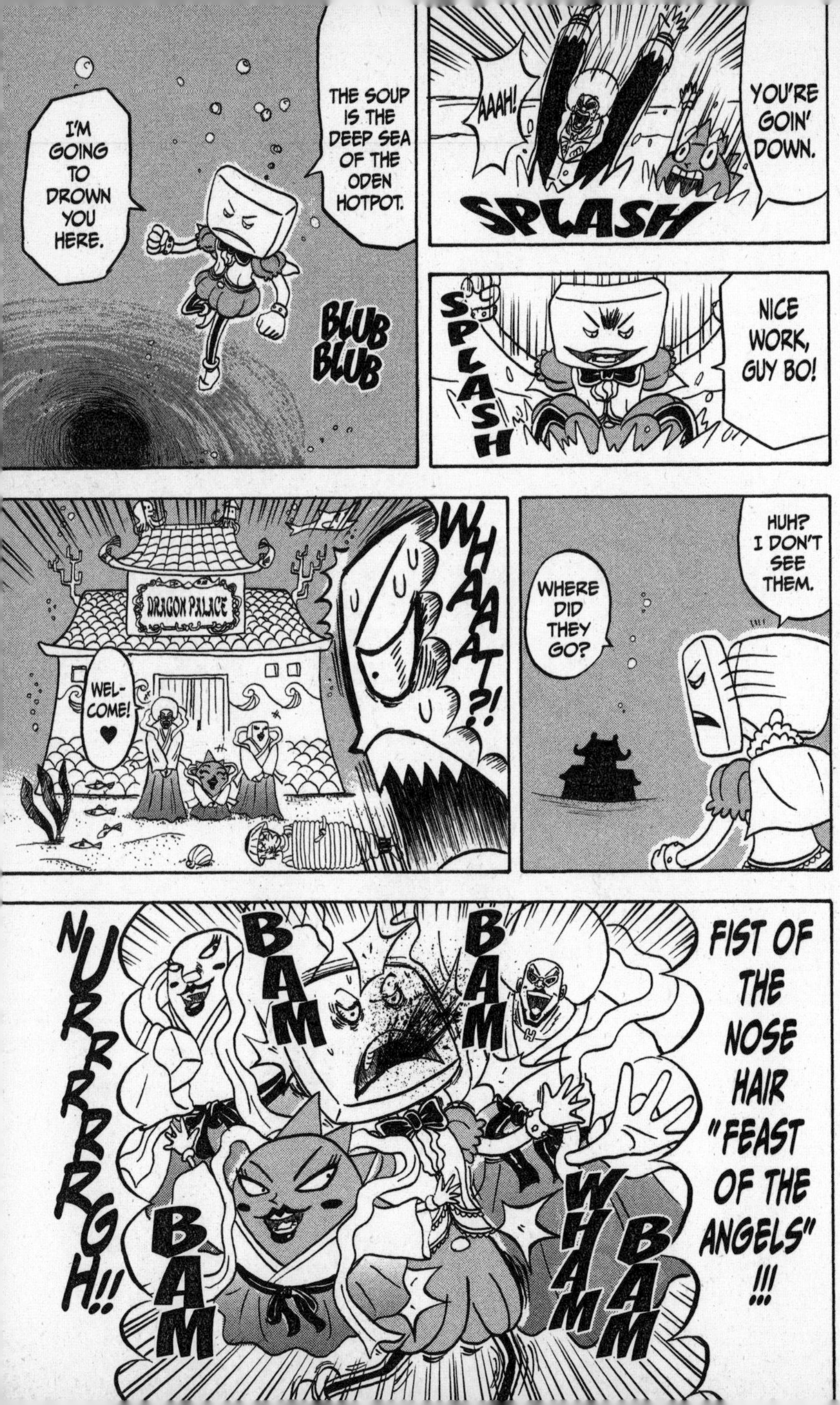
YOU'RE GOIN' DOWN.
AAAH!
SPLASH
NICE WORK, GUY BO!
SPLASH
THE SOUP IS THE DEEP SEA OF THE ODEN HOTPOT.
I'M GOING TO DROWN YOU HERE.
BLUB BLUB
HUH? I DON'T SEE THEM.
WHERE DID THEY GO?
WHAAAT?!
DRAGON PALACE
WEL-COME! ♥
FIST OF THE NOSE HAIR "FEAST OF THE ANGELS"!!!
BAM
WHAM
BAM
BAM
BAM
NURRRRGH!!
BAM

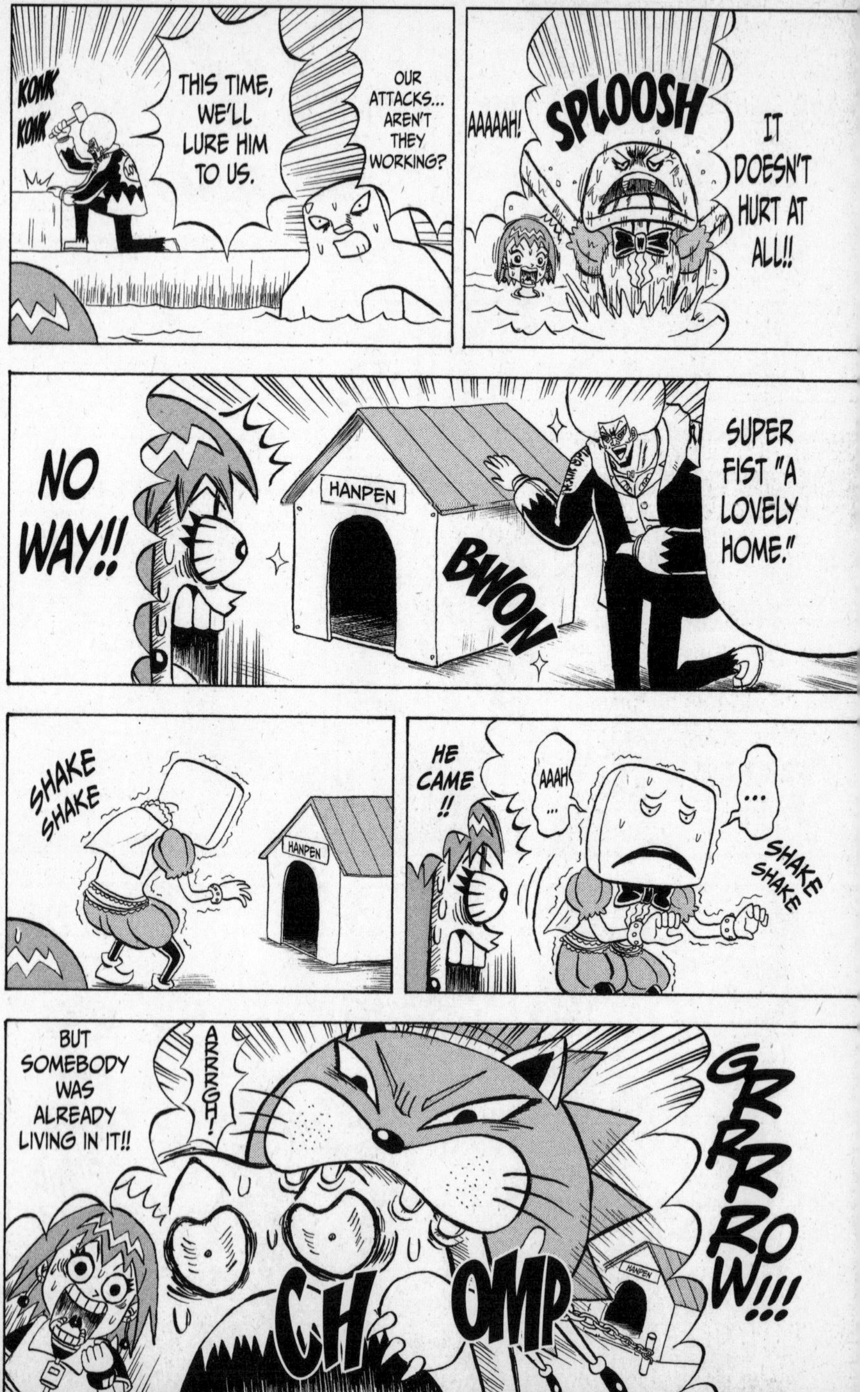
IT DOESN'T HURT AT ALL!!
SPLOOSH
AAAAAH!
OUR ATTACKS... AREN'T THEY WORKING?
THIS TIME, WE'LL LURE HIM TO US.
KONK KONK
SUPER FIST "A LOVELY HOME."
HANPEN
BWON
NO WAY!!
...
SHAKE SHAKE
AAAH...
HE CAME!!
HANPEN
SHAKE SHAKE
GRRRROW!!!
HANPEN
CH OMP
ARRRGH!
BUT SOMEBODY WAS ALREADY LIVING IN IT!!

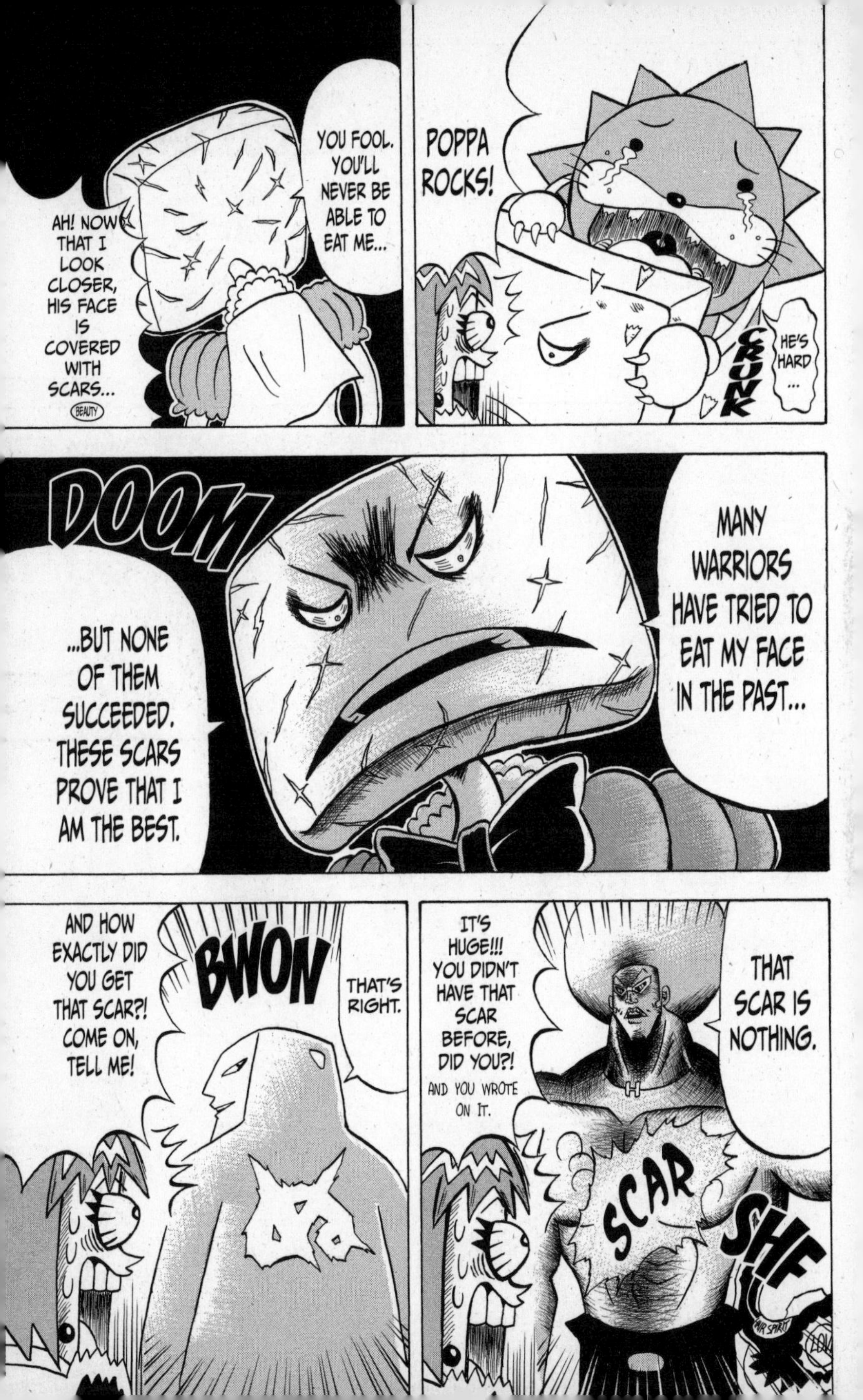
POPPA ROCKS!
CRUNK
HE'S HARD ...
YOU FOOL. YOU'LL NEVER BE ABLE TO EAT ME...
AH! NOW THAT I LOOK CLOSER, HIS FACE IS COVERED WITH SCARS...
BEAUTY
MANY WARRIORS HAVE TRIED TO EAT MY FACE IN THE PAST...
DOOM
...BUT NONE OF THEM SUCCEEDED. THESE SCARS PROVE THAT I AM THE BEST.
THAT SCAR IS NOTHING.
IT'S HUGE!!! YOU DIDN'T HAVE THAT SCAR BEFORE, DID YOU?!
AND YOU WROTE ON IT.
SCAR
SHF
THAT'S RIGHT.
BWON
AND HOW EXACTLY DID YOU GET THAT SCAR?! COME ON, TELL ME!

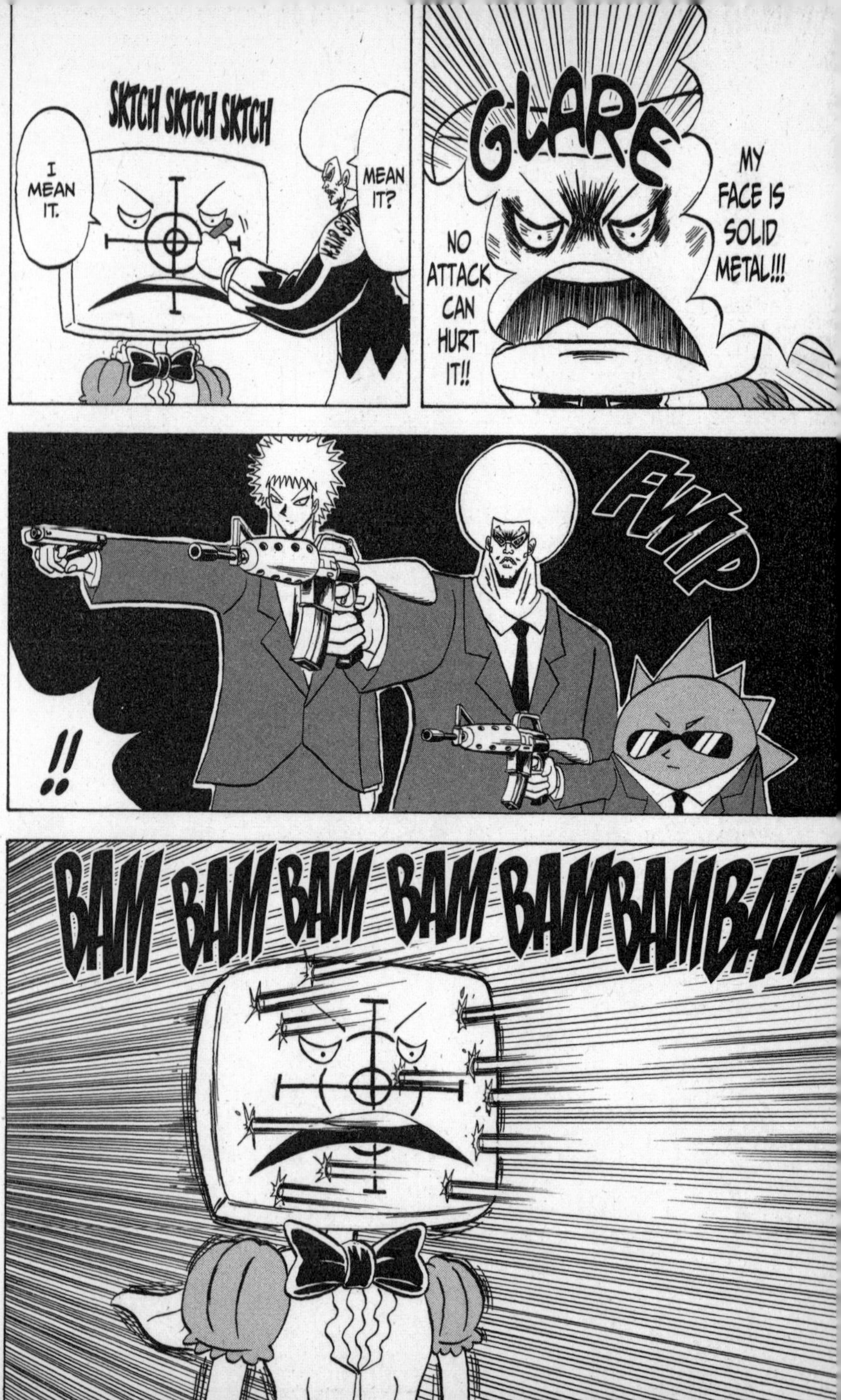
GLARE
MY FACE IS SOLID METAL!!!
NO ATTACK CAN HURT IT!!
SKTCH SKTCH SKTCH
MEAN IT?
I MEAN IT.
FWIP
!!
BAM BAM BAM BAM BAMBAMBAM

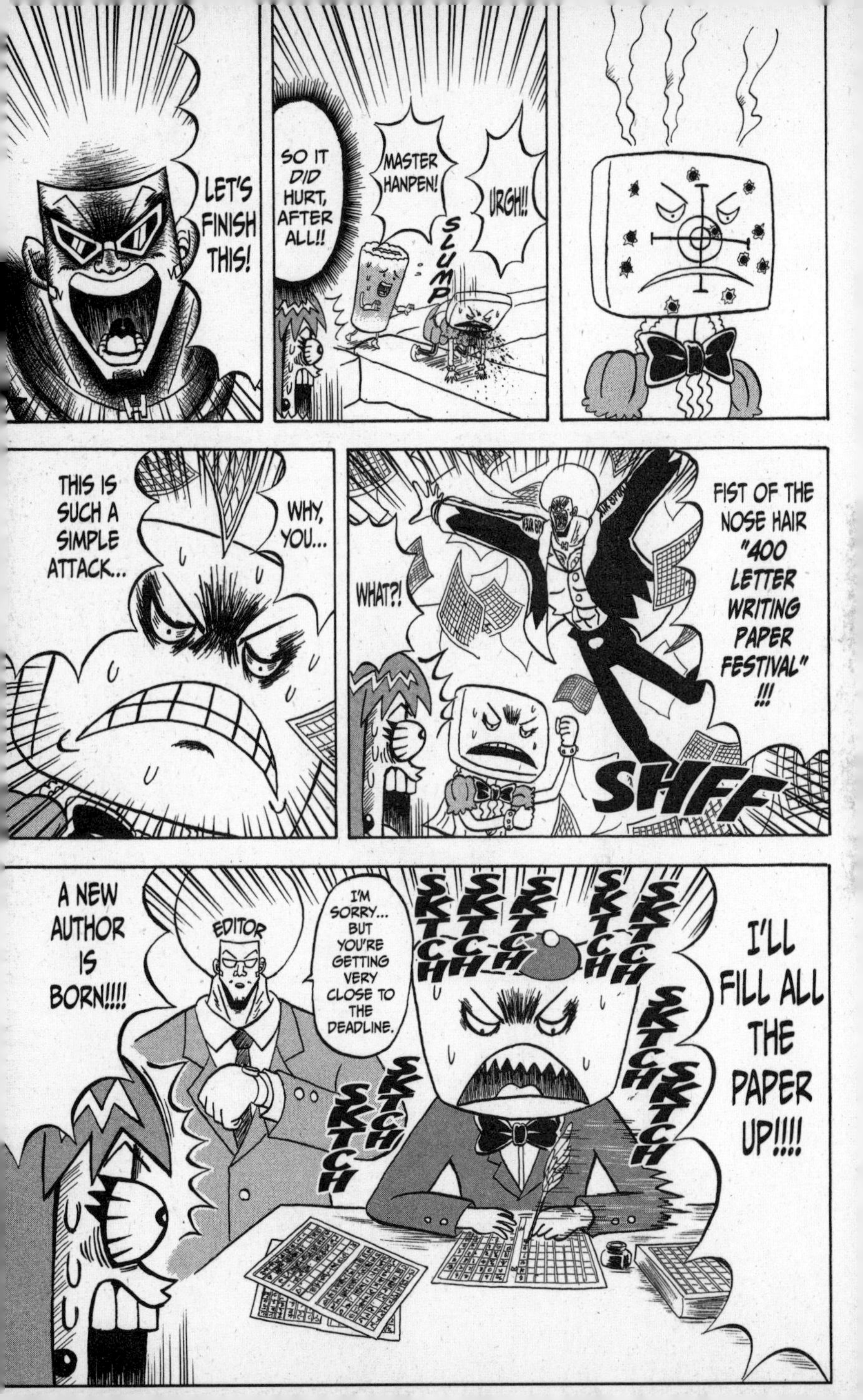
URGH!!
MASTER HANPEN!
SLUMP
SO IT DID HURT, AFTER ALL!!
LET'S FINISH THIS!
FIST OF THE NOSE HAIR "400 LETTER WRITING PAPER FESTIVAL"!!!
WHAT?!
SHFF
WHY, YOU...
THIS IS SUCH A SIMPLE ATTACK...
I'LL FILL ALL THE PAPER UP!!!!
SKTCH SKTCH SKTCH SKTCH SKTCH
SKTCH SKTCH
I'M SORRY... BUT YOU'RE GETTING VERY CLOSE TO THE DEADLINE.
EDITOR
SKTCH SKTCH
A NEW AUTHOR IS BORN!!!!

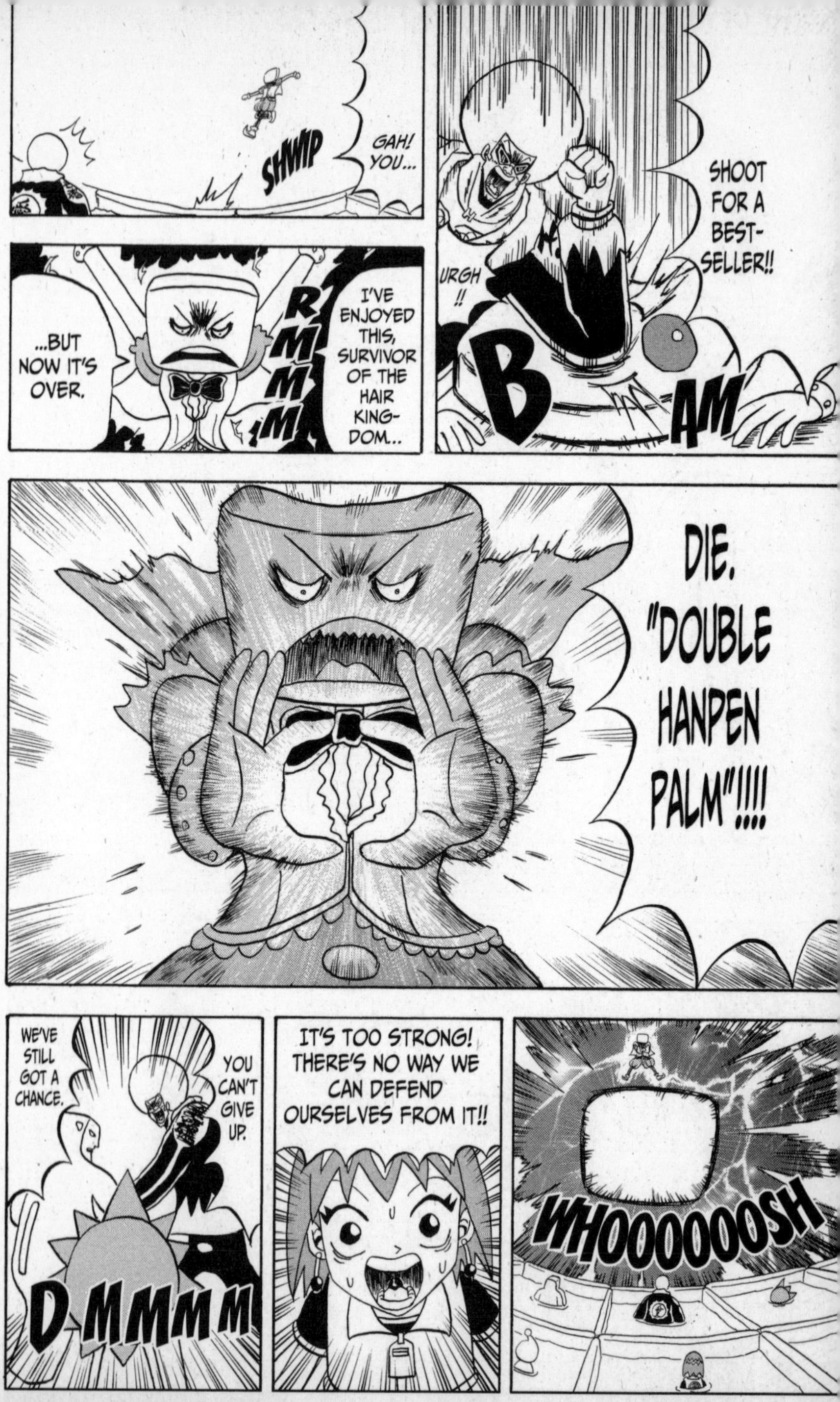
SHOOT FOR A BEST-SELLER!!
URGH!!
BAM
GAH! YOU...
SHWIP
I'VE ENJOYED THIS, SURVIVOR OF THE HAIR KINGDOM..
RMMMM
...BUT NOW IT'S OVER.
DIE. "DOUBLE HANPEN PALM"!!!!
WHOOOOOOOSH
IT'S TOO STRONG! THERE'S NO WAY WE CAN DEFEND OURSELVES FROM IT!!
YOU CAN'T GIVE UP.
WE'VE STILL GOT A CHANCE.
DMMMMM

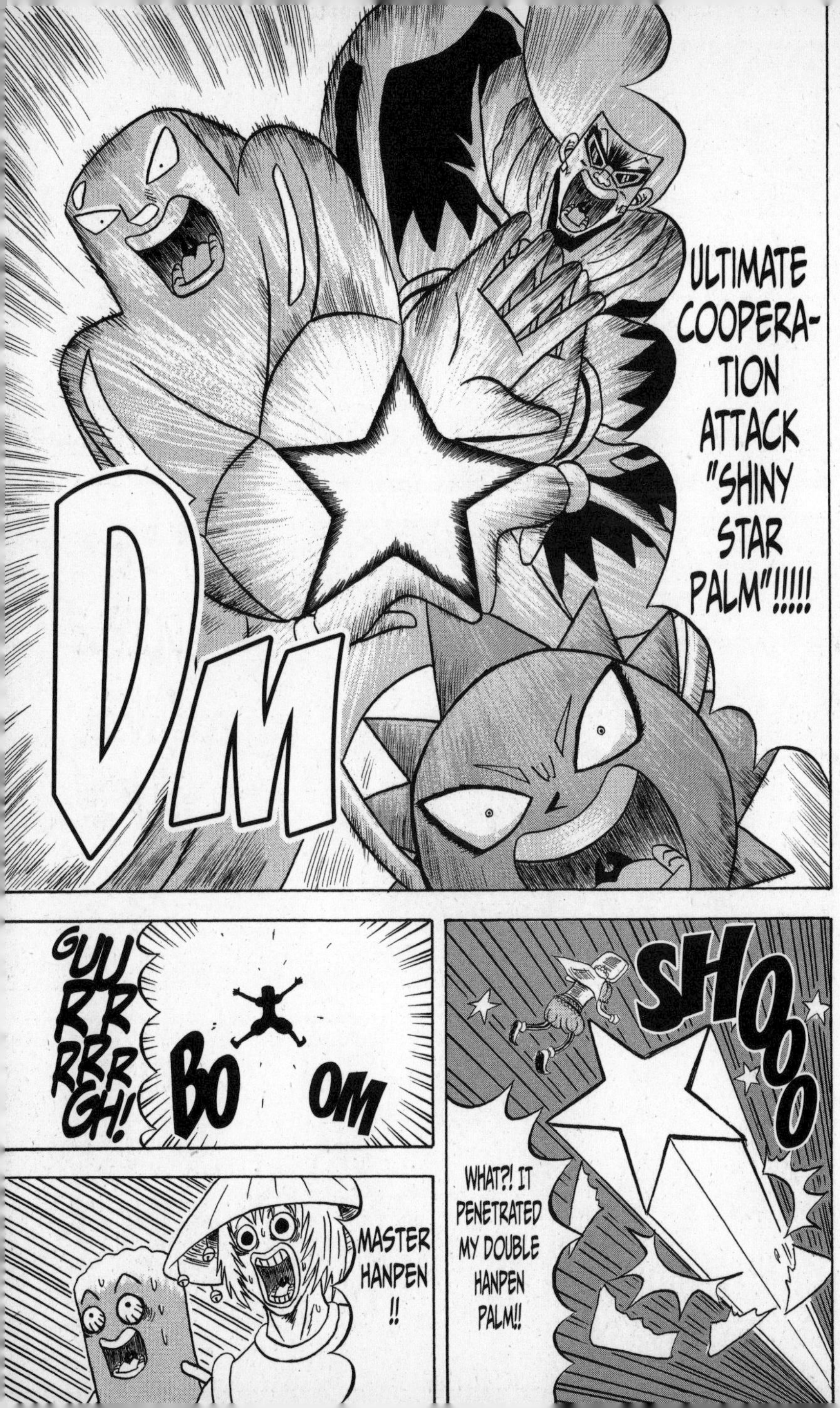
ULTIMATE COOPERATION ATTACK "SHINY STAR PALM"!!!!!
DM
SHOOO
WHAT?! IT PENETRATED MY DOUBLE HANPEN PALM!!
GUURRRRRRGH!
BOOM
MASTER HANPEN !!

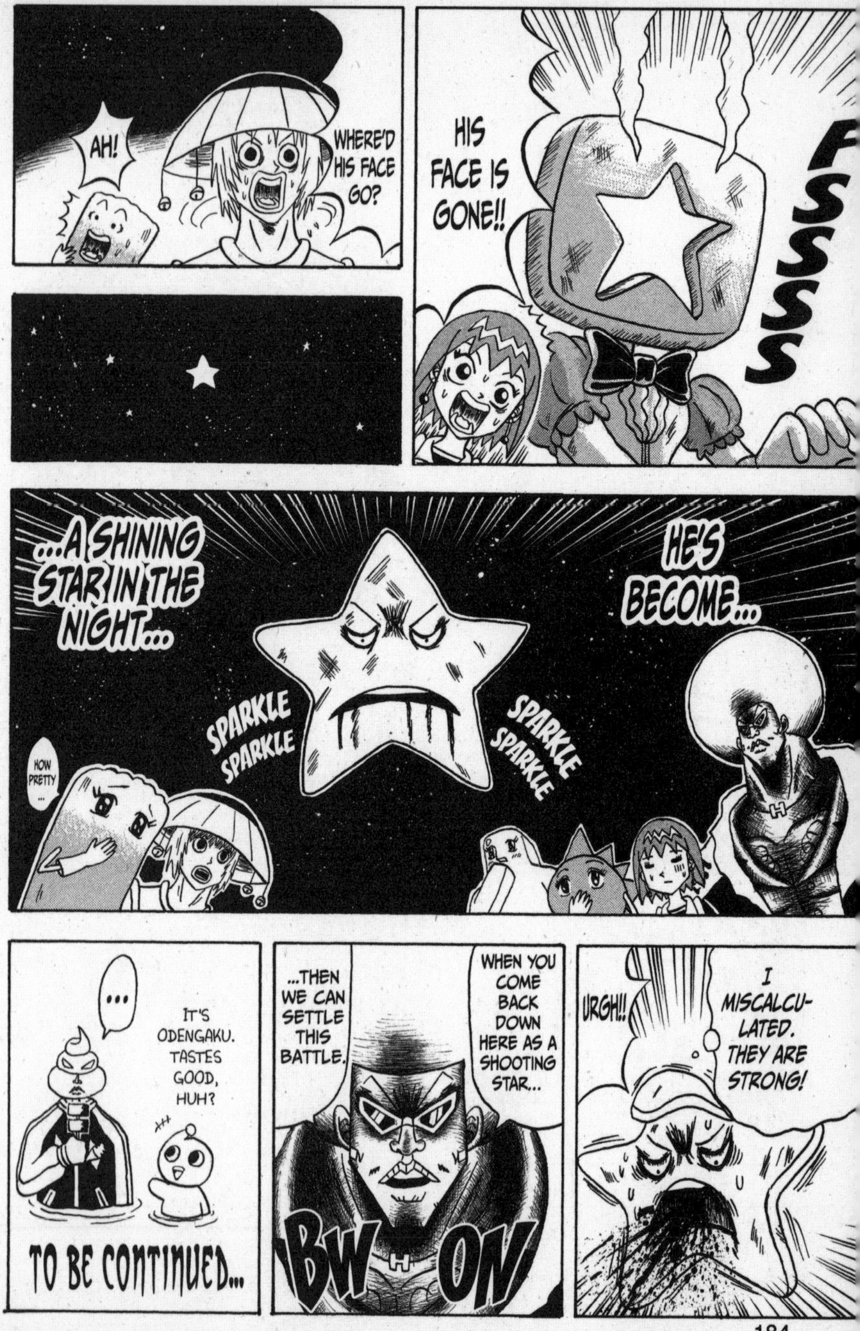
FSSSS
HIS FACE IS GONE!!
WHERE'D HIS FACE GO?
AH!
HE'S BECOME...
SPARKLE SPARKLE
SPARKLE SPARKLE
...A SHINING STAR IN THE NIGHT...
HOW PRETTY...
I MISCALCU-LATED. THEY ARE STRONG!
URGH!!
WHEN YOU COME BACK DOWN HERE AS A SHOOTING STAR...
...THEN WE CAN SETTLE THIS BATTLE.
BWOON
...
IT'S ODENGAKU. TASTES GOOD, HUH?
TO BE CONTINUED...

Bobobo-bo Bo-bobo Extra Story!

Bo-bobo Nose Hair Theater 7: The Reason He Became Their Friend

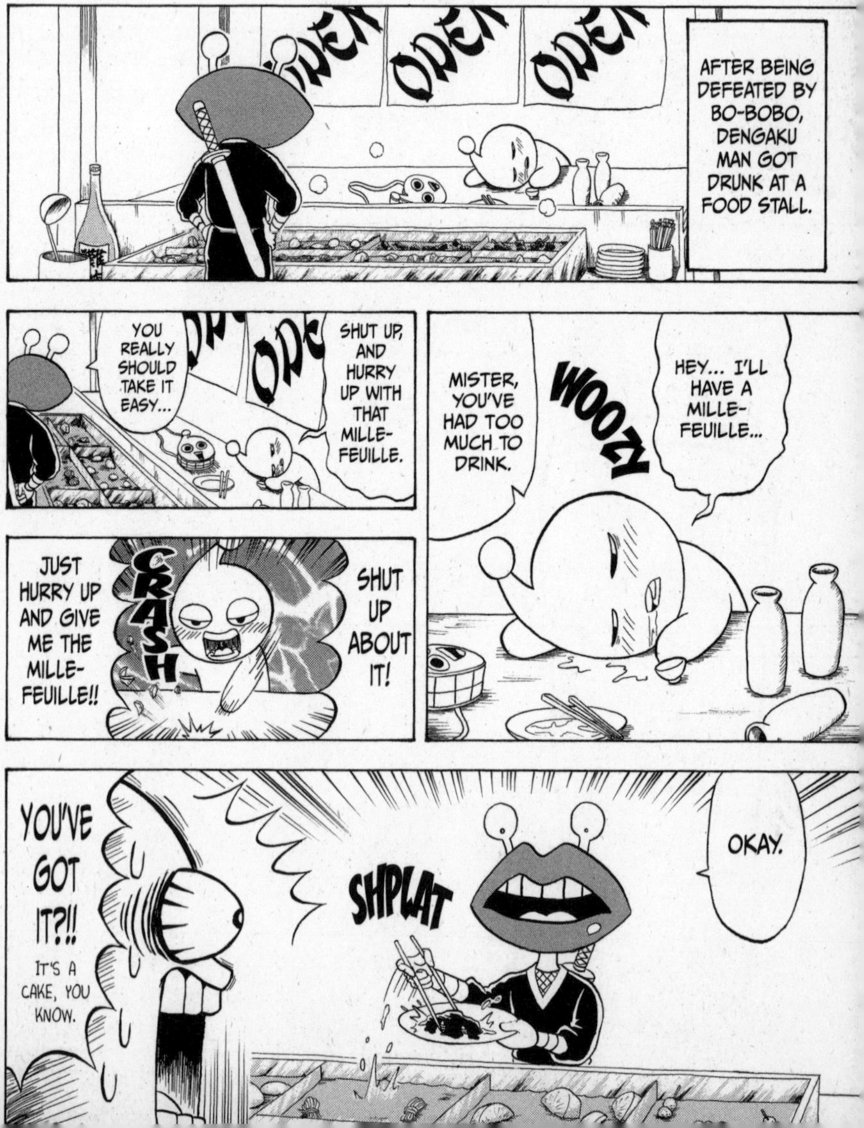
AFTER BEING DEFEATED BY BO-BOBO, DENGAKU MAN GOT DRUNK AT A FOOD STALL.
ODEN
ODEN
HEY... I'LL HAVE A MILLE-FEUILLE...
WOOZY
MISTER, YOU'VE HAD TOO MUCH TO DRINK.
SHUT UP, AND HURRY UP WITH THAT MILLE-FEUILLE.
YOU REALLY SHOULD TAKE IT EASY...
SHUT UP ABOUT IT!
CRASH
JUST HURRY UP AND GIVE ME THE MILLE-FEUILLE!!
OKAY.
SHPLAT
YOU'VE GOT IT?!!
IT'S A CAKE, YOU KNOW.

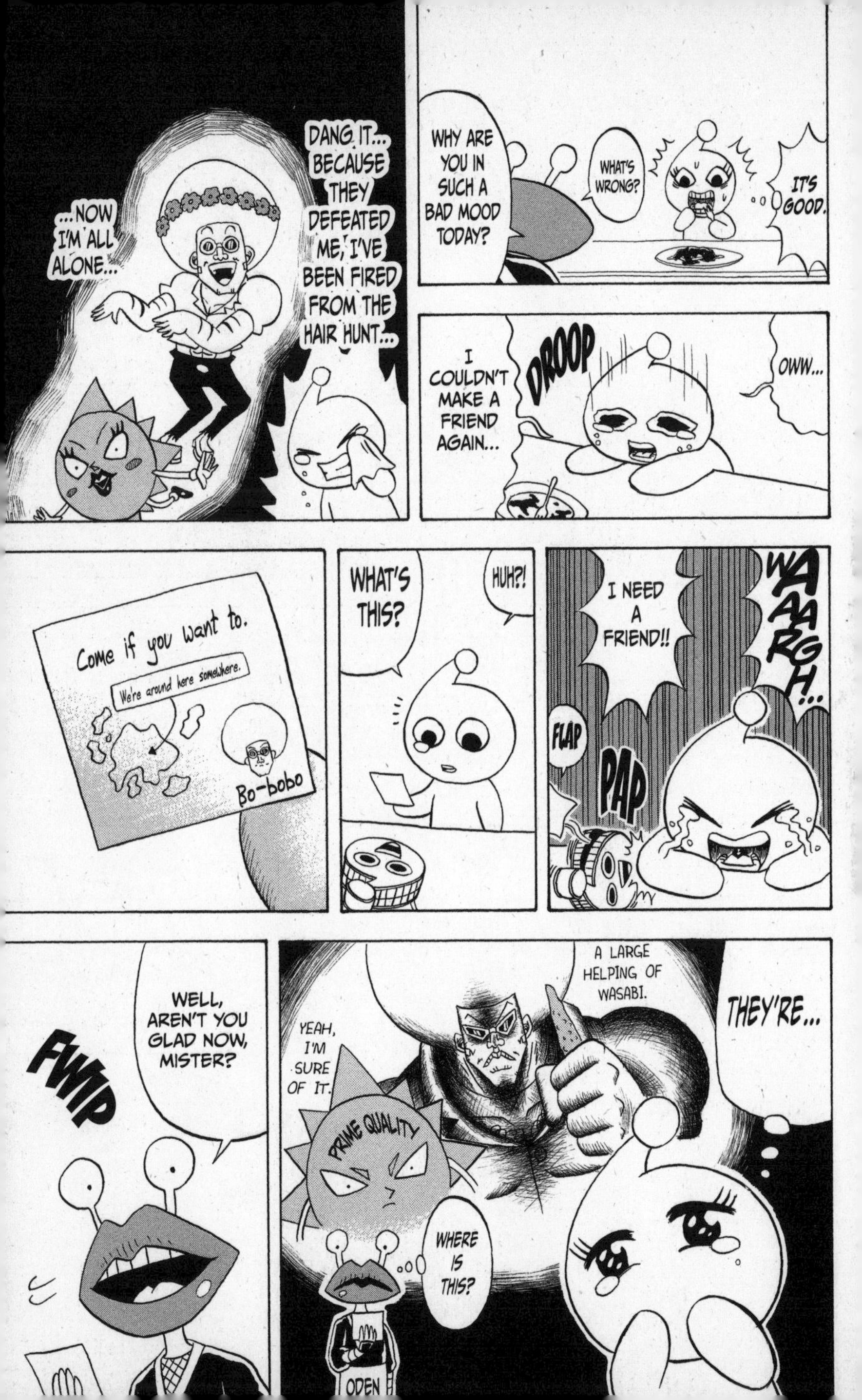
IT'S GOOD.
WHAT'S WRONG?
WHY ARE YOU IN SUCH A BAD MOOD TODAY?
OWW...
DROOP
I COULDN'T MAKE A FRIEND AGAIN...
DANG IT... BECAUSE THEY DEFEATED ME, I'VE BEEN FIRED FROM THE HAIR HUNT...
...NOW I'M ALL ALONE...
WAAARGH...
I NEED A FRIEND!!
PAP
FLAP
HUH?!
WHAT'S THIS?
Come if you want to.
We're around here somewhere.
Bo-bobo
THEY'RE...
A LARGE HELPING OF WASABI.
YEAH, I'M SURE OF IT.
PRIME QUALITY
WHERE IS THIS?
ODEN
WELL, AREN'T YOU GLAD NOW, MISTER?
FWIP

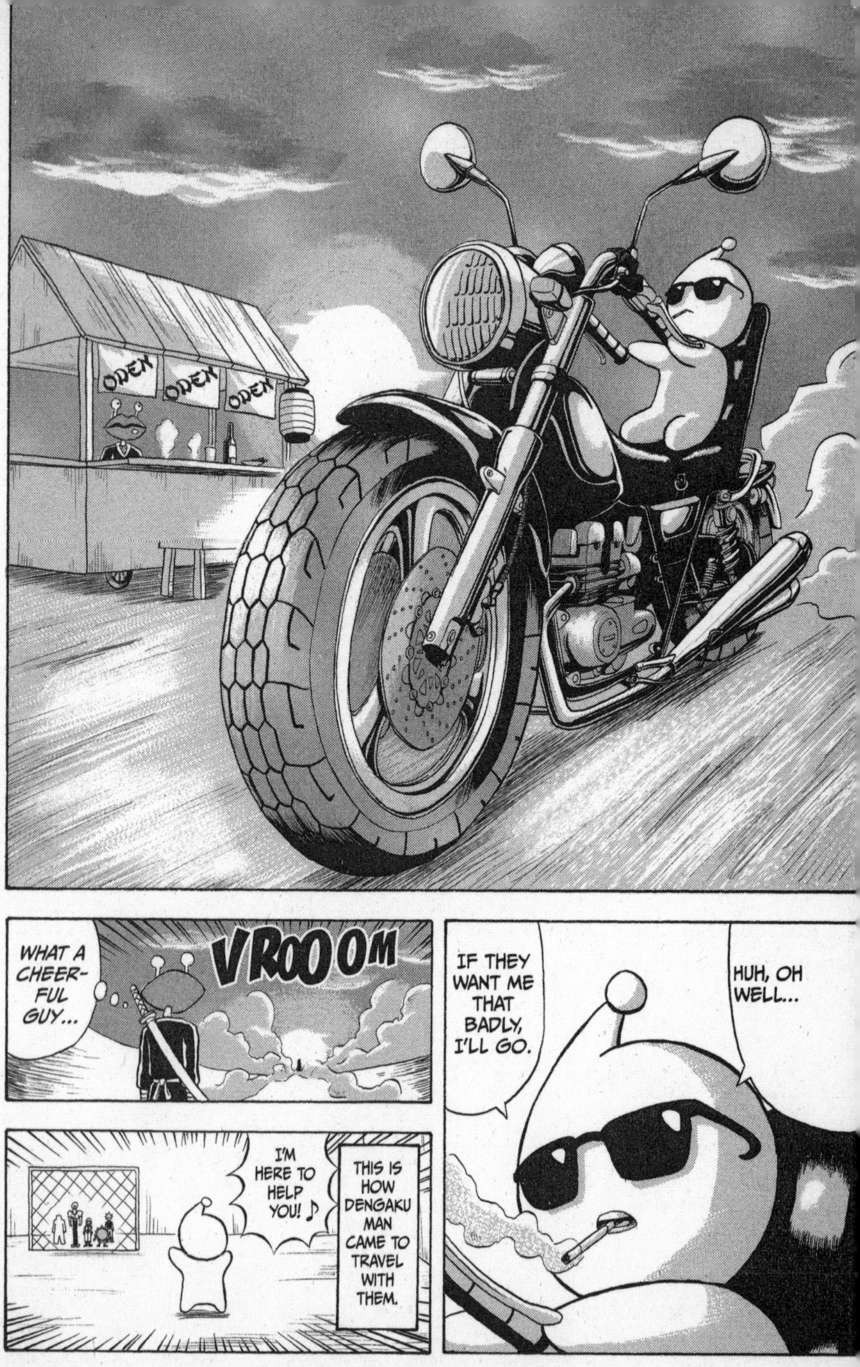
ODEN
ODEN
ODEN
HUH, OH WELL...
IF THEY WANT ME THAT BADLY, I'LL GO.
VROOOM
WHAT A CHEERFUL GUY...
THIS IS HOW DENGAKU MAN CAME TO TRAVEL WITH THEM.
I'M HERE TO HELP YOU! ♪

In the Next Volume

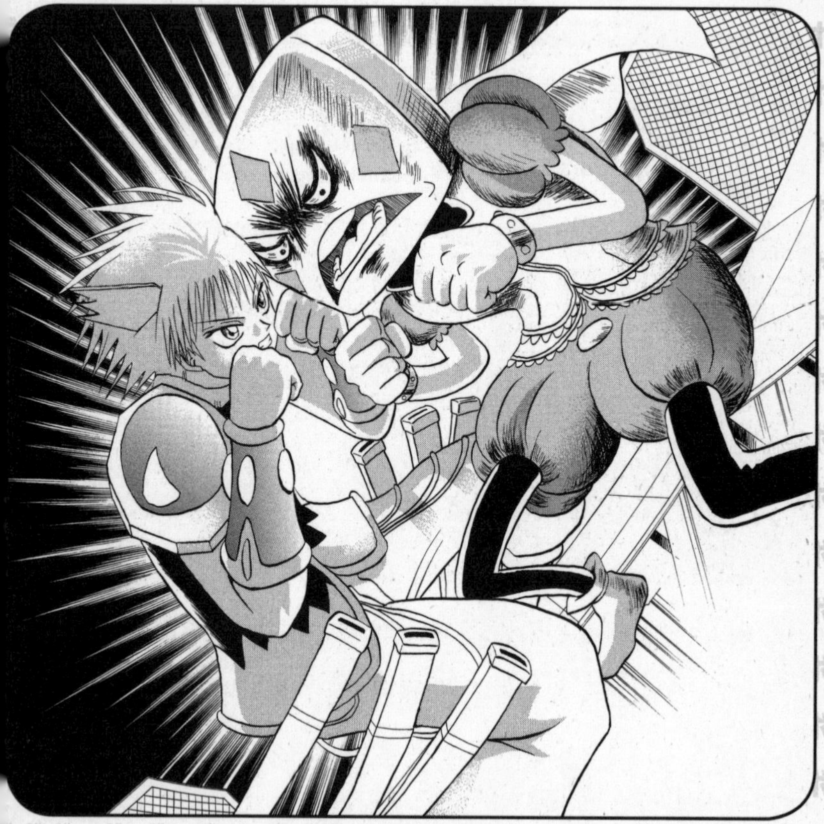

A Deadly Combination

Hanpen's star shoots down from the sky! But little does he know that he's about to go into Food Battle with the greatest combo since rice and fish: Jelly-Bobo!

AVAILABLE OCTOBER 2010!